Church and Settler in Colonial Zimbabwe

Studies of Religion in Africa

Supplements to the Journal of Religion in Africa

Edited by

Paul Gifford
School of Oriental and African Studies, London

VOLUME 34

Church and Settler in Colonial Zimbabwe

A Study in the History of the Anglican Diocese of Mashonaland/Southern Rhodesia, 1890–1925

by

Pamela Welch

BRILL

LEIDEN • BOSTON
2008

This book is printed on acid-free paper.

Library of Congress Cataloging-in-Publication Data

Welch, Pamela, 1950–
Church and settler in colonial Zimbabwe : a study in the history of the Anglican Diocese of Mashonaland/Southern Rhodesia, 1890–1925 / by Pamela Welch.
p. cm. — (Studies of religion in Africa, ISSN 0083-5889 ; v. 34)
Includes bibliographical references.
ISBN 978-90-04-16746-9 (hardback : alk. paper) 1. Church of the Province of Central Africa. Diocese of Mashonaland—History. 2. Anglican Communion—Southern Rhodesia—History. 3. Southern Rhodesia—Church history. I. Title. II. Series.

BX5700.4.A44M37 2008
283'.6891—dc22

2008026945

ISSN 0083-5889
ISBN 978 90 04 16746 9

PRINTED IN THE NETHERLANDS

For Neil and for Lucy

CONTENTS

MAPS AND ILLUSTRATIONS

AUTHOR'S NOTE

This monograph is a lightly revised version of a doctoral thesis in history presented at King's College, London in 2005. Since the material it contains exists in the public domain, footnotes and references to matters of fact rather than interpretation have here been reduced to a minimum, except where a small amount of new matter has been added.

ACKNOWLEDGEMENTS

Many years have gone into the making of this book and as a consequence I owe thanks to many institutions and more individuals than I am able to name. I am grateful to Paul Gifford, Series Editor and Ingeborg van der Laan, Assistant Editor, Brill Social Sciences and Religious Studies, for their assistance with the alchemy by which a thesis becomes a published text. Research was begun with a grant from the Central Research Fund, London University and the King's College Theological Trust supported both early work and completion of the thesis. I have to thank the Department of History, University of Zimbabwe for granting me associate status and the Research Council of Zimbabwe for a research permit, during my original period of research.

For access to collections and permission to quote from material therein, I thank the National Archives of Zimbabwe; the Department of Historical Papers, University of the Witwatersrand Library; the United Society for the Propagation of the Gospel; the Board of TZABA (Transvaal, Botswana and Zimbabwe Association); the Bodleian Library of Commonwealth and African Studies at Rhodes House, Oxford; the Trustees, Lambeth Palace Library; the Record Centre, General Synod of the Church of England; and Derbyshire County Archives. The two maps are reproduced with the permission of the Board of TZABA and the architect's drawing of Salisbury cathedral with the permission of the Department of Historical Papers, University of the Witwatersrand Library. It has not been possible to trace the copyright holder of the photograph of the Salisbury hut church (illustration 1.)

Michael Bullivant and Roger Barker kindly supplied information about the plaques in St. John's, Bulawayo; John Taylor, a reference from the Gell Collection; the Revd J.M. Roden, personal information about Percy Hale, railway missioner. Peter Ewart and Peter Henderson, both of Canterbury, have provided invaluable, new, corroborative information about Nelson Wellesley Fogarty. Miss Olga Ward kindly shared information about her uncle, Archdeacon Upcher and Mrs Nicky Salt gave me use of the Salt Scrapbooks, compiled by her father-in-law, John Salt. The late Canon Richard Holderness generously shared with me his long and unrivalled knowledge of the diocese. I am most grateful to each of these and also to those many other family members, friends, acquaintances, fellow Anglicans and virtual strangers, who have supported or assisted my search in any way.

Andrew Porter, Rhodes Professor in the University of London, supervisor and friend, has provided throughout encouragement, penetrating criticism and an example of the highest academic probity. It is, however, to my husband and my daughter, who have lived patiently and supportively with my pre-occupation for more years than any of us cares to remember, that I chiefly owe my thanks. This book is dedicated to them.

Pamela Welch

LIST OF ABBREVIATIONS

Benson	Edward White Benson papers.
BQP	*Bloemfontein Quarterly Paper.*
CBF	Colonial Bishoprics Fund.
CBM	Central Board of Missions.
CCM	Children of the Church Magazine [SPG].
CCM&PR	*Cape Church Monthly and Parish Record.*
CCR	*Church Congress, Report of Proceedings.*
CE/CA	Church of England, Church [National] Assembly.
CE/CACTM	Church of England, Central Advisory Council of Training for the Ministry.
CE/CA/MC	Church of England, Church Assembly, Missionary Council.
CE/CBM	Church of England, Central Board of Missions.
CE/GS/RC	Church of England, General Synod, Record Centre.
CE/UBM	Church of England, United Boards of Missions of Canterbury and York.
CEYB	*Official Yearbook of the Church of England.*
Ch.Ch.	*Church Chronicle for the Province of South Africa.*
CMS	*Church Missionary Society.*
CMSA	*Church Magazine for South Africa.*
CPSA	*Church of the Province of South Africa.*
CQR	*Church Quarterly Review.*
CR/C.R.	Community of the Resurrection (Mirfield).
CT	*Church Times.*
Davidson	Randall Davidson papers.
DCA	Derbyshire County Archives.
ECMS	*English Church Men's Society.*
ETW	*East and the West: Quarterly Review for the Study of Missions.*
HMss	Historical Manuscripts collection.
JCMA	Junior Clergy Missionary Association.
JCMA (*N*)	Junior Clergy Missionary Association, *Resumé of Proceedings of the Nth Conference.*
LC	Lambeth Conference.
LMS	London Missionary Society.

L.Th.	Licentiate in Theology.
MC: Burgh	St. Paul's Missionary College, Burgh, Lincs.
MC: Canterbury	St. Augustine's College, Canterbury.
MC: Warminster	St. Boniface College, Warminster.
LPL	Lambeth Palace Library.
LRCP	Licentiate of the Royal College of Physicians.
MF	*The Mission Field.*
MMA	Mashonaland Mission Association.
MQP	*Mashonaland Quarterly Paper.*
MRCS	Member of the Royal College of Surgeons.
NAZ	National Archives of Zimbabwe.
RCM	*Rhodesian Church Magazine.*
RHL/USPG	The Bodleian Library of Commonwealth and African Studies at Rhodes House, Oxford, Archives of the United Society for the Propagation of the Gospel.
SACRMQP	*South African Church Railway Mission Quarterly Paper.*
SDC, Lampeter	St. David's College, Lampeter.
SPCK	Society for the Promotion of Christian Knowledge.
SPG	Society for the Propagation of the Gospel in Foreign Parts.
SRQP	*Southern Rhodesia Quarterly Paper.*
Temple	Frederick Temple Papers.
TC: Can. Shol. Linc.	Lincoln Theological College.
TC: Sarum	Salisbury Theological College.
UMCA	Universities Mission to Central Africa.
W/CPSA	University of the Witwatersrand Library, Archives of the Church of the Province of South Africa.

LIST OF OLD AND NEW NAMES

Barue	Barwe
Bechuanaland	Botswana
Enkeldoorn	Chivu
Essexvale	Esigodini
[Fort] Victoria	Masvingo
Gatooma	Kadoma
Gwelo	Gweru
Hartley	Chegutu
Hunyani	Chitungwiza
Inyamwenda's	Norton
Inyanga	Nyanga
Lomagundi	Makonde
Makombi	Macombe
Mangwendi	Mangwende
Marandellas	Marondera
Massikessi	Macequece, Vila de Manica
Matopos	Matobo
Melsetter	Chimanimani
Que Que	Kwekwe
Ramaquabane	Ramokwebana
Rusapi/e	Rusape
Salisbury	Harare
Selukwe	Shurugwi
Shashi	Shashe
Sinoia	Chinoyi
Umtali	Mutare
Umtasa	Mtasa
Umvuma	Mvuma
Umvukwes	Mvurwe

MAPS AND ILLUSTRATIONS

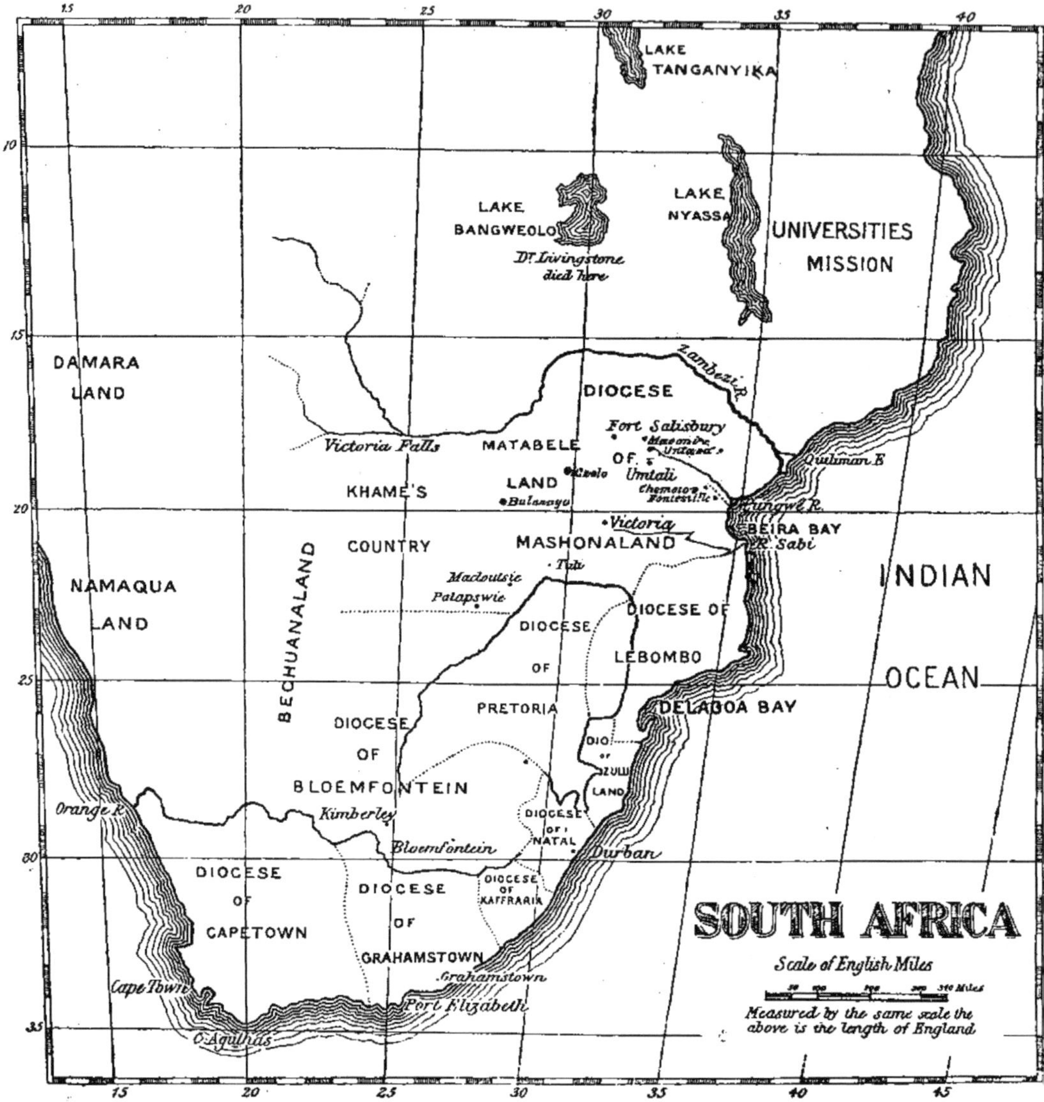

Map 1: The early Diocese of Mashonaland, as published in *Mashonaland Quarterly Paper*, 1893. Used with the permission of the Transvaal, Zimbabwe and Botswana Association.

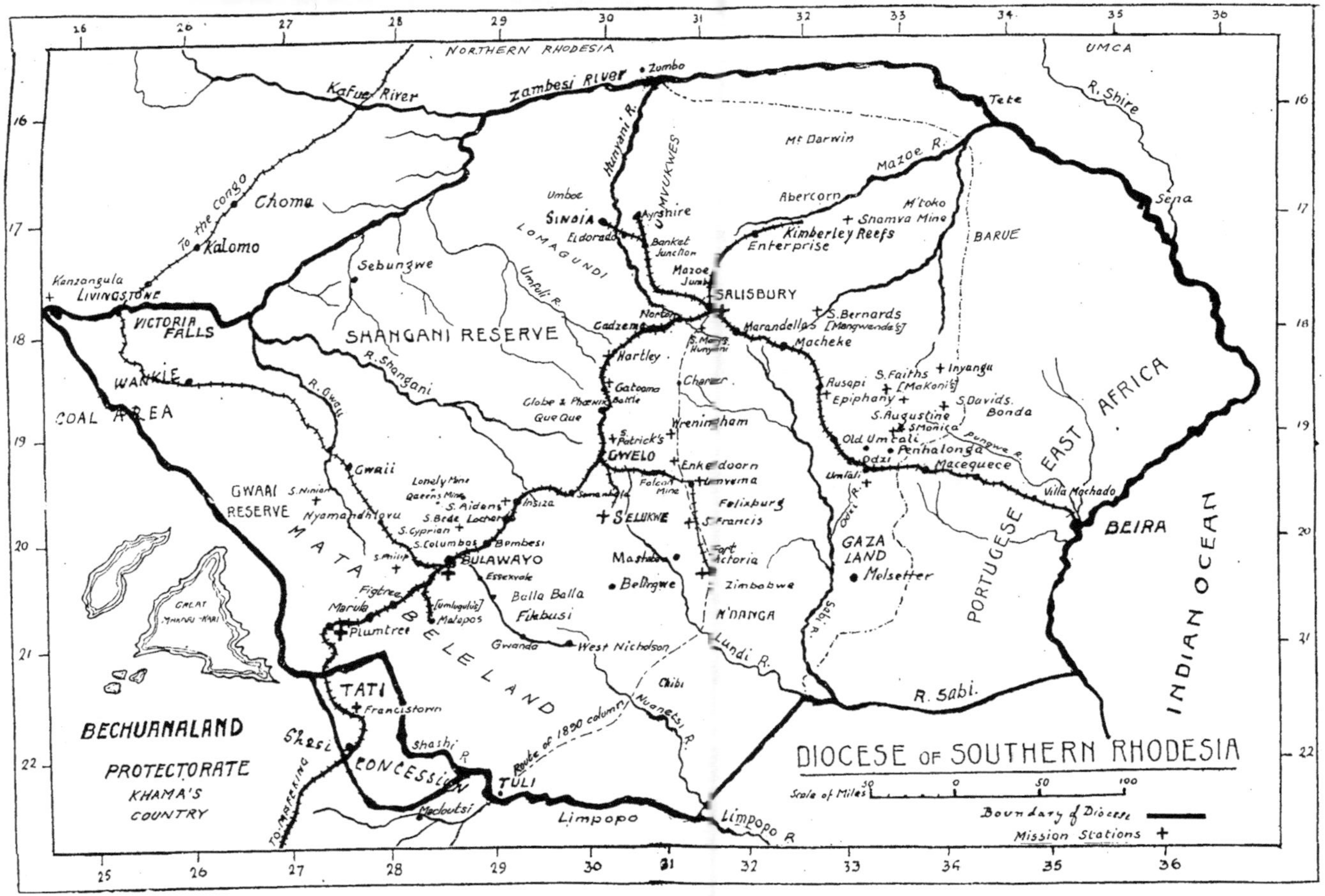

Map 2: The Diocese of Mashonaland/Southern Rhodesia, to 1925, as published in *Southern Rhodesia Quarterly Paper* CXXIV (May 1923) [amended]. Used with the permission of the Transvaal, Zimbabwe and Botswana Association.

Illustration 1: The first church in Salisbury (Harare), 1891, from Mrs O. Gumprich and Mrs E. Yates, compilers, *Women in Central Africa* ([Salisbury]: The Committee of Press, Publicity and Broadcasting of the National Council of Women of Southern Rhodesia, [1951]).

Illustration 2: Sir Herbert Baker, architect's drawing for Salisbury Cathedral, front elevation (c. 1913): cover picture, *Diocese of Southern Rhodesia Church Magazine*, No. 6–Vol. IV (New Series), Jubilee Number, 5th October, 1938. Used with the permission of the Department of Historical Papers, University of Witwatersrand Library.

INTRODUCTION

This book explores the history of the Anglican Diocese of Mashonaland/Southern Rhodesia, a diocese of the Church of the Province of South Africa, in the period 1890–1925 when its institutions took shape and its religious character was formed. It is primarily a study of work among white settlers: detailed consideration of work among indigenous communities, other (minority) groups of settlers, or the migrant labour population lies outside its scope and this work is, therefore, only sketched in outline.

The general history of the diocese in the period has been treated, somewhat briefly, by St. John Evans (1945) and, in more detail, by G.E.P. Broderick (typescript, 1953). Both authors proceed more by way of chronicle and anecdote than analysis, however, and there are large *lacunae* in both narratives. Arnold (1985) merely summarises the work of Evans and Broderick.[1]

Biographies have been published of the catechist-martyr, Bernard Mizeki, and the radical missionary, Arthur Shearly Cripps. Farrant's biography of Mizeki (1966)[2] although now rather dated in approach and occasionally inaccurate in detail, makes sensitive use of sources and so offers considerable insight into the circumstances of the 1890s and into the actions of the first bishop, Knight-Bruce, the third figure of major significance, of whom no adequate study exists.[3] The narrow focus of those who have studied Cripps, however, Steere (1973) and

[1] H.St.J.T. Evans, *The Church in Southern Rhodesia* (Westminster and London: S.P.G. and S.P.C.K., 1945); G.E.P. Broderick, 'A History of the Diocese of Southern Rhodesia (formerly the Diocese of Mashonaland) 1874–1952' (Compiled for the USPG, 1953); W.E. Arnold, *Here to Stay: The Story of the Anglican Church in Zimbabwe* (Lewes, Sussex: The Book Guild Limited, 1985).

[2] Jean Farrant, *Mashonaland Martyr: Bernard Mizeki and the Pioneer Church* (Cape Town, London, Salisbury: Oxford University Press, 1966).

[3] There is one reasonably accurate biographical sketch: R.R. Langham-Carter, *Knight Bruce: First Bishop and Founder of the Anglican Church in Rhodesia* (Salisbury, Rhodesia: Christchurch, Borrowdale, [1975]). There is also a brief, but perceptive, portrait of William Gaul, the second bishop, in A. Pierce Jones, *A Procession of Witness* (Cape Town: [Printed by the Stewart Printing Company, Cape Town], 1947); and a fair memoir of the fifth bishop: Geoffrey Gibbon, *Paget of Rhodesia: A Memoir of Edward, 5th Bishop of Mashonaland* (Johannesburg: Africana Book Society (Pty.) Ltd., 1973).

Steele (1975, 2000) limits their contribution to an understanding of the wider church, post-1901.[4]

The very large number of studies of Christian activity in colonial Zimbabwe, which have been produced since the 1960s also have their limits where the general history of the diocese is concerned, as they either ignore settler religious history or treat it in only one aspect, that of a (stereotypical) failure of settler Christians in their duty towards indigenous communities, whether Christian or not.[5] There is, furthermore, no study devoted to Anglican mission history alone, so even that history has to be gleaned from general and comparative works.

Only the historian John Weller, though much constrained by limitations of space, has offered some balance. In 1984 for example, he pointed out that the Anglican church was, to an exceptional degree (in a racially-divided society), a bi-cultural institution.[6] Weller has also offered a fresh general historiography: in *Anglican Centenary* (1991) he began the story in 1891, with the arrival in the diocese of Knight-Bruce and five (black) catechists.[7] Earlier accounts emphasise a journey of exploration made by Knight-Bruce in 1888 and the entry of Francis Balfour, a (white) clergyman, with the British South Africa Company's 'pioneer column' in 1890.

Stimulating use of Anglican sources has also been made by Terence Ranger in a variety of publications since the 1960s, as he has sought to identify political overtones to missionary activity in Southern Rhodesia and to discern an indigenous response to that activity. He has drawn, in particular, on one of the two main printed records of the diocese, the *Mashonaland/Southern Rhodesia Quarterly Paper*, a compilation of reports and letters, mainly from serving missionaries, published in England between

---

[4] Douglas V. Steere, *God's Irregular: Arthur Shearly Cripps: A Rhodesian Epic* (London: S.P.C.K., 1973); Murray Steele, '"With hope unconquered and unconquerable..." Arthur Shearly Cripps, 1869–1952', in T.O. Ranger and J. Weller, eds. *Themes in the Christian History of Central Africa* (London: Heinemann Educational, 1975), 152–174; Murray Steele, 'Arthur Shearly Cripps' in Daniel O'Connor ed., and others. *Three Centuries of Mission: The United Society for the Propagation of the Gospel 1701–2000* (New York, London: Continuum, 2000), 371–381.

[5] E.g., T. Mcloughlin, 'Teaching the laity: some problems of the Christian Churches in Rhodesia', in A.J. Dachs, ed., *Christianity South of the Zambezi 1* (Gwelo: Mambo Press, 1973), 189–197.

[6] John Weller with Jane Linden, *Mainstream Christianity to 1980 in Malawi, Zambia and Zimbabwe* (Gweru: Mambo Press, 1984).

[7] John C. Weller, *Anglican Centenary in Zimbabwe 1891–1991* (Mutare: (n.p.), 1991).

1892 and 1926.[8] Recently, Ranger has employed the new historiography (of the wide-ranging significance of religious practice, which scholars are using to complement the study of institutions)[9] in studies of the Makoni (1987) and Matobo districts (1999). The influence of the former article is acknowledged in Chapter Six of this thesis.[10]

The principal sources used here are the (published and unpublished) records of the diocese itself, in the National Archives of Zimbabwe; those of the CPSA in the Library of the University of the Witwatersrand; and those of the Society for the Propagation of the Gospel, at Rhodes House, Oxford. A variety of other sources, not used by previous historians, has also been consulted. These include sundry records of the Church of England and the wider Anglican church, many of them published, others to be found in the Record Centre of the General Synod of the Church of England and in Lambeth Palace Library.

This has enabled gaps in the history of the diocese to be filled in and major events to be, not just chronicled, but explained. The methods and approach of the new historiography are also employed: here is traced, not just the development of an institution, with its staff, buildings and Synods but also the emergence of a distinct, local, religious identity. It is hoped, therefore, that this study will contribute both to the new generation of histories of church institutions, which are appearing world-wide,[11] and also to that of the new historiography.

Chapter One examines the episcopate of Knight-Bruce, and the conflict inherent in the attempts of a bishop of the 'English Church'[12] to establish missions in Mashonaland while distancing himself from

[8] The other major printed source is the *Rhodesia Church Magazine*, published primarily for settler congregations in the diocese, 1901–4, and again from 1907–27. In the interval, diocesan news was reported in the (South African) *Church Chronicle*.

[9] See, for instance, David Maxwell, 'The Spirit and the Scapular: Pentecostal and Catholic Interactions in Northern Nyanga District, Zimbabwe in the 1950s and Early 1960s', *Journal of Southern African Studies* 23:2 (June 1997), 283–300; Alison Clarke, *Holiday Seasons: Christmas, New Year and Easter in Nineteenth-Century, New Zealand* (Auckland: Auckland University Press, 2007).

[10] Terence Ranger, 'Taking Hold of the Land: Holy Places and Pilgrimages in Twentieth-Century Zimbabwe', *Past and Present* 117 (November, 1987), 158–194; *Voices from the Rocks: Nature, Culture and History in the Matopos Hills of Zimbabwe* (Harare, Bloomington and Indianapolis, Oxford: Baobab, Indiana University Press and James Currie, 1999).

[11] E.g. Ian Breward, *A History of the Churches in Australasia* (New York, Oxford: Oxford University Press, 2001); David Hempton, *Methodism: empire of the spirit* (New Haven, Conn., London: Yale University Press, c. 2005).

[12] This official alternative title for the Church of the Province of South Africa was used to describe the church, by its members, throughout the period. The term 'Anglican' was rarely, if ever, used.

the British South Africa Company's activities. The evidence of rivalry between him and Cecil Rhodes (a rivalry pointed to by Fripp and Hiller in 1949, but not since explored)[13] is considered in some detail and the starting-point of Anglican activity is once again taken as 1890 but with the entry of two, rather than one (white) clergymen to the territory with the pioneer column. Only one of these was a settler chaplain, however: Balfour's presence is seen, not as an endorsement of company rule but as an attempt to smuggle a missionary into the area.

Chapters Two and Three trace the subsequent uneven development of the diocese under Knight-Bruce's successors (Gaul, Powell and Beaven) and the oscillation in their elections to the bishopric between men of a purely missionary inclination, like Knight-Bruce and those who were at ease with settlers. Two major themes emerge from these narratives: those of the difficulties of obtaining staff and a search for financial security.[14]

The Church of England was the (ultimate) mother-church of the diocese and so the agency which might most be expected to come to its aid. Chapter Four therefore explores the bases and strength of missionary enthusiasm and support, in England, for the overseas church. Chapter Five examines the current supply of clergy to the church in England and abroad, the methods employed in recruiting for work overseas and the obstacles to satisfactory recruitment.[15] An analysis is made of the backgrounds and possible motivation of clergy who were recruited for Mashonaland/SR in the period.

Chapter Six examines the religious practice which developed in the diocese, as English models were retained or modified and new forms of religious expression emerged under the many influences and agents of the new setting: those of the (High Church) tradition of the CPSA; of missionaries, converts and settlers; and the landscape and climate of Central-Southern Africa. A specific study is made of settler religion, which has hitherto received scant attention from scholars.

---

[13] C.E. Fripp and V.W. Hiller, eds. *Gold and the Gospel in Mashonaland 1888: being the journals of 1. The Mashonaland Mission of Bishop Knight-Bruce 2. The Concession journey of Charles Dunell Rudd*. Central African Archives, Oppenheimer Series Number Four (London: Chatto and Windus, 1949).

[14] Weller's assertion (1984), 65, that the diocese was financially dependent upon the settler laity, rather than upon outside agencies, is not correct for this period.

[15] A conference on white settler history in Africa, in 1979, revealed that such history can rarely be understood without an examination of the settlers' society of origin in Europe: Terence Ranger, 'White Presence and Power in Africa', *Journal of African History*, 20 (1979), 463ff.

CHAPTER ONE

OCCUPYING THE GROUND: BISHOP KNIGHT-BRUCE (1891–1894)

In 1891 the Church of the Province of South Africa (CPSA), a daughter church of the Church of England, expanded into Central Africa. A diocese was created by the Provincial Synod for an area north of the Diocese of Pretoria, which ended at the Limpopo River. This diocese, "for Mashonaland and the surrounding territories",[1] was one of the largest Anglican dioceses in the world. It was roughly the size of France, two-and-a-half times the size of Great Britain (see Map 1, p. xx). The central area of the original diocese is today divided into the five dioceses of the Anglican Church in Zimbabwe (Harare, Matabeleland, Mutare, Central Zimbabwe and Masvingo).

Mashonaland itself was little known to the outside world in 1891 and undefined, other than by its general topography and the distribution within it of Shona-speaking peoples ('the Mashona'). At its centre was a large, high plateau, well-wooded and watered. To the north, the land fell away to the Zambezi River; to the east, in the region of the Manyika people rose a mountainous barrier beyond which lay the colony of Portuguese East Africa. Much of the area was dominated by two peoples of Southern, Nguni, origin: the Gaza, in 'Umzila's country' to the south-east;[2] and the Ndebele ('Matabele'), in the south-west (see Map 2, p. xxi).

Ndebele territory (Matabeleland) was itself bordered to the south-west, across the Ramokwebana and Shashe Rivers, by territory known as 'Khama's country': Khama was the leading chief of a number of native polities which had come under British influence, as the Bechuanaland Protectorate, in 1885.[3] To the south-east of Matabeleland and south-west of Gazaland ran the Limpopo River, which served not only as an ecclesiastical boundary between the new Diocese of Mashonaland and

---

[1] 'The Bishop's Letter: Resolutions: Section VII', *CMSA* 6:64 (April 1891), xxxi.

[2] The Gaza people migrated east, just outside the area covered by this study, in 1889: David Beach, *The Shona and their Neighbours* (Oxford: Blackwell, 1994), 137.

[3] Modern Botswana is composed of the former Bechuanaland Protectorate and British Bechuanaland.

that of Pretoria but also as a political boundary: it was the northern border of the Boer South African Republic, or Transvaal.

I *Knight-Bruce and Cecil Rhodes: rival visions*

The immediate cause of the creation of the Diocese of Mashonaland was political rather than ecclesiastical. Lobengula, king of the Ndebele, claimed to rule Mashonaland and certainly exercised effective control over approaches to the area from the south. In October 1888, he granted a mining concession for Mashonaland to agents of Cecil Rhodes, the Kimberley diamond millionaire and Cape politician. Rhodes subsequently formed a large company, the British South Africa Company and the British government, already interested in extending imperial influence in the region, granted the company a charter to exploit the Rudd concession (and any other concessions its representatives were able to obtain from local rulers). In mid-1890, a force of 1,000 men entered Mashonaland: some 200 'pioneers', with their waggon drivers and other employees and a mounted police escort.

The hold these men then established on the area was limited in both extent and effect: indeed, its very precariousness was the reason no resistance was offered to their presence. It is clear that, for some years, local people believed the invaders to be little other than the prospectors and miners they purported to be.[4] By early 1891, nevertheless, 'British Zambezia' was a political fact (from the imperial perspective, at least) and the BSA Company seemingly sufficiently settled for the church to make formal its presence in the new territory, to create a diocese and appoint a bishop.[5]

In forming the Diocese of Mashonaland, however, the church was not simply following the flag. Interest had been shown in the area as early as 1874 by the English missionary society, the Society for the Propagation of the Gospel in Foreign Parts (SPG).[6] In 1886 this interest was revived when a young English clergyman, George Wyndham Hamilton Knight-Bruce, who had long wanted to do missionary work,

---

[4] *Ibid.*, 167.

[5] W/CPSA, AB/1162/A, Diocese of Capetown, Letter-books (1886–1895), Bishops, letters from, 16, to Bishop of Maritzburg, April 17th, 1890, f. 224, to Rev. H.W. Tucker, February 18th, 1891, f. 258.

[6] H.St.J.T. Evans, *The Church in Southern Rhodesia* (Westminster and London: S.P.G. and S.P.C.K., 1945), 9–10.

was appointed Bishop of Bloemfontein, in the Orange Free State.[7] His diocese extended westwards into British Bechuanaland, south of Khama's country and from there a 'road', a rough waggon and major trading route, led to the north (see Map 1, p. xx).

Before his departure for Africa Knight-Bruce consulted the officials of the SPG and laid before them a scheme for a mission to the interior, with himself as its leader.[8] Before he had even taken up his appointment as Bishop of Bloemfontein, therefore, he was dreaming dreams of missionary achievement elsewhere.

After he arrived in Africa Knight-Bruce's ambition crystallized: in the region of Mashonaland he would create a vast area of exclusive missionary influence and thus join the most northerly part of the CPSA to the most southerly stations of the Universities Mission to Central Africa (UMCA), which stretched from the Zambezi to East Africa (see Map 1, p. xx).[9] The English Church, and none other, was to "occupy"[10] the area and be responsible for protecting and converting the local peoples.

Knight-Bruce spent two years in Bloemfontein gathering information about Mashonaland and then in early 1888, with the approval of his metropolitan, William West Jones, the Bishop of Capetown,[11] he embarked on an extensive missionary journey to the north. He travelled first to Lobengula's capital, Bulawayo, for it was unwise to attempt to travel into Mashonaland without the king's permission: the bishop made careful note in his journal of where a party of Englishmen, which included the son of a missionary, had been attacked and killed at Lobengula's command in 1877: but then they had threatened the king.[12]

---

[7] NAZ, HMss, 354, Knight-Bruce, Correspondence and other papers, general, 1885–89, Bishop of Bedford to Archbishop [of Canterbury], November 4th, 1885.

[8] 'The Bishop's Charge, Delivered in the Cathedral, Bloemfontein, at the Opening of the Diocesan Synod, 1890', *BQP* 89 (July 1890), 284.

[9] 'The Bishop's Charge', *BQP* 89 (July 1890), 284, 286–7; 'A Diocese for Mashonaland: The Bishop of Bloemfontein's speech, at a Missionary Meeting at Capetown, February 4th, 1891, during the Provincial Synod', *BQP* 92 (April 1891), 61; G.W.H. Knight-Bruce, *Memories of Mashonaland* (1895) (Facsimile reproduction: Bulawayo: Books of Rhodesia, 1970), 83, 111–2.

[10] Editorial: 'British Responsibilities in Africa', *MF* XXXV:419 (Nov 1890), 402–3.

[11] The title of Archbishop was assumed after the Lambeth Conference of 1897.

[12] C.E. Fripp and V.W. Hiller, eds. *Gold and the Gospel in Mashonaland 1888: being the journals of 1. The Mashonaland Mission of Bishop Knight-Bruce 2. The Concession journey of Charles Dunell Rudd*, Central African Archives, Oppenheimer Series Number Four (London: Chatto and Windus, 1949), 17, 25, nte. 1.

Knight-Bruce took with him several African and 'Coloured' (mixed-ancestry) Christians as servants and companions, a rough map given him by the hunter F.C. Selous and a letter of introduction from Sir Sidney Shippard, Administrator of British Bechuanaland, who was one of his own flock.

He had earlier enlisted the help of missionaries of the London Missionary Society (LMS) who had been working in Matabeleland, without making more than a handful of converts, for almost thirty years. They had, however, gained the respect and so the ear of the king.[13] The LMS, for their part, had long looked "wistfully" at Mashonaland but having been unable to extend there themselves were willing to assist another missionary body to do so.[14] Knight-Bruce obtained permission from Lobengula to proceed and then he made a journey of five months with his companions through Mashonaland, more than 500 miles of it on foot. He penetrated as far north as Zumbo on the Zambezi, exploring (and mapping) areas few Englishmen had ever seen. As he travelled he laid foundations for a future mission, visiting local chiefs and asking their permission to send a teacher to them, should that ever prove possible.

How likely it was, in 1888, that a mission could be established was uncertain. The Scramble for Africa was taking place, the great European powers jostling one another to obtain land, influence and mineral rights in Southern Central Africa as elsewhere in the continent. Lobengula's court was besieged by concession hunters and representatives of governments.

By the time Knight-Bruce first reached Bulawayo in May 1888, the king had signed an exclusive treaty of peace and friendship with the British (the Moffat Treaty) but he and his people were still nervous. They suspected Britain of territorial ambition and were distrustful of anyone seeking gold. In earlier years Lobengula had allowed white men to travel into Mashonaland to hunt and prospect. Now he refused all applications to travel beyond Bulawayo except those of a couple of hunters and Knight-Bruce, who had no interest in gold. Even the bishop's request he parried for two weeks.

---

[13] Knight-Bruce, *Memories*, 56, 83; Fripp and Hiller, *Gold and the Gospel*, 5, 32, 97; C.J.M. Zvobgo, *A History of Christian Missions in Zimbabwe 1890–1939* (Gweru: Mambo Press, 1996), 1, 14.

[14] NAZ, HMss, BR 8/1/1, R. Wardlaw Thompson, Foreign Secretary LMS, to Bishop of Bloemfontein, 23rd June, 1887, f. 8.

When Knight-Bruce then returned to Bulawayo from his journey upcountry in October 1888, he found that pressure on the king had intensified and that among the many men seeking a mining concession in Mashonaland were three agents of Cecil Rhodes. Rhodes, like Knight Bruce, dreamed of expansion. His dream was a secular one, however, although held by him with an almost mystical fervour: he wished to see the empire and British colonisation where it was possible, stretch from the Cape to Cairo. He had already been largely responsible for the spread of British influence into British Bechuanaland and Khama's country: the next step was to cross the Limpopo.[15]

Knight-Bruce, on the other hand, had come to Africa with the "Utopian" dream of establishing a mission in a "purely native" country[16] and he was never to abandon his conviction that missions could have been established in Mashonaland without the BSA Company and its settlers, or even Imperial protection. He had in fact set off on his missionary journey in 1888 earlier than he had originally planned, in the somewhat forlorn hope of obtaining an entry for missionaries to Mashonaland before the gold-seekers. He "did not think the attempt hopeless", however, and believed that Lobengula would have preferred his missionaries to Rhodes's agents but then, as he remarked somewhat tartly, he could not offer "the inducements" that the company could provide—money and rifles.[17]

Knight-Bruce disliked the idea of rule by a commercial company and shared the opinion of many of his contemporaries in Africa and elsewhere—Bishop Key of St. John's, Kaffraria, for instance—who believed that 'civilisation' as represented by settlers, rather than by missionaries, brought little good to local peoples.[18] Contact with civilisation or as Knight-Bruce put it, with "its degraded camp-followers",[19] had been mostly "the curse of the uncivilised".[20]

---

[15] Robert Rotberg, *The Founder: Cecil Rhodes and the Pursuit of Power* (Oxford: Oxford University Press, 1988), 155–66, 159–160, 170–9, 228, 229, 243–5, 682, 686.

[16] Knight-Bruce, *Memories*, 132.

[17] 'The Bishop's Letter', *BQP* 90 (Oct 1890), 330.

[18] Fripp and Hiller, *Gold and the Gospel*, 6–7; 'The Healing of the Nations. A missionary sermon by the Right Rev. Bransby Key, D.D., Lord Bishop of St. John's, Kaffraria, *MF* XXXVI:430 (Oct 1891), 365.

[19] 'The Bishop's Letter', *BQP* 84 (April 1889), 83.

[20] Canon Leigh Bennett, 'Our English Brothers and Sisters beyond the Sea', *MF* XXXVIII:449 (May 1893), 164.

He was prepared to acknowledge that 'civilisation', if carried out by "high-minded" Englishmen and thus "humanely",[21] could eventually be "a blessing" to "lands of darkness" such as Mashonaland but ordinary settlers brought vices with them and the "evils" which accompanied the usual "progress of civilisation" were "neither few nor small".[22] He was one of those who dreaded a repeat in Mashonaland of "the worst mistakes of the past".[23]

Colonisation, moreover, was certain to have a direct effect on his missions, for the bad examples and influence of unregenerate white settlers were widely regarded in missionary circles as one of the chief obstacles to their success. Knight-Bruce also thought that work among local people was likely to be "hindered" and "interfered with" by the presence of settlers, since it would be his duty as a bishop of the English Church to extend spiritual care to them.[24] The last thing he wanted to see in Mashonaland was white settlement.

II *The bishop and the company: Knight-Bruce as political realist*

If British rule in Mashonaland was inevitable, Knight-Bruce favoured a protectorate but it was unlikely that a protectorate would be declared over the area. Rhodes already had the support of local Imperial officials, for one thing: when Knight-Bruce returned to Bulawayo in October 1888, he found there not only Rhodes' agents but also Sir Sidney Shippard, Administrator of British Bechuanaland. Shippard had come, ostensibly, to discuss a boundary dispute between Lobengula and Khama but in reality he was there to lend weight to Rhodes' application for a mining concession in Mashonaland.[25]

Knight-Bruce himself was drawn into the web, visiting the king with Shippard and so lending his credibility to Rhodes' negotiations. Shortly after he and Shippard left for the south, Lobengula signed the Rudd Concession, the basis for the BSA Company's charter.

How aware Knight-Bruce was at the time of the significance of the coincidence of Shippard and Charles Rudd's visits to Bulawayo in

[21] G.W.H. Knight-Bruce, *Journals of the Mashonaland Mission 1881–92* (London: Society for the Propagation of the Gospel in Foreign Parts, 1892), 60, 74.

[22] 'The Bishop's Letter', *BQP* 84 (April 1889), 83.

[23] Editorial: 'The Society's Grants for 1891', *MF* XXXV:415 (July 1890), 250.

[24] Editorial: 'British Responsibilities in Africa', *MF* XXXV:419 (Nov 1890), 403.

[25] Fripp and Hiller, *Gold and the Gospel*, 6–7, 222.

October 1888, and of how he was himself used in some measure to support Rhodes' ambitions, is difficult to tell. The evidence points to his having had very clear suspicions, subsequently if not at the time. His accounts of his exploration were written with an eye to publication in missionary magazines in England[26] and in them he avoided direct political comment but these accounts are significant as much for what they omit as for what they say. Rudd and his companions are barely mentioned, for instance, and then dismissively (as "some" of the Europeans who happened to be at Bulawayo when he was there and who subsequently obtained a concession).[27]

Knight-Bruce was also careful to distance both himself and Shippard from any negotiations connected with the Rudd concession. Knight-Bruce's own relations with Lobengula, he said, had "nothing to do with his relations to the Chartered Company"[28] and he noted in his journal that Shippard had specifically dissociated himself from gold-seekers in their joint interview with the king.[29] Knight-Bruce also referred to Shippard's visit, publicly and somewhat too emphatically, as something in itself and quite detached from anything else, a diplomatic visit to which he attributed "the origin of any friendly feeling that may exist between that chief and the English nation".[30]

Shippard, however, was both a churchman and an official of the Imperial Government and Knight-Bruce always maintained a strictly correct attitude towards him. He made harsh private criticisms of Rhodes and the BSA Company, on the other hand. Rhodes saw missions only as something to be used in his own schemes, as a "political factor".[31] As for the Chartered Company, Knight-Bruce had "a mean opinion of their integrity"[32] and he was irritated by the fact that even some of his clergy were carried away by "the general excitement" roused by the granting of the company's charter and the 1890 expedition to Mashonaland.[33]

---

[26] *The Mission Field* (SPG), July to December 1889; *BQP* 83 (Jan 1889), 8–14, 84 (April 1889), 53–83, 87 (Jan 1890), 192–8.

[27] 'The Bishop's Letter', *BQP* 90 (Oct 1890), 330–1.

[28] *Ibid.*, 331.

[29] Fripp and Hiller, *Gold and the Gospel*, 95.

[30] 'The Bishop's Letter', *BQP* 90 (Oct 1890), 335.

[31] RHL/USPG, D Series, 102(B), 1892, G.H.W. Knight-Bruce to Mr Tucker (n.d.).

[32] LPL, Benson, 79, H.W. Tucker to Archbishop, March 23rd, 1895, f. 141v.

[33] RHL/USPG, D Series, 94(a), 1890, G.H.W. Knight-Bruce to Mr Tucker, February 8th, 1890.

Throughout his involvement with Mashonaland, Knight-Bruce was always careful to distinguish the work of the church from that of the process of colonisation which began in 1890. "Much has been said lately which would give the impression that the Church is going to Mashonaland because the Chartered Company propose going. Nothing could be further removed from the truth."[34] It was "humanly speaking, an accident, that the Chartered Company and the Church should have chosen the same country for their respective purposes".[35]

He insisted, after the company had been granted a charter that attempts would be made to establish a mission in Mashonaland even if the company's venture failed. He was worried by the Bishop of Capetown who seemed "to afect (sic) generally to a closer association with the Company than I advocate" and told him so.[36] In public, he made a pointed distinction between the work of the church and the actions of the company: it remained to be proved (as he wrote in 1891) whether its presence would ultimately "benefit" or hinder the Mission.[37]

Knight-Bruce, however, was a realist: "when we have certain factors to work with, it is idle to theorize as to what would be the best conceivable, and reject anything that does not seem perfect on the hope that something perfect may be found".[38] This realism was just as well for the British government was inclined to back Rhodes' ambitions. Knight-Bruce bowed to the inevitable, even going so far as to use his influence in Rhodes' cause, in Africa and in England—under pressure from Rhodes.[39]

He wrote in support of Rhodes to the English press, for instance and he retracted criticism he had made in public: in 1888, at a church meeting at Vryburg on his return from his journeying in Mashonaland, he had bitterly attacked a clause in the Rudd Concession which allowed for the delivery of large numbers of rifles to Lobengula. Knight-Bruce stigmatised this as a piece of unsurpassed "devilry and brutality". He had seen the effects of Ndebele raiding *impis* on his journey: rifles

---

[34] 'The Bishop's Letter', *BQP* 90 (Oct 1890), 331.

[35] 'A Diocese for Mashonaland' [From the *Cape Times* of February 6th, 1891], *BQP* 92 (April 1891), 57.

[36] RHL/USPG, D Series, 94(a), 1890, G.H.W. Knight-Bruce to Tucker, February 8th, 1890.

[37] 'Going to Mashonaland', [letter from] the Bishop of Bloemfontein, 11th May, 1891, *MF* XXXVI:428 (Aug 1891), 293.

[38] 'The Bishop's Letter', *BQP* 90 (Oct 1890), 317.

[39] Fripp and Hiller, *Gold and the Gospel*, 222.

would allow the Ndebele to slaughter the Shona even more effectively than they were already doing. Knight-Bruce called for British protection over the area, his speech was reported in the papers and led to enquiries uncomfortable to Rhodes by the British government and in the British press.[40]

Knight-Bruce explained his reasons for withdrawing this criticism in a footnote in his diocesan magazine, in 1890. As always was the case when he was uneasy about his actions, his language was obscure but what appears to have lain behind his retraction was practical politics. With the granting of the Rudd concession, Rhodes was about to become the dominant force in Mashonaland and he had put pressure on Knight-Bruce, writing to him on the question of the rifles and making no compromises.[41]

In his footnote, Knight-Bruce explained that he had discovered that the consignment of rifles was not merely part of a payment for mining rights, as he had apparently originally believed but was "a factor in an agreement by which it was intended that the Mashona should be benefited", the action of an "organized system", a company which had been granted a charter by the British government.

This company, moreover, was taking steps to prevent "bad influences" being brought to bear "both on its own men and on the natives" (they were to ban the sale of liquor to 'the natives', for instance) and co-operating "in every scheme for their elevation". Mr. Rhodes had contributed "another" £100 pounds to the mission and its elevating influences, thus setting a good example to other African companies. The bishop "withdrew all reflections" on the matter of the rifles.[42]

The real point, though this can only be inferred from what he wrote, was that with a British presence (of sorts) in Mashonaland, an 'organized system', the Ndebele were not going to be able to use their rifles. The consignment was therefore not likely to be the danger to the Shona that Knight-Bruce had initially believed. He subsequently singled out the BSA Company for praise on this point: with company rule, Ndebele raids on the Shona had (apparently) stopped.[43]

In his support of Rhodes, Knight-Bruce even went so far as to recommend him and his agents as "friends of mine" in a letter to

---

[40] Fripp and Hiller, *Gold and the Gospel*, 6, 222; Langham-Carter, *Knight Bruce*, 23.
[41] Fripp and Hiller, *Gold and the Gospel*, 139.
[42] 'The Bishop's Charge', *BQP* 89 (July 1890), 287, nte. 1.
[43] 'Notes of the Month', *MF* XXXVIII:440 (Aug 1892), 312.

Lobengula, now twisting and turning in attempts to free himself from the Rudd Concession. The bishop's unease in this letter is very evident: "I never said that I should advise you to allow anyone to go through your country to look for gold. However, Mr. Rhodes, Mr. Rudd and Mr. Maguire, are friends of mine, and if you allow anyone to look for gold in Mashonaland, I think that no other people would be better friends to your country than these would be."[44]

Any *rapprochement* between Rhodes and Knight-Bruce was more apparent than real: Knight-Bruce revealed later, in a private letter to the SPG, that he believed that Rhodes "was unlikely to forgive" him for his "opposition" to the rifles.[45] He also appears to have been keen to frustrate Rhodes' territorial ambitions in Portuguese East Africa in 1891 (see, below, pp. 23–4) and while others were fawning or fulsome[46] he held himself aloof from Rhodes. When they met in Mashonaland in 1893, for instance, Knight-Bruce's account of their meeting was of the very barest: he met Rhodes while both were travelling, shared a meal with him in a hut, borrowed a blanket.[47] References to Rhodes in Knight-Bruce's writings are very few and almost entirely confined to brief acknowledgements of help given to the church.

III *1888–1890: A waiting game*

The entry of the BSA Company on to the scene in 1890 complicated Knight-Bruce's plans for Mashonaland but they did not cause him to abandon them. He still wished to send in a mission before the company, not only in order to begin the work of conversion but also to provide protection for the Shona.

If colonisation could not be avoided, he considered that its evils might at least be mitigated by the presence of the church: "the importance of establishing such relations as will open the way to civilising influences, and preventing such misunderstandings as might cause ill-feeling between different races cannot be over estimated".[48] Missionaries should

---

[44] Fripp and Hiller, *Gold and the Gospel*, 139–40.

[45] RHL/USPG, D Series, 106(A), 1893, G.H.W. Knight-Bruce, Bishop, to Mr Tucker, December 12th, 1893.

[46] Cf. Major A.G. Leonard, *How We Made Rhodesia* (1896) (Facsimile reproduction: Bulawayo: Books of Rhodesia, 1973), 338–9.

[47] 'Extracts from the Bishop's Journal', *MQP* VII (Jan 1894), 7.

[48] 'The Bishop's Letter', *BQP* 84 (April 1889), 61.

be there to protect local people from "molestation or annoyance",[49] to act as a "buffer" between the Shona and their colonisers[50] and (as one of Knight-Bruce's obituarists later put it) to prevent them simply exchanging "the tyranny of Lobengula for the tyranny of so-called civilisation".[51]

Until the political future of Mashonaland was settled, however, no movement could be made into the area, by missionaries or anyone else. The BSA Company effectively barred the way and, besides, another entry could not have been made through Bulawayo: Lobengula had not given permission and his people were increasingly restive, fearing that others were about to take their land. Knight-Bruce himself had narrowly escaped attack near Bulawayo in October 1888 and Shippard, in Bulawayo, had been threatened.[52] It was not yet possible to enter Mashonaland from the east, through Portuguese territory overland or up the Zambezi, though Knight-Bruce was early convinced that an eastern route would be the best.

For almost two years, until June 1890, when the BSA Company sent an occupying force into Mashonaland, the Bishop of Bloemfontein was forced to play a waiting game. He published accounts of his journey to arouse interest and support for a mission in England and in Bloemfontein. He negotiated details of the proposed mission with the SPG and his metropolitan, Bishop of Capetown.

Determined to be in control of the new venture, he also played a card which he knew to be a strong one in the circumstances, when the metropolitan was casting about for financial support: in August 1889, he made a private offer to serve as bishop of the new diocese without stipend (for the first three years).[53] This did not secure him the see, for a year later another man, also of independent means, was considered "marked out for the bishopric"[54] but it is evidence of his determination and ambition.

---

[49] *Cape Times* (December 2nd, 1891), in RHL/USPG, D Series, 98, 1891.

[50] 'Notes of the Month', *MF* XXXVIII:440 (Aug 1892), 312.

[51] 'Bishop Knight-Bruce', *MF* XLII:494 (Feb 1897), 50.

[52] Fripp and Hiller, *Gold and the Gospel*, 94; Knight-Bruce, *Memories*, 64–5; NAZ, HMss, BO 11/1/1, John Henry Borrow, Nov 7 1888, f. 461.

[53] LPL, Benson, 79, Draft letter to Bishop of Capetown, August 30th, 1889, f. 252v.

[54] W/CPSA, AB/1162/A, 16, Bishops' circular letter, August 13th, 1890, f. 236. The other candidate was Francis Balfour, then in Mashonaland.

Knight-Bruce also fought off rival bids, for another mission to the interior and for a diocese which was somewhat different from the one he was planning. William Gaul, Archdeacon of Kimberley, initially backed by Shippard, first proposed (in July 1889) that a large mission be sent not to Mashonaland but to an area between the Congo and the Zambezi (subsequently part of Northern Rhodesia, now Zambia). What was envisaged was "a second grand Christian crusade into the strongholds of heathendom in the heart of Africa" like that of the UMCA which had been launched from Oxford and Cambridge earlier in the century, after David Livingstone had appealed to England to free Africa from the curse of the slave-trade through 'commerce and Christianity'. It was believed that this "splendid effort" for the closing years of the century from the Universities would be bound to be met with support by the BSA Company: Rhodes, after all, was an Oxford man and Rudd was from Cambridge.[55]

Gaul's missionary proposal was already with the Archbishop of Canterbury, Edward White Benson, and had been recommended to Rhodes as worthy of support by Shippard before Knight-Bruce knew of it but the knowledge of the interior he had gained stood him in good stead, in helping him to fend off this threat to his own plans. He was swift to point out the impracticability of Gaul's scheme, which Shippard then acknowledged.[56]

A second challenge to Knight-Bruce's plans was offered in 1890. The suggestion was made, also apparently by Gaul, that Kimberley should be removed from Bloemfontein and joined to the proposed Mashonaland diocese. This proposal Knight-Bruce also criticised as impractical: such a diocese would be 1,000 miles long. Kimberley was too far to the south to be a useful base of operations and was settler-dominated: Mashonaland and its missions would be badly neglected.[57]

Gaul's plans, however, were unlikely to succeed even without the vigorous opposition of his own bishop, for money for new ventures was difficult to come by. The Archbishop of Canterbury, for example,

---

[55] LPL, Benson, 79, Shippard to Archbishop, July 18th, 1889, f. 240; Bishop of Capetown to Archbishop of Canterbury, July 24th, 1889, f. 242.

[56] W/CPSA, AB/1162/A, 16, Bishop of Capetown to Bishop of Bloemfontein, July 27th, 1889, f. 189, September 30th, 1899, f. 190; Bishop of Capetown to Archbishop, August 28th, 1889, ff. 247–50.

[57] RHL/USPG, D Series, 94(A), 1890, G.H.W. Knight-Bruce, Bishop, to Mr Tucker, April 5th, 1890, May 25th, 1890; 'The Bishop's Charge', *BQP* 89 (July 1890), 285–6.

thought the Universities were unlikely to support a new mission (as they were already over-subscribed) and although he was willing to negotiate on behalf of a mission with Rhodes and Rudd, who were then in England obtaining the charter, he missed them.[58]

Any large missionary or ecclesiastical schemes, moreover, were scaled down by political as well as financial realities. Rhodes now held the key to Mashonaland and while he seemed "quite disposed to sympathize with, and support, some mission work", he made it clear to the Bishop of Capetown, on his return to South Africa from England in September 1889, that he was not prepared to endorse "a large and thoroughly organized mission". The English Church would have to content itself, "at least for some time to come" with two "chaplains for the police in Khama's country", where the forces of the BSA Company was now gathering.

As to missions, the chaplains might "feel their way to the development of a field of mission work" in Khama's country. Rhodes gave the Bishop of Capetown to understand that he was willing, "to subsidize handsomely, if not entirely to undertake the expense of such a beginning". The chaplains, if Rhodes did provide for them, were to be chosen by him and Knight-Bruce.[59]

Between January and June 1890, therefore, Knight-Bruce licensed three clergyman as chaplains to the forces of the BSA Company and the Bechanaland Border Police, at their camps near the Bechuanaland border. Frank Surridge, an athletic young Englishman who had recently arrived in Cape Town, was recommended to Rhodes as a suitable 'pioneer' by the leader of the expedition[60] and was supported entirely by the company. The other two men came from the Diocese of Bloemfontein: Canon Francis Balfour, the senior chaplain and Wilson Trusted, a young Englishman and recent recruit.

It appeared from these arrangements that Knight-Bruce had accepted a *fait-accompli* and had shelved his plans. He did not give up easily, however, for Balfour, his senior chaplain, was not a colonial clergyman at all but an experienced missionary with little aptitude for colonial

[58] LPL, Benson, 79, Bishop of Capetown to Archbishop of Canterbury, October 2nd, 1889, f. 259; W/CPSA, AB/1162/A, 16, Bishop of Capetown to Bishop of Bloemfontein, September 30th, 1889, f. 191.

[59] W/CPSA, AB/1162/A, 16, Bishop of Capetown to Bishop of Bloemfontein, September 30th, 1889, ff. 190–1.

[60] Lieut-Col. Frank, Johnson, D.S.O. *Great Days: The Autobiography of an Empire Pioneer* (1940) (Facsimile reproduction: Bulawayo: Books of Rhodesia, 1978), 120.

work. Although he was to accompany the BSA Company's pioneer column to Mashonaland in June 1890, acting as chaplain to the police who protected the column (and even accepting a commission, to his bishop's annoyance)[61] Balfour's primary task was to begin a mission to the Shona.

The licensing of Balfour and his two young colleagues illustrates graphically the difficulties which now faced Knight-Bruce in his attempts to plant a mission in the north. Mashonaland was no longer the pure 'native' territory he had dreamed of entering and missionary work had perforce to take second place to colonial work, for the church now had a responsibility to the settlers. He had had to licence two colonial chaplains to one missionary and to get that missionary into the country at all he had to smuggle him in, in the guise of a colonial chaplain.

Knight-Bruce's clergy had also to act as chaplains to a movement the bishop privately feared might become "an ordinary marauding and buccaneering expedition which the Church cannot countenance". He had "protested, and do still against our clergy being committed to any line of action that the Company may adopt". His realism prevailed, however: "We can only accept circumstances as they are—to go along with our fellow-countrymen towards the north so long as nothing is done which would cause us to dissociate ourselves from them".[62] Balfour himself spoke of merely "travelling with" the troops of the BSA Company's police to Mashonaland and "ministering to them on the way".[63]

IV *1890–1: Occupation and a bishopric*

The pioneer column and its escort, led by the hunter Selous, reached their destination in Mashonaland (Salisbury, now Harare, Zimbabwe) on 12th September 1890, without any incident of the kind feared by Knight-Bruce. They had by-passed Matabeleland, cutting a road for their waggons well to the south (see Map 2, p. xxi). A chain of post stations manned by BSA Company troopers had been set up along the route between Salisbury and Tuli, the Company's base camp near the

[61] RHL/USPG, D Series, 94(a), 1890, G.H.W. Knight-Bruce to Mr Tucker, February 8th, 1890.
[62] *Ibid.*
[63] 'From Rev. Francis R.T. Balfour', *BQP* 89 (July 1890), 294.

Bechuanaland border and rudimentary forts had been built at the two camps of Victoria and Charter. Lobengula, though he expressed his anger at the number of white men entering country he regarded as his, when he believed that the Rudd Concession had allowed for ten men only, refrained from giving his regiments orders to attack.

The day after the column arrived at the site of the future Salisbury there was a full dress parade with Balfour, as the senior English clergyman present, standing with Colonel Pennefather, the commanding officer and the staff officer at the flagpole. The British flag was run up. Balfour addressed the force, said the collect "Prevent us, O Lord" ("Go before us, O Lord"), twenty-one guns were fired, all saluted the flag and shouted three cheers for the Queen. The following morning Balfour celebrated Holy Communion in the colonel's tent.

The pioneers fulfilled their contracts with the company by building a fort for the new settlement and then dispersed to look for gold. Surridge, their chaplain, attempted to follow and minister to them but he had great difficulty in doing so. Their camps were widely scattered and his horse had died. Surridge himself was, as he put it, "let loose on the veldt with three pounds of meal, two pounds of sugar and one pound of tea as my only means of existence."[64]

He spent time at gold claims in the Hartley Hills, some 60 miles to the south-east of Salisbury and "endeared himself" to the men working there by his kindness to them.[65] Within two months, however, he had walked out of the country in company with another young man, his boots tied up with strips of ox-hide to keep them together and a worthless BSA Company cheque in his pocket. The expected mining boom had not occurred, there was no second Rand in Mashonaland and there was nothing to be bought, even with a company cheque.

The BSA Company itself had gambled on a rapid development of the country by others and the arrangements it had made to supply the pioneers with food and the necessities of life were entirely inadequate. The occupation had also taken place just before an extremely heavy rainy season: the rivers rose and few waggons were able to make their

---

[64] NAZ, HMss, BR 3/1/1, Frank Surridge to G.E.P. Broderick, November 20th, 1945, ff. 3–5.

[65] Adrian Darter, *The Pioneers of Mashonaland* (1914) (Facsimile reproduction: Bulawayo: Books of Rhodesia, 1977), 113.

way into the country. Even the company's police were almost without boots within six months of the occupation.[66]

The church was therefore attempting to establish itself within a colonial venture which was, for the immediate future, a failure and Surridge was the first, but not the last, member of the staff of the Mashonaland Mission to sever his connection with the mission early because of impossible or deeply discouraging conditions of service.

Knight-Bruce was subsequently to write in the strongest terms (but privately, to the SPG) about "the extraordinary way in which the difficulties of Mashonaland" had been "concealed from the public".[67] "[F]alse impressions", he said, had "gained ground owing to the prominence of the commercial aspect of Mashonaland".[68] The BSA Company had needed to retain the confidence of their shareholders and news of the early failure of Mashonaland was suppressed.

The consequences of this failure for the church were serious. For all his dislike of colonisation, Knight-Bruce had seen the advantage to his missionaries of an organised system of transport and supplies, of colonial stores and hospitals. In early 1891, in Bloemfontein, he worried about Balfour: what was he eating?

By this stage Balfour was the only remaining member of the mission. Surridge had gone and Wilson Trusted, at Tuli, had died within four months of dysentery. His illness and death illustrate further difficulties Knight-Bruce had to contend with in his efforts to establish a mission in Mashonaland, besides the presence of settlers and BSA Company's failure. Disease was to reduce his own efficiency and the efficiency of his staff, death to reduce their numbers.

The Mashonaland plateau was said to be healthier than Bechuanaland, where Trusted had died. Dysentery, however, was prevalent and the cause of malaria had not yet been discovered. Deaths from disease and privation were common among the settlers. At Salisbury in 1893, for example, the clergyman was to record one marriage, three baptisms

---

[66] Cf. Archibald Colquhoun, *Dan to Beersheba* (London: William Heinemann, 1908), 287–8, 293–4; Ethel Tawse Jollie, *The Real Rhodesia* (1924) (Facsimile reproduction: Bulawayo: Books of Rhodesia, 1971), 16–7.

[67] RHL/USPG, D Series, 102(B), 1892, G.H.W. Knight-Bruce to Mr Tucker, November 24th, 1892.

[68] RHL/USPG, D Series, 106(A), 1893, G.H.W. Knight-Bruce, Bishop of Mashonaland, to Mr Tucker, February 9th, 1893, f. 3.

and twelve deaths for a population of 300, most of whom were young men.[69] At Umtali in 1892, a grave was always left ready dug.[70]

Knight-Bruce's immediate missionary ambitions were also not realised but had to give way to the needs of settlers for Balfour was unable to devote himself to evangelizing, let alone to begin a large central mission station for the Shona as had been hoped. His time was taken up with colonial work for two clergymen who were supposed to relieve him of this work, soon after he reached Mashonaland, never arrived.

At Fort Salisbury in 1890–1, therefore, Balfour built a 'pole-and-dagha' (hut) church with the help of a handful of settlers and the labour of local people (see photograph, p. xxii). He equipped it with furniture made out of packing cases and calico and held services for the few in the small settler community "who cared for holy things".[71] He also attempted to visit the new and constantly shifting mining camps near Salisbury, in the Mazoe Valley, for instance. The only missionary work he was able to do was near Salisbury: he made a few short forays to Shona chiefs and villages near the colonial camp.

The Provincial Synod of the CPSA met in February 1891 and agreed to create the new diocese of Mashonaland. The SPG offered a grant of a thousand pounds a year for the first seven years and Knight-Bruce was invited to become the first bishop.

He was the leading candidate, having initiated the work there and offered to serve without stipend and Rhodes, now Prime Minister of the Cape, wished him to remain in charge of English Church affairs in Mashonaland:[72] it is evident that Rhodes believed he knew how to deal with Knight-Bruce. Bloemfontein was unlikely to protest: Knight-Bruce had not been popular in the diocese because too much of his energy had been given to his dream of a Mashonaland mission.[73]

---

[69] RHL/USPG, E Series, 48, 1893, J.H. Upcher, Return, Salisbury, October 1893.

[70] NAZ, HMss, PE 3/1/1, Douglas Raymond Pelly, Correspondence, 1892–1934, December 18th, 1892, f. 173, May 15th, 1893, f. 224.

[71] 'From the Rev. Canon Balfour', *BQP* 91 (Jan 1891), 14.

[72] RHL/USPG, D Series, 94(a), 1890, G.H.W. Knight-Bruce, Bishop of Bloemfontein, to Mr Tucker, October 28th, 1890.

[73] LPL, Benson, 79, A. Mason to Archbishop, October 9th, 1889, f. 263; W/CPSA, AB/1162/A, 16, Bishop of Capetown to Mr Tucker, February 18th, 1891, f. 258, to Archbishop of Canterbury, April 25th, 1892, ff. 339–40.

Knight-Bruce accepted Mashonaland with the proviso that he be allowed first to view his new diocese and in the meantime set about planning his mission strategy and attempting to raise enthusiasm and support, while at the same time countering criticism that more should already have been done, that he had been slow off the mark.

He defended himself on the ground that to have taken hasty action would have been to invite failure[74] but what was to follow was almost constant failure. Virtually all his plans were to go awry, partly because of conditions in Mashonaland, partly because of miscalculations and mismanagement by Knight-Bruce himself and failures among his staff.

In South Africa in early 1891, however, he began recruiting, with an eye primarily to the establishment of mission stations rather than work among the settlers. Most of his recruits were laymen. Some were artisans: he recruited two carpenters, for example, on a year's contract each, to work on the proposed mission buildings. He also employed a Free State farmer for one year and bought livestock for the mission, for he intended his mission stations to be self-sufficient so that his staff could survive if lines of supply and communication were ever cut off.

It had also been suggested to Knight-Bruce, by Rhodes, that he establish a hospital in Mashonaland and he therefore recruited a doctor, as well as three nurses from a church hospital in Kimberley. For the spiritual side of the work, he engaged a young clergyman, J.R. Sewell and a couple of laymen who wished to be missionaries. Most important of all, he found five African catechists willing to accompany him to the north. Africa, he believed, would only be won by Africans, who could understand and live beside their own people. He expected his mission stations to be run by clergy. Around these stations, however, and in close connection with them, were to be African catechists, living with the local people.[75]

One party of staff was sent up to Mashonaland by the southern route from Mafeking, with waggons, supplies and the livestock. Knight-Bruce himself set off with a second party by sea from Durban, in an attempt to enter Mashonaland from the east. This party consisted of the two carpenters and the catechists, besides Knight-Bruce himself.

[74] 'A Diocese for Mashonaland' [From the *Cape Times* of February 6th, 1891], *BQP* 92 (April 1891), 57–9.

[75] 'The Bishop's Letter', BQP 90 (Oct 1890), 315, 324–5; Peter Hinchliff, *The Anglican Church in South Africa: An account of the history and development of the Church of the Province of South Africa* (London: Darton, Longman and Todd, 1963), 167, 171.

The nurses and a young English layman waited behind in Durban, to follow on with the doctor.

Knight-Bruce's party reached Beira, then an embryo port on the Portuguese East African Coast, a few tin shacks on a spit of sand and managed to obtain places on a launch going up to 'Mpanda's, a Portuguese post several days' journey up the Pungwe River. From 'Mpanda's there was supposed to be a waggon route to Umtali (Mutare), a camp on the eastern border of BSA Company territory. The company with the contract to make the road had, however, failed to do so, beyond a certain point and since the area was a (tsetse) fly belt, all the trek oxen had died. There was no way either passengers or supplies could be carried by waggon to Mashonaland and there was a shortage of local bearers.

Knight-Bruce had brought with him large supplies of food to feed his staff and building materials for his mission station. He was forced to leave most at Beira and the rest at 'Mpanda's. He also left at 'Mpanda's the two carpenters of the party (E. Wilson, J. Wilkins) to look after the stores and to wait for the rest of the second party to join them.

He himself walked on into the interior, once again with only African Christian companions but this time they were not servants but catechists, members of the mission. Their route lay through very difficult terrain, thick, semi-tropical vegetation and mountains rather than the lightly-treed grasslands of the Mashonaland plateau. Because there were Portuguese posts along the way there little fear of attack by local people, though plenty from lions.

The Portuguese and the Chartered Company had also just become engaged in a minor local war. A filibustering expedition of company men, having routed the Portugese in a skirmish at Massikessi (Macequece; Villa de Manica) was making its way towards the coast: Rhodes had his eyes on Beira and an eastern route into company territory which he could control.[76] Knight-Bruce had been advised at 'Mpanda's not to attempt to try for Umtali.

Characteristically he refused, for he wished to get to his new diocese without loss of time. He also had an ulterior motive: on the journey with him was the Military Secretary to the High Commissioner, Major

[76] J.G. Lockhart and The Hon. C.M. Woodhouse, *Rhodes* (London: Hodder and Stoughton, 1963), 232–3.

H.L. Sapte, bearing news that Britain and Portugal had agreed to resolve their differences over where the border of Mashonaland should lie. The company's filibusters were therefore out of order.[77]

Knight-Bruce set off with Sapte but outstripped him. At a point south-east of Massikessi he and his men met the company's force and halted their advance. If he had been used in 1888 to assist Rhodes gain Mashonaland, Knight-Bruce had the satisfaction of being on the spot in 1891, to help thwart him in this attempt to gain part of Portuguese East Africa. Knight-Bruce's own accounts of the incident are disingenuous[78] but his motive can be discerned from Rhodes' reaction: Rhodes believed that, had his forces reached Beira, the conquest would have stood and that Knight-Bruce, with Sapte, had lost him the route into the interior. He never forgave him.[79] Knight-Bruce for his part had a poor opinion of Rhodes and loathed colonial 'buccaneering' and land-grabbing. He was also openly pleased to have prevented the shedding of blood, especially that of Portuguese who had treated him kindly on his journey upcountry.

At Umtali, Knight-Bruce took a service in the camp, suffered a bout of fever, then hurried on with his companions to Salisbury. From there, in June 1891, he wrote to his fellow bishops in South Africa, formally accepting the bishopric of Mashonaland.

V *Land acquisition and its significance*

Knight-Bruce's first objective in his new diocese was to find many and prime sites for mission stations. He conferred with Balfour and, to his satisfaction, obtained permission from the Administrator, Dr. Leander Starr Jameson, to mark out a 'mission farm' wherever he could establish work. The tone of his remarks about the BSA Company became noticeably warmer as a result of Jameson's co-operation in this and other matters. Jameson was "most kind" and had offered "everything I can possibly want for our work".[80] Knight-Bruce was also greatly reassured by the calibre of the officials he had met in the country: he wrote that, the movement of the white man northward in Africa being

[77] Langham-Carter, *Knight Bruce*, 45–6.
[78] Knight-Bruce, *Journals*, 24–5, 79–80; *Memories*, 89–90.
[79] Lockhart and Woodhouse, 233.
[80] Knight-Bruce, *Journals*, 29.

"inevitable", he was "thankful that a Company, having such a class of officers...is the power which has moved up".[81]

His next move was to attempt to establish an ascendancy for his mission among the local people. He therefore despatched Balfour on a visit to significant chiefs to the north-east of Salisbury and having purchased one of the few 'salted' horses available, in order to travel more quickly, set off himself back towards Umtali, visiting the leading chiefs of the intervening district as he went and choosing sites for stations near their villages. He left two of the catechists, Bernard Mizeki and Frank Ziqubu, to begin work 30 miles north-west of Umtali, near one of the most important chiefs, Chief Makoni, with goods to barter for food. There was a BSA police post not far away and a trooper who was interested in missionary work.

This first journey of Knight-Bruce's was one of three made during his short stay in the country in 1891. As a result of these journeys and further journeying in 1893, he obtained the rights to more than 25 'farms' of 3,000 acres each and he was able to report back to England that 30 of the 35 major chiefs of the country were willing to receive his teachers.

He was subsequently criticised for his policy in Mashonaland, for attempting too much, spreading too wide. He defended himself on the grounds that he had created a broad framework for the future[82] and where land was concerned he had several motives.

In the first place, he wanted the English Church to hold "the principal position" in Mashonaland, though he could no longer hope for an exclusive one.[83] Land and plenty of it needed to be obtained quickly, for other missionaries were coming into the country and the Roman Catholics, the only other denomination to have sent a cleric into Mashonaland with the pioneer column, had already begun a mission at Chief Chishawasha's, fifteen miles from Salisbury and had sent emissaries to Chief Mtoko in the east.

Secondly, Knight-Bruce saw these 'mission farms' as future sources of support for the church. In England, the Church of England's wealth lay primarily in land, in her ancient connection with agriculture, with tithes, the parson's glebe and the income they generated. If land in

---

[81] Knight-Bruce, *Memories*, 97–8.
[82] Knight-Bruce, *Memories*, 108, 112.
[83] RHL/USPG, D Series, 102(B), 1892, G.H.W. Knight-Bruce, Bishop of Mashonaland, to Mr Tucker, October 26th, 1892.

Mashonaland could be developed, Knight-Bruce believed the church's finances would be secure and when he returned to England in 1892, to recruit more staff and raise funds for the mission, he made a separate (and unsuccessful) appeal for what was then the enormous sum of £10,000, just to develop his mission farms.

His last motive was born out of his South African experience and the driving force of his missionary instinct to protect 'native' peoples. The company's right to grant land at this point was more than dubious: Knight-Bruce believed that the incoming forces had no more right to take land to which local people laid claim than they had to take the acres of someone in England. Land perceived as unclaimed or unused, however, he believed might fairly be distributed among settlers (and missions). He feared though that with an increase of colonial settlement local people might be forced off the land and he intended his mission farms to be sanctuaries for them, should this ever happen.[84]

The new Bishop of Mashonaland, on this initial visit to his diocese, had also to choose a place for his own headquarters. He had originally intended to make his own 'central' mission station to the south-west of Salisbury, near the Hartley Hills, where the gold-mining centre of the new territory was supposed to be, where supplies could be found and settlers would need the services of the church. He had expected to place his nurses there, or at Salisbury.

Hartley, however, was not a significant settlement as sufficient payable gold had not been found. At Salisbury, he had been forestalled by the Roman Catholics: Dominican nuns had just begun nursing there. The BSA Company had already suggested Knight-Bruce's nurses go to Umtali and Jameson now agreed to pay them and provide them with a hospital.

This arrangement fell in with Knight-Bruce's own preference for a headquarters in the east. The area was high and so believed likely to be a healthy spot, relatively free from fever. There was a large 'native' population: the camp was near the village of the most important of the Manyika chiefs, Mtasa ('Umtasa'). There was also an expected ease of supply: the cost of bringing in goods by the east was supposed to be a seventh of that via the southern route.

---

[84] Knight-Bruce, *Memories*, 97–9, *Journals*, 34–5, 79–80.

It was, and is, usual for an Anglican bishop to have his seat at the chief administrative centre of a country (or county). Even Balfour had assumed that Knight-Bruce's headquarters must be at Salisbury. To Knight-Bruce, however, "no one place" was "much better than another".[85] Umtali made a convenient headquarters for a mission and he intended to be a bishop living among his missionaries. His 'central' mission was to be central, not to the new colonial state but to his missionary work.[86]

Knight-Bruce might have been speaking more favourably about the BSA Company in 1892, therefore, but he was still determined to make plain the difference between his work and their actions and accompanying colonisation. The distinction was intended, moreover, to be a permanent one. He had "no wish to change to another headquarters"[87] and while other settlers were living in pole-and-dagha huts or tin shacks and the mission was almost at the point of collapse for lack of money, Knight-Bruce planned and eventually carried out (in 1893) the erection of a solid brick building for his headquarters.

VI *1891–3: Preliminary work, Knight-Bruce's absence in England*

In Umtali in 1891, Knight-Bruce chose a site for a hospital near the camp and about two miles away found a large piece of land, very well situated and with its own source of water, for his mission farm and headquarters. Here, with help of a young settler, Walter Sutton (the son of an English archdeacon) and the labour of local men, he began to construct huts for his mission workers, most of whom were yet to arrive in the country.

The waggon party which had left Mafeking some months before had not yet arrived. The group which had come in by the eastern route and now included the nurses, doctor and the young layman, William Wilson, was still at 'Mpanda's. Knight-Bruce made attempts to have them brought up but there were no carriers. They finally had to walk

---

[85] 'The Bishop's Letter, No. IV. RMS 'Roslin Castle', February 1893', *MQP* IV (April 1893), 1.

[86] RHL/USPG, D Series, 102(B), 1892, G.H.W. Knight-Bruce to Mr Tucker, 27th February, 1892; 'The Bishop's Letter', *BQP* 90 (Oct 1890), 335.

[87] RHL/USPG, D series, 106(A), 1893, Yearly Report for the Society for the Propagation of the Gospel in Foreign Parts from the Mashonaland Mission. G.H.W. Knight-Bruce, Bishop of Mashonaland, November 1893, f. 3.

into the country, as he had done and then had to borrow or share huts in the camp, because the mission huts were unfinished. One man, the doctor, Doyle Granville, tendered his resignation to Knight-Bruce immediately on arrival and then died in an attempt to travel on alone to Salisbury. The nurses settled down to nurse both settlers and local people in a small hut hospital.

The other men joined Knight-Bruce on the farm, working on the huts and bricks for his house, even blasting rock for its foundations. Periodic and largely unsuccessful attempts were made to try and retrieve the stores from 'Mpanda's. The party therefore had to rely on make-shift tools and, for supplies, on the company and whatever local people wished to sell. Knight-Bruce longed for some soap, but there was none to buy.

When he managed to procure sufficient supplies, however, he set off on another missionary journey of 280 miles, this time to the south of Umtali where he penetrated to areas few white men ever reached: one village reported having last seen a white face thirty years before. Knight-Bruce himself excited as much interest, he wrote, as a new animal at the zoo.[88]

He returned to Umtali to note progress: 50,000 bricks had been made and the nurses had new huts. He then set off on another journey, back to Salisbury, calling on new chiefs and visiting the catechists he had left at Makoni's a little while before (see above, p. 25). He found that Mizeki had moved 60 miles away, near to another important chief, Mangwende ('Mangwendi') of the Nhowe people. Mizeki joined Knight-Bruce for the rest of this journey.

William Wilson, the lay missionary, with the catechists Thomas Maho and Charles Makolami, also accompanied Knight-Bruce on the journey from Umtali and when Salisbury was reached, these three men set off to find a station for the catechists at one of the chiefs to the north of the camp. Knight-Bruce himself (with Selous) chose a farm for the mission near Salisbury, then travelled down to Fort Charter in an unsuccessful attempt to meet the waggon party.

He returned to Umtali to find that the township had been moved: the original camp had been on a gold belt, which had now been pegged. Though Knight-Bruce was swift to claim the best sites in the new township, the move of the camp involved the church in additional expense

---

[88] Knight-Bruce, *Journals*, 65.

and inconvenience: the mission farm was now five-and-a-half miles away, too far to serve as a suitable headquarters. Knight-Bruce was also met in Umtali by the remnants of the waggon party, three men whom he had missed on the road and who had had to walk for the last 400 miles of their journey. Sewell, the young parson, was following with the waggons. Knight-Bruce then left for England, in October 1891, without waiting for Sewell to arrive.

He had spent about five months in his diocese and was now to be away for a year and a half, not returning until April 1893. In England, he raised money to pay off the debts of the mission. From England, he despatched more workers, intending them to be reinforcements for staff already in the field. They found when they arrived that almost all the other staff had left or were about to leave.

One of the new men, Douglas Pelly, arriving at Umtali in May 1892 found "a sad moral chaos"[89] instead of the flourishing industrial mission station he had been led to expect. On the mission farm, there were only three huts and the grave of one of the carpenters, John Wilkins. The other carpenter, Edward Wilson, having by now fulfilled his year's contract with the mission, waited only for Pelly to arrive before moving into Umtali and setting up in business with another man.

At Beira on his way in, Pelly had been startled to meet two other members of the mission on their way out, Sewell, the clergyman and J.W. Jagger, the ordinand and intending missionary. Sewell "damned the Bishop, the Mission and the country" and tried to persuade Pelly to return with him to England.[90]

He had had, however, a long and difficult journey upcountry with the waggons, half of his party had deserted and the livestock had died or been sold. He had only reached Umtali in late 1891 and had then, in company with the other members of the mission, nearly starved. Most of the mission's stores were still at Beira or 'Mpanda's and the workers had been left with insufficient money to buy food. Sewell went "mad with worry" (by Knight-Bruce's own account)[91] and left a reputation behind him of having done little in Umtali but "drink and swear", while Jagger, who had been supposed to take charge of the

[89] J.H Upcher, 'Southern Rhodesian Memories', *SQP* C (May 1917), 13.

[90] NAZ, HMss, PE 3/2/1, Douglas Raymond Pelly, Reminiscences, 1891–1900, f. 3.

[91] RHL/USPG, D Series, 102(B), 1892, G.H.W. Knight-Bruce to Mr Tucker, November 23nd, 1892.

practical management of the mission, had apparently done nothing but "smoke and sleep".[92]

The only people Pelly found working for the church in May 1892 were the five catechists; Balfour at Salisbury; and two white lay missionaries. One of these men, William Wilson, who had been working at 'Sosi's' town (near Marandellas, now Marondera) and at Makoni's, was to leave the country within months because of fever. The other man was a volunteer, Frank Edwards who, though much in earnest, was unstable. He also left the country within months and ended up in a lunatic asylum in Britain from which he wrote increasingly demented letters to the SPG.

Pelly had been sent out by Knight-Bruce to rescue the mission's stores and join the 'industrial mission'. What could be salvaged of the stores he collected with carriers but the mission was now non-existent. He therefore conferred with Balfour and then proceeded to become to the small and rowdy camp of Umtali what Sewell might have been, an "influence for good".[93] The mission station was abandoned. In the camp, Pelly built a small hut church with the help of Edward Wilson, the carpenter who had formerly belonged to the mission and his business partner. At the opening service there were only three people, Pelly and the two carpenters. The mission's nurses disdained the ministrations of this new young layman, preferring to ask the Resident Magistrate to read Sunday services in their hospital instead.

A year after Pelly's arrival, however, half the camp was attending his services (although not the nurses). Pelly messed with some other young men, joined them on lion shoots and in sports but continued to keep up the character of a Christian layman: he was the son of an English vicarage and subsequently took orders. He even began mission work among local people in a small way in Umtali itself, using the little hut church.

More workers followed Pelly out in 1892. A priest and a deacon, James Hay Upcher and Alfred Dykes Sylvester arrived in July, having travelled together from England and come up from the south through Pretoria, to which there was now a railway. Sylvester was meant to go to Tuli, where there had been no clergyman since Trusted had died

[92] NAZ, HMss, PE 3/1/1, Pelly, Correspondence, 1892–1934, July 14th, 1892, ff. 75–77.

[93] Rose Blennerhasset and Lucy Sleeman, *Adventures in Mashonaland* (1893) (Facsimile reproduction: Bulawayo: Books of Rhodesia, 1969), 214.

almost two years before but the camp was now almost empty, barely a dozen people there. Since a goldrush was under way in the Fort Victoria area and the settlement now held 400–500 people, he went to Victoria instead. Upcher, having seen his younger colleague settled, travelled on to Salisbury to relieve Balfour.

Another man, an ordinand, Frederick Lawrence arrived, supposedly to work at Tuli, in November 1892. He also did not stay: there were now 200 officers and troopers of the Bechuanaland Border Police at Macloutsie, to the south of Tuli, so he moved his base there. He had travelled with a Church Army layman, J.R. Burgin, who worked with him while he waited for his bishop to return from England and arrange his sphere of work: Knight-Bruce had at last been able to set aside a man for missionary work.[94]

VII *1893: Knight-Bruce returns to the diocese; Anglo-Ndebele War*

In April 1893 Knight-Bruce returned to his diocese, travelling up from the south because entry from the east was still difficult. This meant that he had first to attend to the colonial settlements through which he travelled. At Macloutsie, he ordained Frederick Lawrence deacon (this was the first ordination in the new diocese) on Easter Day, in the reading room of the camp, "in the presence of a congregation composed...entirely of officers, non-commissioned officers and troopers".[95] He also formed a church committee led by Sir Frederick Carrington, the commander of the police and made arrangements for the building of a church.

At Fort Victoria Knight-Bruce held a confirmation. Church life there had got off to a good start: ninety-per-cent of the people were nominally members of the English Church. Balfour had visited the camp, formed a church committee composed of the leading men of the settlement and lent money for the building of a mud-brick church. It could hold a hundred people, had a thatched roof and a Gothic screen. Sylvester had planted a garden round it of bright flowers, zinnias and marigolds.

---

[94] Lawrence, Upcher and Walker (below, p. 36) were also recruited as missionaries but colonial work had to take precedence.

[95] Knight-Bruce, *Memories*, 206–7.

He himself had been faced with "the usual opposition" to religion but, in his bishop's judgement, was "living it down".[96]

At Salisbury, Upcher had obtained a new and better site for a church and organised the erection of a brick building to replace Balfour's hut. He had also, immediately upon arriving, begun a mission service for local 'Mashona'. Balfour had been a rather lonely figure at Salisbury but Knight-Bruce found that Upcher was very well respected and attracting good congregations to his services. He wrote to his wife that the people were "as fond of [Upcher] as they could be of anything that [was] not gold or whiskey".[97] A schoolmaster, engaged by Knight-Bruce, had also arrived to begin a school for settler children.

In the east of the diocese, Pelly was about to be relieved by a deacon, F.R. Ritchie, who was also expected to minister to the large numbers of men now at Beira and on the railway which was being constructed from Beira to Umtali. Fresh nurses had replaced the original nurses. Knight-Bruce's time in England had been fruitful: there were a dozen staff in Mashonaland and more were on their way.

The spiritual needs of the colonial communities having been attended to, the bishop was able to turn his attention to missionary work. He had already sent Burgin, the lay missionary, to begin work among both local people and settlers in Gazaland, about 100 miles south of Umtali. He now visited Bernard Mizeki and Frank Ziqubu, who were persevering at their posts. Thomas Maho and Charles Makolami were working under Upcher's supervision near Salisbury but the fifth of the original band of catechists, Samuel Makosa (or Koring) had ended up in prison early in 1893, for shooting and killing a 'Mashona' thief.[98] One new catechist, Jacob Dyasi, was sent to another important chief, Mapondera, then at Mazoe.

Two lay missionaries were among the new staff on their way out and work was soon to be started at Chief Mtasa's by Pelly and the mission's new doctor, Dr. Rundle. All was also in readiness for the building of the mission's brick headquarters. With the bishop's return and a new wave of staff the work of the diocese had received a fresh beginning.

---

[96] W/CPSA, AB/355f, Knight-Bruce, Papers, Letter to his wife, April 30th, 1893.

[97] *Ibid.*, June 17th, 1893. For Balfour, see H.M. Hole, *Old Rhodesian Days* (1928) (Facsimile reproduction: Bulawayo: Books of Rhodesia, 1976), 26.

[98] NAZ, HMss, PE 3/1/1, Pelly, Correspondence, 1892–1934, February 2nd, 1893, f. 201, February 26th, 1893, f. 204.

War had been threatening with the Ndebele, however, ever since the occupation of Mashonaland and it broke out within months of Knight-Bruce's return, in September 1893. Two columns of settlers made their way to Bulawayo, defeating Ndebele regiments in battles on the way. Lobengula set fire to his capital and then retreated northwards towards the Zambezi. Bulawayo was occupied, Lobengula died while retreating and Chartered Company rule (of a sort) was asserted over Matabeland.

The Anglo-Ndebele War ('Matabele War') divided Christian opinion. Many church leaders were as convinced as the majority of settlers that the power of the Ndebele should be crushed. A friend of Rhodes, William Alexander, the Bishop of Derry, preached a blood-thirsty sermon in Westminster Abbey, urging on the attack.[99] Sylvester, parson at Fort Victoria, stood on an ammunition box in the parade ground and "bellowed that the sons of Ham should all be cleared out".[100] He had seen his own servant speared to death in front of his eyes, when an Ndebele force had pursued fleeing Shona into the settlement. The Jesuit, Fr. Prestage, gave his unqualified support (but privately) to the "smashing up" of the "infamous rule" of Lobengula.[101] At a public meeeting in Salisbury, Upcher and the Wesleyan Methodist minister, Isaac Shimmin, urged the settling of "the Matabele question once and for ever".[102]

Others condemned the war. Lord Northbourne, a prominent supporter in England of the Mashonaland and other missions, declared that "the real interests of Christianity were by no means likely to be promoted by the sword".[103] Knight-Bruce was vehement: "I entirely and emphatically repudiate any share in the sentiment that the "sword" is a necessary factor in the Christianising of the savage nations: or that the only road for the preaching of Christianity is cleared by destroying their power... no letter written or speech made urging on a war with

[99] 'Extracts from the Bishop's Journal', *MQP* VII (Jan 1894), 9; RHL/USPG, D Series, 106(A), 1893, G.H.W. Knight-Bruce, Bishop, to Mr Tucker, December 12th, 1893, ff. 2–3.

[100] K. Sayce, *A Town called Victoria: or the Rise and Fall of the Thatched House Hotel* (Bulawayo: Books of Rhodesia, 1978), 43.

[101] Zvobgo, *A History of Christian Missions*, 6–7.

[102] John Weller & Jane Linden, *Mainstream Christianity to 1980: in Malawi, Zambia and Zimbabwe* (Gweru: Mambo Press, 1984), 202.

[103] 'Home Notes. Second Annual Festival' [Mashonaland Mission Association], *MQP* IX (July 1894), 16.

the Matabele had ever had any sympathy whatever from me. I hoped to the last it would be avoided".[104]

He was, however, the only cleric to accompany a settler column to Bulawayo although he refused to take an official position with the force and travelled at his own expense. He was, in this, explicitly following the example set by Selwyn, first bishop of New Zealand, during the Anglo-Maori Wars: he went, not as chaplain to the settler force but as bishop of the country and therefore of both parties to the war. If there had to be war, then he would do what he could to prevent unnecessary bloodshed, procure a just solution to the conflict and protect the interests of the Ndebele.[105]

Knight-Bruce used his waggon as a hospital waggon for wounded Ndebele 'enemies' and Shona 'friendlies' fighting alongside the settlers; he rescued a wounded black man under heavy fire; and he offered to go alone after the fleeing Lobengula to treat for peace. After Bulawayo had been taken he held a church parade but made it very clear that thanksgiving was being offered, not for victories won but for mercies shown. He recorded that, while many of the combatants thought his "neutral" position "all wrong", they grumbled but acquiesced. Others, the "very many high-minded" men in the columns, were "very fair to the Matabele" and would gladly have seen peace "and on very just terms".[106] Rhodes, in contrast to Knight-Bruce, when he reached Bulawayo a little later, was to praise the settlers as the conquerors of Matabeleland, the destroyers of a "ruthless barbarism".[107]

Most contemporary settler accounts of the conquest of Matabeleland and the settlement of Bulawayo are characterized by a similar sense of triumph. A feared enemy had been defeated and a new impetus given to a faltering and foundering colonial venture.[108] Knight-Bruce's accounts are subdued, unhappy.

During the campaign he was torn between pride and distress: pride that the English Church could claim the leading men among the colonial

[104] RHL/USPG, D Series, 106(A), 1893, Yearly Report for the Society for the Propagation of the Gospel in Foreign Parts from the Mashonaland Mission. G.H.W. Knight-Bruce, Bishop of Mashonaland, November 1893, f. 11.

[105] 'The Bishop's Letter, No. VII. Fort Charter, September 22nd, 1893', *MQP* VII (Jan 1894), 6; Knight-Bruce, *Memories*, 220–2.

[106] 'Extracts from the Bishop's Journal', *MQP* VII (Jan 1894), 9, 12–4.

[107] Rotberg, *The Founder*, 443–44.

[108] Cf. C.H.W. Donovan, *With Wilson in Matabeleland* (1894) (Facsimile reproduction: Bulawayo: Books of Rhodesia, 1979), 175–6, 272.

forces (both the columns of settlers and a column coming up from the south, from Bechuanaland, were led by members of his church committees)[109] and distress that that the war had happened at all. He found it, for instance, a most "painful incongruity" to say morning service and then be told that Ndebele had been killed in an engagement.[110]

His own position with the column was an extremely difficult one: he was, after all, in almost the exact position he had feared Balfour and his colleagues might be, in 1890, accompanying an expedition of which he could not approve.[111] The attack on the Ndebele was condemned by a Radical critic in the House of Commons as a free-booting and marauding expedition, the very thing Knight-Bruce had feared the pioneer column might become.[112]

He was pathetically anxious to record that Lobengula thought no ill of him, that he was believed not to be accompanying the king's enemies to Bulawayo, for he was well aware that Lobengula would be incapable of understanding that he was accompanying the company's forces as a 'neutral'.[113] The king's own behaviour he admired, for Lobengula, although he had fired Bulawayo before retreating, had honoured his word not to harm any of the white traders who lived in or near his capital. Knight-Bruce described this as a "lesson in chivalry" for king's colonial conquerors.[114]

After Bulawayo was taken Knight-Bruce remained there for a short while, hoping to influence peace negotiations but his offer to go alone to the king was refused. This did not surprise him: he wrote, "I don't know that I should be of any value to the Company by going: for I could only recommend Lobengula to accept terms that I considered as advantageous to him as to them".[115] No negotiations took place with Lobengula and the result of the war for the Ndebele was punitive: they lost their cattle and their land on a vast scale.

---

[109] 'Home Notes. Second Annual Festival' [Mashonaland Mission Association], *MQP* IX (July 1894), 18.

[110] 'Extracts from the Bishop's Journal', *MQP* VII (Jan 1894), 8.

[111] *Ibid.*, 6; and see Knight-Bruce, *Memories*, 220–1.

[112] Sir Lewis Michell, *The Life of the Right Honourable Cecil John Rhodes*, Vol. II (London: Edward Arnold, 1910), 89.

[113] 'Extracts from the Bishop's Journal', *MQP* VII (Jan 1894), 12.

[114] *Ibid.*, 13–4.

[115] RHL/USPG, D Series, 106(A), 1893, Yearly Report for the Society for the Propagation of the Gospel in Foreign Parts from the Mashonaland Mission, G.H.W. Knight-Bruce, Bishop of Mashonaland, November 1893, f. 11.

Knight-Bruce took no part in the land-spree that followed the war. He recorded only that he did pastoral work in Bulawayo immediately after it was taken, visiting the makeshift hospital and the groups of young men in their tents and 'messes'. Most of the 'mess' with whom he felt most at home were soon to die. They were among a detachment of men sent after Lobengula, not to negotiate with him but to capture him. Thirty-four of the detachment, led by Allan Wilson, a member of the Victoria Church Committee, were cut off by Ndebele at a bend in the Shangani River, surrounded and killed one by one. The death of such men was a real loss to the church, their bishop recorded.[116]

Knight-Bruce returned across country to Umtali, making no attempt to put work in Bulawayo on a permanent basis but then the church had no money to provide an extra member of staff for "this necessary and precarious work".[117] He was also not convinced that Bulawayo would be a permanent settlement. Although Lobengula's capital had become, almost overnight, a colonial encampment of more than 1,000 people, other settlements had swollen and shrunk very rapidly: Fort Victoria, for instance, was now almost empty. Macloutsie, when Knight-Bruce visited it after leaving Bulawayo was also virtually deserted, its little church not quite finished.

In Umtali, in December 1893, the bishop moved at last into his brick headquarters. He gathered Mizeki and Ziqubu, a newly-arrived layman (James Walker) and one of the first local catechumens, Shoniwa Kapuya, to begin translation of the New Testament into 'Chiswina' (Shona).[118] In early March 1894, however, Knight-Bruce had to abandon this work for he was invalided out to England with blackwater fever, less than a year after he had returned to Mashonaland.

Most of the work he had initiated on his return was also collapsing. Burgin, the missionary, had left Gazaland because it turned out that he had been working in territory granted by the BSA Company to another missionary body. The mission at Mtasa's had also been given up: Knight-Bruce had himself buried Dr. Rundle and Pelly had left for

---

[116] 'Central Sale', *MQP* IX (July 1894), 18.

[117] RHL/USPG, D Series, 106(A), 1893, Yearly Report for the Society for the Propagation of the Gospel in Foreign Parts from the Mashonaland Mission, G.H.W. Knight-Bruce, Bishop of Mashonaland, November 1893, f. 13.

[118] 'The Bishop's Letter, No. VIII. Mission House, Umtali, January 9th, 1894', *MQP* VIII (April 1894), 5. In old age, Kapuya mistakenly attributed this translation work to Gaul: Jean Farrant, *Mashonaland Martyr: Bernard Mizeki and the Pioneer Church* (Cape Town, London and Salisbury: Oxford University Press, 1966), 140.

England, having agreed to finish his two-year contract in fund-raising there for Mashonaland. Maho and Makolami, having fulfilled their contracts, had returned to South Africa.

Lawrence, who had served at Macloutsie, had been invalided home to die. The two new lay missionaries (p. 32) had come and gone and Sylvester, at Fort Victoria and Ritchie, at Beira, had neither of them been much of a success[119] and had left. Only seven members of staff remained (apart from two nurses at Umtali): a priest, Upcher, at Salisbury; Walker, now ordained deacon; the catechists Mizeki, Ziqubu and Dyasi; Burgin, who with the shortage of other staff was having to do colonial work (he and Walker had to cover Fort Victoria and Umtali between them); and W. Mitchley, an ordinand, who had replaced Ritchie at Beira. He was to leave under a cloud before the end of the year, reducing the staff to six.[120]

Knight-Bruce left a diocese in considerable disarray: the numbers of staff had been halved and work abandoned. The situation seemed almost as bad as it had been two years before when Pelly had arrived to find a virtually deserted diocese. It was, in fact, worse, for with a colonial spread into Matabeland, the area of the diocese which could be worked had more than doubled. This now stretched along the line of colonial settlement from Beira to Bulawayo and down into Bechuanaland.

VII *Resignation*

From England, in October 1894, the first Bishop of Mashonaland resigned his see. Resignation from the sacred responsibility of a bishopric was and is a very grave matter. It was only relatively recently that bishops in England had been able to retire and it was still common for bishops there to die in office. In the Anglican churches abroad, with their different constitutions and often very difficult conditions of work, resignation was acceptable but premature retirement was deeply frowned upon.

Knight-Bruce's resignation was offered and accepted on medical grounds. It is evident from the correspondence, however, that his resignation was likely in any case, for by early 1894 the condition of the diocese was so scandalous that public criticisms were being made. The

---

[119] NAZ, HMss, PE 3/2/1, Pelly, Reminiscences, f. 13.
[120] *Ibid.*, f. 27.

first two Umtali nurses published a jaunty and somewhat unfriendly account of their experience in the service of the mission.[121] A Cape newspaper suggested that there was something "radically wrong in the management" since nearly every white man who entered the service of the mission had left, or died. There were few in Mashonaland who were "prepared to support and uphold the way in which the Church of England mission is managed there".[122]

West Jones of Capetown wrote most unhappily and anxiously about the state of Mashonaland to Knight-Bruce and to the SPG.[123] To Upcher, in Salisbury, he confessed astonishment at the assurances Knight-Bruce had given him "that everything was being done that could be done": he could not "in the least understand it".[124] He sent William Carter, the Bishop of Zululand, up to Mashonaland to relieve Upcher and to investigate. He also sent Upcher funds (£500 supplied, of all people, by Rhodes) because there was no money. When Knight-Bruce resigned, the diocese was in debt.

The SPG had made their annual grant of £1,000, the BSA Company had provided funds for colonial chaplains and an association in England (the Mashonaland Mission Association) had collected money for the work, but no-one in 1894 knew what had happened to this money. Supporters of the mission complained, the Archbishop of Canterbury and the Secretary of the SPG conferred but found that no adequate records of expenditure had been kept.[125]

Knight-Bruce admitted to both mistakes and failures and a large expenditure of money, while defending himself on familiar grounds, that the expenses of the mission and the difficulties of the work had been very much greater than had been expected.[126] He had also, earlier, pointed out that conditions in Mashonaland were more like those of

[121] Blennerhasset and Sleeman, *passim*.

[122] RHL/USPG, D Series, 110, 1894, cutting, *Cape Times* (March 21st, 1894).

[123] W/CPSA, AB/1162/A, 18, Bishop of Capetown, to Knight-Bruce [November] 1894, f. 118, to Mr Tucker, SPG, October 10th, 1894, f. 87.

[124] W/CPSA, AB/1162/A, 18, Bishop of Capetown, to Ven. J.H. Upcher, October 19th, 1894, f. 99.

[125] RHL/USPG, D Series, 110, 1894, A.C.W. Upcher to H.W. Tucker, October 17th, 1894, f. 141; LPL, Benson, 141, H.W. Tucker to Archbishop, March 23rd, 1895, Benson, 142, A.C.W. Upcher to Archbishop, December 4th, 1894, ff. 58–64, Lord Northbourne to A.C.W. Upcher, December 3rd, 1894, f. 60.

[126] 'The Bishop's Letter, No. VIII. Mission House, Umtali, January 9th, 1894', *MQP* VIII (April 1894), 7; 'The Bishop's Letter, No. IX. Bovey Tracey, June 18th, 1894', *MQP* IX (July 1894), 6.

the UMCA to the north than the other South African dioceses and so required more money than had been provided. The UMCA received £17,000 a year: the £1,000 a year given by the SPG for Mashonaland was, therefore, entirely inadequate.[127]

Knight-Bruce had already argued, in fact, that he himself had had to find such large sums of money that the Mashonaland Mission was virtually "a private mission"[128] and that the venture had only survived because of his long absence in 1892–3, fund-raising in England.[129] The two accounts he gave of monies received appear to substantiate his claim. One is for 1892 and 1893 combined: it shows a total income of just under £6,000: the SPG contributed £2,000; other societies in England £1,000; "other" (probably the BSA Company) £100; and £2,843 is attributed to special funds raised (by Knight-Bruce) in England. The second account, apparently for 1892 alone, shows a total of just under £5,000, £1,080 of which was contributed by missionary societies.[130]

Knight-Bruce likened the work of founding the diocese to building the foundations of a pier: a great deal of work and expense was incurred but nothing could be seen. He argued that commercial companies expected to sink a great deal of capital before they reaped any profits and that the church should expect to do the same.[131] He clung to his belief that he had created the framework of a vast mission which was not unworthy to take its place by the side of the UMCA.[132]

He had his defenders and what he had attempted to achieve was acknowledged: his had been the 'courageous pioneer work' of the Church in Mashonaland.[133] Tucker, Secretary of the SPG, declared that the attacks on him were "unfair and ungrateful" and no other man

---

[127] RHL/USPG, D Series, 102(B), 1892, G.H.W. Knight-Bruce to Mr Tucker, February 27th, 1892, October 26th, 1892, November 24th, 1892; 106(A), 1893, G.H.W. Knight-Bruce, Bishop of Mashonaland, to Mr Tucker, February 9th, 1893, f. 3.

[128] RHL/USPG, D Series, 106(A), 1893, G.H.W. Knight-Bruce, Bishop of Mashonaland, to Mr Tucker, February 9th, 1893.

[129] United Festival of the Home Organizations in Aid of the Funds of the Ten Dioceses of the Province of South Africa, *Combined Report* (London: [The Committee], 1893), 30–31.

[130] RHL/USPG, D Series, 106(A), 1893, Schedule (for Mashonaland), 3rd March, 1893; 'Annual Report: Summary', *MQP* III (Jan 1893), 29.

[131] 'The Bishop's Letter, No. IX. Bovey Tracey, June 18th, 1894', *MQP* IX (July 1894), 6; 'The Bishop's Letter, No. X. Coombe, Lustleigh, October 3rd, 1894', *MQP* X (Oct 1894), 6.

[132] 'Mashonaland', *MF* 138:447 (Mar 1893), 90.

[133] RHL/USPG, X363, MMA, Executive Committee, Minute Book, Council Meeting, October 31st, 1894.

would have done all that Knight-Bruce had done. Tucker suspected that the criticism had been orchestrated, that "a dead set" had been made against Knight-Bruce in South Africa and England.[134] It was certainly true that the Bishop of Derry, one of Knight-Bruce's most active critics, was a friend of Rhodes[135] and had a daughter married to a Mashonaland pioneer.

What was not made public was Knight-Bruce's own loss of interest in Mashonaland, as early as April 1892. Then in England, he had proposed to the Archbishop of Canterbury and George Howard Wilkinson, Bishop of Exeter, a friend of the CPSA, that a second diocese be set up in Natal, the corollary being that he would be its first bishop. The Bishop of Capetown had had to write to England to quash this proposal and to point out how "unhappy" such an appointment would be.[136]

Diocese-hopping (premature translation) is almost as great a scandal in the church as the resignation of a see. Knight-Bruce had himself elected to move to Mashonaland, after a very short episcopate in Bloemfontein and had now barely "passed though" his new diocese. His fellow bishops had only agreed to his move to Mashonaland because it was believed that a man of his interests and gifts was needed there: "his genius lay wholly in the direction of pioneer missionary work". He had also made it clear while at Bloemfontein that he had "a most decided distaste for the quiet and even work of a settled Diocese": the scandal of another move aside, he was not the right man for a settled area like Natal.[137]

That Knight-Bruce was prepared to contemplate such a move in 1892 is evidence of his very early disillusion with Mashonaland. The truth is that not only were conditions there extremely discouraging but, with colonisation, the country had lost its appeal for him. He wrote in his memoirs, "my friends in Africa know that it is Africa wild rather than Africa civilised that attracted me". For him, the "great charm" of Mashonaland had "vanished with the coming of the white men". The "whole face of the country" seemed different, the old order had changed, and "the romance had gone".[138]

---

[134] LPL, Benson, 141, H.W. Tucker to Archbishop, March 23rd, 1895.

[135] RHL/USPG, D Series, 106(A), 1893, G.H.W. Knight-Bruce, Bishop to Mr Tucker, December 12th, 1893.

[136] W/CPSA, AB/1162/A, 16, Bishop of Capetown to Archbishop of Canterbury, April 25th, 1892, ff. 339–40.

[137] W/CPSA, AB/1162/A, 17, Bishop of Capetown to G.H. Wilkinson, October 10th 1892, f. 43.

[138] Knight-Bruce, *Memories*, 2–3.

Knight-Bruce was not naïve about 'natives'. Face to face with 'savage Africa' for the first time, in 1888, he had been appalled[139] and he was fiercely critical of those who opposed missions on the grounds that indigenous peoples should be left to their own way of life. To these theorists Knight-Bruce opposed his own experience. The 'native' in his natural state was not "the sober innocent person the mission-haters would have us believe".[140] He could "conceive no more ludicrous assertion" than that the "raw native is better than the Christian or educated one".[141] He saw the potential of the indigenous people of his diocese, however, and wished nothing more than to be an agent in their conversion.[142]

He had little interest in settlers, unless they were men of his own rank, gentlemen and behaved as gentlemen ought to behave. For colonials in general and the "lower moral stratum of the European population in Africa", he felt distaste.[143] In public, he stated his belief that ministry to settlers was as valuable as missionary work: "no work, if honestly done for Christ, is of less importance than any other".[144] One built up the faithful and kept the truth before their eyes, the other spread the gospel. He himself did his duty by white men wherever he found them, in Mashonaland and elsewhere but, as his own obituarist admitted, Knight-Bruce had an "unconciliatory manner" and while he "did everything that was right... did it, unfortunately, in the wrong way".[145] His own preference for work among 'natives' could not be concealed. It was clearly shown, for instance, in his *Memories of Mashonaland*, published in 1894: the one chapter on 'European Work' is second to last, following eight on missionary work. The frontispiece is a photograph of his ideal, the black "Christian gentleman"[146] Chief Khama. "Very few colonists", Knight-Bruce confided to his journal, were Khama's "equal".[147]

[139] NAZ HMss, BR 8/1/1, Knight-Bruce, Correspondence, cutting from *Diamond Fields Advertiser*, December 18th, 1888.

[140] Knight-Bruce, *Memories*, 139; and see *ibid.*, pp. 120–3.

[141] 'The Bishop's Journey', *BQP* 83 (Jan 1889), 12.

[142] Fripp and *Hiller, Gold and the Gospel*, 114–5; Knight-Bruce, *Journals*, 28–9, 33.

[143] Knight-Bruce, *Journals*, 47; see also, W/CPSA, AB/355f, Knight-Bruce, Papers, Letter to his wife, April 26th, May 7th, 1893.

[144] 'The Bishop's Charge', *BQP* 89 (July 1890), 278.

[145] 'Bishop Knight-Bruce' [from the Church Times], *BQP* 115 (Jan 1897), 23.

[146] Knight-Bruce, *Memories*, 156.

[147] Fripp and *Hiller, Gold and the Gospel*, 114.

To the settlers of Mashonaland his opinions and his preference were evident and he was attacked in their papers for neglecting them in favour of 'the INFERNAL MASHONA'.[148] Pelly wrote, in 1893, that he was almost universally disliked;[149] Carter of Zululand, in 1894, that scarcely anyone seemed to have a good word for him.[150] He was dismissed (privately) as "that damned Bishop".[151]

VIII *Knight-Bruce: achievements and failures*

Knight-Bruce died from pneumonia following a recurrence of malaria in 1896, in Devon, where he had been serving as assistant bishop to the Bishop of Exeter. He was forty-four. His death naturally halted criticism. What were remembered were his courage and his dedication to missions.[152] His immediate legacy to Mashonaland, however, was failure.

He had not implemented his grand scheme of missionary work. Even his title to his mission farms turned out to be flimsy, for he was away in England when the country was being surveyed and titles granted. The church ended up with only 12 farms, not 25 or 28, or even 40, as Knight-Bruce had once believed he held. Most of them were also in the east of the country, which left the diocese with a lopsided missionary influence. Land and work elsewhere, especially in Matabeleland, had to be established with great difficulty, if at all, by his successors.

His episcopate, however, did ensure that the English Church in Mashonaland bore from the outset a strong missionary character and was not merely a colonial chaplaincy, with perhaps some missionary work attached. It was also not entirely without direct missionary fruit, for while few of his other staff fulfilled their contracts, most of his catechists adjusted to local conditions, were not invalided out either by fever or deprivation.

---

[148] Weller and Linden, *Mainstream Christianity*, 68.

[149] NAZ, HMss, PE 3/1/1, Pelly, Correspondence, 1892–1934, February 2nd, 1893, f. 202.

[150] W/CPSA, AB/186, W.M. Carter, Papers 1891–1930, Letter to Johnnie Cox, December 14th, 1894.

[151] Maurice Heaney, in NAZ, HMss, BO 11/1/1, Henry John Borrow papers, letter to Borrow, April 3rd, 1890.

[152] Langham-Carter, *Knight Bruce*, 63–4.

As they were left very much to their own devices, several of them strayed. Frank Ziqubu, for instance, became more of a farmer than an evangelist.[153] The first two conversions among local people, nevertheless, were the result of their presence and both converts then themselves became catechists: Sahanya Watu, baptised as Raymond in 1897, had attached himself to Charles Makolami and then worked for Douglas Pelly in Umtali. Shoniwa Kapuya, baptised some months earlier as John, had been a catechumen under Bernard Mizeki.

Mizeki himself was murdered in a rising against colonial rule in 1896. He was mourned by those who knew him as a remarkable man, highly intelligent, deeply devout but, initially, as just one of several workers who had "quietly and humbly" given their lives for the church.[154] A simple, local pilgrimage to the site of his death was then begun in the early 1900s and a shrine was erected on the site in 1938. The eighteenth of June, the anniversary of his death, or martyrdom, has been kept ever since as a major festival and day of pilgrimage by Anglicans throughout Central and Southern Africa.[155]

When Knight-Bruce resigned in 1894, however, there were no mission stations in existence in Mashonaland and no converts, only three catechists living near local chiefs. The majority of the settlers were members of the English Church and most were living without pastoral care, without the sacraments, even without proper burials. It was clear to Knight-Bruce's successor that work had survived in the area only because of the leadership of first, Balfour and then Upcher, at Salisbury.[156]

---

[153] For his dismissal in 1897 and a later episcopal encomium, see below, pp. 56, 61.

[154] J.H. Upcher, *Notes toward the history of the Church in Mashonaland* (Salisbury: Diocese of Southern Rhodesia, 1903), 2.

[155] Farrant, 236–42; for varying significance attributed to Mizeki since 1933, see T.O. Ranger, 'Taking Hold of the Land': Holy Places and Pilgrimages in Twentieth-Century Zimbabwe', *Past and Present* 117 (November 1987), 186–90, 192–3.

[156] RHL/USPG, D Series, 114, 1895, Will. Mashonaland to Mr Tucker, May 25th, 1895.

CHAPTER TWO

A BASE OF OPERATIONS: WILLIAM GAUL (1895–1907)

I *1894–5: Appointment of a new bishop*

The Diocese of Mashonaland in 1894 needed a new bishop who could rescue it from the perilous position in which it had been left by Knight-Bruce. To be able to do so, he needed to be not only an effective leader but also a cleric who could exercise his office fruitfully among settlers and work with the BSA Company.

The Bishop of Capetown's first choice for the vacant see was James Hay Upcher, Archdeacon of Mashonaland and Vicar-General of the diocese since Knight-Bruce's departure for England in March 1894. Upcher, as we have seen earlier (p. 32) had been successful in ecclesiastical terms, in drawing settlers to church in Salisbury, beginning 'town mission work' and supervising work elsewhere. He was also highly thought of by the administration. He, however, refused to be considered for the office of bishop either in 1894 or subsequently, as his only desire was to be a missionary.[1]

William Thomas Gaul, Archdeacon and Rector of Kimberley, was then invited to become the second bishop of Mashonaland. He was a man who was unlikely to have risen to episcopal office under normal circumstances. The bishops of the CPSA, like the bishops of the Church of England, were usually drawn from the English upper-classes. They were public school men and graduates of either Oxford or Cambridge, like Knight-Bruce or William Carter, Bishop of Zululand, who on his visit to Mashonaland in 1894 was agreeably surprised to discover a fellow-Etonian in the acting administrator, Colonel Frank Rhodes.[2] Upcher was a member of the Norfolk squirearchy and a Cambridge man.

Gaul, by contrast, was of Irish origin, a graduate of Trinity College, Dublin and had begun his working life as a teacher in Battersea. He

---

[1] W/CPSA, AB/1162/A, 18, Bishop of Capetown to Revd B.C. Durrad, October 24th, 1894, f. 106; to Ven. J.H. Upcher, December 1st, 1894, f. 147.

[2] W/CPSA, AB/186, W.M. Carter, Papers 1891–1930, Letter 'to Algy', 2nd December, 1894.

was a colonial priest, that is, he had been ordained in South Africa (in 1874): this was the first time a man ordained in South Africa had been considered for the episcopate there.[3] It was also very rare indeed for an Irishman to become a bishop in the 'English Church': Gaul believed (incorrectly) that he was the first to do so since the disestablishment of the Church of Ireland or even since the Reformation. He was, moreover, personally unconventional to the point of eccentricity.[4] It is a measure of how serious the situation was in Mashonaland that he was offered the bishopric in spite of these disadvantages.

His chief qualification lay in the fact that he had worked for twenty years in the Bloemfontein diocese, most notably in the extremely difficult conditions of the Kimberley diamond fields. He had proved himself there to be a clergyman of "outstanding vigour and leadership", among both settlers and 'natives':[5] Knight-Bruce had made him an archdeacon in recognition of his excellent work.

Gaul had also taken a keen interest in developments north of the Limpopo. As we have seen in Chapter One, his vision and inventiveness had posed a threat to Knight-Bruce's plans for the area in 1889–90. He had also shown a pastoral concern for the new society which was to be created to the north: he had given a prayer book to each man leaving Kimberley to join the pioneer column.

He was a man likely to work well with local officials for he did not share Knight-Bruce's distrust of the BSA Company. On the contrary, he was known to be on excellent terms with the directors,[6] was a personal friend of Rhodes and the Fourth Earl Grey, of Jameson and Alfred Beit (he was to be named in his will as one of the Beit trustees). Rhodes himself had suggested to Gaul that he "come up" to Mashonaland and "bring the Church" with him when its occupation was in prospect.[7] It is probable that Rhodes himself had some influence in Gaul's appoint-

---

[3] A. Pierce Jones, *Procession of Witness* (Cape Town: [Printed by the Stewart Printing Company, Cape Town], 1947), 24. Gaul was ordained deacon in Ireland, priest in South Africa.

[4] W/CPSA, AB/1162/A, 24, Bishop of Capetown to Coadjutor, October 6th, 1908, f. 472.

[5] Henry Paget Thompson, *Into All the Lands: The History of The Society for the Propagation of the Gospel in Foreign Parts 1701–1950* (London: S.P.C.K., 1951), 315.

[6] W/CPSA, AB/1162/A, 18, Bishop of Capetown to Ven. W. Gaul, December 3rd, 1894, f. 152, December 11th, 1894, f. 163; to Bishop of Grahamstown, December 11th, 1894, f. 165.

[7] 'The Bishop's Charge (continued): Rhodesia and our Responsibilities', *MQP* XLVI (Nov 1903), 5.

ment.[8] He was an appropriate person to become bishop in a colony now to be known officially (from late 1895) as Rhodesia. (The diocese, which extended far beyond the bounds of the colony, retained the title of Mashonaland until 1915.)

Gaul, furthermore, did not share Knight-Bruce's distaste for the generality of settlers: on the contrary, they produced in him great sympathy and even admiration. He knew their lives to be strenuous and often sacrificial: it was, after all, by their "pluck and staying power" that the Empire was being extended in Africa and elsewhere.[9] Gaul wrote feelingly, for example, of the men building the railways, men "from Harrow—from the University, and this one and that one from anywhere and everywhere, on this or that side of the equator, all pushing on the rail through Africa, from Cape to Cairo, for their old mother England, with "hard berth and bitter fare", and often leaving a lonely grave in the bush to mark the Empire's progress".[10]

He characterised a group of young officials, in early North-West Rhodesia, as "ably representing England at its best—self-reliant, eager and with ideals worth having"[11] and wrote on his retirement, "The Bishop never feels more at home in a billiard room with his friends than when he leads public worship there and is allowed to "say his say". If there be one thing more than another he will miss... it will be his camp services among his good friends, the miners, railwaymen and police of Rhodesia, who always hit hard and straight themselves, and always take kindly to the Bishop's humble attempts from the shoulder. May God bless them all—men and women in their tussle with life and its trials, in the shaft, the workshop and the home."[12]

The needs of Mashonaland in 1895 were very specific and William Gaul was able to meet them as a man direct from England would have been unlikely to do. The news was greeted with delight in the South African press: there could be "no more popular appointment". Now, it was prophesied, "the black past" of the diocese would be "wiped

---

[8] W/CPSA, AB/186, W.M. Carter, Papers 1891–1930, Letter to Johnnie Cox, December 9th, 1894.

[9] 'Letter from the Bishop, No. XIII. Umtali, April 14th, 1898', *MQP* XXV (Aug 1898), 6.

[10] RHL/USPG, D Series, 126(b), 1898, Will. Mashonaland, Report, December 31st, 1898.

[11] 'North-West Rhodesia', *Ch.Ch.* (July 12th, 1905), 427.

[12] 'The Bishop's Notes', *RCM* 4:4 (April 1907), 1.

out"[13] and this prediction was to be fulfilled: Gaul was to be as successful and as popular among the settlers of Mashonaland as he had been in Kimberley.

Gaul was no more naïve about settlers, however, than Knight-Bruce was about 'natives'. He had worked in South Africa since the early days of the diamond diggings, "when most men were chiefly eager to secure the riches of this present world" rather than the things of God, as his fellow-bishops put it.[14] He knew at first hand that life in Africa was "a battle, morally, physically and spiritually",[15] that there were "manifold powers of evil associated with the early days of pioneer civilisation"[16] and he could be very fierce about unrepentant sinners, men who became the "devil's missionaries" through their "drunken and immoral lives". One of the functions of the church, he stated, was to be a "standing protest" against such men and a check to all other forms of evil.[17]

He believed hardened sinners to be in a minority in the settler community, however, and that many young men went astray simply because they came out from England "utterly untrained to *resist* evil".[18] The role of the church, moreover, was to touch and reclaim men of 'all sorts and conditions'. Gaul said in 1908, "do not suppose that everybody who goes to South Africa who calls himself a pioneer, or a miner, or a prospector, is altogether bad, for there is not an altogether bad man in the world, and if you go the right way to work you will find among these men some of the finest traits of self-denial and generosity and receptiveness".[19] He himself had the gift of speaking as "man to man not from saint to sinner"[20] and his directness did him no harm in a society where a clergyman could be instructed to admonish his congregation:

---

[13] 'The Friend of the Free State', *Cape Times*, in *MQP* XIII (July 1895), 6.

[14] 'Copy of letter, Bishops of the Province to Bishop of Mashonaland, March 1st, 1907', *MQP* LX (May 1907), 5.

[15] Bishop of Mashonaland, 'South African Church Festival', *Guardian*, June 17th, 1896, reprinted in *MQP* XVII (Aug 1896), 26.

[16] 'Letter from the Bishop, No. IV. Latitude 2°S Longitude 42°, November 1895', *MQP* XV (Feb 1896), 5.

[17] 'Letter from the Bishop, No. VIII. Umtali, March 1st, 1897', *MQP* XX (May 1897), 4.

[18] 'Letter from the Bishop, No. XIII. Umtali, April 14th, 1898', *MQP* XXV (Aug 1898), 7.

[19] 'The Annual Meeting', *SARWMQP* 19 (April 1908), 12.

[20] 'Mrs Mary Blackwood Lewis's letters about Mashonaland, 1897–1901', *Rhodesiana* 1:5 (1960), 28.

"I hope you'll give us "gip", we need it badly".[21] One of his clergy characterized Gaul in 1904 as "popular but...hits out...expects to get his head punched".[22]

In Kimberley, he had had at least one celebrated run-in with Rhodes (over the matter of Sunday observance)[23] and he was quite ready to criticise the BSA Company or any other government or society, when he felt criticism to be necessary. In 1897, for example, he encouraged a black priest to preach, to the settler congregation in Salisbury, a sermon which included references to "dishonest or merely expedient legislation", unfair working practices, racial prejudice and unacknowledged half-caste children.[24] Gaul's comment was that such sermons "ought to do good...Educated natives, and especially Christian natives are...measuring us by our own bushel of the Gospel, and testing us by its standard".[25]

Gaul was also better suited than Knight-Bruce to be a bishop among pioneers because his imagination was caught, not by the 'wild' Africa which had so appealed to his predecessor, but by that which had repelled him, by Africa 'civilised', by the progress of the Empire, the extension of British rule, technology and colonisation. The railways, for instance, were for Gaul, as for many of his contemporaries, an object of wonder, "carrying the religion and politics and commerce and enterprise and hopes and fears of the Empire...into and through the great, dark Central African Continent".[26] He was someone who had "a sympathetic attitude towards every form of modern life, individual, social or national",[27] a bishop who, on being shown around a new mine, secretly blessed the machinery.

The new bishop's eccentric style was also an asset in early Mashonaland, where settlers revelled in the freedom of a "shirt-sleeve"

---

[21] 'Diocese of Mashonaland. Letter from H.P. Hale, Missioner', *SARWMQP* (July 1904), 8.

[22] Over the question of importing Chinese labour for the mines: NAZ, Hmss, HA 4/1/1, H.P. Hale, Letterbook, ff. 10–11.

[23] Pierce Jones, *Procession*, 77.

[24] RHL/USPG, D Series, 138(b), 1901, Rev. Hezekiah Mtobi, sermon manuscript.

[25] RHL/USPG, D Series, 122(b), 1897, Will. Mashonaland to 'Sir', March 13th, 1897.

[26] 'North-West Rhodesia', *Ch.Ch.* (July 12th 1905), 427.

[27] J.T. Darragh, *Johannesburg Times*, in *MQP* XIII (July 1895), 10.

society.[28] It was no place for a "stiff ecclesiastic", as Upcher put it.[29] Knight-Bruce had been unable to adapt himself to the "rough and ready" attitudes of a pioneering society[30] but Gaul saw "the ABC" of colonial life as the willingness to be unconventional[31] and was himself praised as "splendidly" so.[32] He was happy to describe himself as a "Bush Bishop" rather than a "regular" bishop,[33] to wear a khaki version of episcopal clothing, to ride a bicycle, carry his own bags, fetch his own bathwater.

In 1895, therefore, Mashonaland exchanged a bishop who was attacked in the settler press for one who was already admired for the keen interest he took in all matters affecting the progress of the colony. When Gaul retired in 1907, 1,500 'Rhodesians' from all walks of life subscribed to a purse of £330 and a heartfelt tribute of thanks to him and regret at his leaving.[34]

Earlier, a settler publication had written of him, "If there is one man Rhodesians are proud of it is their Bishop, Dr. Gaul, of Mashonaland. His stories are as good as his sermons. As much at home in the fighting column, if duty calls, as in church he is loved as a stalwart, saint-like Christian by all sorts and conditions. Those who have been in Rhodesia and missed meeting Dr. Gaul bring home one kindly memory the less."[35]

William Gaul was consecrated bishop in Bloemfontein cathedral in April 1895. He had a magnificent send-off from Kimberley and equally enthusiastic farewells in Bloemfontein and Johannesburg. He then arrived in the dusty township of Bulawayo, in May 1895, to a warm welcome: there was a public *conversazione*, at which the entire settlement

[28] Hugh Marshall Hole, *Old Rhodesian Days* (1928) (Facsimile reproduction: Bulawayo: Books of Rhodesia, 1976), 74–5.

[29] NAZ, HMss, ANG 1/4/4, First Diocesan Conference, St Augustine's, Panhalonga, August 21st, 1902, f. 1.

[30] 'Bishop Knight-Bruce', [Obituary, *The Church Times*], *BQP* 115 (Jan 1897), 23.

[31] RHL/USPG, D Series, 142(b), 1902, W. Mashonaland to the Right Rev. the Secretary, SPG, November 17th, 1902.

[32] F.A. Rogers, 'Letters from the Line. Diocese of Grahamstown', *SARWMQP* 19 (April 1908), 3–4.

[33] 'Bishop's Letter No. XXI. Church House, Bulawayo, 28th September, 1900', *MQP* XXXIV (Nov 1900), 5.

[34] [J. Hallward], 'The Bishop's Farewell', *RCM* 4:7 (July 1907), 9–10.

[35] 'The Bishop of Mashonaland and the Company Promoter', *Rhodesia Review: An Independent Quarterly for Settlers and Shareholders* (June 1905), 236.

appears to have been present. With his advent, relationships between settlers and bishop had already changed.

So had relationships with other religious bodies. Knight-Bruce had wanted an exclusive sphere of operations for the English Church in Mashonaland and regarded other missions as little more than intruders. Both the local Methodist minister and Jesuit priest were present at Gaul's welcoming *conversazione*, however, to his pleasure. Gaul still claimed pre-eminence for the English Church but official relations with other churches now took on a friendlier tone.[36]

The English Church's own structures also changed. Knight-Bruce had chosen Umtali in the east for his 'central station' but Gaul promptly set up headquarters in Salisbury, the settler capital. For his predecessor's vision of a bishop living among his missionaries, Gaul substituted the usual English pattern: the bishop was to have his seat at the administrative centre of the country. The church needed to be to be concerned, not just with the religious life of the new colony but also with its social and political life and progress.

Knight-Bruce had also attempted to centre the ecclesiastical life of the diocese on a mission station. For Gaul, the heart of diocesan life was to be a cathedral. 'Home', or English, patterns were for him the norm: "Our aim with regard to the white population is to reproduce among them that English home life of which we are justly proud, and the basis of which is the Christian religion".[37] The little church at Salisbury began to be referred to as 'the pro-cathedral' and in 1903, Lady Milton, the wife of the then Administrator, began a fund for the building of a proper cathedral.

II *1895–8: Re-construction*

On his arrival in his diocese in 1895, Gaul found, as Knight-Bruce had found before him and succeeding bishops were to discover, that the immediate needs of Mashonaland resolved themselves very quickly into two which were pressing and over-riding, men and money, staff and the wherewithal to support them.

---

[36] See, RHL/USPG, D Series, 163b, 1905, W. M'land to Dear Bishop, Sept 2nd, 1905.

[37] 'Diocese of Mashonaland', South African Church Festival, *Combined Report* (London: [The Committee], 1896), 28.

The diocese now held a settler population of about 5,000. There were six colonial settlements of any size, Salisbury, Bulawayo, Beira, Umtali, Fort Victoria, and the new mining centre of Gwelo, half-way between Salisbury and Bulawayo. Tuli, on the Bechuanaland border and Macloutsie, over the border, though still in existence, were very much depleted. Indigenous peoples numbered some 500,000, and were distributed over an area ten times the size of England. Many people from the surrounding territories were also employed on mines and in the settlements. The Roman Catholics, moreover, now posed a threat not just to the English Church's missionary plans but, through their schools and nursing sisters, to its assumption of "influence and power" among settlers.[38] The diocese had only six members of staff: a priest, a deacon, a layman, and three catechists. There were also three nurses at Umtali.

One commentator described Mashonaland as being in a state of "utter degradation and collapse".[39] Gaul himself characterised Bulawayo as a "spiritual wilderness", on his arrival in 1895.[40] It was the most important town in the country and was growing rapidly: the settler population doubled between late 1894 and late 1895 (numbers rose from 1,000 to 2,000). Bulawayo, however, had seen no English clergyman between Knight-Bruce's departure in October 1893 and a visit by Upcher a year later, in November 1894.

Since then Upcher had been attempting to look after both settlements. They were a four-day, rough and expensive post-cart journey apart and while he was in one town, the other had been left untended. Though lay people in both places had rallied and held services (with varying success) and in Bulawayo had even built a church, there was no-one to do the pastoral work, to deal with "sickness, fever, death, sin".[41] The new bishop, on his arrival in his diocese, found himself obliged to act as the parish priest of Bulawayo until a clergyman arrived from England some months later to relieve him.

---

[38] RHL/USPG, D Series, 122(b), 1897, Will. Mashonaland to Rev. H.W. Tucker, April 27th, 1897.

[39] RHL/USPG, D Series, 114, 1895, Bishop of Derry to Rev. H.W. Tucker, March 20th, 1895.

[40] RHL/USPG, D Series, 134(A), 1900, Will. Mashonaland, Annual Report, January 19th, 1900.

[41] RHL/USPG, D Series, 114, 1895, Bishop of Derry to Rev. H.W. Tucker, March 20th, 1895.

Of the other significant colonial settlements, Fort Victoria and its district were being looked after by Burgin, the layman and Umtali by Walker, the deacon, that is, by a junior cleric who ought not to have had sole charge of a church. Since neither settlement had the services of a priest, neither congregations nor ministers were able to receive the sacraments. At Beira, which had many British inhabitants and a high mortality rate, there was no minister at all and men were "living and dying like heathen".[42] Nor was there a parson in the huge mining district of Gwelo. Missionary work was also weak, for there were only two catechists at work in the east of the diocese and one at Mazoe, 30 miles or so from Salisbury.

The situation was also changing rapidly, for settlers were streaming in, prospectors spreading out all over the country. In the Salisbury area, farmers were scattered 10 to 20 miles from the town and settlements were developing at Mazoe and at Hartley, 60 miles to the south-west. Umtali, in August 1895, had a settler population of 100 in the town but 126 in the district. By February 1896, there were 150 in the town and 150 in the district. Within two years, by 1897, Gaul was to reckon that there ought to be four clergymen for the Bulawayo district alone, if the work there was to be done properly.

The surrounding territories were also developing. A railway was pushing up from Mafeking though Bechuanaland and was to reach Bulawayo in November 1897. Bechuanaland was already nominally part of the Diocese of Mashonaland and when the railway arrived the territory became accessible and therefore a real responsibility. Though most of the colonial settlements were very small and were on or near the line of rail, there were 400 miles of rail between Bulawayo and Ramatlabama, the southernmost point of the diocese, on the border with the Cape Colony and all along the line were gangers and their families. Far beyond the line of rail, up to 500 miles away, were occasional settlers and traders.

A significant settlement, Francistown, was to spring up on the railway line near the Monarch Mine in the Tati Concession in 1897 and the railway itself was to be continued beyond Bulawayo, reaching the Victoria Falls in 1904 and then extending into North-West Rhodesia. With it were extended the responsibilities of the Diocese of Mashonaland.

---

[42] 'Letter from Rev. A. Walker. Church House, Umtali, June 16th, 1897', *MQP* XXI (Aug 1897), 13.

Gaul's first task was to attempt to increase his tiny staff. Two of the six had left the diocese almost immediately after he arrived: Upcher went on a six-month furlough and Burgin returned to England to train as a clergyman, with the hope, which was never fulfilled, of returning to Mashonaland. A parson recruited in England for Bulawayo was on his way out, however, and Gaul had found a few members of staff in South Africa, two colonial clergymen and two missionaries: Hezekiah Mtobi, a 'Fingo' (Mfengu) from the Grahamstown diocese; and Douglas Pelly, who had been since 1894 a sugar planter in Natal but had now been persuaded (by Balfour) to return to Mashonaland and prepare for ordination.[43]

Gaul was therefore able to place parsons at Bulawayo, Salisbury and Gwelo and send Mtobi and Pelly (whom he ordained deacon) to reinforce mission work in the east of the country. There was still no-one for Beira or Fort Victoria. With his handful of new staff installed, Gaul then left his diocese in January 1896 and travelled to England, as Knight-Bruce had done before him, in search of more staff and funds.

He left a troubled country. In some areas, locusts had destroyed crops, in others drought had been severe. A new and terrible cattle disease, rinderpest, was sweeping through the country and decimating stock and transport oxen. More significantly, perhaps, resentment was growing in local communities at the taxes, impositions and abuses of colonial rule. Then, at the end of 1895, Dr. Jameson, the Administrator, and many of the young men of the colony had made an ill-advised and unsuccessful raid (in which Rhodes was implicated) into the Transvaal, in an attempt to assist British there to unseat the Boer government.

Jameson was captured with his men, among them many of the BSA Company's police (and he and Rhodes were disgraced). With the Administrator and the bulk of the police out of the country (and defeated) the Ndebele rose against their colonial conquerors, in March 1896, a couple of months after Gaul had left for England. They were followed in June by many of the Shona polities. About 10%, some 590, of the settlers, men, women and children were killed, in outlying districts, on mines and farms. The others withdrew into laagers in the settlements for safety. Lines of supply were cut, however, and there was little food and much illness in the laagers.

[43] NAZ, HMss, PE 3/2/1, Douglas Raymond Pelly, Reminiscences, ff. 22–4.

The effect of the risings (Umvukela/Chimurenga) on the church was felt most directly by the catechists, in Mashonaland, who, like other 'foreigners' associated with the settlers, were prime targets. At Mangwende's, Bernard Mizeki was murdered. Ziqubu had to be smuggled to safety by Chipunza, a friendly sub-chief, for Makoni was one of the leaders of the rising. He and Chipunza later helped to lead imperial forces to Makoni's strong-hold and the chief was executed.

Jacob Dyasi, who had been working near Chidamba's, in the Mazoe area, found safety in the 'native corps' of the colonial forces. Douglas Pelly was also affected (his hut was ransacked) but he himself was away from Makoni's when the rising began. He became chaplain to the Rhodesia Horse, a mounted settler militia, as he was the only one of Gaul's clergy who was available and fit enough to do so. One of his chief offices was to bury the remains of murdered settlers.

Gaul returned to the diocese in late 1896 as the rising in Matabeleland was being brought to an end, partly by the personal intervention of Rhodes, who negotiated unarmed with Ndebele leaders in the Matopos Hills (and thereby restored, in part, his political reputation). In Mashonaland the struggle dragged on and was only finally quelled in mid-1897.

On his journey, Gaul stopped and prayed at the graves of settlers who had been murdered but he had also hastened his return in order to be on the spot, like Knight-Bruce in 1893, to do what he could to see that full justice was done to 'the natives' at the conclusion of hostilities.[44] What influence he was able to exert is not known although it was his friend, and a member of the Mashonaland Mission Association council, the Fourth Earl Grey who now became Administrator in Jameson's stead.

Gaul himself stated that he regarded the conflict as "most lamentable".[45] He refused publicly to "take sides", was prepared only to "*state* and *teach* principles", however unpopular such a course was, when men on both sides "were exasperated and vengeful,—and both of them with cause to be so". "In such a situation", he wrote, "who and what but

[44] 'Annual Council Meeting. July 6th, 1896', *MQP* XVII (Aug 1896), 22.

[45] 'Letter from the Bishop of Mashonaland. Salisbury, November 25th, 1896', *MQP* XIX (Feb 1897), 10.

the Church of God can mediate?" His was, he believed, the gospel method, and would win in the long run.[46]

The immediate work of the church, however, was greatly weakened by the conflict. At Mangwende's and Makoni's, work was abandoned and most of the people themselves were moved into 'reserves', away from their original villages near the colonial lines of communication. Only in the extreme east of the country did mission work continue. A lay steward, C.A. Franklin, who had been employed in 1895 to develop the agricultural potential of the land, was still farming on Knight-Bruce's original farm at Penhalonga. Mtobi, although distressed by the conflict, had also worked on at Mtasa's where he had been stationed for Mtasa, though a difficult chief for missionaries to deal with, had not taken part in the risings.

Gaul's small colonial staff was also in the process of being depleted once more, by privation, fever and discouragement. Griffiths, the man at Gwelo and Hammick, at Bulawayo, left. Upcher, who had returned to the diocese just before the risings and Walker (at Umtali) were invalided out. Only one of the clergy who had been doing colonial work remained, Herbert Foster, at Salisbury

There was no immediate prospect of replacing the workers who had left, let alone finding extra staff to expand the work, for seven months of hard work by Gaul in England had yielded no clerical recruits, bar a man who had only lasted six months. He had only been able to secure promises of future service from a couple of young men still in training. There were now so few clergy in the diocese that Pelly, one of the two mission clergy (and now a priest) had to be sent to a colonial post, at Umtali.

Mashonaland was thus in at least as bad a state as it had been two years before, when Gaul had first arrived. He wrote to the SPG in late 1896 that he had "hardly yet made sure of the base of operations"[47] and things continued to be very shaky: 1897 was "a very dark year".[48] Gaul himself had to act as parish priest of Bulawayo and people began once again to ask what the matter was with the English Church, as

[46] RHL/USPG, D Series, 122(b), 1897, Will. Mashonaland to the Rev. Secretary SPG, October 6th, 1897.

[47] RHL/USPG, D Series, 118(b), 1896, Will. Mashonaland, Report, December 21st, 1896.

[48] RHL/USPG, D Series, 122(b), 1897, Will. Mashonaland to the Rev. Secretary SPG, 6th October, 1897.

they had done during Knight-Bruce's episcopate: there was only one clergyman and the bishop in the huge stretch of country between South Africa and Salisbury and only the priest at Salisbury for the whole of Mashonaland proper. The English church claimed 80% of the settler population, yet the Roman Catholics and Nonconformists, with 20% between them, had twice the number of staff.[49]

Though the numbers of English clergy then began to build up from this low point, they did so painfully slowly. An additional difficulty was that the majority of recruits were young or not yet ordained and so could not be sent to a sole charge: three young men arrived in 1897, for instance, two ordinands and one junior clergyman, Nelson Fogarty, who became Gaul's chaplain. Only one experienced clergyman was recruited in the course of the year, from South Africa and he was sent to look after the urgent needs of Beira.

Missionary work remained in a very precarious state. 'Offence' (unspecified) removed the two remaining catechists, Ziqubu and Dyasi, in late 1897. An attempt to begin a medical mission on a church 'farm' at Zimunya's village, near Umtali, also failed: a (lay) missionary doctor from England, Dr. Dunley Owen, resigned within months of his arrival with his wife in mid-1897, after a midnight attack on their huts by local people. (The station remained open but not as a medical mission, in the care of a new catechist, Alfred Gadeza.)

Foster, the clergyman at Salisbury, then broke down so badly that he was compelled to leave the diocese for almost two years (August 1897 to June 1899) and Gaul himself was invalided out for several weeks at the end of 1897. At Salisbury, work survived the emergency only because a former colleague of Foster's, Herbert Selmes, was despatched from the CPSA to take his place, for a year. Bulawayo by early 1898 was in the charge of an elderly English clergyman who was very nearly blind and who had agreed to go to Mashonaland, also for one year, because nobody else was prepared to volunteer. From Bulawayo, he wrote to England, "everything shrieks for help".[50]

---

[49] 'Letter from Rev. H. Foster, Salisbury, June 16th, 1897', *MQP* XXI (Aug 1897), 11.

[50] 'Letter from Canon Bathe, Bulawayo, February 28th, 1898', *MQP* XXIV (May 1898), 9.

III *1898: Missionary work; the 'Native Question'*

By the end of 1898, however, the diocese was in a very much better position, at least in the matter of staffing, partly because its plight became a matter of major concern to the CPSA and supporters in England. The parish of Claremont, in Cape Town, for instance, which had already supplied four clergymen for Mashonaland (Surridge, in Knight-Bruce's time; Foster, Selmes and Fogarty) now supplied another, Walter Leary and encouraged Selmes to remain in the diocese. In England, a very capable clergyman, William Roxburgh was found with the help of the SPG and a group of lay missionaries were recruited from the Lichfield diocese.

Men who been invalided out also returned, others were ordained and there were no further losses. By the end of 1898 Gaul could look back to the beginning of his episcopate and report that he had increased the numbers of his clergy from two to twelve in three-and-a-half years. The chief colonial towns now had clergy, all but tiny Victoria and a 'railway mission' had been begun: Fogarty was now working down the line south of Bulawayo.

It was possible, therefore, in 1898 to move forward and begin new missionary work, to Gaul's satisfaction for he, although popular with settlers, did not regard himself narrowly as a settler bishop. He certainly believed that settlers, as the "elder children" of the church, should have first claim upon her ministrations[51] but he also had an unmistakable "zeal and enthusiasm" for missions.[52] The second task of the church in Mashonaland was to be an "uplifting and civilising influence" on the local population.[53]

Gaul's sympathies were thus broader than those of Knight-Bruce who had only wanted to be a missionary: Gaul described the vocation of a man like himself as that of a "Colonial Mission priest".[54] The two aspects of the work were for him indivisible and the task before

[51] 'Letter from the Bishop, Salisbury, Easter Eve, 1907', *MQP* LX (May 1907), 5.

[52] 'The Friend of the Free State', *Cape Times*, in *MQP* XIII (July 1895), 9.

[53] 'Diocese of Mashonaland', South African Church Festival, *Combined Report* (London: [The Committee], 1896), 28.

[54] RHL/USPG, D Series, 148(b), 1903, W. Mashonaland, Annual Report, 10th March, 1903.

the church in Mashonaland was really a single one: that of "teaching, disciplining and perfecting Nature (whether Native or European)".[55]

His missionary strategy also differed from that of Knight-Bruce who had placed his catechists in 'native' villages, away from the colonial camps. For Gaul, missionary work in the 'locations' of colonial towns was as important as work out in villages little touched by a settler presence. Colonial settlements could and should be the "spiritual watersheds" of a country.[56] He also believed that the church had a responsibility to protect local people from the corrupting aspects of modern life where they were most likely to come in contact with it, in the towns.

Gaul as a result put a strong emphasis upon work in the settlements. In late 1897, for instance, he assigned a catechist, Josiah Kubevana and a missionary with experience in the UMCA, James Gillanders, to develop a church, St. Columba's, in the Bulawayo location (now Makokobo) among the people from many tribes and territories living there. For Gaul, the "first-fruits" and the "turning point"[57] of the church's missionary work in the diocese were not the first two or three converts baptised in the east of the country in 1896/97 but the forty baptised at St. Columba's at Christmas 1899, the ninety-nine baptised at Easter 1901.

He also attempted to build upon Knight-Bruce's missionary beginnings in the east of the country but did so by concentrating rather than dispersing workers. The stations at Makoni's and Mangwende's remained closed although Mtobi and Gadeza worked on at Mtasa's and Zimunya's. A group of workers was placed near them, however, at Penhalonga: two new catechists and the laymen from the Lichfield Evangelistic Brotherhood, under the leadership of Douglas Pelly (and Pelly's newly-married wife) in order to create a 'strong centre' of work there.

A strategy of concentration gave way to opportunity, however, in areas other than the east of the country. In Matabeleland, where Gaul was as eager to establish an ascendency among the Ndebele as Knight-Bruce had been among the Shona, he appears to have been met by a

---

55 RHL/USPG, D Series, 118(b), 1896, Will. Mashonaland, Report, December 21st, 1896.

56 RHL/USPG, D Series, 134(A), 1900, Will. Mashonaland, Report, 19th January, 1900.

57 Bishop of Mashonaland, 'Notes of the Month', *MF* XLV:535 (July 1900), 272.

desire among the Ndebele themselves and particularly among the elite, to ally themselves with the church of the English monarch.[58] This was not a passing inclination as a Bulawayo clergyman was to confirm in 1911, "they want the King's Church: they do not like other bodies. They believe greatly in Royal Authority and command".[59]

Three leading Ndebele 'indunas', 'Umlugulu' (Mlugulu), 'Manyagavula' and 'N'yanda', in response to an emissary, invited Gaul to begin work near their villages some thirty miles to the south of Bulawayo. He despatched a solitary missionary, with a catechist, to begin work there in 1898.

A second mission was founded in the Charter district in the following year, as the result of a growing enthusiasm for missionary work on the part of the Salisbury clergyman, J.H. Selmes, who raised the necessary funds himself in England. He had in the earlier part of 1898 explored the possibility of developing work on a church farm not far from Salisbury, at 'Inyamwenda's' (Norton), where a catechist, John Mazoe, had been recently stationed. His attention was then diverted to a much more densely populated 'native' area in the Charter district by a chance encounter with the local Native Commissioner, which resulted in an invitation to begin work at 'Headman Gabajena's village', forty miles from Enkeldoorn (Chivu). Upcher took part in the foundation of this new mission and it was named Wreningham, after his family village in Norfolk.

Attempts were also made to reach 'Makombi' (Macombe) of the 'Barue' (Barwe), a powerful independent chief in Portuguese East Africa who was seeking British allies against the Portuguese and sent repeatedly to Gaul, asking for missionaries. Upcher made two or three journeys in an attempt to reach him from Umtali, as did W.H. Robins, the clergyman at Beira. They failed to do so, however, largely because of the reluctance of porters to venture into territory perceived as hostile.

We have seen above that Gaul differed with Knight-Bruce as to missionary strategy. He also held a different view as to the aim of missionary work. Knight-Bruce's aim had been primarily the strictly religious one of conversion: his ideal was the Christian chief of a distinctly 'native'

[58] 'A Little Help. Letter from the Bishop of Mashonaland', *CCM*, X:115 (July 1901), 80.

[59] RHL/USPG, D Series, 208(B), 1911, H.H. Foster to Bishop Montgomery, September 19th, 1911.

polity, Khama. Neither conversion, nor the economic and social betterment which he believed would inevitably follow, needed to entail the loss of "those qualities that commend themselves to us in an untamed savage".[60] The essentials of local cultural identity ought to remain undisturbed. Gaul, on the other hand, while he believed the "good" in existing 'native' customs should be retained[61] was firmly convinced that the 'natives' needed to "advance". The only true "protection" for "living men or things" was "growth, development, and progress, physical, mental and spiritual". Africa needed to undergo profound social and economic change as well as religious transformation.[62]

Gaul also believed that with missionary work (on the right lines) lay the solution to the difficult 'Native Question', the conflict of interest between local peoples and the settlers. He was in fact something of a leading thinker in these matters: his ideas, codified at a conference of some of the Mashonaland clergy in 1902 as "Resolutions on the Native Question",[63] were adopted not only by his own Synod (in 1906) but by the Province and attracted favourable comment in Britain.[64]

Gaul ruled out any immediate equality between the two groups but he also envisaged a future in which local people would be not in a state of "helotism" and mere sources of labour for settlers[65] but would form modern, self-sufficient communities alongside settler communities. For this to happen, African "kraals" needed to become Christian homes, "irresponsible nomads" to become "responsible citizens", able to claim the place of "political and social equality" which was "intended for them in the Commonwealth".[66] The matter concerned not just the church but also the state and could affect the entire social and political future of Central and Southern Africa.

Gaul believed colonization to be a constructive rather than a harmful agency in this transformation of Africa. He saw a consonance, for

[60] G.W.H. Knight-Bruce, *Memories of Mashonaland* (1895) (Facsimile reproduction: Bulawayo, Books of Rhodesia, 1970), 184, and see 119, 198–201.

[61] Bishop of Mashonaland, *Ch.Ch.* (March 22nd 1905), 174.

[62] William Gaul, Bishop of Mashonaland, 'The Possibilities of an African Kraal', *East and the West* III (April 1905), 128.

[63] The resolutions are reproduced in H.St.J.T. Evans, *The Church in Southern Rhodesia* (Westminster and London; S.P.G. and S.P.C.K., 1945), 31.

[64] 'The Church in South Africa,' (n.a.), *Church Quarterly Review* 114, (Jan 1904), 245.

[65] RHL/USPG, D Series, 138(b), 1901, Will. Mashonaland to Rev. H.W. Tucker, June 6th, 1901.

[66] Evans, *The Church*, 31.

instance, between the need of the settler economy for labour and the creation of 'responsible citizens' for he held as firmly as any other Victorian to the conviction that there was a primary civilising and character-building discipline in hard and regular work. Gaul also shared the contemporary settler belief that local people did not know how to work. They needed, he believed, to move from "the false dignity of loafing to the true dignity of labour".[67]

Labour (under principled employers) was, however, only a "preparatio evangeli".[68] The real development of 'responsible citizens' could not take place without the church. Gaul wrote in 1896, "With regard to the natives I should like to bear testimony to the fact that the only possible uplifting and civilising influence for them is the Church of GOD. People talk of teaching them to labour—and I intend and hope to have industrial teachers at Mission Stations—but something more is needed, and that is the Church of the living God, with its daily discipline of life and character, and the uplifting power of its worship".[69] He pointed to the examples of Frank Ziqubu, catechist become successful tenant-farmer on church land in Rusapi and Simon Mooti, a former servant of Gaul's from Kimberley, now the cook at the church house in Salisbury and founder of a night school for town 'natives': for Gaul, the religion of these men shone through their work.[70] Gaul's ideal was not a Christian chief like Khama but a working man like Ziqubu or Simon Mooti. And he was not alone in this: the Salisbury clergyman, Frank Urch, for instance, wrote in 1903, "If we could secure an indefinite number of Simons the much vexed Native Question would be solved in a generation".[71]

The corollary to this vision was that the society for which the local people were to be prepared should be one in which there was "justice for all, irrespective of colour",[72] and the point of maturity towards which Gaul looked and worked, for his settler congregations, was that

---

[67] RHL/USPG, D Series, 134(A), 1900, Will. Mashonaland, Report, January 19th, 1900.

[68] RHL/USPG, D Series, 142(b), 1902, Will. Mashonaland to Secretary, January 12th, 1902.

[69] South African Church Festival, *Combined Report* (London: [The Committee], 1896), 28.

[70] RHL/USPG, D Series, 142(b), 1902, Will. Mashonaland to Secretary, January 12th, 1902.

[71] 'Salisbury', *RCM* 3:2 (Feb 1903), 2.

[72] 'Notes at a Missionary Meeting to welcome the Bishop Elect of Mashonaland', *CCM&PR* III:4 (April 1895), 51.

they should become missionary-minded, actively engaged in bringing about this new state of affairs. Nothing gave him greater pleasure as a bishop than indications of growth in "intelligent interest"[73] or a missionary spirit, as when (unusually for Southern Africa) some 'native' and mixed-ancestry Christians occasionally worshipped alongside settlers in St. John's Bulawayo, as they had done at St. Cyprian's Kimberley when Gaul had been the priest there.

During his episcopate some of the settler laity became sufficiently emboldened to involve themselves in the development of 'native' churches and night-schools in Bulawayo, Salisbury and Umtali. In 1906, the laying of the foundation stone for a new 'native' church in Salisbury was attended by Lady Milton, the wife of the Administrator, by the Mayor and some of the town council, members of the Salisbury Mission Board and 30–40 members of the settler congregation of the pro-cathedral. In the districts, here and there, to Gaul's delight, a Native Commissioner knelt to be confirmed beside a convert on a mission station.

These events were signs to Gaul that the general settler distrust of missions was beginning to be moderated and the work of the church to this end was having some success. He watched and worked as keenly for any evidence of a more enlightened vision in government, evidence, as he put it, of "true statesmanship".[74]

IV *1899–1902: Second Anglo-Boer War and its aftermath*

In May 1899, Gaul reported to English supporters that the diocese was emerging from the "rough pioneer stage".[75] There were still difficulties: the priest at Gwelo, for instance, was attempting the impossible in a district which was bigger than England. For the east of the country, there was only one missionary priest at Mtasa's and one colonial clergyman at Umtali. Nevertheless, staff numbers had built up since the low point of 1896 and new work had been undertaken. The second phase

---

[73] 'The Bishop's Notes', *RCM* 3:3 (March 1903), 2.

[74] RHL/USPG, D Series, 178(b) 1907, W. Mashonaland to the Rt. Rev. the Secretary SPG, January 13th, 1907.

[75] 'Letter from the Bishop, No. XVII. Salisbury, March 21st, 1899', *MQP* XXVIII (May 1899), 4.

of Gaul's episcopate, the period 1899–1907, had begun hopefully. "All looked well" as he reported back to the SPG.[76]

Then came another war. Anglo-Boer relations had continued to smoulder since the Jameson Raid at the end of 1895 and in October 1899 they flared up into open conflict. Gaul deplored the war: he saw it as a judgement upon both Briton and Boer. All war came from sin and repentance was needed by both sides in this conflict for the covetousness, corruption and irresponsibility which had led to the war. Britain, in particular, had "played wiggle-waggle with her White Man's Burden".[77] The war was a rebuke and one which should be heeded.

His opinions about the war notwithstanding, Gaul did his episcopal duty. He and Upcher, his archdeacon and two other members of staff took turns serving as chaplains and ambulance workers to the imperial troops from the early stages of the war to the relief of Mafeking in February 1900. One man, Walter Leary, was wounded and taken prisoner and did not return to the diocese until 1901. Gaul himself and Upcher, with their ambulance railway coach, were at the relief of Mafeking.

It was inevitable that the outbreak of war would have a direct effect on the work of the diocese. Leary had just begun the new mission at Umlugulu's in Matabeleland. The mission was first left in charge of the catechist, Edwin Dondashe and then abandoned. The railway missioner, Fogarty, had his coach commandeered as an ambulance coach and then Kitchener borrowed it to pursue the Boer leader de Wet. Incoming clergy were unable to reach the diocese when expected and those who were there had increased duties when imperial troops were stationed near colonial settlements, near Bulawayo and Umtali. The cost of living, always high, rose further.

A slump then followed the war and the church experienced something similar: spiritual depression accompanied commercial depression.[78] Development was constrained by a lack of money and of men. Gaul had commented in 1898 that he ought to have "an army" of clergy but was expected to occupy his diocese with an allowance of men that

[76] RHL/USPG, D Series, 134(A), 1900, Will. Mashonaland, Report, January 19th, 1900.

[77] 'Letter from the Bishop, No. XX. Bulawayo (n.d.)', *MQP* XXXIII (August 1900), 3.

[78] RHL/USPG, D Series, 142(b), 1902, W. Mashonaland to Bishop Montgomery, February 25th, 1902.

would be required to run "a third-rate creamery".[79] In 1902, Mashonaland was "at a standstill for want of clergy and catechists".[80]

Only in missionary work were there some developments. The bright spot of the diocese was St. Columba's in the Bulawayo location, founded in 1897: in 1902, the building had to be enlarged to accommodate a congregation of 800. St. Columba's had also begun to be the 'watershed' Gaul had hoped it would become: a twin mission developed in 1901 at Bembezi (Lochard Siding) from two outstations, one at a 'Fingo' (Mfengu) settlement (St. Bede's), one (St. Aidan's) among local people at 'Chief Marzwi's' village. In the east of the diocese, Upcher was able to re-occupy Makoni's (the mission of the Epiphany, Rusapi) in 1902.

The total number of stations, however, was not increased for as these new missions opened, others closed. Bembezi was staffed by Leary and Dondashe, who had worked with him at the now defunct Umlugulu mission. When Mtobi, at Mtasa's, left the diocese in 1901 he was not replaced.

A variety of factors contributed to the closures: the mission at Umlugulu, for example, was on land which had been earlier alienated to settler agriculture (the Essexvale Estate) and the people had moved, or been moved, out of the area by 1901 but the perennial shortage of clergy and a new staffing policy with regard to catechists were among them. Gaul had a very high regard for the work of catechists but was becoming increasingly unwilling to subject them to the strain of working in isolation. (The majority, at this stage, were from South Africa and had left their wives and families there). There had been the two distressing 'failures' in 1897 and there were two more in 1901: Gadeza at Zimunya's (which now also closed) and John Kapuya, the first Shona convert who had been sent as catechist, a year before Upcher, to re-open Makoni's.[81]

The changes and closures meant that in 1904 there were only four rural missions in the diocese: St. Augustine's, Penhalonga, near Umtali; Epiphany at Makoni's; St. Aidan's, Bembezi; and Wreningham, near Enkeldoorn. All of them, with the partial exception of St. Augustine's, Penhalonga, were very small and had a tiny staff: a single missionary,

[79] RHL/USPG, D Series, 126(b), 1898, Will. Mashonaland to Mr Tucker, May 4th, 1898.

[80] 'The Bishop', *MQP* XXXIX (Feb 1902), 3.

[81] Kapuya periodically returned to the service of the church thereafter. He was buried, at his own wish, at the Mizeki shrine in 1968.

with the assistance of a catechist or two. They were a far cry from the industrial missions Gaul had hoped to found.

By the time Gaul retired in 1907 there were three additional stations, all on the same limited scale. A second mission at Makoni's, St. Faith's, had been founded in 1903 and another in the Victoria district, the Mission of the Transfiguration, in 1905. Upcher also re-opened Mangwende's, Bernard Mizeki's station, in 1907.

Four places were once more in the care of catechists: the first two missions of the English Church in Bechuanaland, one at Moroka's Stadt, 30 miles from Francistown and another at Francistown itself; the 'native' church, St. Michael's, at Salisbury, established in 1906–7; and St. Mary's, a mission near 'Chief Chihoro's' on the Hunyani river, twelve miles from Salisbury. The Salisbury clergyman, however, shared and closely supervised the work of the catechists at St. Michael's and St. Mary's. The railway missioner watched over the catechists at Francistown.

Gaul's episcopate also saw the beginning of work among women. An attempt was made to provide nursing and pastoral care, primarily for settler women, from a centre in Salisbury (St. Mary's Hostel) between 1902 and 1904. This failed, mainly because of personal conflict among the staff. Work among indigenous women, however, moved forward in 1904. Such work had long been desired, for it was firmly believed that no race could rise above the level of its women. Christian wives were needed for converts and only Christian women, Gaul held, could turn pagan huts into "Christian homes".[82] It was also hoped that the missions would produce nursemaids to care for the growing number of settler children, a hope that was not fulfilled, in the event, as local communities proved reluctant to expose their daughters to the corrupting influences of the colonial towns.

Some work among indigenous women had been carried out at St. Columba's in Bulawayo since 1900 but this was not on a very large scale. In 1904, however, St. Monica's, a school for women and girls was opened at Penhalonga and then in 1907 women's work was begun at St. Faith's, Rusapi by one of the first pupils at St. Monica's, Lily Mutwa, Bernard Mizeki's widow. It was only possible to establish St. Monica's, however, because the missionary in charge, Mother Annie Dalby, (the

---

[82] Bishop of Mashonaland, [Annual Meeting of the SPG], *Ch.Ch.* (May 27th, 1904), 333.

former head of St. Mary's Hostel) was possessed of an independent income and able to raise support from friends in England.

V *Itinerating work—"defending the outposts"; role of the laity*

In the post-war period Gaul had not only the needs of new missions but also the calls of new colonial towns and centres to answer for, in spite of the slump which had followed the war in South Africa, colonial immigration into the diocese continued. By 1904 the settler population of Rhodesia alone had more than doubled: there had been about 5,000 settlers in early 1896 and there were 12,623 in 1904. When Gaul retired in 1907 the depression affecting the country had begun to lift and the colonial population was set to all but double again.

There was no corresponding increase in the numbers of clergy arriving and not many more clergy in the diocese in 1904 than there had been in late 1898: there were 12 clergymen at the end of 1898 and still only some 14 in 1904. By the time Gaul retired three years later there were 18–19. He spoke passionately, in England in 1904, of the "desperate sense of helplessness" which overcame men in his position who had to watch "great stretches of country being occupied, men and women pouring in and forming new communities and were unable to respond to their call for clergy and helpers".[83] In that very year an opportunity to place a parson in the growing mining town of Que Que (originally Sebakwe, now Kwekwe) was lost because there was no clergyman to be sent. The post and the attached subsidy (offered by the BSA Company) went to a 'dissenting' minister instead.

This difficult situation was made more difficult still for the church by the fact that the newcomers were settling primarily in the districts rather than in the existing towns, where the few churches and their clergy were. At Hartley, the mining settlement 60 miles from Salisbury and part of the Salisbury ecclesiastical district, the settler population increased from 100 to 600 in the four years between 1904 and 1908. Only 50 of the settlers were in the township itself by 1908, however, and the rest, the majority of 550, were scattered throughout the district. By 1906 the farthest part of the Hartley ecclesiastical district was 120 miles from Salisbury.

[83] Bishop of Mashonaland, 'Annual Meeting, Society of the Sacred Mission', *Ch.Ch.* (December 14th, 1904), 787.

Gaul, however, had seen the results of dedicated district work in the Bloemfontein diocese, of "colonial visitation" in a "land of far distances",[84] visits to a handful of miners or down a railway line. In the colonial work of Mashonaland he placed particular value on 'itinerating', visiting small settlements, mines, railway employees, police camps, even individual settlers on their farms. Itinerating was his solution to the problems posed by colonial work—the paucity of clergy and the scattered nature of settlement. Such work he declared, "DEFENDS THE OUTPOSTS".[85] It dispelled prejudice,[86] meant far-flung settlers experienced the Church as "a live workaday power"[87] and knew where to find their clergyman when they needed him. It also secured the future. As Gaul pointed out, the prospectors' camp of two or three might become the mining camp of hundreds and it in turn might become the mining town of thousands.

It proved impossible to find or finance clergy specifically for itinerating work although Gaul sighed for "an order of priests on the tramp"[88] and made constant appeals to the SPG for clergy to do this work. Only along the railways was itinerating carried out at all regularly, south of Bulawayo by the railway missioner of the diocese and north of Bulawayo by clergy from the South African Church Railway Mission, who came in to assist the diocese after 1903, at Gaul's request.

Wherever possible, the ordinary clergy itinerated. They were licensed to districts, not to parishes, which meant that every part of the vast diocese was in the charge of someone, even if that charge was nominal. The missionary clergy were also involved: they were given pastoral charge of the small settlements and scattered farmers or miners in their mission district. When the Umlugulu mission was begun in 1898, for instance, Leary, the missionary there, also had responsibility for the nearest township, Gwanda (seventy-five miles away) and the miners at the Geelong and other mines surrounding it. When Leary moved

---

[84] RHL/USPG, E Series, 54(A), 1899, Will. Mashonaland, Report, July 31st, 1899.

[85] RHL/USPG, D Series, 163(b), 1906, W. Mashonaland, Report, January 26th, 1906.

[86] RHL/USPG, D Series, 134(A), 1900, Will. Mashonaland to Mr Tucker, October 13th, 1900.

[87] RHL/USPG, D Series, 142(b), 1902, W. Mashonaland to the Right Rev. the Secretary, SPG, November 17th, 1902.

[88] *Ibid.*

to Bembezi in 1901, he had responsibility for the mines and farms in that district.

Of the fourteen clergy at work in the diocese in 1903, seven were colonial clergy and seven were missionaries but all the missionaries were engaged in ancillary colonial work. This ancillary work could be very effective, as can be seen in the fact that the only buildings erected for settler use outside the main towns, in Gaul's episcopate, were two in areas cared for by missionaries: in 1902, a church hall was built in Rusapi (Rusape) and regular services held by the missionary from Makoni's; and in 1907 a church was built by the miners of Penhalonga Valley, who were cared for by the missionaries of St. Augustine's, three miles away.

Even so, there were too few clergy to carry out the work properly and the strain imposed upon them was acute. They could not afford horses or carts or, sometimes, railway fares, if there was a railway. Bicycling or walking along many miles of rough 'roads' and narrow tracks required considerable physical strength. And time was required to do itinerant work properly. In 1905, for instance, it took Gaul and the Salisbury parson ten days to visit the various mines and centres in the Hartley district alone.

The shortage of clergy also meant that remote districts could go for long periods without visits, if there was no-one to relieve the town parson and free him to itinerate. Melsetter (Chimanimani), a colonial farming area 100 miles south of Umtali and nominally in the care of the parson there, had only three English Church services in the nine years 1900–1909.

The work everywhere outgrew the ability of the church to keep up and the clergy had to "spread themselves like butter", as Gaul put it.[89] Work in one place frequently had to be "weakened" in order to "save extinction" in another.[90] The archdeacons of the diocese had to do duty for ordinary clergy, Upcher so frequently that he referred to himself as "the Diocesan football".[91] He was rarely able to carry out his duties as Archdeacon of Mashonaland properly. His counterpart Frederic Beaven, the first Archdeacon of Matabeleland (appointed 1903), spent most of his time as an itinerant priest, filling gaps left by the railway

[89] Ralph S. Seacombe, 'Railway Mission', *RCM* 15:7 (July 1918), 9.

[90] RHL/USPG, E Series, 60(A), 1905, J.H. Upcher, Rusapi, November 20th, 1905.

[91] 'Bulawayo', *RCM* 7:12 (Dec 1910), 11.

missioners: he was almost entirely responsible for beginning the work of the church in North-West Rhodesia (modern Zambia).

Gaul also had to fill gaps: he had to serve as a sort of "relieving curate" between Salisbury and Bulawayo in 1900[92] and the "odd man" of the diocese in 1902.[93] He likened himself to a general compelled to go onto the battlefield because of a shortage of soldiers. This was not only absurd in itself but serious in its effects as he could not travel and supervise his isolated staff properly. He was unable to visit the new (and precarious) mission begun at Penhalonga for two years from its foundation in 1898, for instance, while he acted as either a colonial parish priest or an army chaplain. By the time he was able to make a visit, there were only two (lay) missionaries left of the original staff of five.

The shortage of clergy also meant that something of a shift occurred, in perception and roles, from those pertaining in England where 'the parson' was 'the Church'. In Mashonaland, leading lay people come into sharp focus as the comrades and not merely the supporters of the clergy. There were not many of them for although a majority of the settlers were "educated" young Englishmen,[94] many discarded the habit of church-going once in Africa as they discarded other conventions.[95] The "*really faithful*" were few.[96] Their "keenness and enthusiasm", however, were considered "astonishing" by workers newly out from England.[97]

They were also acknowledged as having a distinct effect upon the communities in which they lived. "Determined" lay people could have a "definite spiritual influence" on colonial society[98] (and upon 'the natives')[99] especially when they were already in positions of influence as so many were, for the English church, accustomed to pre-eminence

---

[92] 'Letter printed by request of the Bishop if too late for the May magazine', 18th April 1900, (loose in *MQP* XXXII (May 1900), 4.

[93] 'The Bishop's Notes', *RCM* 2:9 (Sept 1902), 2.

[94] James Hay Upcher, *Notes on the Story of the English Church Mission in the Diocese of Mashonaland* ([Salisbury, Diocese of Southern Rhodesia, 1903]), 11.

[95] In 1901, 20% of settlers attended services. Only 8.5% were communicants: RHO/USPG, D Series, 138(b), 1901, Will. Mashonaland, Report, February 28th, 1901. Church attendance in England, for a roughly comparable group, was 30–40%: Adrian Hastings, *A History of English Christianity 1920–1990* (London and Philadelphia: Collins, 1991), 37–8.

[96] 'Letter from the Bishop, No. XVIII. June 28th, 1899', *MQP* XXIX (Aug 1899), 5.

[97] E.W.L[loyd], 'The Railway Mission, 1899–1902', *MQP* XLIII (Feb 1903), 20.

[98] E.N. Parker, Railway Chaplain, 'A Visit to Khama's Country', *MQP* L (Nov 1904), 21.

[99] Fr. Hallward, C.R. 'Vocation of the Laity', JCMA *53* (Nov 1923), (n.p.).

'at home', drew naturally in Mashonaland (as we have seen in Chapter One) upon the influential, upon colonial substitutes for the upper classes such as members of the administration, managers of mines or businesses.

The Administrator, many senior officials of the BSA Company, the judges and the Resident Commissioner normally had their seats in the pro-cathedral in Salisbury. In smaller centres the Church Council usually included the Resident Magistrate and other officials, the Inspector of Police perhaps or the Native Commissioner. The first meeting of the Umtali Church Committee, on July 25th, 1894, for example, was held in the office of the Resident Magistrate and included the Civil Commissioner.

These members of the laity, unlike laity in England, assumed responsibility for such matters as the finances of the parish (see, below, pp. 73, 75). Some also shared in the provision of worship. Military men, in particular, company officials and magistrates, would read the service on a Sunday if there were no parson available, as was the custom of similar officials throughout the Empire. The Inspector of Telegraphs, a Captain in the Mashonaland Horse, held a church parade on his own initiative in the tiny Fort Charter laager in 1896 where there was no parson, for instance. The Resident Magistrates took services in early Umtali, in Tuli, Fort Victoria, Gwelo and Salisbury.

The laity also often took leading roles in such matters as the building of churches and founding of schools, which in England were normally the preserve of the clergy. We have seen above (p. 51) that the first church in Bulawayo was built entirely by the laity. Similarly, the founding of a school at Plumtree south of Bulawayo in 1902, for the education of the children of railway employees and other isolated settlers, was as much the result of the determination of laymen as that of the clergy. Plumtree was a customs post and the school and a Sunday service were begun in the office of the customs officer T.J. Wadeson, with the support of E.C. Baxter, Comptroller of Customs, a leading layman in Bulawayo.

In some settlements where there were no resident clergy, a few outstanding laymen came to exercise a role that was pre-eminently clerical 'at home', that of chief moral and spiritual exemplar and minister to the local community. In Francistown, Andrew Murray, the Secretary of the Tati Concession was churchwarden from 1898 to 1906 and was credited, by the itinerant parson, with being (together with his wife) the most significant single influence on the township in its progress during those years from a place with a very bad reputation towards one with a "surprisingly good" "outward moral tone" and Sabbath observance (of a sort).[100] J. Haddon, manager of the Globe and Phoenix mine from 1906, was praised for having a similar effect upon Que Que.

In Beira, where there was no parson after early 1901, the British consul held the congregation together, arranged and prepared a meeting place and played full choral evensong on the piano when the parson visited from Umtali. The work of such laymen showed what "a strong good man in a responsible position" could do "if he had the courage of his convictions".[101] Without them, Gaul confessed that the clergy "could have done little".[102]

The influence of the women of the church was similarly acknowledged: "a pure, good, cultured woman" exerted considerable "power" in the "rough world" of the colonial frontier.[103] Even a "nice" woman could change the tone of a tiny settlement.[104] In several instances, the outstanding religious and moral influence in a settlement was acknowledged to be that of a woman, a school-teacher perhaps, a nurse or the founder of a Sunday School.

VI *Finance: external income and self-support*

We have seen above that a lack of staff was one major difficulty faced by Gaul. The other was a lack of money, although Gaul on the whole found money easier to find than men. There were several points in his episcopate where a stipend or part-stipend could be found for a clergyman in the out-districts (Gwanda in 1904, for instance) or for a second priest at Bulawayo or Salisbury but no clergymen could be found willing to serve. The respect and affection in which Gaul himself was held also meant that he was able to attract financial support from individuals, such as the Fourth Earl Grey, who would provide a catechist's salary for him or pay the fees of a scholar at a mission school.

---

[100] RHL/USPG, E Series, 57(A), 1902, J. Hallward, Report, Francistown, Michaelmas 1902.

[101] [J.F. Salt], 'Gwelo', *RCM* 6:4 (April 1909), 11.

[102] 'Diocese of Mashonaland', *Ch.Ch.* (Sept 5th 1906), 9–10.

[103] The Hon. Sir Arthur Lawley, 'Annual Meeting', *SARWMQP* 43 (April 1914), 16.

[104] RHL/USPG, E Series, 58(B), 1903, E.N. Parker, Railway Mission, Report, December 31st, 1903.

When he became bishop, however, the diocese was in debt to the tune of £200. Gaul considered that one of the primary tasks of his episcopate was to put the finances of Mashonaland on as secure a footing as possible and to do so "through the principles of self-sacrifice, economy and efficiency".[105]

The only guaranteed sources of income were the annual grant for general purposes from the SPG and lesser annual sums raised by the Mashonaland Mission Association, the organisation set up by Knight-Bruce on his visit to England in 1891–3. The amounts given by these two bodies were not large. The SPG grant was also reviewed annually and instead of increasing with the development of the diocese was subject to threatened or actual cuts. Even when the effective work of the diocese had doubled or trebled, and subsequently, the SPG grant for general purposes did not rise above £1,100 in spite of constant pleas from Gaul for considerably increased support.

The Mashonaland Mission Association produced an average of £700 p.a. between 1895 and 1905 for general funds but there were considerable annual fluctuations: in 1900, £948 was sent but in 1902 only £315. This was largely because the association, though it was concerned with general fund-raising, also undertook to pay the passages and expenses of staff travelling between the diocese and England and to contribute to the support of others on furlough. A high turnover of staff could make considerable holes in funds raised by the association in any one year and so limit the amount of money remitted to Mashonaland for general expenditure. The amount raised in England in 1906 was £800 but over £500 went on passages, outfits and staff on furlough so only £300 was remitted to Mashonaland for general purposes.

The SPG grant and the sums sent by the association were also entirely swallowed up by stipends and salaries. If there were to be any developments in the work of the diocese additional income had to be found. Gaul, therefore, while he made persistent attempts to increase external support for Mashonaland, also saw the need for self-help.

This meant in first instance colonial self-help, for Gaul aimed very early on to make colonial congregations self-supporting, as he saw no reason why missionary supporters in England should pay for religious privileges for settlers where the settlers could afford to pay for their

[105] 'The Bishop's Charge, First Diocesan Synod, Salisbury, April 19th, 1903', *MQP* XLV (Aug 1903), 7.

own. As a result, Salisbury, Bulawayo and Umtali were each providing a priest's stipend of £200 p.a. by 1896. Newer or smaller centres and areas where the settler population was much scattered were only able to provide a part-stipend: Gwelo in 1898 and Selukwe in 1904 were able to raise only £100 towards the support of a clergyman.

Gaul also gathered leading laymen together to assist him, appointing an Honorary Diocesan Accountant in 1900 (and a Diocesan Board of Finance in 1903). He engaged the energies of a wider group through the diocesan Synod which he summoned for the first time in 1903, once a completed railway system made travel within the diocese relatively easy. The Synod met again in 1906. Without the "devotion" of the laity who served on these and local councils, the bishop and clergy would have been "very helpless", as Gaul wrote in 1907.[106]

This policy of self-support, however, though reasonably successful in its own terms, had one disadvantage: it meant that the local finances of the church were closely tied to the fortunes of the colony of Rhodesia, the dominant economy within the diocese. And the new colony struggled, not only against the social and economic dislocations caused by the risings of 1896–7 but also with drought; fever; disease and pests; recurrent cattle sickness which destroyed stock and paralysed transport; a perennial shortage of labour; delays in the building of railways (there was no railway through the country from Umtali to Bulawayo until 1902); exorbitant freight charges once the railways were built; and the effects of the South Africa War and the slump which followed it.

The colony had also been founded on speculation and so was subject in its early years to all the vagaries and uncertainties of gold fever and 'boom or bust'. Large fortunes were made out of speculation and company-mongering—but in England, not in Africa. A political and economic struggle also developed very early between the settlers and the BSA Company, representative of external, and monopoly, capital.[107]

A modern economy securely based on paying mines and productive farms only developed very slowly. In 1905, as Gaul pointed out, the settler community was not even growing enough food to feed itself.[108] Not until 1908, after he retired, did the country begin to make something

[106] RHL/USPG, D Series, 178(b), 1907, W. Mashonaland to the Rt. Rev. the Secretary SPG, January 13th, 1907.

[107] Ian Phimister, *An Economic and Social History of Zimbabwe 1890–1948: Capital Accumulation and Class Struggle* (London: Longman, 1988), 20ff., 29, 34–6.

[108] 'The Bishop of Mashonaland and the Company Promoter', 236.

of a move forward with a re-structuring of the mining industry and the beginnings of effective agriculture.

All this reacted upon the work of the church, both missionary and colonial. The virtual failure of the colony had been a very large factor in the wreck of Knight-Bruce's plans for Mashonaland and it affected his successor almost as severely, for the capacity of the diocese to generate funds from within in Gaul's time was limited by the slow and unsteady growth of the economy. The price of any development throughout his episcopate (and beyond) was also extremely high. A sovereign, for example, was reckoned as worth 7/6 (about a third of its English value) in Rhodesia in 1895 and again in 1904. The cost of living in the Salisbury of 1902 was considered to be three times that of London.

The result, as far as colonial work went, was that the English Church was unable to provide anything other than an attentuated version of 'home life'. There was only money for churches and parsons and there were few enough of those. In education, while attempts were made to provide church schools on the English model, the tiny schools at Salisbury (1896–9) and Francistown (1899–1905) were closed during Gaul's episcopate. Those at Fort Victoria (1902–8), Umtali (1904–9) and the largest school, St. John's, Bulawayo (1895–1910) lasted a few years longer. Plumtree, the railway school founded south of Bulawayo in 1902, survived because the BSA Company, the railways and the parents contributed to its support.

It was also found necessary in 1899 to close down the nursing operations of the church which had been begun by Knight-Bruce at Umtali: the diocese had since then provided a fresh supply of nurses every couple of years. Gaul considered that they had cost the diocese a considerable amount of money without providing a concomitant religious advantage.[109]

Money was in such short supply that the smaller colonial settlements could not put up church buildings without external help. Others could not support parsons: Fort Victoria, for example, could do neither. It remained too small a settlement, with a settler population of about one hundred, to be able to replace the church building unaided (the original church had fallen into ruin in 1895) or to pay a clergyman. A parson was placed at Victoria in 1900, after a lapse of six years, only

[109] 'Letter from the Bishop, No. XVII. Salisbury, March 21st, 1899', *MQP* XXVIII (May 1899), 4.

because a BSA Company grant for chaplaincy work provided half of his stipend.

Nevertheless, and in spite of these constraints and difficulties Gaul's policy of local self-support was remarkably successful. In Knight-Bruce's time all funds for the diocese had come from external sources but during Gaul's episcopate funds came as much from within the diocese as without. By 1900 half of the money spent in Mashonaland was raised locally, in that year £3,043 out of a total of £6,286.

Some help was received within the country from non-ecclesiastical sources for colonial church work: the schools received some assistance from the BSA Company; land was often given, by the Company and individuals, for church buildings in settlements; the railway authorities provided a subsidy for the work of the railway missioner; and between 1899 and 1906 the administration made grants to the diocese for itinerant chaplaincy work by the town clergy in the districts. The bulk of the money however, was raised by members of the settler laity who gave "largely and at great personal sacrifice" to the work of the church.[110] It was estimated that they gave, in proportion, ten times as much as church people did in England.

The growth of settler self-help in Mashonaland meant that external funds could be progressively released for missionary work: by 1904 the colonial side of the work was virtually self-supporting and a practical distinction could be made between colonial (or parochial) and diocesan funds. Diocesan funds were by then largely devoted to the support of missionary work.

The financing of missions remained acutely difficult however, as income received from external sources (from the SPG and the 'home' association) remained static or even diminished in any one year and continued to be entirely swallowed up by the stipends and salaries of clergy and catechists. There was no surplus for development or extension, for buildings, educational work, transport, more or larger stipends.

Self-help within the diocese for missionary work was attempted but with the exception of St. Columba's, Bulawayo, the mission stations had too few converts to even approach self-support in Gaul's time. There was not a great deal of help to be had from the colonial community for even ardent advocates of missions conceded that it was beyond the

---

[110] South African Church Festival, *Combined Report* (London: [The Committee], 1896), 22.

capacity of the settler congregations to do much more than they were doing and to give large support to missionary work.[111] Only in the largest town, Bulawayo, did a colonial congregation give regular support to a mission: half of the stipend of the missionary at St. Columba's was paid by St. John's, the settler church and (most unusually, for a white clergyman) half by his own (black) congregation.

VII *Finance: Capital funds*

Gaul had written in 1897 to the SPG: "Difficulties are splendid and one is used to them, but there are limitations which paralyse".[112] In the next year, he re-opened missionary work (at Umlugulu's and Penhalonga), without sufficient funds or staff. The entire external income of the diocese in that year was £2,000, the amount he estimated should have been spent on the setting up of a single mission station. He worried, and with justification, that the work would be "crippled" and workers "killed off" without greater support.[113]

Since greater regular support from outside the diocese was proving very difficult to obtain, Gaul became determined to create a reserve fund for Mashonaland which would enable the diocese to meet challenges and crises and to "buy up opportunity" when it arose, without having to turn to England for support which might or might not come. The diocese needed to become, as he put it, "its own SPG".[114]

When there was a relatively large opening balance in the books of the diocese at the begining of 1900, £1,708 of unexpended revenue which had accumulated over the several years when it had not been possible to find sufficient staff or expand the missionary work of the diocese, Gaul put this money aside as the basis of a reserve fund and managed to add to it to bring it up to £2,000. Without this fund, most of the subsequent development of the diocese in his time (and beyond it) would not have been possible. The fund was small in comparison

[111] RHL/USPG, D Series, 156(b), 1904, J.H. Upcher to Bishop, 19th December, 1904.

[112] RHL/USPG, D Series, 122(b), 1897, Will. Mashonaland to Secretary, July 7th, 1897.

[113] RHL/USPG, D Series, 126(b), 1898, Will. Mashonaland, Report, December 31st, 1898.

[114] RHL/USPG, D Series, 163(b), 1905, W. Mashonaland, Report, January 26th, 1906.

with the need of the church to expand in every direction. That it was of such importance only reveals how scanty the church's resources were.

It was also only because of irregular extra-diocesan help received that Gaul was able to leave this reserve fund to his successor, for there was an excess of diocesan expenditure over normal income from 1900 to 1907. The reserve fund was drawn upon to carry the diocese between 1900 and 1904. Only small amounts were needed to supply the 1900–02 deficits but those of 1903 and 1904 were large, nearly £600 in 1903 and over £300 in 1904. If the reserve fund had not been used, mission stations would have had to be closed. It meant, however, that the fund had been severely depleted by early 1905 and Mashonaland had to be rescued by Alfred Beit from "a crack in the floor", as Gaul put it.[115] Beit, hearing how heavily the fund had been drawn upon, gave Gaul a cheque for £1,000 to replace the capital.

In the years 1905–7 deficits were only prevented by a combination of non-recurring grants from the BSA Company for chaplaincy work, which were put to general funds and extra grants from the SPG: unappropriated funds from its Bi-centenary appeal (1901) were allocated to Mashonaland, for those three years only.

Gaul also had to provide for his own needs as well as those of his diocese and clergy. When he became Bishop of Mashonaland in 1895 there was no bishop's stipend and no bishop's house. Money was subsequently put aside to build a house (from £1,000 compensation received from the BSA Company for damage done to church property during the risings of 1896–7). This sum was insufficient to build an adequate house in Salisbury, the see town. When he was in Salisbury Gaul slept, first in the church vestry and then in a couple of rooms tacked on to the church. In Bulawayo he had to live in a three-roomed tin cottage, which he described as "a cross between a canal boat and a cloak-room".[116]

This lack of adequate accommodation meant that he had to endure a virtual and painful separation from his wife for the twelve years he was Bishop of Mashonaland: he was physically resilient but she was not, her health was poor and she needed decent housing. She spent the

[115] RHL/USPG, D Series, 163(b), 1905, W. Mashonaland to Bishop Montgomery, 8th July, 1905.

[116] 'Letter from the Bishop, No. XIII. Umtali, April 14th, 1898', *MQP* XXV (Aug 1898), 4.

years of his episcopate in South Africa, collecting an additional £1,000 for a bishop's house. One was bought for Gaul's successor.

Gaul also had to provide for his own income. Knight-Bruce had served without stipend and had refused to divert attention from the general (and critical) needs of the diocese, in his time, towards the raising of a episcopal stipend. This left Gaul, who had no private income, to raise a capital sum which when invested would provide an episcopal income. The SPCK (Society for the Promotion of Christian Knowledge) and a fund which had been set up in England in 1841 to assist the development of new overseas bishoprics, the Colonial Bishoprics Fund, pledged sums of money, if they could be matched: this Gaul had to do himself.

He raised more than was necessary (£4,000) in South Africa before leaving for Mashonaland in early 1895. His supporters in Kimberley and Johannesburg were enthusiastic: Rhodes, Beit, mining companies, subscribed.[117] The fund was completed in 1896, during his visit to England, largely by the gifts of Southern Africans resident there. The Mashonaland Bishopric Endowment Fund then stood at £10,000, which produced an income of £400–450 a year, an entirely inadequate income for a diocese where the cost of living was so high. Gaul's income had to be supplemented by the SPG, to the tune of £200 a year and by a tithe from the Bulawayo congregation, but even then was inadequate.

The exigencies of the diocese also meant that there were times when Gaul gave up part of his small income to subsidise other work. In 1898, his £200 from the SPG had to be used for the new missions established in that year and the diocesan deficit of 1904 (£300) would have been larger if Gaul had not diverted this portion of his income to general funds.

Gaul managed to add to the Bishopric Endowment Fund (it was over £12,000 by the time he retired) but he himself believed that the minimum endowment for any new bishopric in the province ought to be £20,000, which would bring in an income of £1,000. Knight-Bruce, on his private income, had been criticised for living far more luxuriously than his staff.[118] Gaul, on the Mashonaland episcopal income, lived as hard a life as any of his clergy.

[117] RHL/USPG, D Series, 114, 1895, Will. Mashonaland to Mr Tucker, May 25th, 1895.

[118] NAZ, HMss, PE 3/1/1, Douglas Raymond Pelly, Correspondence, 1892–1934, July 14th, 1892, ff. 77–8.

When he was in charge of the Bulawayo parish, for example, living with Fogarty in the tin house in 1897, they could not afford to eat meat or eggs. When Mrs Gaul was with her husband in 1899, in one of the attempts they made to live together in Salisbury, they could not afford to housekeep, nor to eat properly: once again, eggs were luxuries. They had meals sent in from a nearby boarding house but only ate one meal between the two of them.

William Gaul retired from the bishopric, exhausted by his labours, in June 1907. He had taken over a diocese with two clergy on the staff. There were now 18, as well as a greatly increased number of layworkers and 'native' teachers. The organs of self-government were also in place: Mashonaland had become a duly constituted diocese within the CPSA, able to frame its own canons and regulations, with the calling of the first Synod in 1903.

Gaul had also found the diocese in debt. He left it with a capital sum for the income of the bishop and another for the diocese. There was £2,000 towards a bishop's house. Permanent buildings had been erected at most of the centres of mission work and in the colonial townships. Where early buildings needed to be replaced, in Salisbury and Bulawayo, funds for new churches were already in hand. There were 12 mission farms and 52 town plots.

Gaul reported, with modest pride, that his successor would find "a base of operations fairly sure" and with outposts established,[119] that "the bush" had "been cleared a bit and humble but strong foundations laid".[120] The local verdict was that his achievements had been "stupendous",[121] his episcopate "magnificent".[122] Who now would "bend the bow of Ulysses"?[123]

---

[119] RHL/USPG, D Series, 178(b) 1907, W. Mashonaland to the Rt. Rev. the Secretary SPG, January 13th, 1907.

[120] LPL, Davidson, 132, W. Mashonaland to Archbishop, January 1st, 1907, f. 199.

[121] Geo. Bowen and E.A. von Hirschberg, Church Wardens, 'To the Parishioners, S. Mary and All Saints, Salisbury', *RCM* 4:4 (April 1907), 6.

[122] [H.H. Foster], 'Bulawayo', *RCM* 7:6 (June 1910), 10.

[123] [J.H. Upcher], 'Rusape', *RCM* 4:3 (March 1907), 6.

CHAPTER THREE

UNHAPPINESS AND PARADOX: EDMUND NATHANAEL POWELL (1908–10) AND FREDERIC HICKS BEAVEN (1911–1925)

I *Powell: election, consecration and first impressions*

On 11th September 1907, the first elective assembly of the Synod of the Diocese of Mashonaland met to choose a successor to Gaul. There were 16 lay electors and 17 clergymen, few of whom, if any, had participated in such an assembly before. Several of the clergy were relatively young and somewhat disconcerted to find themselves exercising such solemn responsibilities as the nomination and election of a bishop.[1]

The assembly was not able to secure either its first or second choice of candidate. Archibald Ean Campbell, who had visited the diocese in 1904 and had made a very good impression, had only been Bishop of Glasgow and Galloway for three years and considered it his duty to remain in Scotland. Frank Weston, a missionary with the UMCA and a personal friend of some of the Mashonaland clergy, also refused the bishopric as he was destined for higher things within the UMCA: before many months were out, he had been consecrated Bishop of Zanzibar and so become leader of that mission. The third candidate, however, an English parish priest, Edmund Nathanael Powell, accepted the call to Mashonaland.

In Powell, the diocese reverted to a bishop with a more conventional background than Gaul had possessed. He had been educated at Winchester and at Trinity College, Oxford, which had produced many members of the English episcopal bench. His school-fellows had included the current High Commissioner of South Africa, Lord Selborne and the Bishops of Kaffraria and Natal.[2] Powell also had many years of experience in the London slums, experience which was almost a prerequisite for an invitation to episcopal office in the CPSA,

[1] [Editorial] 'Notes', *RCM* 4:10 (Oct 1907), 9.

[2] 'The New Bishop of Mashonaland', *South Africa*, 76 (Oct–Dec 1907), October 19th, 1907, 157.

especially in missionary areas. Knight-Bruce, for instance, had worked in the London slums as a clergyman, Gaul as a layman. The Bishops of Pretoria, Lebombo, Zululand and Bloemfontein in 1908 all had previous experience of settlement or slum work in East or South London.

Powell had none of the foreign experience which might given him an additional qualification for the bishopric and he confessed that his knowledge of Africa was very slight but he did have missionary credentials, apart from his work in 'home missions'. He had grown up with the foreign missionary cause and his father had been the treasurer, for twenty years, one of the most important missionary societies of England, the SPCK. He himself was a leading member of the Junior Clergy Missionary Association, a society of clergymen associated with the SPG and he had been the commissary (or agent) in England for the bishop of another South African diocese, St. John's, Kaffraria.

He also had a connection with Mashonaland through a training home for women missionaries which had been established in a neighbouring parish in the East End of London and had supplied workers to Mashonaland (Annie Dalby, for example). His nomination to the bishopric was proposed by the two leading missionaries of the diocese, James Hay Upcher and Harold Etheridge, the man now in charge of the largest rural mission station, St. Augustine's at Penhalonga.

Powell was also thought to be suitable for the demands of the post in that he was "strong...morally and spiritually",[3] young enough (he was 48), a bachelor and so free from family responsibilities, had "a massive but athletic frame"[4] and, by his own account, had a "capacity for eating anything and sleeping anywhere".[5] He was consecrated in Cape Town cathedral on 24th February 1908 and arrived in his new diocese in March. His first reaction to his new surroundings was rhapsodic: "[N]o-one who could live in Africa would ever want to live in England".[6] He made a favourable impression himself, with his "commanding presence", "freshness and energy", his "straightforward" and "manly" approach and was judged to be "the right man in the right place".[7]

---

[3] 'Letter from Bishop Gaul', *RCM* 4:12 (Dec 1907), 3.
[4] 'The New Bishop of Mashonaland', *South Africa* 76, October 19th, 1907, 157.
[5] LPL, Davidson, 158, E.N. Powell to Archbishop, August 1st, 1910, ff. 342–3.
[6] 'Letter from the Bishop. Salisbury, March 27th, 1908', *MQP* LXIV (May 1908), 3.
[7] 'Umtali', *RCM* 5:4 (April 1908), 6.

Powell's tenure of the bishopric, however, was to be short and unhappy. Within a year he had attempted to resign, much as Knight-Bruce had done and, like Knight-Bruce, had been prevented by his fellow-bishops in England and the CPSA.[8] One year further on, he had also been invalided out to England and some months later had resigned.

His unhappiness appears to have had several causes. In the first place, the wide-open spaces of the diocese affected him, after his initial rapture, as monotonous, depressing and lonely. He admitted that he had "no sportsmanlike or adventurous tastes",[9] which might have enabled him to enjoy them and he missed the crowded streets of the East End of London, the buildings, cathedrals and the rich and varied city life of England.[10]

He was also unable to reconcile himself to the work of a bishop, especially a bishop of such a diocese: he "could not find enough to do".[11] He had been used to the work of an urban parish priest and such work in those days was busy and highly organised. Parishes also had large staffs: at St. Stephen's, Upton Park, Powell had worked closely with four curates, whereas the entire clerical staff of the huge diocese of Mashonaland in his episcopate numbered twenty. When his desire for an early resignation was brought to the attention of the Archbishop of Canterbury, Randall Davidson, by the Bishop of London, a former bishop and confidante of Powell's, they came to the conclusion that it was perhaps a mistake to offer a bishopric in a place as lonely as Mashonaland to a man used to city work and that a country parson might have been more suitable.[12]

Powell was also, like Knight-Bruce, unable to make common cause with settlers[13] but he appears to have been daunted chiefly by the

---

[8] LPL, Davidson 158, Correspondence relating to the proposed resignation of Bishop Powell, 12 Feb 1909–9 Dec 1909, ff. 38–47.

[9] 'Letter from the Bishop Elect', *RCM* 4:11 (Nov 1907), 2.

[10] 'The Bishop's Letter. Buckhurst Hill, July 22nd, 1910', *MQP* LXXIII (Aug 1910), 4.

[11] W/CPSA, AB 186, W.M. Carter, Papers 1891–1930, Letter to 'My dear Algy', September 8th, 1909.

[12] LPL, Davidson, 158, Memo from Bishop of London [A.F. Winnington-Ingram], received September 11th 1909, f. 43, Archbishop of Canterbury, Randall Davidson, to Bishop of London, September 13th, 1909, f. 44.

[13] NAZ, HMss, ANG 1/10/1, Bishop E.H. Etheridge, Memoirs, 1954, f. 50; and see, below, pp. 88–89.

sheer difficulty of the circumstances under which he had to work. He was shocked by the state of the diocese on his arrival: he did not see the evidence of Gaul's labour, only that "we need everything, and at once".[14]

To the SPG and the Mashonaland Mission Association, therefore, Powell wrote very much as his predecessors had done: an immediate and significant increase of staff and the money to support them were needed, if the church was really to attempt "the conversion of the heathen—the bringing about of a Christian Rhodesia".[15] This was particularly true of the missions, where the work, to his eyes, had barely begun. The most urgent need of the diocese was more missionary work and this included greater pastoral care of the mission priests, whom Powell perceived as lonely and isolated. One of his first acts as bishop was to appoint a dean for the pro-cathedral at Salisbury, in order to free himself to travel around the missions.

A major difficulty, though, lay in the fact that the building up of missions, however urgent and however much Powell was drawn to such work, could not be his primary task. In his first report to the SPG, he identified the "supreme problem of the diocese" as being "how best to reconcile the claims to spiritual help of the white man and the native"[16] and came to the conclusion that work among settlers had to come first, as it had done in Gaul's time.

As far as numbers went, the country was mainly a black man's country and would continue to be so: there were over 600,000 'natives' and only a few thousand settlers. Gaul had envisioned large-scale emigration into Rhodesia which would turn it into "another America", with a white population equal to the black[17] but Powell believed the local people were likely to increase "enormously and perpetually and at a far faster rate than any possible increase among the whites". He acknowledged, nevertheless, that Rhodesia was "sufficiently a white man's country" to make the distinctively "white" work "most necessary most important"

---

[14] 'Letter from the Bishop. Salisbury, March 27th, 1908', *MQP* LXIV (May 1908), 3.

[15] RHL/USPG, E Series, 63(B), 1908, From the Bishop, Victoria, May 20th, 1908.

[16] *Ibid.*

[17] 'Notes at a Missionary Meeting to welcome the Bishop Elect of Mashonaland', *CCM&PR* III:4 (April 1895), 51; RHL/USPG, D Series, 126(b), 1898, Will Mashonaland to Mr Tucker, May 4th, 1898.

(sic).[18] Church schools were needed, new and better churches and clergy to reach the scattered settlers outside the towns.

The tragedy of Powell's episcopate was that he was able to develop neither side of the work significantly because the income and staff of the diocese remained static, while its responsibilities increased even more dramatically than they had done during Gaul's time. One observer had said in 1907 that if the country developed, the church would not be able to cope and in 1908, as Powell became bishop, it began to enjoy a modest prosperity and to fill up with new settlers. The 12,603 settlers of 1904 had all but doubled (to 23,606) by 1911.

The problem caused by numbers was further exacerbated by the fact that such a large proportion of the immigrants continued to settle in the districts, away from the main settlements. Even where the church made some headway it was quickly swamped. By early 1909, for instance, Hartley, with a population of 600, was able to build a church and support a clergyman and was therefore separated from Salisbury. The area then continued to develop so rapidly that before the end of the year ecclesiastical sub-division was mooted: there had been four places at which services were held in 1908 and by late 1909 there were nineteen.

In the Victoria area, Powell on tour stumbled across areas of settlement which had never been visited by a parson, such as Felixburg with a colonial population of some 100. Remote and inaccessible Inyanga (Nyanga), north of Umtali, was now developing as a farming area. Other areas, Marandellas (Marondera) (near Mangwende's), 50 miles or so south-east of Salisbury; Melsetter (Chimanimani), 100 miles south of Umtali; Figtree and Marula, in Matabeleland, were filling up with farmers and traders. Gwanda district, 100 miles south-east of Bulawayo, had a settler population of 700 by early 1909 and no parson.

There were also acute pressures for an expansion of the Church's missionary work. The primary pressure came from the indigenous people themselves. The risings of 1896–7 had been succeeded by a decade of resistance to missions but now, usually with the sanction of their chiefs, many people and particularly the younger generation were turning to the missions for the combination of education and religion they offered. In the east, in Manicaland, there was a huge wave of

[18] RHL/USPG, E Series, 63(B), 1908, From the Bishop, Victoria, May 20th, 1908.

conversions and the missionaries were being overwhelmed. The people themselves were saying, "the earth is shaking".[19] Mashonaland and parts of Matabeleland were also judged to be becoming "ripe".[20]

Other areas of the diocese had no missions at all, or at least none belonging to the English Church. Powell estimated that three-quarters of his diocese was untouched. There were 15,000 'natives' and no English Church missions in the Hartley area, for instance. In the Victoria district, the most densely populated and so most important district, there was only one missionary who also had colonial responsibilities and there were only two clerical missionaries for the whole of Matabeleland, at St. Columba's, Bulawayo and at Bembezi.

Local people, in some areas of the central watershed, were also on the move, because their villages were on land allocated much earlier for settler or company agriculture. As this part of the country was now filling up with settlers, the people were being moved into designated 'reserves', away from the vicinity of the church's missions, to make way for the newcomers. The reserves were already causes of "grave anxiety and heart-searching",[21] simply because they were untouched by the church. Now it was becoming necessary to follow people who were already church members to their new homes, if they were not to be abandoned and lost.

Opinion in official and business circles was also changing in favour of missionary work, which brought increased opportunities and increased pressure to bear upon the church. The BSA Company, in 1908, ceased to give grants for colonial chaplaincy work but increased grants to mission schools. More Native Commissioners were asking for missionaries, especially for missionaries of the English Church (as it was perceived to be on good terms with the government)[22] and particularly where people were being moved into reserves. Preference was shown, for example, by Native Commissioners at Ndanga, Que Que and Lomagundi.

---

[19] 'Letter from the Revd. H.E. Etheridge. Penhalonga, September 24th, 1907', *MQP* LXII (Nov 1907), 11.

[20] 'Letter from Archdeacon Upcher, Rusape, July 1909', *MQP* LXX (Nov 1909), 7.

[21] 'Letter from the Revd. G. Ashworth. Selukwe (for mail leaving Christmas Day, 1909)', *MQP* LXXI (Feb 1910), 8.

[22] RHL/USPG, D series, 193(B), 1909, E.N. Mashonaland to Bishop Montgomery, January 14th, 1909; Editorial, *RCM* (Aug 1912), 3.

On the mines too, there were new opportunities. Many of the employees were Christian migrants from neighbouring territories[23] and increasing numbers of local labourers were converts. Mine mangers had hitherto forbidden missionaries access to their large labour forces but it now became apparent, to some, that the provision of religious privileges led to a more contented and stable work-force and that there were advantages in opening their compounds to teachers and catechists.[24] Specific opportunities were therefore offered to the church to begin work in mine compounds, at Penhalonga Valley, for instance, and Selukwe.

Vastly increased missionary opportunities and rapid colonial immigration into the districts posed acute problems, however, for an institution with an income and staff that did not increase correspondingly, especially since neither new mission work nor colonial district work could pay for itself for the first few years.

The older missions, which had been aiming at self-support since Gaul's day, had achieved a measure of financial independence by 1909. St. Augustine's, Penhalonga, for instance, was producing a proportion of its own income (£1,000 by 1909), from fees from pupils at the mission schools, offerings from congregations and government grants for education. The mission was also growing food worth £500 per annum.

Mass 'conversions', however, meant an increased demand for teachers, missionaries, new buildings and schools, by people, most of whom were part of a rural and peasant economy and could only contribute to the support of the church in kind and in labour, not in cash. In areas untouched by the wave of conversions and where missions were in the formative stage, such as the Victoria district, or potentially, in the 'reserves', they still needed full external support. And the existing missionaries were badly-fed and badly-housed, condemned, as Powell put it, to "slow but certain suicide" on a diet of "corn and pumpkin".[25]

The conditions of work in Mashonaland, Powell wrote in 1909, were as "difficult as they possibly can be".[26] He deplored the financial state of the diocese, declared that advance was everywhere frustrated for lack

---

[23] By 1922, about 66% of labourers were from surrounding territories—Mozambique, Northern Rhodesia (Zambia) and Nyasaland (Malawi): Ian Phimister, *An Economic and Social History of Zimbabwe 1890–1948: Capital Accumulation and Class Struggle* (London, Longman, 1988), 85.

[24] 'Letter from the Bishop. Hawstead, Buckhurst Hill, April 14th, 1910', *MQP* LXII (May 1910), 4.

[25] 'Letter from the Bishop. A Dirge and a Call. (n.d.)', *MQP* LXX (Nov 1909), 4.

[26] 'The Bishop's Charge', *RCM* 6:6 (June 1909), 3.

of funds and was full of gloom.[27] There were no workers in Portuguese East Africa, only one (the railway missioner) in Bechuanaland, only two mission priests in Matabeleland and he could have found work immediately for an additional ten in Mashonaland, yet he was faced with the prospect of retrenching workers rather than employing more.

II *Powell and the settlers*

Powell attempted to increase the external income of the diocese, as his predecessors had done, in order to supply its needs. He pleaded with the SPG for an increased grant and protested when the extra-ordinary grants of 1905–7 came to an end in 1908. He wrote despairing and appealing letters to the Mashonaland Mission Association. He also tried to generate an increased income within the diocese and failed to do so.

The missions could do no more for themselves than they were already doing, so Powell attempted to raise support for mission work from his settler congregations. He pointed out to them that retrenchment would be "disastrous"[28] when the country was advancing and there were so many new openings. Since, however, external funds were not increasing and Mashonaland was going to be thrown on its own resources more and more, the general support of the diocese was now needed. At this point, 1909, the only regular contributions to diocesan expenses by settler congregations were made by St. John's, Bulawayo and the pro-cathedral, Salisbury, which both contributed a tithe of their receipts towards the bishop's income.

Powell therefore brought the needs of the missions before his settler congregations. He preached on the duty of supporting missionary work and published his sermons in the diocesan magazine. He made practical suggestions as to how help might be given, while acknowledging that a colonial population estimated at 15,000 in 1909, which was already entirely supporting ten clergymen, could not support any more.

He believed, however, that they could support catechists for him. In April 1909 he pointed out that a catechist's salary was 50 shillings a month. If the church's catechists could be supported locally, income

---

[27] RHL/USPG, D Series, 193(b), 1909, E.N. Mashonaland to Bishop Montgomery, August 10th, 1909.
[28] [Editorial], *RCM* 6:12 (Dec 1909), 2.

from England would be freed to pay more missionary clergy. In May 1909, he suggested that the 1,000 settler communicants of the church should each contribute £1 a year, which would bring in £1,000 for the support of catechists.

This appeal fell on stony ground. Only one pound was contributed by one communicant and the closure of a mission in that year was only prevented by one clergyman forgoing his stipend and another pledging his credit.[29] The truth was that Powell had badly misread his audience and underestimated the lack of interest, or even hostility, that existed within the church where missions were concerned.[30] Settlers who became personally involved in such work were still very rare: the one farmer in the period who did so, for example, Howard Marshall, a neighbour of Upcher's at Rusape, was described by Powell as "an absolute exception".[31]

Powell's episcopate also coincided, not with a convergence of action and interest but with an increasing separation between settler and indigenous communities (particularly in the central part of the diocese, the colony of Rhodesia). In the out-districts, the movement of people into reserves meant that fewer and fewer white farmers had black neighbours. An increased physical or geographical separation was also taking place in the colonial settlements. Earlier, the make-shift huts in which the settlers lived and the hastily-erected shelters of 'native' town-dwellers, had been randomly placed. These haphazard arrangements were now giving way to ordered towns, with permanent buildings and gardens, and made-up roads. There was an increased concern for sanitation and fear of the spread of infectious diseases from the local peoples.[32] 'Native' locations were created (where they did not already exist), outside the colonial towns.

Separation also took place within the church. Congregations which had shared buildings moved into separate buildings: in Gwelo, for instance, in 1909. In Umtali, where the indigenous congregation had

---

[29] NAZ, HMss, MS 1036/3, Diocese of Mashonaland/SR, Board of Finance, Minute Book (1903–1925), November 11th, 1909, f. 118; 'Diocesan Board of Finance', *RCM* 6:12 (Dec 1909), 4; 'Letter from Archdeacon Upcher. Rusape, July 1909', *MQP* LXX (Nov 1909), 6.

[30] Cf. Percy F. Hone, *Southern Rhodesia* (London: George Bell and Sons, 1909), 77–84.

[31] 'Letter from the Bishop. (n.d.), (n.p.)', *MQP* LXXI (Feb 1910), 5.

[32] L.H. Gann, *A History of Southern Rhodesia* (London: Chatto and Windus, 1965), 192–3; Hone, *Southern Rhodesia*, 16.

already moved into a separate building on the same stand, the 'native' church was now moved (or built) further away.

Powell's own actions also reduced his ability to elict support from settler congregations for, like Knight-Bruce, he alienated them by his opinions and by sharp criticism of them and their Christianity. In the diocesan magazine for July 1908, for example, he wrote that his first Harvest Festival in Africa had left "a strong and sad impression" upon him: "Very few at the Eucharist poor collections no offerings either in money or in kind miserable congregations" (sic).[33] He also wrote back to England about incidents of settler ill-treatment of local people, the brutal labour practices of some, for example.

He branded racial prejudice as un-Christian. One of his very first sermons was on the temptation of a conquering people to "racial arrogancy" and the need to replace this "arrogancy" by "the great grace of chivalry" and so win the "good esteem, the gratitude, the admiration" of a "conquered race".[34] He urged upon settlers the "essential duty" of finding and serving Christ in the poor, the needy and "all strangers", particularly those "of strange race and strange tongue in our midst...who will need all our gentleness and mercy".[35]

The settlers, for whom another bloody rising against colonial rule remained a real possibility, reacted to his criticisms and to these novel ideas by withholding their money and voting with their feet: in Powell's time, services at the pro-cathedral were thinly attended—one of his grounds for criticism of settler religion. Not very long after he left the diocese, however, it was necessary to extend the building because it was not possible to seat everyone who came.

The Diocese of Mashonaland ended 1908, Powell's first year in office, with a large deficit and the Central Reserve and Sustentation Fund had to be drawn upon to the tune of £800. Similar deficits and retrenchment of staff were only prevented, in 1909 and 1910, by extra fund-raising efforts made by the Mashonaland Mission Association, in response to Powell's desperate appeals to them and by an additional £400 found by the SPG for 1910. Powell himself was only able to initiate four new pieces of mission work, only one of which was conspicuously successful: an increase in the numbers of (self-supporting)

[33] E.N. Mashonaland, 'Harvest Festival', *RCM* 5:7 (July 1908), 3.
[34] 'Christian Chivalry', *RCM* 5:4 (April 1908), 2.
[35] 'The Bishop's Letter', *RCM* 5:3 (March 1908), 2.

female missionaries and so the beginning of work among women at St. Faith's and Wreningham.

He also began a mission, St. Matthias at Umgusa, outside Bulawayo, (that is, he sent a missionary to upgrade an existing out-station) in 1908 and he founded an additional mission in the densely-populated Victoria area at Ndanga, 40 miles beyond Victoria, in 1909. Both of these ventures closed within the year. The Umgusa mission was on private land, which was sold and Umgusa was reduced once more to an outstation. The Ndanga mission was run by Upcher but was too remote to allow him to function as an archdeacon and his health broke down. He could not be replaced, as he worked without stipend and there was no money to pay another missionary. The fourth initiative undertaken by Powell, the provision of a new 'native' church in Umtali to replace the old building, which he found offensively shabby, was of dubious benefit to the congregation, for it left them with a large debt which they found difficult to service.

The one successful new station begun during Powell's episcopate, St. David's, Bonda, north of Penhalonga was created by the pressure of conversions in mid-1910, when Powell himself was no longer in the diocese and was financed by an independent appeal to sympathisers in England. In Matabeleland where the church's missionary work was already very sparse, Powell alienated and so lost Walter Leary, the very able man appointed to Bembezi by Gaul.

Leary, with Gaul's encouragement had managed to begin the first real 'industrial' missionary work in the diocese. He had borrowed money, erected tobacco barns, bought cattle and was just about to reap a good crop of tobacco and repay his debts, when his operations were closed down by Powell. Farming was not, in Powell's book, a suitable activity for a missionary.[36] Leary, however, had not only believed in the value of the 'industrial' training he offered but had looked forward to the time when his efforts would make his mission self-supporting and so release funds for work elsewhere in the diocese.[37]

[36] NAZ, HMss, MS 1036/3, Diocese of Mashonaland/SR, Board of Finance, Minute Book (1903–1925), March 9th, 1908, f. 28, June 29th, 1908, f. 86; LE 4/1/1, Walter Leary, Reminiscences, ff. 11–14, 23.

[37] 'Letter from the Rev. W. Leary. Bembezi, July 5th, 1903', *MQP* XLVI (Nov 1903), 18; Alan G.S. Gibson, Bp., Victoria West, August 12th, 1904, 'From Pretoria to Bulawayo', *Ch.Ch.* (August 26th, 1904), 534.

Such progress as was made in Powell's episcopate was largely self-financing and the result of local rather than episcopal initiative. Mission congregations and their priests were responsible for building permanent churches at Selukwe, Gwelo, Rusape (Epiphany) and the mine compound at Penhalonga Valley. In colonial work, two new ecclesiastical districts with permanent churches were created at Hartley (1909) and Selukwe (1909) (hitherto part of the Gwelo district) and the first suburban chapel was built in Salisbury, at Avondale (1910). The two very capable men Powell had appointed to Salisbury and Bulawayo also began vigorous campaigns to replace the dilapidated pioneer churches in those towns with worthier buildings.

Powell left Mashonaland early in 1910. He had been ill, since the previous December, with rheumatic fever and sciatica and returned to England to recuperate. In England, he recovered for a time then developed an ulcer and resigned in August 1910.[38] In his letter to the diocese, he expressed his gratitude that his resignation was not of his own making but had come from God through sickness.[39] He was a man of principle and it is clear that his illness was a relief to him, in that it enabled him to resign with some grace.

He was very much like Knight-Bruce. He had come out to his diocese full of plans for missionary work, only to find that resources were scanty and colonial work had to take precedence. A fascination with Khama of Bechuanaland re-appears in his writings[40] and he, like Knight-Bruce and unlike Gaul, identified real missionary work with rural missions, 'veldt' missions, not with town work. As far as settlers went, he did not shirk his responsibilities to them but he found himself unable to understand them and was critical, dismayed or saddened at what he saw in colonial life and religion (or lack of it).

He seems to have found a kindred spirit in only one man, Arthur Shearly Cripps, missionary at Wreningham since 1901. Cripps was a poet and writer, a violent (and erratic) critic of settler life and ways, who lived in Franciscan simplicity on his mission station and attempted to serve a "Black Christ" in the people around him.[41] His was the only

[38] LPL, Davidson, 158, Correspondence relating to the proposed resignation of Bishop Powell, 1st August, 1910–16th August, 1910, ff. 342, 343, 346, 349, 350.

[39] 'Letter from the Bishop. To the Clergy and lay Electors and others in the Diocese of Mashonaland, July 31st, 1910', *RCM* 7:9 (Sept 1910), 2.

[40] 'Letter from the Bishop. Bulawayo, (n.d.)', *MQP* LXVII (Feb 1909), 3.

[41] D.V. Steere, *God's Irregular: Arthur Shearly Cripps: A Rhodesian Epic* (London: S.P.C.K., 1973), 56.

work to draw an accolade from Powell: he called it "magnificent".[42] Cripps himself dedicated one of his anti-settler writings to Powell, with "esteem and affection" and an inscription from the book of Ezekiel, "And they, whether they will hear, or whether they will forbear, (for they are a rebellious house) yet shall know there hath been a prophet among them".[43]

III *1911: Frederic Beaven, the settlers' choice*

Powell was succeeded by a man already on the staff of Mashonaland, Frederic Hicks Beaven, the man whom he had brought to Salisbury as dean in 1908 in order to free himself to concentrate on missions. Beaven had been Vicar-General since Powell's departure for England in late 1909.

He was an Englishman from a military family and a man of private means but, like Gaul, was neither a public school nor a 'University' man. He had trained for the ministry at St. Bee's, a non-graduate theological college in the North of England and as a non-graduate, briefly, at Durham University. These facts alone would have prevented him rising to high office in the 'home' church, since non-graduates and colleges such as St. Bee's were not held in high regard.[44] Beaven, however, had been a highly successful parish priest at Stafford in the diocese of Lichfield, before going out to South Africa as a chaplain to the imperial troops in 1901. He had then stayed on to do district work in the Capetown diocese, become Archdeacon of Matabeleland in 1903 and was responsible for beginning and sustaining church work in North-Western Rhodesia.

He was the choice of the laity in the elective assembly of the diocese, who made it clear that they wanted no-one else. The clergy, especially the missionary clergy, were less enthusiastic for Beaven had no missionary experience at all.[45] Powell, however, had greatly diminished the

---

[42] NAZ, HMss, MS 1036/3, Diocese of Mashonaland/SR, Board of Finance, Minute Book (1903–1925), June 30th, 1908, f. 90.

[43] A.S. Cripps, *The Brooding Earth* (Oxford: B.H. Blackwell, 1912), frontispiece.

[44] Alan Haig, *The Victorian Clergy* (London and Sydney: Croom Helm, 1984), 116, 122ff.

[45] NAZ, HMss, ANG 1/10/1, Bishop Etheridge, Memoirs, 1954, f. 51.

prestige of the church among the settlers and Beaven "possessed to an extraordinary degree" their confidence and affection.[46]

Just as parallels can be made between Powell and Knight-Bruce, so they can be found between Beaven and Gaul. In the succession of each to the bishopric, a man with settler credentials replaced a man with missionary aspirations who had alienated his colonial flock. Gaul's appointment in 1895 had met with settler acclaim and in 1911 the announcement of Beaven's election was awaited in "a tense silence" by the elective assembly[47] and greeted with relief and barely-restrained jubilation by settler congregations.

He was at heart a colonial chaplain. Powell's pastoral instincts when he became bishop had been touched by his isolated missionaries but Beaven's were stirred by the lonely lives of his settler flock on the veld. Settlers, he declared, needed the ministrations of the church "as much as if not more" than "the heathen" did[48] and in his enthronement sermon the new bishop spoke plainly of his admiration for the "splendid heroism" shown in settlers' "ordinary lives".[49]

Beaven did not deny that particular "race difficulties" had to be faced in the diocese[50] and he feared the attitudes of the more exploitative settler societies to the South.[51] Rhodesians, however, he considered, were sometimes "judged a bit harshly by the world[52] and he was among those, such as Lord Buxton (Governor General and High Commissioner of South Africa, 1914–20), who were ready to defend or praise them publicly.[53] In 1920, when two of his own missionaries, Edgar Lloyd and Arthur Shearly Cripps, spoke at a meeting in England about racial conflict, labour exploitation and land-grabbing, Beaven in closing the meeting asserted that he had seen "a great improvement" in the

---

46 'Letter from the Archdeacon of Matabeleland. Bulawayo, December 29th, 1910', *MQP* LXXV (Feb 1911), 7.

47 'Election of the Bishop', *RCM* 7:11 (Nov 1910), 1.

48 'Letter from the Dean. (n.p.), March 20th, 1910', *MQP* LXXII (May 1910), 6.

49 'Address by the Bishop. Enthronement, February 21st, 1911', *MQP* LXXVI (May 1911), 5.

50 *Ibid.*

51 CE/CBM, Missions Overseas, Annual Review (London: 1920), 109.

52 'Address by the Bishop. Enthronement, February 21st, 1911', *MQP* LXXVI (May 1911), 5.

53 Earl Buxton, Chairman, 'Annual Festival' [Mashonaland Mission Association], *SRQP* CXXV (Aug 1923), 1.

attitudes of the settlers and that "the vast majority" were "kindly and considerate" towards "the native races".[54]

He believed that the British Empire, which the settlers represented, was "the world's greatest secular agency for good"[55] and among the personal heroes he listed in his enthronement sermon was Cecil Rhodes, in company with King Alfred, St. Augustine, David Livingstone, Bishop Gray (first Bishop of Capetown) and the seventeenth century Anglican divine, William Law. So great was Beaven's admiration for Rhodes that, when he was Dean of Salisbury and raising funds for a cathedral, he proposed at one point that one of its chapels be dedicated as a memorial to Rhodes alone, as founder of the country.

Beaven had no corresponding indigenous hero, neither a Christian chief, like Khama nor a working man, like Frank Ziqubu or Simon Mooti and he knew his own "shortcomings" as far as missionary work went.[56] In 1919, however, he ordained the first black clergyman to serve in the diocese since Mtobi had left in 1901, Samuel Muhlanga, an Ndau ('Shangaan') who had worked as a catechist-teacher in the Salisbury district for many years. During Beaven's episcopate indigenous Christians were also given a voice in the affairs of the church: a conference for missionaries and village teachers was instituted in 1914 and indigenous lay representatives attended Synod from 1924.

He himself believed that the "first duty" of the church was to evangelise the world, and to create a "bond of spiritual fellowship" between "East and West, Europe and Africa".[57] He was kindly in all his dealings, punctilious in carrying out his duties and during the course of his episcopate even began to take a personal interest in missionary work: now and then, he would slip in, unannounced, to a mission service.

Nevertheless, when he became bishop he made a structural change which was the reverse of Powell's. He himself had been appointed Dean of Salisbury, in order to free Powell to give more time to missions. He himself appointed a Superintendent of Missions, as was the custom elsewhere in the CPSA, to take charge of the missionary side of the work and thus allow him to spend more time with settlers. This appointment, while bringing a new energy and unity to missionary work

---

[54] 'Annual Meeting [Mashonaland Mission Association]. Work in Southern Rhodesia', *SRQP* CXII (May 1920), 8–9.

[55] 'Diocesan Synod', *RCM* 18:10 (Oct 1921), 4.

[56] 'The Bishop's Charge', *RCM* 21:10 (Oct 1924), 7.

[57] 'Synod: Part of The Bishop's Charge', *SRQP* XC (Nov 1915), 9.

also had the effect of further separating the interests of the two wings of the church: the superintendent travelled the country visiting missions, Beaven normally visited settler congregations and only travelled to missions for special occasions such as confirmations.

Beaven's episcopate therefore presents something of a paradox: he presided over a considerable advance in missionary work and at least nominally in the status of indigenous Christians in the life of the diocese[58] while at the same time endorsing settler withdrawal from contact with indigenous groups.

Separation within the church was not complete, however, certainly not as complete as outside it. Synod was no longer an entirely white body from 1921, for instance, once Muhlanga was ordained. Such a racially-mixed gathering was so unusual at the time that once this was the case, Synod no longer sought the hospitality of the Bulawayo or Salisbury Clubs. The subsequent admission of indigenous lay representatives to Synod aroused considerable settler criticism.[59]

The clergy also continued to serve both mission and settler congregations, in contrast to practice elsewhere in the CPSA where the ministry and organisation of colonial parishes and missions were quite distinct. To clergy coming in from South Africa, the "unity" of the work of the diocese was, in fact, quite striking.[60]

This impression was no doubt reinforced by the fact that the period also saw some softening of attitudes among the laity and in the settler community generally, towards missionary work. Evidence given to the Committee of Enquiry into Native Affairs for Southern Rhodesia (1910–11) bore "abundant and... surprising testimony to the change of view".[61] Settler newspapers began to pronounce in favour of missions and a very positive debate on missionary work took place at Synod in 1912, something that would not have been possible ten years before.

This change in attitude, however, was connected primarily with the perennial settler demand for labour: products of the missions were no

[58] Representation of settler and indigenous laity in Synod was not on the same basis: each major mission was entitled to send one representative, whereas settler representation was based on the number of communicants in a parish. Indigenous communicants, by 1923, out-numbered settler communicants by 4 to 1 (8,000:2,000).

[59] 'Letter from the Archdeacon of Mashonaland. Salisbury, September 27th, 1921', *SRQP* CXVII (Nov 1921), 8.

[60] RHL/USPG, E Series, 80(A), 1925, Edward Paget, Bishop of Mashonaland, First Report, (n.d.) [1925].

[61] 'Missions' [Report to Synod], *RCM* 9:11 (Nov 1912), 6.

longer stereotyped as rascals, as had been the case earlier but as good employees. Missionaries, who had been working towards such a change in attitude for many years, accordingly welcomed it while pointing out its limitations: the Archdeacon and Superintendent of Missions, for instance, was constrained to remark that missions did not exist to provide settlers with "good cooks and smart waiters" but to draw people into union with God.[62]

Others pointed out that few settlers ever visited a mission (and that not all missions were situated in remote areas). The increased distance which had grown up between settler and indigenous groups was, in fact, becoming formalised in this period, outside the church as well as within it, largely as the result of the committee of enquiry of 1910 (and an earlier South African enquiry of 1904). These committees had investigated the effects (mostly judged deleterious) which colonisation had had upon indigenous societies and they had come to the same conclusions as Gaul, that the transforming and educating agents of those societies ought to be Christian missions.

Responsibility for the welfare of 'natives' was now delegated, not just to the members of the Native Department but also to official representatives of the churches, the professional missionaries. Serious discussion of matters of interest to indigenous communities thereafter took place at the biennial meetings of the Southern Rhodesia Missionary Conference, to which most of the major churches belonged and was largely removed from the assemblies of individual bodies, such as the Anglican Synod.

While, therefore, a handful of settlers continued to be involved in the development of mission churches and night schools, for most of the settler laity local lives and concerns remained unknown, opaque. Entirely typical is the account in a settler memoir of an office messenger known for over fifty years (from 1896) to his employer and family (who were exceptionally kindly church people) without their being aware "of the other life he had been leading all the time as the gentle patriarch of a whole clan and a Methodist lay preacher".[63]

Newcomers could find the degree of separation within the church quite shocking. A recently-arrived English railway missioner conducted

---

[62] Archdeacon Etheridge, 'Methods of Missionary Work in Rhodesia', *RCM* 14:3 (March 1917), 9.

[63] Hardwicke Holderness, *Lost Chance: Southern Rhodesia 1945–58* (Harare: Zimbabwe Publishing House (Pvt.) Ltd., 1985), 21.

a service of Holy Communion for a settler family in their home, in the Gwanda district, in 1924, for instance. He found, to his utter dismay and their unconcern that their devout old servant had been kneeling in the passage outside for the entire service, knowing he would not be allowed in. To the missioner, the church of such settlers seemed to be that "of a race, a nation" and their God "little removed from the tribal deities of old".[64]

IV *A smaller diocese, greater prosperity and resilience*

In many respects, Beaven faced fewer practical difficulties than any of his predecessors. Although his episcopate was to see the outbreak of yet another armed conflict, World War One in 1914, the diocese was rather better established and reasonably resilient by that point and so (as we shall see below) its ministry, while greatly stretched, did not break under the demands of the war.

Beaven himself was relieved, by the appointment of a Superintendent of Missions, of part of the now very large task of diocesan administration. His private resources enabled him to work and travel freely within the diocese and the diocese itself was reduced to a more manageable size during his episcopate.

Sub-division had been mooted since Gaul's time but it proved impossible (until 1952) to raise the necessary endowment for a second bishopric. In 1909, however, a bishop was appointed for North-West Rhodesia which meant that the Bishop of Mashonaland no longer had to oversee work beyond the Zambezi. In 1915, a new Diocese of Kimberley and Kuruman was formed to the south-east and virtually all of Bechuanaland was incorporated into it (see Map 2, p. xxi). Mashonaland was now re-named Southern Rhodesia.

In its work among settlers the diocese still had to contend with rapid immigration, as the influx into Southern Rhodesia which had begun in 1908 continued. This influx was then halted by the outbreak of World War One and the country lost some 20% of its settlers to the war effort.[65] Immigration resumed after the war but the 42% increase

---

[64] 'Letter from Mr. Beresford', *SARWMQP* 79 (April 1924), 5.

[65] 5,716 settlers served in the war, mainly in the East and South-West African campaigns. Over 700 (12%) died: Peter Mclaughlin, *Ragtime Soldiers: The Rhodesian Experience in the First World War* (Bulawayo: Books of Zimbabwe, 1980), 140.

in the settler population between the censuses of 1911 and 1921 (when numbers rose from 23,606 to 33,650) was by no means as startling as earlier increases had been and much of the increase was attributable to the growth of a young Rhodesia: the settler community was beginning to reproduce itself.

The pre-war influx of Beaven's episcopate also presented less of a problem to the church than earlier immigration had done: settler congregations, for one thing, were better able to support the work of the church because with the new immigrants came a modest prosperity. The re-construction of the mining industry which had been begun in 1904 and the first real attempts by the BSA Company to encourage settler agriculture, which had been made in 1907, were having their intended effect.

Agricultural production, mainly of maize and tobacco, rose sharply as did the output of gold: output in 1900, before re-construction, had been 54,9891 oz of gold whereas 854,480 oz was produced in 1914.[66] This greater (but uneven) prosperity then continued and even increased during the early stages of the war, when gold and the base minerals now also being mined in the country were at a premium, although there was a down-turn, especially in gold mining, from 1915. A partial recovery in gold only began in 1920.

The economy was also affected by post-war uncertainties and a political debate surrounding the future of Southern Rhodesia. The BSA Company's charter had been renewed in 1914 for a further nine years. In 1923, after considerable discussion and a referendum, the charter was not renewed and Southern Rhodesia became a self-governing colony within the Empire. The economy then began (apparently) to pick up once more.

The settler community in Beaven's time also passed out of the 'pioneer' stage. There were more women, marriages and children even on some of the remoter mines. The tone of such a society was more conducive to successful church work than that of a moving frontier society composed almost entirely of young men.[67] The presence of women and families also appears to have counteracted, to some degree,

---

[66] Phimister, *An Economic and Social History*, 60; Gann, *A History*, 160, nte. 1.

[67] In 1911, the ratio of men to women in Rhodesia was 66:34, in 1921 it was 56:44. The percentage of women in congregations, in 1921, was 49.64% and 53.98% of communicants were women: *Report of the Director of Census for 1921* (Salisbury: 1922), 2, 21.

a post-Victorian drift away from church-going which was beginning to spread from England to British communities abroad.[68] Many of the incoming settlers, moreover, particularly farmers from the Cape, were members of the English Church.

Colonial settlement also became denser in the period, which lessened difficulties. In the chief mining area, particularly, the Midlands, the many small mines of the immediate post-reconstruction years tended now to be replaced by larger mines and mining communities, which were easier for the clergy to reach and work amongst than the many scattered camps of small-workers. At Selukwe, for instance, there were three or four large mines (though some 30 in the district). Gatooma grew up around one large mine, the Cam and Motor, Umvuma was synonymous with the Falcon, a copper (and gold) mine. The Midlands towns were also relatively close together, only some 30 or 40 miles apart.

Travel and communication also improved because branch railways spread to service the mining industry. Settlements hitherto reached only by road or track became accessible by rail: the Salisbury parson on a district visit in 1916, for instance, was able to reach Bindura and Shamva by rail instead of push-bike or motor-bike. Even forlorn Fort Victoria was reached by the railway in 1914.

The increasing number of settler farmers posed more of a difficulty for the church than the miners, although the very rapid increase which had given rise to perturbation during Powell's brief episcopate slowed somewhat. By 1921, nevertheless, there were more farmers than miners, civil servants and BSA police combined.[69]

The land that they were taking up, however, tended to be relatively accessible, near the line of rail and farming areas were being more densely settled than hitherto. In 1904, there had been only five farms between the outskirts of Salisbury and Mazoe, thirty miles to the north. By 1909, there were eighty and by 1913 settler farmers occupied the land to 120 miles away. This meant that the isolated farmers of earlier years were being replaced by recognizable farming communities. Where once the travelling parson would only have been able to visit and hold services on individual farms, he could now arrange to meet his flock at a central point, a hotel or a Farmers' Hall, at Bindura or Tafuna,

---

[68] Percentages for church attendance, and the committed, are similar for 1901 and 1921: see p. 69, note 95; *Report of the Director of Census for 1921* (Salisbury: 1922), 20.

[69] Phimister, *An Economic and Social History*, 100.

north of Salisbury, for instance, at Marandellas to the south-east, or Figtree and Marula in Matabeleland.

The early part of Beaven's episcopate therefore saw much consolidation of colonial church work in the small mining towns and agricultural areas. Church councils were formed and buildings, churches or church halls and rectories were erected in Gatooma (1911), Que Que (1913), Enkeldoorn (1914), Umvuma (1915) and Sinoia (1915). In one area, Marandellas, the church lent money to the farmers to build a Farmer's Hall that could also be used for worship.

Beaven himself was able to oversee the building of the first part (the sanctuary and choir) of a magnificent cathedral in Salisbury, in 1914 and a fine building, on a new and central site, was completed for St. John's, Bulawayo in 1913. The very "solidity" of these buildings could be seen as testimony to the fact that the English Church was now "firmly established" in Rhodesia.[70]

Four churches were then opened after the war, in 1922: one at Inoro, part of the Marandellas district, built by the missionary at Mangwende's; the first English Church in Beira, St. George's, built as a war memorial; a tiny church erected by members of the farming community in Essexvale (Esigodini); and the first part of a building on a new site, in Gwelo, to replace the pioneer church.

In mining districts, however, the down-turn which began in 1915 produced radical changes. Selukwe, once the centre of a busy mining area, had been separated from Gwelo as an ecclesiastical district with a resident parson and a new church in 1909. When the mines of the area began to close in 1916, Seluke lost its resident priest to mission work in the nearby Selukwe Reserve. By 1919, there were only a few farmers in the district and Selukwe returned once more to the care of the priest at Gwelo.

Hartley, separated from Salisbury in 1909, was left with large building debts it was unable to service when mining became depressed. It was grouped first with Que Que in 1920 and then with Gatooma and Que Que in 1925. Several other colonial parishes received subsidies from central funds or were grouped together after the war because no one centre could now support a clergyman. Victoria, Umvuma and Gwelo, for example, were grouped in 1920.

---

[70] [H.H. Foster, Archdeacon of Matabeleland], 'Bulawayo', *RCM* 10:5 (May 1913), 10.

V *Corporate life; education*

The most distinctive feature of Beaven's episcopate, ecclesiastically speaking, was that the church began to acquire more of an institutional character: corporate life began to replace individual, unco-ordinated endeavour. Beaven himself regularly consulted the Diocesan Board of Finance, instituted by Gaul and a Bishop's Senate (later Cathedral Chapter), begun by Powell. Members of Synod were better accustomed to debate and decision: there were "fewer rambling speeches"[71] by 1912. Members of the missions met in conference with their missionaries and their bishop and, by 1924, in Synod.

Organisations and societies familiar from England were established among the settlers. An English Church Men's Society was formed in Mashonaland, as elsewhere in the CPSA, in 1909 and continued in existence until World War One. The society had been founded in England in 1900 (as the Church of England Men's Society) because men had begun to fade out of parish life, leaving active work (teaching in Sunday Schools, or work among the poor) largely to women. The society was designed to draw them back.

In Mashonaland/SR, leading laymen were themselves the chief instigators and the organisers of the ECMS and used it as a vehicle to draw other, less committed, men into the service of the church. The society provided an opportunity for men to worship together, a forum for learning and debate and opportunities for 'good works': the branch in Bulawayo came to the rescue (financially) of the Bethlehem school for 'coloured' children, in 1916, for example. The Salisbury branch raised money in 1910 to purchase a motorbike for the itinerant clergyman.

Corporate attempts were also made to address social concerns. In 1910, leading churchwomen began a Rhodesian Women's Union, affiliated to the English Mother's Union and open to settler women of all denominations (renamed the Church Woman's Society in 1913) as part of a campaign against "impurity... temper, swearing, drinking and debt"[72] amongst their men as well as to encourage the proper care and upbringing of children. Branches of the Girls' Friendly Society were begun in the same year to offer moral protection and encouragement

[71] 'Letter from the Archdeacon of Mashonaland. Victoria Falls Hotel, Zambezi, September 21st, 1912', *MQP* LXXXII (Nov 1912), 10.

[72] Georgina B. Beaven, 'Rhodesia Women's Union. Presidential Letter', *RCM* 8:2 (Feb 1911), 6.

to young, single, settler women; and in 1914 an order of nuns, the Community of the Resurrection of Our Lord (Grahamstown), founded St. Gabriel's, a home for settler orphans who had previously had to be sent out of the country to South Africa.

The church also gave support to other attempts to re-shape the morals and perspectives of the frontier. At a time when settler feeling ran particularly high on the subject of the 'Black Peril' (sexual 'outrage' offered to white women by black men), for example, the diocesan magazine gave considerable space to those who pointed out that a 'White Plague' was far more extensive and that indigenous communities were powerless to combat it.

In 1915, Synod supported a recommendation before the Legislative Assembly that penalties which already existed for sexual intercourse between black men and white women (outside marriage) be extended to such intercourse between white men and black women and a resolution to that effect was conveyed personally to the Administrator, by a delegation led by Beaven. The legislation did not pass, however: the matter was not just one of casual exploitation, for a number of white men (particularly in Matabeleland) kept black concubines or common-law wives.[73]

Anxiety also surfaced about the children produced by black/white relations, who tended to be rejected by the societies of both parents and had been a cause for concern since Gaul's day. Attempts (short-lived) were made, at Bulawayo and Bembezi (1911), to provide schooling for them.

Efforts were made to minister to other minority groups. There were, for example, a handful of 'Chinamen' and a few Indians in Bulawayo and Salisbury and church night schools were now provided for them. Concern had also long been felt for people of mixed ancestry, particularly those known to white settlers as 'Coloureds' or 'Cape Coloureds' and to themselves as 'Cape Folk' (since many of them were originally from the Cape). They occupied an uncertain position on the fringes of colonial society and many (835 of the 1,998 'Coloureds' in Rhodesia in 1921) were members of the English Church.

The majority lived in Bulawayo, where St. Cyril's (a church hall built in 1899, at the south end of the town) which had earlier served

---

[73] Philip Mason, *The Birth of a Dilemma: The Conquest and Settlement of Rhodesia* (Oxford: Institute of Race Relations and Oxford University Press, 1958), 240–47.

a double function (as a school, for 'coloured' children and a church, for white railwaymen) was now reserved for their use. In 1912, in Bulawayo the nuns from Grahamstown founded Bethlehem School for the more respectable 'coloured' children. Work in Salisbury included a school (1911–15) and a mother's meeting. In Gwelo, by 1926, a black catechist/teacher (with a "Cape Pupil Teacher's Certificate") ran a day school for a group of children, who were described as "pure African, Eurafrican, Indian and St. Helenan".[74] Down the railway line, the missioners who had struggled for years to found a boarding school for the children of 'coloured' gangers, who were running wild and without any education, finally succeeded, at Shashi (Shashe), in 1916.

Missionary work also began to display institutional characteristics in addition to those noted above, even though most stations continued to be run by solitary missionaries. Several of these men, long-serving and highly idiosyncratic in personality and method, themselves became virtual institutions: James Hay Upcher, between 1916 and 1931, at Hunyani (Chitungwiza); Edgar Lloyd at Rusape (1903–36); and Arthur Shearly Cripps, in the Charter district (1901–1952). The appointment of a Superintendent of Missions however, meant that this side of the work received a degree of central co-ordination and direction for the first time.

An institution of another kind was acquired in 1915 when a religious order, the Community of the Resurrection (Mirfield) took charge of St. Augustine's, Penhalonga. The CR 'Fathers' were to have a profound influence upon the diocese: here it can only be noted that their arrival was to lead to raised standards of education and ministerial training (see, below, p. 114).[75] St. Augustine's, under the community, also became the first mission of the diocese to rival well-manned, 'show-piece' missions long-possessed by denominations which had had concentrated most of their missionary efforts on single, central stations rather than attempting the wide—and very thin—spread of the Anglicans.

A religious order also became the dominant influence in work among women during Beaven's episcopate: the Grahamstown nuns took over work at St. Columba's, Bulawayo (1914); St. Faith's, Rusape (1916); and

---

[74] 'Letter from Rev. T.O. Beattie. St. Patrick's, Gwelo, February 22nd, 1926', *MQP* CXXVI (May 1926), 9.

[75] Alan Wilkinson, *The Community of the Resurrection: A Centenary History* (London: SCM Press Ltd., 1992), 238–51; RHO/USPG, E Series, 79(B), A. Cotton C.R., Report, Penhalonga, December 31st, 1924.

St. Monica's, Penhalonga (1919). Women's work had already grown substantially: by 1911, at St. Monica's, Annie Dalby and her helpers were caring for 70 boarders and 30 day-scholars, as well as a group of orphaned infants of both sexes. Other female missionaries, most of them also single and honorary, worked at Bonda; Wreningham; and St. Mary's, Hunyani, as well as Bulawayo and Rusape. Missionary wives made significant contributions (as such wives did throughout the mission field): Mea Broderick, for example, at Bonda between 1910 and 1916. Elaine Lloyd, wife of Edgar Lloyd, at St. Faith's between 1909 and 1928, became a leading figure in missionary circles.

More 'industrial' work, in fact, was achieved among women than among men: spinning, weaving, dairying, were taught, as well as laundry and domestic work. However, as was the case with clergy, it was never possible to find workers in sufficient numbers and very few women gave long service. Although some two dozen served in the diocese (over the period 1904–25), many came and went within a couple of years, or less.

In education, the church in Beaven's episcopate had finally to accept a state of affairs quite unlike that of 'home', where the schools were "the chief bulwark" of the Church of England and the church the chief educator of the people.[76] It was possible to maintain some pretensions to a dominant position in the education of local people, at least until about 1920. By this point, however, not only had the Anglicans been outstripped by the Roman Catholics but the government itself was moving into the field of (industrial) education, since that offered by the missionary bodies had proved inadequate.

In settler education, any lingering pretensions had early to be abandoned. At Plumtree, one of the two schools the English Church had founded which remained open, a new headmaster, R.W. Hammond, had been appointed in 1906 and was to serve for thirty years. Hammond created a school with a unique 'bush' ethos and very high standing: in 1924, Plumtree was to be judged one of the "top ten great schools of the Commonwealth".[77] In 1908, however, Hammond insisted upon the chapel becoming undenominational (in spite of the fact that he was the son of an English parson and took, and preached at, the school

[76] 'Letter from Archdeacon Upcher. Rusape, July 1909', *MQP* LXX (Nov 1909), 9.

[77] Jill Baker, *Beloved African* (Weltevreden Park, South Africa: Covos-Day Books, 2000), 64, 85–6.

Evensong regularly himself).[78] In 1914, financial stringency led to the school being taken over by the government. The diocese did not own or finance Plumtree and so had of necessity to acquiese in both instances. A chaplaincy and leadership on the school board were retained, however, and so the church continued to exert a dominant religious influence at Plumtree, without being able to claim an exclusive one.

Then, in 1910, the last of the church's schools for settler children, at St. John's, Bulawayo, closed. Successive rectors of St. John's had fought hard to keep it open but on the recommendation of an Education Commission of 1908, BSA Company assistance had been withdrawn from all denominational schools and a system of secular education was established for settler children throughout the country. The church could not afford to keep St. John's open without subsidy: the pupils were largely children of miners and farmers and were mostly "very poor".[79] The only schools for settler children with a definite religious foundation to survive were Roman Catholic, run by religious orders with an efficiency and lack of expense the English Church had long envied but could not emulate.[80] Members of the church chafed at the spectacle of English Church children being educated, albeit on English public school lines, by Dominican nuns and French and German Jesuits.[81]

The church attempted to counter the loss of St. John's (and Plumtree) with two different strategies. One was a refusal to jettison English tradition entirely: many members of the church did not believe that there could be a "great white Christian civilisation" in Rhodesia without English Church schools.[82] After the closure of St. John's, therefore, Herbert Foster, then rector at Bulawayo, brought the nuns from Grahamstown to the town, in order that a church education might be provided for at least one section of the colonial young. They established St. Peter's,

---

[78] J.B. Clarke, 'The Early Years of Plumtree School', *Heritage of Zimbabwe* 4 (1984), 1,8.

[79] 'Letter from the Rev. G. Broderick. The Rectory, Bulawayo, March 30th, 1907', *MQP* LX (May 1907), 16.

[80] RHO/USPG, D Series, 122(b) 1897 Will. Mashonaland to Revd. H.W. Tucker, April 27th, 1897.

[81] NAZ, HMss, Misc, BE 4/1/1, Thomas Oliver Beattie, Reminiscences, 1910–22, f. 4.

[82] 'Letter from the Archdeacon of Matabeleland. March 26th, 1909', *MQP* LXVIII (May 1909), 11–12; Messers Bell and Winslow, 'European Education', *RCM* 6:6 (June 1909), 9.

a "purely select" school[83] for girls from the upper echelons of colonial society, in a Bulawayo suburb in 1911.

St. Peter's flourished, with very little financial help from the diocese: the community had its own sources of support and the school attracted pupils who would otherwise have been sent to the Cape for a convent education. In 1921, an attempt was made to provide a similar education for boys: Cedric School was founded by a layman, also in Bulawayo, at the urging of "numerous parents" who wanted a school for "decent children", compelled to attend the government schools for lack of any acceptable alternative. Cedric had no official church sanction but claimed to be a "definite" Church school.[84]

The second strategy involved embracing the new order, forsaking English ideals in education and accepting that new (and narrower) ones had to be provided, if the majority of settler children were to receive, if not a church education, at least a degree of religious nurture. In Bulawayo, therefore, the teachers and children of St. John's transferred together to the new schools. There and elsewhere the parish clergy maintained close links with the pupil bodies of the new schools. Boarders, children from the out-districts in particular, swelled Sunday Schools and confirmation classes.

The clergy also utilised a tool already to hand, which had been provided by the foresight of Gaul. He had persuaded Rhodes to secure a 'right of entry' to settler schools (for ministers of all denominations) so that the children might be taught their religion.[85] This responsibility had always been taken seriously by the English clergy and so, while many settler children remained both uneducated and uncatechized (schooling was non-compulsory until 1930) creditable efforts were made to provide regular religious instruction for those at school in the main centres of Bulawayo, Salisbury, Gwelo and Umtali, where there was a continuous clerical ministry.

Through these methods, pastoral work and regular teaching within the new order, the English Church was able to re-claim something of a leading role in the religious nurture of settler children. By the 1920s,

---

[83] 'Letter from the Archdeacon of Matabeleland. Bulawayo, Dec 29th, 1910', *MQP* LXXVI (Feb 1911), 6.

[84] RHL/USPG D Series, 269 1920, B. Chard, letter to The Secretary, SPG, July 10th, 1920.

[85] A. Pierce Jones, *Procession of Witness* (Cape Town: [Printed by the Stewart Printing Company, Cape Town], 1947), 77.

although the clergy were now being overwhelmed by the growing numbers in the schools, Beaven was able to comment very favourably on their tone and on progress made since the early days of the colony.

VI *Familiar problems: finance, the needs of rural missions*

In Beaven's time, as we have seen above, the work of the church in the colonial settlements saw an overall development and consolidation. The same was true of the main centres of mission work: the erection of permanent church buildings by congregations, for instance, which was characteristic of settler work in this period was also characteristic of mission work. Existing churches were enlarged. New churches were built, at Hunyani (1911); Gatooma (1914); by Cripps at his new mission, Maronda Mashanu (1914) and at Enkledoorn (1917); at Sinoia (1915) and Mangwende's (1923); in the Selukwe (1920) and Que Que (1924) reserves; in the Chiduku reserve (St. Faith's district) (1911) and at St. Faith's itself (1913).

Two large and familiar problems continued to haunt the diocese, however, the funding of new missions, especially rural missions and the desperate shortage of clergy, particularly for itinerant and missionary work.

The irresistible pressures to expand missionary work which had faced Powell also faced Beaven and his Superintendent of Missions. A massive turning to the church continued, with all of its attendant demands and anxieties. Settler immigration continued to cause movement of local people into reserves and away from the neighbourhood of missions. St. Aidan's, Bembezi, for instance, was by 1916 entirely surrounded by settler farms. By 1922, 63.5% of the local people lived in reserves[86] and some of these were very remote and difficult of access, particularly in Matabeleland: it took the priest from St. Columba's, Bulawayo, three months in 1918 to do a trip of some 750 miles, visiting out-stations in the Gwaai and Shangani reserves.

The BSA Company was also said to be giving "whole-hearted support" to missionary work,[87] particularly after the adoption of the recommendations of the Native Affairs Commission of 1910. The

[86] Phimister, *An Economic and Social History*, 67.

[87] Archdeacon of Matabeleland, 'Annual Meeting [Mashonaland Mission Association], Friday, May 2nd, 1913' *MQP* LXXXIV (May 1913), 21.

Native Commissioners continued to ask for missionaries and teachers. A more positive attitude among settlers also meant more openings, more demands upon the church. Here and there, farmers were following the example of mine managers and offering the church access to their labour forces.

The style of existing missionary work was also changing in such a way as to strain the resources even of the older missions: missionaries were no longer caring for large numbers of people at a central station but having to travel many miles round a network of small outstations. By 1921, Lloyd, at St. Faith's, had to undertake regular three-month journeys of five hundred miles on a donkey, round the neighbouring reserves, in order to visit all the members of his mission.

More money was needed both for new work and also to maintain established work, for even where efforts were made, as on some of the older missions, to become self-supporting, these were limited in effect. The grants made by the government, for all their new enthusiasm, were also judged "woefully inadequate", far too small a proportion of that paid in 'native' taxation.[88] The stipends of the missionary clergy had still to come from central funds, if they came at all. At St. Faith's, Rusape in 1912, only one of the priests was receiving the tiny stipend customary in the diocese (£200 p.a.), another received only £50 and was subsidised by friends in England, the third worked for no pay. Four of the other missionary clergy of the diocese did not receive stipends.

Beaven did as his predecessors had done: he appealed to England for more support for missionary work and at the same time attempted to raise funds locally. He did both with some degree of success.

The only guaranteed sources of regular income remained the SPG and the Mashonaland Mission Association. The Association only managed to provide an average of £461 p.a. between 1911 and 1924 but the SPG block grant for general purposes was increased significantly for the first time in the history of the diocese. It rose from the usual £1,000/1,100 to £1,650 in 1915; £1,722 in 1916; and £1,800 in 1921. Expenditure on the stipends and pay of missionary clergy and teachers alone exceeded the income of the diocese from these two sources, however, in all but one year of Beaven's episcopate (1915) and money to cover the short-fall had to be found within the diocese.

[88] [Ven. H. Etheridge, Superintendent of Missions], 'Native Missions: Report to Church Synod', *RCM* 12:11 (Nov 1915), 6.

Beaven attempted to increase local giving and also to systematise the finances of the diocese (although he was unable to achieve a complete centralisation of finance). He also followed Gaul's policy of adding to the Central Sustentation and Reserve Fund any capital sums, donations or legacies received by the diocese. By this means he doubled the fund: it was £2,181 at the beginning of 1911 and £4,269 by the time he retired in 1925.

New policies of local support were also adopted. In 1911, for instance, on the missions, a system of assessments, i.e. regular giving by individual members, 5/—per annum for a man and 2/—for a woman, which was standard practice elsewhere in the CPSA, was introduced and very successfully. By 1915, over £1,000 a year was being contributed by members, through collections and assessments, for the support of mission work.

Beaven also introduced tithing, to both colonial and mission congregations, in 1912. Until then only the Bulawayo and Salisbury congregations had tithed their incomes consistently, to supplement the episcopal income. Beaven re-directed these tithes to general funds and then in 1912, through the Diocesan Synod, introduced a system of tithes on all parish and mission income (other than that for capital expenditure). Over the years 1912–1924, these tithes brought in an average of £485 a year to general funds but payment was very uneven: some parishes and missions paid regularly, some were constantly in arrears. Most of the colonial parishes and some of the mission churches laboured under heavy building debts incurred before the outbreak of the war and all struggled in the difficult economic climate of the immediate post-war years.

In 1915, when the economic downturn which was to last until the early 1920's began, the financial situation of the diocese was such as to cause real anxiety and the Synod of that year gave detailed consideration to finance. The Diocesan Treasurer pointed out that insolvency was only being staved off by the voluntary renunciation by the bishop and the archdeacon (the Superintendent of Missions) of part of their incomes and a very large reduction in the numbers of catechist-teachers since the beginning of the war. Synod then requested Beaven to lead an appeal for funds and he launched a Bishop's Diocesan Fund early in 1916, soliciting the support of individuals, companies and mines and contributing generously to the fund himself.

Beaven's popularity in the settler community can be gauged by the relative success of this fund, for his appeal did not fall flat as Powell's appeals had done. This was no doubt partly because settler opinion on the subject of missions was changing but largely because the appeal was made by Beaven personally. His gentle but assiduous promotion of the Cathedral Building Fund was similarly successful: the debt for the first part of the building, erected in 1914, (over £14,000) was paid off by the time Beaven retired from the bishopric in 1925, in spite of the economic difficulties faced by the country.

Beaven also went about the matter indirectly: while Etheridge spoke of the needs of the missions and the duty of supporting them, Beaven emphasised the need for an increased diocesan income, not just increased funds for missions and he appealed to the church on the basis of principle, on the essential unity of the church's work. He worked with, rather than against, the attitudes of the settlers. In appeals for his Bishop's Diocesan Fund, for instance, he emphasised the fact that more money was needed for many reasons, including the support of poor colonial parishes and not just for the support of missions. Contributors were even allowed to earmark contributions for colonial or mission work.

Beaven was not able to raise anything like the sum wanted: he had hoped to increase the income of the Diocese by £2,000 a year. The fund began with a flourish, for nearly £1,000 was raised in the first year but contributions then rather petered out in the economic downturn, with an average of some £240 being contributed in a normal year. It was, however, rather more successful than three funds launched purely for missionary work, the Native Development Funds A (1913) and B (1914) and the Native Ministry Fund (1919), which were able to attract very little money.

Beaven's popularity also meant that larger sums could be raised in a crisis, as in 1923, when £557 was raised in response to a special appeal made necessary by a particularly large deficit (£584) incurred the previous year. Similar deficits in 1920 and in 1924 (as in 1912) were only prevented because the bishop raised extra funds on visits to England.

In nine of the fourteen years of Beaven's episcopate the diocese ended the year with a deficit, usually a small one, which was written off to the Central Reserve and Sustentation Fund. There was a significant surplus, which was used to replenish the fund, only three times, in 1916, 1917 and 1923, when the bishop himself was responsible for raising the extra money through his Bishop's Diocesan Fund.

The struggle to survive financially could be most clearly seen on the missions. Missionaries continued to be paid tiny stipends and were working with the barest equipment. When, for instance, a new mission was begun near Gwelo in the Que Que Reserve (St. Patrick's, Gwelo) in early 1925 (at the initiative of members of St. Matthew's, the 'native' church in Gwelo), the missionary's wife, a trained nurse who was supposed to begin medical work, had no medical supplies, no drugs, not even disinfectant. What little local support the mission could raise came from St. Matthew's.[89]

It was only Beaven's personal popularity, moreover, which kept the diocese afloat: the future of the Diocesan Fund, for instance, was not assured beyond his episcopate. He left the diocese early in 1925 and his successor, arriving in October, found the diocese heading for a deficit of £1,000.

VII *Staff: a perennial problem*

During Beaven's episcopate, the diocese had some success in balancing its books but staffing remained an acute problem, in both sides of the church's work for, although converts ensured that the church grew in both colonial towns and rural areas and settlers spread into new districts, few additional clergy could be found.

This meant, in missionary work, that the opening of a new station continued to cause the effective closure of another. The one remaining mission near Victoria, begun by Gaul in 1905, for instance, closed in 1912 as another mission, St. Francis, opened in the Selukwe Reserve. When St Patrick's, Gwelo was opened in 1925, St. Francis, Selukwe was reduced to an out-station.

In colonial work, the few clergy there were had their hands full, attempting to cope with the larger towns and settlements: the work loads of the Salisbury and Bulawayo clergy were variously described in 1911–2 as "preposterous"[90] and "utterly impossible".[91] As a result, settlers in outlying or remoter areas, whether miners or farmers, were not being reached, certainly not regularly.

Itinerant work in the Bulawayo area suffered particularly badly as the two clergy there, unlike the Salisbury clergy, had no resident

---

[89] NAZ, HMss, Misc BE 4/1/1, T.O. Beattie, Reminiscences, f. 1, 4.

[90] 'Archdeacon Foster's Letter. Bulawayo, 25th February, 1912', *RCM* 9:3 (March 1912), 9.

[91] 'Salisbury', *RCM* 8:9 (Sept 1911), 5.

"dignatories" to give them occasional relief: the only dignatory in Bulawayo was the archdeacon who was also the Rector of St. John's.[92] Most of the itinerant work, including work on mines and farms, was done by the railway missioner, who worked off the line until 1918 (when all the missioners reverted to strictly railway work). The areas which he did not cover could only be visited by the Bulawayo clergy very rarely, once in every two to three years, perhaps (Lonely Mine and Queen's in the Inyati area) or once in two to five (Belingwe).

Colonial district work in Salisbury was more regular, as the clergy there could be relieved from Sunday duties by the bishop and the Superintendent of Missions. But even in the Salisbury district, the coming of the railway and the increase in the number of settlers meant that areas difficult of access became neglected. To the north and east of Salisbury, whereas the parson had once visited Mazoe itself, Arcturus and Goromonzi, he was now usually forced to confine his attention to the miners and farmers of Bindura, Shamva, Concession, Tafuna, all of them on the line of rail.

Farmers in the remoter areas were visited very irregularly, if at all, unless they were near the railway. The farming area of Umboe, for example, in the Lomagundi area, seventy miles or so beyond the railhead at Sinoia, saw a parson perhaps once a year. Mount Darwin, over 110 miles of rough track to the north of Salisbury, was visited by clergy only for specific occasions such as farm weddings, at two, three or four-year intervals.

In Beaven's episcopate, the pre-war high point of clergy numbers was reached in 1912, when there were 23 clergy on the staff, yet this was the point when the need to increase staff was "never so sore".[93] Only four new missionaries had joined the staff in the previous eight years (and two of those were completely inexperienced). In colonial work, the Rector of Gwelo was looking after Que Que and Umvuma in addition to Gwelo; there was no priest for the whole of Bechunaland, for the settlements, the railway, the growing 'native' work in and near Francistown and for the school at Plumtree; Victoria rarely saw a parson and the Rector of Bulawayo broke down under the strain of coping with only one other priest to help him.

---

[92] 'Bulawayo', *RCM* 11:10 (Oct 1914), 16.

[93] F.H. Beaven, 'The Annual Meeting [Mashonaland Mission Association]. The Needs of Mashonaland', *MQP* LXXX (May 1912), 19.

The years of World War One and Beaven's enthusiastic support of the war effort (he vigorously encouraged his clergy to volunteer as chaplains) then increased the strain on an already very inadequate staff. Four colonial priests and five of the six lay missionaries then at work in the diocese left for war service in Europe. Five clerical missionaries left for work elsewhere and only three were replaced. Two of the remaining mission priests did spells of several months' duty as chaplains to the forces, in South-West and East Africa.

The clergy who were left and who were usually already doing the work of several men then had additional duties. The priest in charge of Hartley had to add Que Que, for example. The parson at Gwelo, who was already at breaking point with the work there and at Umvuma, undertook Victoria as well. The Archdeacon and Superintendent of Missions had to take entire charge of the Salisbury district mission work in addition to his diocesan duties as his assistant had to be sent to fill a gap elsewhere.

Where missions were run by solitary missionaries (everywhere, with the partial exception of Rusape and Penhalonga) these men carried an increasingly heavy priestly load. At St. David's, Bonda the priest had to care for over 1,000 communicants by 1918 and they were spread out over villages up to 120 miles from the central station and in very rugged terrain. By 1922, communicants numbered 2,400 and there was still only one priest.

Matabeleland was particularly badly off for clergy. Ernest Harker, who became the new Archdeacon of Matabeleland and Rector of Bulawayo in 1912, worked there single-handedly for three years and had had only four months' holiday in nine years by the time he was able to take leave after the war. There had been only two clerical missionaries and one of them was transferred to colonial work because of the shortage of colonial clergy. This left one man, at St. Columba's, to cover the whole of the priestly town and rural work of Matabeleland from 1914 until 1925 (and beyond).

After the war extra clergy were recruited (there were 28 clergy in 1921 and 30 in 1924) but mission congregations continued to grow and colonial settlement was by then spreading to new areas. Even the Victoria area began to prosper, with flourishing asbestos mines and incoming farmers.

The clergy, where they were able, continued to itinerate. The figure of Ernest Parker (at Salisbury, 1904–32) on his bicycle, was already a familiar one throughout that vast district. Ernest ("Pop") Simpson, missionary at Mangwende's (1907–32), his station entirely surrounded by settler farms, became more of an itinerant farmer's padre than a missionary. Beaven himself was an indefatigable traveller. He spent almost his entire episcopate itinerating, travelling thousands of miles around his diocese every year (16,000 miles in 1916), constantly criss-crossing the country, visiting mines and settlements, doing twice-yearly confimations on the major missions, filling gaps for his clergy, opening up new areas.

The shortage of clerical recruits did have one positive effect, in that it hastened the development of an indigenous ordained ministry: when Samuel Muhlanga was ordained in 1919, several other men were in training at Penhalonga. Three of them were ordained deacon when Muhlanga was priested, in 1924; Stephen Hatendi; Gibson Nyabako; and Leonard Sagonda. Peter Sekgoma, a nephew of Khama, was ordained deacon in Matabeleland in the same year. The settler community also produced its first clergyman in the period: Lionel Borrodaile Bell, born in Bulawayo, who had been at university in England (at Oxford) and been ordained priest there in 1922 but returned to work in the diocese (at Plumtree) in 1925.

A handful of local ordinations, however, could hardly begin to counter the effects of a desperate shortage of clergy. One of the new deacons of 1924, Sekgoma, had to be given sole charge at St. Carantoc's, Francistown, an expedient which had been frowned upon as far back as 1895, when Gaul had first arrived in the diocese.

The lack of clergy also resulted in the extension of lay ministry, particularly among indigenous congregations. Originally, as we saw in Chapter One, catechists were recruited in South Africa but St. Augustine's began to send out local men, trained as village teachers, in 1903. There were 149 such teachers working in the diocese in 1918 and 205 by 1924.

These men carried the chief burden of the missionary work of the diocese, as their counterparts did elsewhere in sub-Saharan Africa. They were also, because of the role played by the churches in indigenous education in Southern Rhodesia, responsible to a far greater degree than catechists elsewhere for the education of their people.[94] In the Salisbury district after 1905, for example, two or three congregations in

[94] Bengt Sundkler and Christopher Steed, *A History of the Church in Africa* (Cambridge: Cambridge University Press, 2000), 803.

the care of teachers grew up at Hunyani, Seki's and Shiota. In 1914, there were 8 such congregations or out-stations in the Salisbury area and by 1923 there were 29.

Matabeleland, in this as in other respects remained weak, largely because until the end of the period, when St. Patrick's was founded in the reserve near Gwelo (1925) (see, above, p. 111), there was no equivalent of St. Augustine's to produce the teachers who were constantly asked for but to no avail.

The shortage of clergy also resulted in some extension of lay ministry among settlers. Earlier, as we saw in Chapter Two, settler laymen, particularly officials or military men, had been accustomed to read the services in the absence of the clergy. Now several such men (there were 13 lay-readers by 1918) were licensed to take regular services and do some pastoral work. Their ministry could be very vigorous: at Sinoia, Harry Keigwin, magistrate and Native Commissioner, built and looked after not only a settler but also a mission church. The lay ministry of the period could also have severe limitations: in 1917, Thomas Beattie, Rector of Gwelo, returned from itinerating in the district to find that in his absence an infant of Christian parents had died without baptism, an adult Christian been buried without a funeral service.

Most settlers in the out-districts (and fully half the settler population lived outside the main settlements by 1911) showed a similar reluctance to take responsibility even for ordinary worship. If a clergyman were present, they would support him, often enthusiastically: in 1913 for instance, farmers in the Nyamandhlovu district, Matabeleland, came from 34 miles around for a service taken by the railway missioner. Some walked 20 miles to get there. Yet, without a parson, settlers might meet regularly for tennis but rarely for worship.

They were in this, however, not unusual: as we have seen earlier (Chapter Two, p. 69) in England, in this period, 'the parson' was 'the Church'. Anglicans world-wide and particularly new immigrants, tended to be "extraordinarily sacerdotal",[95] to wait for a clergyman to arrive, rather than take an initiative in church matters themselves. In the CPSA this "preference for the ordained ministry" was said to be "far more pronounced" than elsewhere, the people particularly unwilling to offer

[95] William Carter, Bishop of Pretoria, *Official Report of the Pan-Anglican Congress*, VI, (London: S.P.C.K., 1908), 33; cf. H.St.J. Woollcombe, *Beneath the Southern Cross: being the impressions gained on a tour through Australasia and South Africa on behalf of the Church of England Men's Society* (London: Longmans and Co., 1913), 125–6, 130.

or accept lay ministry.[96] No commentator appears to have attributed this unwillingness to the fact that the CPSA was a High Church or Anglo-Catholic stronghold and that a discouragingly elevated doctrine of priesthood, or the parson's role, prevailed.[97]

Beaven retired from the bishopric of Southern Rhodesia to an English parish in early 1925, at the age of seventy. He was succeeded by another Englishman who had been working for some years, very successfully, on the Rand: Edward Francis Paget, an Oxford man, son of one English bishop and nephew of another. He, on arrival in the diocese, promptly offended settler sensibilities by threatening to be enthroned in St. Michael's, the mission church in Salisbury, unless indigenous representatives were invited to the ceremony in the cathedral.[98] In Paget's election to the bishopric the pendulum had swung again.

He was to be the dominant ecclesiastical figure of the area for the next 30 years, finally retiring as Archbishop of a new Province of Central Africa in 1957. In 1925, however, Paget toured his diocese after his enthronement as his predecessors had done and came to the conclusion, like them, that a great increase in staff and a vast increase in income were needed. He then, like each previous bishop, turned to England in search of them.

[96] Ven. A.B. Sidwell, Archdeacon of Pretoria, Bishop-Elect of George, 'The Work of the Church among the White Settlers of South Africa', *Official Report of the Pan-Anglican Congress*, VI, (London: S.P.C.K., 1908), S.E.1(c), 4.

[97] Wilkinson, *The Community of the Resurrection*, 98.

[98] Geoffrey Gibbon, *Paget of Rhodesia: A Memoir of Edward, 5th Bishop of Mashonaland* (Johannesburg: Africana Book Society (Pty.) Ltd., 1973), 29–30.

CHAPTER FOUR

FINANCE IN CONTEXT: MASHONALAND/SOUTHERN RHODESIA AND THE EXPANSION ABROAD OF THE 'ENGLISH CHURCH'

I *The Background*

We have seen in the previous chapters that one of the most serious hindrances to the development of the Diocese of Mashonaland/SR, between 1891 and 1925, was a lack of money. We have also seen that successive bishops looked to England to remedy this deficiency and that they did so with limited and varying success. If this failure to find support on the scale desired and the persistence with which it was sought nevertheless are to be understood, they have to be seen in a larger context. They are therefore examined here against the background of recent history and contemporary developments in both the mother church, the Church of England and also in other extensions of the church overseas.[1]

The Church of England, in the course of the nineteenth century, had experienced comprehensive reform and revival. A drastic overhaul of the institution was begun by Parliament in the 1830s. Within the church itself, religious movements such as the Evangelical and the Tractarian and Oxford Movements had led to a resurgence of religious fervour and understanding. Changed circumstances were then encountered towards the turn of the century, particularly where the clergy were concerned and these will be examined in the next chapter. The church considered as a whole, however, remained a very large and vigorous institution and the afterglow of the Victorian revival finally died out only in the trenches of World War One.

The history of the church abroad on the other hand, both within and outside the British Empire, was more uniform: a considerable and rapid expansion began in the mid-to-late nineteenth century and continued until well after the period of this study. The extension of the CPSA

[1] The Protestant Episcopal Church of America is excluded from this study, as being wholly independent of the Church of England.

into Central Southern Africa, which resulted in the formation of the Diocese of Mashonaland/SR, was therefore not something isolated but part of a much greater and world-wide movement.

The movement had two main engines. The first was an increased enthusiasm for missionary enterprise which followed the Victorian revival of religion: from the 1860s 'missions to the heathen', or 'foreign missions', multiplied markedly both within and outside the British Empire. At the same time as Knight-Bruce was exploring the possibilities of Mashonaland, for example, four other Anglican missionary bishoprics were being planned, for Corea (Korea) (1889); Lebombo, in Portuguese East Africa (1893); New Guinea (mission 1891, bishopric 1898); and Chota Nagpur (1892), the first missionary bishopric in India. These five dioceses, moreover, were not the only new missionary jurisdictions in immediate prospect for the church abroad: another Indian missionary bishopric, Tinnevelly and Madura (1896) soon followed, as did three new Japanese dioceses.

Ecclesiastical expansion also took place in response to a great increase in national activity overseas. We have seen, in Chapter One, that national activity was a secondary cause operating in Mashonaland: the foundation of the diocese followed the BSA Company's advance of 1890. The occupation of Mashonaland, however, was only one aspect of the Scramble for Africa and British expansion in Africa itself part of a greater, world-wide, territorial extension of the empire. British trade and influence abroad also increased greatly and large-scale immigration took place within the Empire, from Britain to existing colonies of white settlement. Bishoprics were therefore created for new territories brought under the British flag such as Bloemfontein in 1863 or Damaraland (South-West Africa, now Namibia) in 1924. Bishops were appointed for British communities in foreign lands: in South America, the jurisdictions of the Falkland Islands (1869) and Argentina (1910). New sees multiplied in Australia and Canada: there were 9 Canadian dioceses in 1870 and 22 in 1900; 10 in Australia in 1870 and 21 by 1909.

The pace of this ecclesiastical expansion increased significantly as the end of the nineteenth century approached. When Mashonaland/SR was created in 1891 it became one of 82 colonial and missionary dioceses of the English or Anglican Church abroad. Ten years later, in 1901, there were 101 overseas bishoprics; by 1914, 122; and by 1930, 135. Mashonaland/SR was thus only one of fifty-three new dioceses founded between 1891 and 1930 and one of forty founded between

1891 and 1914 alone. In Southern Africa, there had been one bishopric in 1847 and there were 14 in 1924.

II *Financing expansion*

The rapid growth of the church overseas was a matter for gratification and gratitude at home. Nowhere in the religious revival of the nineteenth century, it was said (in 1897), had the church "shown more vitality than in the Colonies and Missions"[2] but the particularly rapid expansion which began in the late nineteenth century created formidable difficulties, both for the Church of England and for her extensions. Expansion had to be financed and the Bishops of Mashonaland/SR were not alone in looking to England for support.

There was no help to be found from the state although the earliest overseas bishoprics had been founded and paid for by the state. In the course of the nineteenth century, however, a general dis-entanglement of church from state had taken place in the Empire. Only (partly) in India and in Barbados did establishment remain.

It was also not easy to procure help from the mother church, for the Church of England was a highly de-centralised institution and there was no one body to which overseas dioceses could appeal, bar a (voluntary) fund begun in 1841 for the endowment of overseas bishoprics, the Colonial Bishoprics Fund. Central, representative organisations for the Church of England were only created towards the end of the period covered by this study and then partly as a result of pressures exerted by the overseas church, which are considered below. In the late nineteenth century, however, support of the church abroad was the preserve of voluntary societies, which raised their own funds, administered their own affairs and were organised on party lines. The church party to which an overseas mission or bishopric belonged was therefore the first determinant of the support it was able to find in England.

Party also decided the extent of the support which could be found. Missions of the Evangelical party enjoyed generous funding, so generous in fact that they (and kindred Nonconformist missions) were drawing stinging criticisms even from within missionary circles themselves by

[2] 'Notes of the Month: The Queen's 60th Anniversary Celebrations', *MF* XLII:499 (July 1897), 272.

the 1890's, for the luxury and comfort in which many workers were said to live in the field. The "modern professional missionary", the man who became a "Sahib", "with his punkah and his bungalow and his pony carriage" was attacked for his failure to make converts and the expense of maintaining him in the field: these men, it was charged, were simply "costly encumbrances" to missions.[3]

Work carried out by others, however, particularly those in association with the largest of the non-Evangelical societies, the Society for the Propagation of the Gospel in Foreign Parts (SPG), was more often than not described as "precarious"[4] or "starved,[5] a far cry from the well-supplied missions of the Evangelical camp. A typical (Evangelical) Church Missionary Society party to the Sudan included three clergymen, one medical man, an agriculturist and a carpenter.[6] In 1905, in Mashonaland, a clergyman was fortunate if he had the assistance of even one lay missionary.

There were several reasons for this disparity of provision. In the first place, the Evangelical societies were able to raise large amounts of money in England because support of missions was part and parcel of Evangelical self-understanding: the missionary enthusiasm which became so marked in Britain in the late nineteenth century was largely an Evangelical phenomenon.

The way in which Evangelical societies were organised and administered also contributed to their success. Expansion was carefully controlled: the work of the largest of the Evangelical Societies, the CMS, for instance, was directed from London. Even bishops connected with the CMS could be subject to a considerable degree of control from laymen on the central committee at home. Evangelical societies, moreover, with one exception (The Colonial and Continental Church Society) confined their energies to 'missions to the heathen' and did not engage in colonial work.

The SPG, however, as the largest and the oldest of all the English missionary societies (founded 1701), already had very wide responsibilities abroad when the rapid expansion of the late nineteenth century

[3] Isaac Taylor, 'The Great Missionary Failure', *Fortnightly Review* 44:CCLXII (Oct 1888), 488–500.

[4] E.J. Palmer, Bishop of Bombay, JCMA *30* (April 1909), 9.

[5] H.H. Montgomery, Secretary of the SPG, JCMA *32* (April 1910), 10.

[6] H.C. Jackson, *Pastor on the Nile: Being some account of The Life and Letters of Llewellyn H. Gwynne, C.M.G., C.B.E., D.D., LL.D., Formerly Bishop in the Sudan and Deputy Chaplain-General in France in the First World War* (London: S.P.C.K., 1960), 74.

began: while CMS was connected with work in some 20 or so dioceses, the SPG was currently involved in more than 50.

The SPG, moreover, though founded to minister to colonists, had engaged in missionary work since its foundation. The world-wide expansion of both types of work which occurred in the late nineteenth century, therefore faced the society with a constant dilemma: "When new lands open the Society is called upon to enter: it cannot refuse even though wisdom dictates abstention".[7]

The SPG, unlike the CMS, found it difficult to limit local initiatives from London for the society held to a high doctrine of episcopacy and resolutely eschewed any attempt to exert control where a bishop held authority. It was powerless in 1900, for instance, to prevent Gaul embarking on new missions at Bembezi and Wreningham and then appealing to the society for extra funds to support them.

The late-nineteenth century SPG, however, was unable to raise sufficient money to meet its ever-increasing obligations. Few members of the Church of England were interested in the colonial church[8] and, outside Evangelical circles, interest in 'missions to the heathen' or 'foreign missions' was at a "very low ebb", as the Archbishop of Canterbury, E.W. Benson, pointed out in 1888.[9] Ten years later, in 1898, the vast majority of laymen were still giving "small support to missions—at home or abroad".[10]

Support of the SPG was also affected by party battles within the Church. Traditionally, the society had been supported by those of 'moderate' or 'non-party' views and by the High Church party but as the end of the nineteenth century approached the moderates become alienated, as the influence of the extreme High Church, or Anglo-Catholic, party grew. As a result the SPG, though its responsibilities abroad were about twice those of the CMS, was only able to raise an income which was less than half that of its rival: in 1897, the income of the General Fund of the SPG was £80,000 and that of the CMS was well over £200,000. How, the SPG asked, was it possible to evangelise the world on £80,000 a year?[11]

---

[7] 'Report, Annual Meeting [SPG], May 5th, 1898', *MF* XLIII:510 (June 1898), 217.

[8] C.O.L. Riley, Bishop of Perth, *CCR* (1897), 231.

[9] CE/GS/RC, UBM/BD/1, Minutes of the Board of Canterbury Province from 4th July 1887–16th May 1895, July 23rd, 1888, *Printed report*, 1.

[10] *Church Times* (June 17th, 1898), 685.

[11] Editorial: 'The Year 1897', *MF* XLIII:505 (Jan 1898), 3.

The hey-day of the SPG, however, was just beginning, for as the Anglo-Catholic party rose in importance and numbers in the Church of England, the fortunes of the SPG revived with it. The missionary fervour of the Anglo-Catholics nevertheless never matched that of the Evangelicals as, like their predecessors in the Tractarian and Oxford Movements, they were largely absorbed by matters (and party battles) at home.

It was not until just before World War One that a greater awareness of the needs of the church abroad began to arise in Anglo-Catholic circles[12] and even then active missionary work, and so active support of missions, was left very largely to the new religious orders which had been formed in the wake of the Oxford Movement (approximately half of the members of the English religious communities were stationed abroad in the early 1920's).

There were not many of these orders, however, and they were principally concerned to raise money for their own work abroad rather than for the general fund of the SPG. When the Community of the Resurrection (Mirfield) took charge of St. Augustine's, Penhalonga in 1915, for example, they made their own, entirely separate appeals for funds, even though they received grants from the diocese and so from the SPG. Most of the Anglo-Catholic missions had a limited success in raising funds, for by the mid-1920's they were all said to be in a distressingly "starved condition".[13]

In missionary theory, new branches of the church overseas were expected to become independent. The CMS encouraged its missions to become "self-supporting, self-governing and self-extending".[14] The SPG similarly, from its formation, "had adopted the principle that there should be no pampering" of the overseas church[15] and believed that the "surer way of spreading the Gospel to the uttermost parts of the earth" was by building up local colonial churches as missionary centres.[16]

---

[12] F.L. Cross, *Darwell Stone: Churchman and Counsellor* (Westminster: Dacre Press, 1949), 20.

[13] *C.R.: Chronicle of the Community of the Resurrection*, 91 (Michaelmas 1925), 13.

[14] Gordon Hewitt, *The Problems of Success: A History of the Church Missionary Society 1910–1942: Volume II, Asia, Overseas Partners (1972)* (London: SCM Press Ltd.), 420.

[15] Rev. Leonard Dawes, SPG, *CCR* (1897), 231.

[16] C.F. Pascoe, *Two Hundred Years of the SPG: An historical account of the Society 1701–1900: Based on a digest of the Society's Records* (London: Published at the Society's Office, 1901), ix.

A breakdown of these theories against the facts was observable world-wide in the late nineteenth century. In Southern Africa, the northward extension of the CPSA into Mashonaland in 1891 and a similar extension eastwards into Portuguese territory (the Diocese of Lebombo, 1893) should have been financed by the CPSA itself, as the SPG pointed out in 1894. If the responsibility could be seen as a shared one, then South Africa's was the larger share.[17] We have seen in Chapter One, however, that the Mashonaland venture only took place because a small annual grant was made by the SPG. The same was true of extension into Lebombo. No help was given to either diocese by the CPSA until 1915, when an attempt was made to raise money to help impoverished Lebombo meet its missionary responsibilities and also to extend the CPSA further, into South-West Africa. Mashonaland/SR, itself a "poor relation" of the other dioceses,[18] was then asked to contribute to the support of these two ventures.

Central funds of any kind were not easy to raise in the CPSA, however, for the majority of the dioceses were struggling financially and faced with pressures for internal expansion similar to those experienced in Mashonaland/SR. And, as in Mashonaland/SR, settler prejudice against missions meant that difficulty was experienced throughout the province in raising money for such work. The CPSA, throughout the period 1890–1925 and well beyond, remained heavily dependent on the support of the SPG: the society's grants were the "life-blood" of the Province.[19]

Varying degrees of dependence could be seen elsewhere. The Canadian church, after the turn of the century, faced the challenge of rapid and enormous immigration into the prairies and was unable to extend to meet it. Australia turned to England for help with widely-scattered immigrants in the 1930's. In other areas, mass movements towards Christianity, as occurred in parts of India in 1913 or Lebombo in 1924, flooded missions with converts. Dependence inevitably continued: in 1931, 104 out of the 146 overseas dioceses were still in need of some degree of help from societies in England.

---

[17] SPG, [Annual] *Report* [for 1894] (1 May 1895), 23.

[18] RHO/USPG, D Series, 217, 1912, J.H. Upcher, (enclosure) in Frederic H. Mashonaland to Bishop Montgomery, 21st September, 1912.

[19] *Official Report of the Tenth Provincial Missionary Conference of the Church of the Province of South Africa, Holden at Port Elizabeth October 25th–28th 1933* (Johannesburg: Imprinted at the C.R. Press, Rosettenville, 1933), 8.

From the late nineteenth century onwards, therefore, appeals for aid were received, by the SPG in particular, from increasing numbers of dioceses all over the world and the effect was "overwhelming", as an editorial in *The Mission Field*, an organ of the SPG, pointed out:

> In its colonial work... the Church has to deal with colonisation proceeding at a rate surpassing all previous experience. Formerly even the quickest rush to the colonies presented no such problem: it was easy for the Church to keep pace with it. Now railways traverse uninhabited prairies in the Dominion of Canada, a year or two sees thousands of square miles not occupied but sparsely dotted over with the settlers. How is the Church to follow them? She tries but the effort is one of incalculable difficulty.
>
> In Africa huge districts, till the other day hardly known, are annexed to the Empire. They are occupied, not as several of our earlier colonies were by the poorer members of the English race moving forward by degrees but by rich companies who are able to advance as fast as human ingenuity and enterprise backed by capital can press forward. And on the Missionary side, who can fail to be touched by the often recurring message of the willingness of the heathen to receive many more teachers than we can send?[20]

III *Reform of the SPG, an increase of interest in missions, special funds*

The truth was, however, that when the rapid expansion of the church overseas began in the late nineteenth century the SPG was ill-equipped to respond to it. The society was dominated by caution and precedent, an "old guard" in control.[21]

The faint interest in the church abroad displayed by many of its members was also of long-standing: missionary work, in particular, had never been widely popular in England, either in church or in country. On the contrary, the first missionary enthusiasts, early in the nineteenth century, had been mocked and ridiculed and not only "by ribald persons of small repute".[22] In the 1860s, missionaries had been described in the House of Lords, as "imposters or fanatics".[23] Missions

---

[20] Editorial: 'The Year 1891', *MF* XXXVII:423 (Jan 1892), 3.

[21] M.M. Montgomery, *Bishop Montgomery, A Memoir* (Westminster: Society for the Propagation of the Gospel in Foreign Parts, 1933), 52.

[22] Sir Harry Johnston, 'Are Our Foreign Missions a Success?', *Fortnightly Review*, 45: CCCXVIII (April 1889), 481.

[23] The Revd. H.W. Tucker, M.A., *Memoir of the Life and Episcopate of George Augustus Selwyn D.D.: Bishop of New Zealand, 1841–1869; Bishop of Lichfield, 1867–1878* (London: William Wells Gardner, 1879), *Volume II*, 305–6.

were still hardly taken seriously outside missionary circles: they were said to be "exceedingly unpopular" at home and abroad, "even among people given to benevolence"[24] and the newspapers were accustomed to sneering at them. After all, as we have seen above, current practice (although not the necessity of missions themselves) was coming under fire in the 1890's within missionary circles themselves.

It was evident to those concerned with the overseas church that of all the needs of the missionary cause, perhaps none was greater than that of a growth in the missionary spirit in England. "One of the crying needs of the Church of England", it was said, was to create at home "a living, practical, effective sympathy with the Church abroad".[25] Even the clergy, it was pointed out, knew very little about the subject (candidates for Holy Orders needed to know no church history after that of the reign of Queen Anne, who died in 1714) and most of them regarded support of missions as being no part of their ordinary work.[26]

A series of initiatives designed to transform public opinion was therefore launched in the late nineteenth century by the supporters of missions. Boards of Missions were formed by the Convocations of Canterbury and York, at first severally, then jointly, to bring together and to publicize within the Church of England the work and interests of the missionary societies and the churches abroad. This was in response to pressure, from some missionary enthusiasts, for central organisations that would not be subject to the rivalry of the party missionary societies and so, it was believed, would engage the interest of the whole church. Diocesan Boards of Missions were set up in the majority of English dioceses. A Missionary Council to represent the interest of the whole church was created when the Church Assembly came into being after World War One.

A major missionary conference was held in London in 1894, by the United Boards of Missions of Canterbury and York, because of "an admitted lack of enthusiasm, and a consequent measure of failure, among Churchmen in the recognition and discharge of the solemn obligation under which the Church is placed, to minister to the Spiritual

---

[24] R.N. Cust, *Notes on Missionary Subjects I* (London: Elliot Stock, 1888), 36.

[25] J.E.C. Welldon [Bishop of Calcutta, 1898–1901], 'An "Imperial Conference" of the Church and its Significance', *The Nineteenth Century and After*, LXII:376 (June 1908), 900.

[26] Rev. L.F. Crawford, JCMA *29* (Nov 1908), 16; Sir Arthur Hirzel, *The Church, the Empire and the World: Addresses on the Work of the Church Abroad* (London: S.P.C.K., 1919), 20.

needs of the inhabitants of our Colonies and other British dependencies" and "in the hope of kindling a wider and warmer zeal in this respect".[27] A much larger attempt to inform and rouse consciences was held in 1908, the Pan-Anglican Congress, masterminded by a new and energetic Secretary of the SPG, involving delegates from every branch of the overseas church and intended "to open a fresh, concerted, statesmanlike advance all along the Church's line".[28]

Missionary literature was improved. A journal was begun for the open discussion of missionary problems and to encourage a "wider outlook".[29] Serious studies of missionary work were published, of a type hitherto produced only in America and Germany.

The missionary societies also widened their scope and appeal. Associations for children were begun and the august SPG unbent, ceased to rely exclusively on the "guineas of the clergy and the pence of the poor"[30] and began to welcome the shillings of women and laymen of small means, as the CMS had long done. Missionary study circles were begun and associations formed to promote interest in missions. Missionary exhibitions were held, and even 'missionary missions'.

It was observed that interest in missions within the Church of England widened and grew from the 1890's, no doubt partly as a result of these efforts. By 1901, it was said, there existed "in some quarters a more pacified feeling"[31] towards them. They were beginning to receive their proper degree of attention in the Church and among the clergy. A new Evangelical revival also crossed and re-crossed the Atlantic and affected the universities in particular (which had been earlier dead to mission). By 1909, missionary enthusiasm in the 'home' church had reached unprecedented levels.

Missionaries were also being publicly defended by many officials and others who travelled abroad[32] and even in government circles at home, a more positive attitude was developing. At the beginning of the

---

[27] Preface, *CEYB* (1895), v.

[28] Louisa Creighton, 'Ministry of Women: Its relation at the present time to work done by men', in *Official Report of the Pan-Anglican Congress*, IV (London: S.P.C.K., 1908), S.C.iii(a) I, 7.

[29] [Editorial note], 'Our Tenth Year', *East and the West, A Quarterly Review for the Study of Missions*, X (Jan 1912), 93.

[30] 'Notes of the Month', *MF* XXXII:CCCLXIV (March 1887), 90.

[31] E.T. Churton, Bishop of Nassau, *Foreign Missions* (London: Longmans, Green, 1901), 1–2.

[32] CE/CBM, *The Foreign Missions of the Church, First Annual Review* (London, 1908), 62–4; Johnston, 'Are Our Foreign Missions a Success?', 481–6; C.I.E. Scott Moncrieff,

modern missionary enterprise, governments had thrown "all manner of official obstacles...in the way of the troublesome missionaries"[33] and by the end of the nineteenth century there was still considerable ambivalence towards them in government circles. Lord Salisbury, for instance, a good churchman, was hesitant about the value of missions, "as possibly a perplexity" to the British government (and this at the Bi-Centenary celebrations of the SPG in 1901).[34]

The beginning of a change of attitude was already discernible nevertheless and by the 1920s, while the value of missions to governments could still be called into question,[35] within the Empire they had largely proved their worth, chiefly by extensive co-operation with governments in the provision of education and medical care. We have seen, in earlier chapters, the growth of support for missions by the BSA Company in Mashonaland/SR and the co-operation of church and administration in the field of education.

By the outbreak of World War One it was evident that the missionary cause was beginning to gain recognition in the home church and the impetus was not lost. The cause was taken up again with fervour immediately after the war. In the mid-1920's, a collection of reports covering the needs of every part of the church overseas was produced by the Missionary Council and presented with much publicity to the whole church. These reports were hailed as the first official (or corporate) recognition by the Church of England of her responsibilities to her extensions abroad:[36] the series was called "The World Call to the Church", and the call came from every quarter, from India, from Africa, 'The Far East', and from 'Moslem Lands'.

The growth of interest in the church overseas resulted in a substantial increase in financial support: contributions from parishes for missions rose by 56% between 1899 and 1929; contributions by individuals direct to the missionary bodies grew by something like 62% in the

---

Eastern Missions from a Soldier's Standpoint (London: The Religious Tract Society, 1907), 11–5.

[33] C.F. Gordon-Cumming, *The Last Commandment: A word to every Christian* (London, [Church Missionary Society], 1887), 4.

[34] H.H. Montgomery, *The Spirit of the SPG* (London: S.P.C.K., 1929), 19.

[35] A.N. Porter, 'Religion and Empire: British Expansion in the Long Nineteenth Century', *JICH* XX:3 (1992), 373–4.

[36] G.A. Gollock, comp. *In the Year of the World Call* (London: Overseas Council [Church of England], 1927), 3.

same period. In 1881, £350,000 had been raised for missions in the Church of England. In 1920, £975,000 was raised.

The difficulty, however, was that even this increase in income at home did not suffice to meet the needs of a rapidly expanding church abroad and the primary problem of missionary finance therefore remained what it had always been outside the Evangelical camp: money raised at home was never adequate to meet the needs of the church abroad. The income of the SPG, for example, may have doubled between 1901 and 1927 but so did expenditure.

Even Evangelical missions began to feel the draught. Between 1880 and 1911, the CMS was able to finance rapid expansion. The fortunes of the Evangelical party, however, had begun to wane after the turn of the century, as those of the Anglo-Catholic party rose and by 1911 the CMS, while reporting its largest annual income ever, was forced to retrench and suspend the sending out of new missionaries. In 1926, the CMS was operating in deficit.

Since any increase in the income of the main missionary societies at home was rapidly outstripped by a growth in the needs of the church abroad, the practical results of increased enthusiasm over the period 1890–1930 were minimal for the majority of the extensions of the church overseas. As a result, the overseas bishops and particularly those in association with the SPG were driven to make their own individual appeals for support in England.

The SPG disapproved of this fundraising, believing that it drew funds away from the society itself but was powerless to prevent it. The bishops defended their actions, out of need and also in the belief that they attracted support from people who would not normally give to missions. One of the Knight-Bruce's first initiatives, as the new Bishop of Mashonaland, was to form a diocesan association (or 'home society') to raise funds in England, particularly from people who might have an interest in the area but no general interest in missions.[37]

Diocesan associations had by then been in existence for more than half a century (the first was formed for the new diocese of Capetown in 1847). Among the problems created by increased ecclesiastical activity abroad in the late nineteenth century, however, was the fact that

[37] RHO/USPG, D Series, 114, 1895, Mrs L. Knight-Bruce to Mr Tucker, December 7th, 1895.

the very increase in activity could itself hinder fund raising: so many appeals, from dioceses and individual missions, began to reach the home church from all over the world that complaints began to be made of their bewildering multiplication and the "distraction and despair" this engendered.[38] There were 70 individual societies known to the SPG in 1857 and 335 by 1881. Twice the experiment was tried of having a full or part-time clerical secretary of the Mashonaland Missionary Association, in 1892 and 1912–3, in the belief that this would produce a larger income for the diocese. Neither was able to generate much support.

This difficult situation was made worse by the fact that many other good causes were also making public appeals for support. The nineteenth century had seen a great awakening of the corporate social and religious conscience of England and philanthropic societies to address home problems had proliferated. The result was an intense competition for funds and since home needs were both pressing and well-publicised, home societies were usually able to elicit more support than the missionary societies or churches abroad, a contemporary growth in missionary enthusiasm notwithstanding. The annual income of a home society could equal or even exceed the income of one of the great missionary societies itself, let alone that of an overseas diocese. By 1894, for instance, Dr. Barnado's Homes were receiving some £150,000 a year, whereas, as we have seen above, the income of the SPG's general fund in 1897 was just over £80,000.

The success of a specific diocesan or mission association could also depend upon its being able to find suitable person to lead its appeals. The chairman of the British Columbia and Yukon Association between 1910 and 1926 was Arthur Foley Winnington-Ingram, an immensely popular and long-serving Bishop of London (1902–1939). To his energy and charm was attributed much of the success of the association in raising an average of £15,000 a year while he held office.[39]

Most associations, however, raised very much less: the Mashonaland/SR Mission Association only raised £800 to £1,000 per year between 1892 and 1926 (when the association merged with the home societies of two other South African dioceses). The bishops of the diocese, like

[38] W/CPSA, AB/1162A, 24, Archbishop of Capetown to Bishop of Grahamstown, September 1st, 1902, ff. 61–2.

[39] S.C. Carpenter, *Winnington-Ingram* (London: Hodder and Stoughton, 1949), 99, 262, 265, 315.

many overseas bishops, were unable to attract much personal support in England or to find well-placed friends to act for them.

Only Knight-Bruce had many wealthy or influential connections. The first chairman of the Mashonaland Mission Association, for example, was Mandell Creighton, one of the leading figures of the Church of England and bishop, first of Peterborough and then of London. He had been Knight-Bruce's tutor at Oxford. Creighton died, however, in 1901. He was succeeded as chairman by suffragan bishops of Northern dioceses: the Bishop of Derby, then Stafford; and the Bishop of Hull.[40]

Even during Knight-Bruce's episcopate, moreover, he (and his immediate family) had to find the bulk of financial support for the diocese, as we saw in Chapter One, for the existence of an association did not normally spare an overseas bishop from the burden of being his own chief fundraiser. Every few years he had to travel 'home' and make an exhausting tour: in 1925, for example, the new Bishop of Kaffraria, E.H. Etheridge, on a tour of Scotland, had 90 services, addresses and speeches in 64 days.[41] Without such personal contact with the nebishop, supporters tended to lose interest and funds began to dwindle. Bishops of Mashonaland/SR found it necessary to visit England in 1891–3, 1896, 1904, 1910, 1912, 1923, 1924 and 1925. Knight-Bruce was not the only overseas bishop to spend a year or more fund-raising and looking for staff: E.F. Every, the Bishop of the Falkland Islands, spent the whole of 1911 in England, in a largely unsuccessful attempt to garner support.[42]

IV *Protest against underfunding*

This system, which sent bishops abroad and then abandoned them, began to produce an ever-louder chorus of protest from the overseas bishops and their friends. Anxiety about finance was said to be so acute as to endanger the lives of the bishops[43] and their resignation or breakdown became all too common. We have seen, in earlier chapters, the burden laid upon the Bishops of Mashonaland/SR by inadequate funding.

[40] Edward Ash Were, Bishop of Derby (1889), Bishop of Stafford (1909); Francis Gurdon, Bishop of Hull (1913).

[41] 'Editorial', *RCM* 22:6 (June 1925), 3.

[42] *Guardian* (August 16th, 1912), 1061.

[43] W/CPSA AB/1162A, 24, H.H. Montgomery, Hon. Sec. Colonial Bishoprics Fund, to Archbishop of Capetown, June 1st, 1904, f. 420(1).

The custom of beginning new dioceses without an income other than that of the bishop had been criticised since the mid-nineteenth century: by 1906, it was described by the secretary of the Colonial Bishoprics Fund as "almost a crime".[44] Reproaches, often anguished and bitter, began to be sent back to the home church from men with dioceses and responsibilities as widely separated as Labuan (Borneo) and the Falkland Islands, from Japan, from Mashonaland/SR.[45]

Critics declared that Church of England ought to make some adequate provision for the future working of a new diocese, not just "block off a huge area" on the map and leave a bishop "marooned" there.[46] As things now stood, there the matter ended for the church and trouble began for the unfortunate bishop. Supporters protested: it was "cruel" to send out a bishop to "the firing line" and then desert him.[47]

Such accusations of dereliction of duty by the 'home' church were not entirely new. One of the earliest public denunciations of the Church of England's failure to support work abroad adequately had been made in the 1850s, when the first Bishop of New Zealand, George Augustus Selwyn, re-visited England and administered "the most terrible" rebuke to his fellow-countrymen for their neglect of the wider church.[48] As the pressures upon them intensified, Selwyn's successors in the foreign field became increasingly vocal.

They and their supporters inveighed vigorously, trenchantly, against the failure of the home church to support her extensions adequately. The Church of England was charged with "spiritual apathy",[49] with "indifference and neglect",[50] with "slackness"[51] and "coldness"[52] towards

[44] *Ibid.*

[45] LPL, Davidson, 425, Memo from Bishop of Labuan and Sarawak to Summer Meeting of CBM, June 1912, f. 98; *Guardian* (August 16, 1912), 1061; CE/GS/RC, UBM/BD/1, Minutes of the Board of Canterbury Province from 4th July 1887–16th May 1895, June 20th, 1893, f. 52.

[46] LPL, H5691.S7, Preliminary Expedition, Mission of Help to South Africa, *Report* (Private and Confidential) (1903), f. 14.

[47] The Archdeacon of Stow (the Ven. J. Wakeford), 'The Church in Mashonaland', *MQP* LXXXVIII (May 1914), 22.

[48] S.C. Carpenter, *Church and People, 1798–1889: A History of the Church of England from William Wilberforce to "Lux Mundi"* (London: Society for Promoting Christian Knowledge, 1933), 440.

[49] Bernard Wilson, 'The Church and the Empire', in Herbert Hensley Henson, *Church Problems: A View of Modern Anglicanism: By various authors* (London: J. Murray, 1900), 374.

[50] Preface, *CEYB* (1901), vii.

[51] CE/CBM, *Third Annual Review of the Foreign Missions of the Church* (London: 1910), 82.

[52] Churton, *Foreign Missions*, 2.

the church abroad. She was said to be unconcerned about the colonial church and her neglect of her emigrants was declared "scandalous".[53] The "want of sympathy" with missionary work in England was harder to bear than the dangers and difficulties of the work itself, said Knight-Bruce.[54] The chief "hindrance" to the success of foreign missions was the lack of interest in them in England.[55] Great possibilities lay before the colonial church, which could not be taken up because of the "supineness" of the church at home.[56]

To such critics, the mother church seemed to be self-absorbed and preoccupied with trivia (battles over ritual, for instance) as the Bishop of London pointed out in 1907: "The Missionary and Colonial Bishops who often stay with me from different parts of the world are pained and astonished beyond measure at finding the Home Church convulsed over the colour of a garment or the use or non-use of some help to worship, and so little interested in the conversion of the world".[57]

At the Lambeth Conference of 1897, foreign bishops were blunt: the Church as a whole had failed "to realise her bounden duty to be the great Missionary Society of the world".[58] The portion of the Lambeth Encyclical dealing with "the Duties of the Church to the Colonies" made much the same point, although the language was more restrained. "The colonists are our own kin, and we cannot leave them to drift away from the Church of their fathers... Our duties to the Colonies in all spiritual matters are undeniably heavy."[59]

Bishops were joined by Archbishops. In 1897, a disciple of Selwyn's, Frederick Temple, then Archbishop of Canterbury, made a passionate indictment of the Church of England in a sermon at the dismissal service of the Lambeth Conference: it was time for the church to awake, he said. The duty of spreading the gospel "had been taken up

---

[53] W.T. Thornhill Webber, Bishop of Brisbane, *CCR* (1897), 229.

[54] 'Notes of the Month', *MF* XXXVIII:440 (Aug 1892), 313.

[55] Editorial: 'Missionary Encouragements', *The Net, Cast in Many Waters*, 30:1 (January 1895), 1.

[56] RHL/USPG, X1002, H.H. Montgomery, Bishop of Tazmania, Federation of JCMAs, Tenth Annual Report (Advent 1904–1905), 16.

[57] [A.F. Winnington-Ingram], *Guardian* (April 24th, 1907), 657.

[58] H. Thomas, comp. *The First Five Lambeth Conferences etc.* (London: S.P.C.K., 1929), 238.

[59] Thomas, *The First Five Lambeth Conferences*, 192–3.

by devoted men, and by associations of devoted men; but as a body the Church had left it quite alone".[60]

The Archbishop not only preached on the subject, he himself wrote the section of the Lambeth Encyclical devoted to the neglect of the Church, as a body, in the matter of missions: and had to moderate it, in deference to the wishes of the conference because it was felt that the strength of his remarks would "greatly grieve the keen supporters of missions without having any useful effect upon such as were negligent".[61] Support of missions should not be left only to the societies, had said Frederick Temple's predecessor, Archbishop Benson, a few years earlier.[62] Missions, said his successor, Randall Davidson, in 1910, should hold the "central place" in the life of the Church and no other.[63]

These loud calls to duty were not sufficient to rouse the church at home, however, for the same assertion had to be made in 1932 as had been made before the turn of the century, that there was a "definite obligation to the missionary work of the Church" resting on all Church people and that it was not "a hobby confined to a few enthusiasts".[64]

The representatives and supporters of the overseas church therefore argued for support on other grounds, such as the well-being of the Church of England herself. Her extensions abroad were a sign of the vitality of the church: if these extensions were prosperous and efficient, they would bestow a "reflex blessing" on the church at home.[65] Successes in the mission field, similarly, resulted in a greater "vigour" at home.[66] It was even suggested that the very existence of the Church of England in the future might depend upon the colonial and foreign churches she had established abroad.[67]

---

[60] E.G. Sandford, ed., *Memoirs of Archbishop Temple, By Seven Friends* (London: Macmillan, 1906) *I*, 55, *II*, 275.
[61] *Ibid.*, *II*, 277.
[62] 'A New Plan for Increasing Interest in Missions', *The Net, Cast in Many Waters*, 30:2 (Feb 1895), 21.
[63] Gordon Hewitt, *The Problems of Success: A History of the Church Missionary Society 1910–1942: Volume I, In Tropical Africa, The Middle East, At Home* (London: SCM Press Ltd., 1971), 412.
[64] CE/CA/MC, *Missionary Finance: Being the report of the Missionary Finance Commission set up by the Missionary Council of the Church Assembly* (London: Overseas Council, 1932), 28.
[65] Thomas, *The First Five Lambeth Conferences*, 280.
[66] B.F. Westcott, Bishop of Durham, 'Notes of the Month', *MF* XXXV:416 (August 1890), 308.
[67] Rev. J.H. Simpson, 'Interest in Foreign Missions', *MF* XXXVI:432 (Dec 1891), 443.

This second argument seems to have made as little headway as the argument from duty, however, for it was as necessary to warn in the 1920s, as in the 1870s, that the continued well-being, both spiritual and material, of the Church of England were dependent on her being unselfish and sharing her wealth of resources with the Church abroad.[68]

A further line of reasoning concerned the inherited wealth of the Church of England. Beaven of Mashonaland pointed out in 1914 that past generations had endowed the church plentifully. It behoved present members of the Church of England, who "benefit[ted] so richly by the generous gifts of pious benefactors", to be liberal to the churches abroad, which were receiving no direct benefits from the endowments of a common past. He also pointed out that the possession of endowments by the Church of England also meant that the offerings of her members, who had no need to contribute to the support of their own church, were "set free" for the support of church expansion.[69]

The overseas churches also emphasized the contrast between their poverty and the comfort enjoyed by the home church. In Mashonaland/SR, the church was living "from hand to mouth",[70] often lacking "bare spiritual necessities", while the Church of England enjoyed every "spiritual necessary and even luxuries".[71] It was noted in 1914, that a wealthy English parish church could spend £1,000 a year on music and £1.3.2 on missions.[72] In 1920, the diocese was hindered from making a particular missionary advance for the want of as little as £12 a year, something the "elder Brethren" at home simply failed to understand.[73]

These two arguments were applied with diminishing effectiveness in the period 1890–1930, as the Church of England herself faced changing circumstances and the need for financial reform. Income from endowments was proving to be no longer adequate and members of the Church of England were having to follow in the footsteps of the members of the church abroad and learn to undertake regular sup-

---

[68] C.R. Sumner, Bishop of Winchester, *Chronicle of Convocation*, Upper House, February 11th, 1870, 153; *Church Times* (September 2nd, 1927), 254.

[69] CE/CBM, Missions Overseas, Seventh Annual Review (London: 1914), 110.

[70] 'Establishment and Endowment', *RCM* 7:5 (May 1910), 7.

[71] 'Letter from Rev. P.E. Knyaston. Church House, April 3rd, 1913, Umtali', *MQP* LXXXIV (May 1913), 8.

[72] 'A Missionary's Groan', *MQP* XC (Nov 1914), 20.

[73] 'Letter from Rev. J.W. Wilson, St. Columba's Mission, Bulawayo, July 14th, 1920', *SRQP* CXIII (Aug 1920), 13.

port of their parishes and dioceses. The clergy, moreover, had always formed the bulk of the non-Evangelical missionary supporters and the increasing poverty of the English clergy from the late nineteenth century was giving rise to serious concern.

Nevertheless, to the struggling churches and missions abroad, the large and continuing disparity in wealth between them and their mother church meant that an argument for generosity, if not for an equitable share of inherited wealth, retained considerable force. Talk of diminished resources at home did not convince. The "income-tax returns, wages, and savings-banks returns of England alone" showed that the money was there and was "available".[74]

Those concerned with the churches and missions abroad also applied to the relations between the church there and the English people at home, a "principle of Christian economy" which was accepted at home, that those who made money from an area, such as the owners of large properties in cities, should contribute to its well-being and "do good" with the wealth so gained.[75]

In the same way, it was stated, "those who belong to great empires and partake of their advantages" were "accountable in full proportion":[76] those who derived their wealth from the empire ought to contribute to the provision and support of the church in the empire. Gaul, addressing a meeting at the Mansion House in 1896, suggested that everyone who was making profits out of Mashonaland should give one tenth of those profits for the work of the church there. The hope had earlier been expressed that the church would receive its "due share" of what was being put into the country for its development.[77]

It was declared that this 'principle of Christian economy' was not being honoured. Certain parts of England, particularly the ports and manufacturing towns, drew their wealth largely from 'the heathen

[74] 'Church Finance in the Colonies and Mission Field. A Paper read at the Swansea Church Congress in October, 1909, by Bishop Gaul. (From the *Guardian*)', *RCM* 6:11 (Nov 1909), 4. Cf. John R. Mott, *The Home Ministry and Modern Missions* (London: Hodder and Stoughton, 1908), 93–99. For a rare dissent from this opinion, see Churton, *Foreign Missions*, 9.

[75] A. Blomfield, ed., *A Memoir of C.J. Blomfield, Bishop of London: edited by his son, A. Blomfield: With Selections from his Correspondence, II* (London: John Murray, 1863), 237.

[76] Churton, *Foreign Missions*, 6.

[77] Bishop of Zululand [W.M. Carter], 'Notes of the Month', *MF* XL:473 (May 1895), 186.

world' yet gave back little in support of missions to the heathen.[78] Elsewhere, as in South America, huge dividends were being earned by British capital, yet nothing proportionate was given back for the spiritual welfare of the British living in the area or for church's mission to the local people.[79]

The Lambeth Conference of 1897 made this point very clearly with regard to the colonial churches:

> While the duty of the whole Church in assisting the colonics financially is... plain... there is one point on which clear and decided teaching should be constantly given at home viz.: the manifest duty of those who derive income from colonial property or securities to contribute to the furtherance of the Church's cause where such property is situate. There are colonies where the church is struggling with difficulties, and yet from which large revenues are drawn by men and women who live in England, and who give their money, if and when they give it, rather to the place where they live than to the supply of spiritual privileges to the toilers who contribute to their fortunes.[80]

The conviction was echoed, time and time again, from those concerned with the church overseas, from Africa, from Australia, from South America. The wealth of the Empire flowed home and therefore the wealth of the church and the people should be shared with the Empire.

Argument was also taken beyond questions of duty, spiritual self-interest, fairness, or generosity to the church abroad. An appeal was made to the financial self-interest of those who drew their wealth from the empire.

It was firmly believed that the prosperity of the empire, like the prosperity of England, depended upon the well-being of the church. At home, churchmen agreed, the country's Christianity was the foundation of her happiness and wealth. Similarly, the "energy" which had "inspired the English nation... to discover the world" sprang from the "sense of freedom" which only Christianity could give[81] and it followed that the English, in going abroad, must carry the English

---

[78] E.A. Knox, *Reminiscences of an Octogenarian 1847–1934* (London: Hutchinson, 1935), 270.

[79] E.F. Every, *The Anglican Church in South America* (London: S.P.C.K., 1915), 154–5.

[80] Thomas, *The First Five Lambeth Conferences*, 279.

[81] RHO/USPG, X1001, Mandell Creighton, Bishop of Peterborough, 'The Church and the Mission Field', London Junior Clergy Missionary Association (in Association with the SPG), Great Evening Meeting, St. Andrew's Eve, 1894, 5.

faith with them if they wished to prosper. The needs of the colonial church might form the higher ground of the argument for support but the lower ground was the continuing prosperity of the empire, upon which wealthy individuals were dependent: "if the Church was not...planted in the colonies, the Empire of England [would] sink", as Gaul put it, in 1896.[82]

It was also declared that there seemed to be a misunderstanding in England about the extent of colonial wealth in Mashonaland/SR, as elsewhere. Because some men returned to England from the colonies rich, the assumption was made that the colonies were rich and that the church there was not in need of support whereas the contrary was, in fact, true: most of the colonies and so the colonial churches were poor because their wealth was almost entirely in the hands of men resident in England. The appeal for help from home was, therefore, "a just and strong one".[83]

In some dioceses abroad, such as Mashonaland/SR, there were "no wealthy benefactors";[84] from Bloemfontein came the plea, "please do not think we are rich";[85] from Goulburn (Australia) "the people are very poor";[86] from Algoma (Canada) "wealthy English Churchmen ought to do more for the Church here" as "our immigrants are of slender means" and "with difficulty exist".[87] In other dioceses, what wealth did not flow back to England was in the hands of men who did not recognise any obligation to the church and so the colonial churches tended to gain little from increasing colonial prosperity. The development of goldfields in Australia, for example, did not enrich the local church.[88] In Southern Africa, most of the capital which produced large incomes was English capital and nearly all the wealthier men of the country left for England and spent their money there. Of those who remained, very few were members of the English Church and many were not Christians, so the church had no claim upon them. The lack

---

[82] 'Some items of the Society's work', *MF* XLI:486 (June 1896), 233.

[83] Bishop of Rockhampton [N. Dawes], *CEYB* (1899), 245.

[84] Bishop of Mashonaland [F.H. Beaven], CE/CBM, *Missions Overseas, Seventh Annual Review* (London: 1914), 110.

[85] Bishop of Bloemfontein [G.W.H. Knight-Bruce], *BQP* 95 (Jan 1892), 54.

[86] Bishop of Goulburn [W. Chalmers], 'Notes of the Month', *MF* XLIII:510 (June 1898), 236.

[87] 'Notes of the Month', *MF* XXXVI:421 (Jan 1891), 37.

[88] Bishop of Adelaide [J.R. Harmer], 'Notes of the Month' *MF* XLI:488 (Aug 1896), 315.

of generosity and piety among the rich of South Africa was clearly revealed, it was said, by the lack of fine churches in the country, the lack of cathedrals.[89]

In Mashonaland/SR, the poverty of the church made it evident that none of the famed Rhodesian wealth went to support its work. The Rector of Bulawayo wrote in 1909, "the poverty of Lazarus is the judgement of Dives. In our case both Diocese and Parish are in want, fed, alas!, only too truly by crumbs from the rich man's plenty. It is sad for Diocese and Parish, it is sadder for those who are making money in this country and will not give their dues to God... Something is much amiss when the country generally is advancing, as all will allow it is, while the Church has to threaten serious retrenchment".[90] The Bulawayo parish was finding it hard to pay the salaries of the clergy and there was no money for even the most necessary repairs to church property.

Clergymen in Mashonaland/SR longed for rich and pious patrons like those they had known in England. They dreamed, of "some kind English millionaire or even a less important person than that"[91] or of "some wealthy person with that imagination and vision which is so often dimmed by worldliness"[92] to give them the money they needed to erect church and mission buildings or save a school from closure. Gaul, begging for more help from the SPG's "cruse of oil" in 1898, apologised for the fact that he needed to do so and would need to continue until "a Pentecost came to Millionaires who take all their money to England to spend it on Deer Forests and Banquets".[93] He also mentioned, with some asperity, people who wrote to him complaining of the spiritual destitution of their relatives but who did not enclose cheques.

It can be safely assumed that, behind some of the wistful statements made about wealthy men and the poverty of the church in Southern Africa, lies a regret that one of the richest and most powerful of South Africa's millionaires, Cecil Rhodes, was no great supporter of the English Church, although he had been born in an English vicarage:

89 'Letter from Canon Bathe, Bulawayo, February 28th, 1898', *MQP* XXIV (May 1898), 9; 'Cathedrals in South Africa' (from *Ch.Ch.*), in *RCM* 7:9 (Sept 1910), 2.

90 [J. Hallward], 'Bulawayo', *RCM* 6:10 (Oct 1909), 10.

91 'Letter from Rev. A.S. Robins, Salisbury, June 22nd, 1901', *MQP* XXXVII (Aug 1901), 12.

92 [J. Hallward], 'Bulawayo', *RCM* 6:10 (Oct 1909), 11.

93 RHO/USPG, D Series, 126(b), 1898, Will. Mashonaland to Mr Tucker, January 17th, 1898.

his remark, that the English Church "never knew its own mind" and so did not interest him, was widely quoted.

Rhodes did give occasional support to the diocese, as we have seen in Chapter One and he would help individuals of whom he approved, such as Gaul or Upcher (he paid for a house to be built for Upcher in Salisbury in 1895, when he found him living in the church vestry, for instance) but in general he preferred organisations he judged more practical and business-like, such as the Salvation Army or the active Roman Catholic orders.[94]

Only in the German Jews Alfred and Otto Beit did Southern Africa produce patrons somewhat on the English model. Both men had a great respect for Gaul and contributed handsomely to the Mashonaland Bishopric Endowment Fund. Alfred Beit rescued the diocese from financial trouble in Gaul's time, as we have seen earlier; Otto contributed smaller sums in Beaven's episcopate, but it was principally in the provisions of Alfred Beit's will, of which Gaul was an executor, that 'the principle of Christian economy' was honoured. Most of the wealth he had gained was poured back into the welfare of Southern Africa, particularly into transport and education

The Beits were exceptions to the general rule. Neither in Africa nor in England did many of the very rich contribute largely either to the missions or the colonial churches and money for Mashonaland/SR as for most work overseas came, as it had always done, largely from "narrow incomes".[95]

The bulk of the fund-raising was done by the families and friends of the bishops and long-serving clergy, chiefly by the women in those families and the amount raised was correspondingly small. Of the wealthy and titled whose names adorned the original council of the Mashonaland Mission Association, including several directors of the BSA Company, none appears to have made other than small contributions to its work.

The directors may have had particular reasons for withholding funds: one of them, Philip Lyttelton Gell, a prominent churchman in England, the son of a parson and something of an authority on church finance, was prepared to make the right noises in public, to commend the idea

---

[94] J.G. Lockhart and C.M. Woodhouse, *Rhodes* (London: Hodder and Stoughton, 1963), 209.

[95] Gollock, *In the Year*, 35.

of supporting the diocese. Privately, however, he was unmoved, as by an appeal for funds from St. John's, Bulawayo, in 1911. He complained about a "deliberate animosity on the part of the clergy" towards the BSA Company and of their practice of communicating with the Imperial government direct, rather than through the local administration. He cited, in his note, the radical missionaries Cripps and Edgar Lloyd but also the more conservative Upcher and Samuel Christelow.[96]

V *Competition for funds, the power of romance*

We have seen that advocates of the overseas church marshalled a considerable array of arguments in their attempts to persuade the Church of England to supply the needs of her extensions. They also made many and detailed suggestions as to how the whole process of fund raising might be reformed. Missionary finance, it was declared, should be central to the life of the Church of England, not something extraneous. Support also needed to be systematically organised and it was frequently suggested that a centralised collection for the support of the overseas Church (such as existed in the Episcopal Church of America, or in Canada and Australia), should replace English haphazardness.

What the overseas church needed was money "without the miserable devices to get it", which grew "more and more prevalent".[97] "I hate this begging business" wrote Edward Paget, the new Bishop of Southern Rhodesia, in 1926.[98]

The Church of England did make moves towards greater centralisation in the period in her own life: most significant of these was the formation of a central governing body, the Church Assembly, subject to Parliament and so with limited powers of self-regulation, after World War One. Attempts were also made to deal with matters affecting the overseas church centrally, as we have seen above (p. 125, ff.). These attempts, however, came up against the complex and de-centralised nature of the Church of England itself and the resistance of the voluntary societies. Even after a Missionary Council was formed by the Church Assembly it could only inform and appeal on behalf of mis-

---

[96] DCA, Gell Collection, BSA Company, Native Taxation and Labour, marked *Private* (draft), P.L. Gell to (?), Middlesex, c. 1911.

[97] 'A New Plan for Increasing Interest in Missions', *The Net, Cast in Many Waters* 30:2 (Feb 1895), 21.

[98] 'The Bishop's Letter, R.M.S. "Kenilworth," At Sea, 8th May, 1926', *SRQP* CXXVI (May 1926), 5.

sions to the members of the Church of England. It had no mandate to raise or distribute funds.

The overseas church was therefore largely left with the existing and unsatisfactory system of rival appeals by missionary societies and associations. One of the worst aspects of this system was that it had no rational basis: the success of an appeal, as we have seen above, could depend on whether it was led by someone who had an attractive personality or wealthy and well-placed friends, rather than upon the actual needs of the church in that area. This was offensive in principle and could have alarming repercussions. If a particular bishop died, retired or moved to another diocese, for example, the support of his friends could disappear or move with him. Knight-Bruce took many of his supporters with him when he left Bloemfontein for Mashonaland. Branches of home associations could also transfer their support elsewhere if they lost their personal connection with an area: the Hampstead branch of the Mashonaland Mission Association transferred its support to British Honduras in 1908, because its vicar had just been appointed bishop there.

Work, at home or abroad, which was considered 'interesting' or, more often, 'romantic' was also more likely to attract volunteers and to gain financial support than work that lacked such appeal. This deeply distressed those who supported missions out of conviction: "interest", said the SPG, was "a mischievous word".[99] Those attempting to attract funds for their work nevertheless had to reckon with this very powerful motive for support, and with its various forms.

In the love of adventure and tales of adventure, for instance, there was a strong link between missionary enthusiasm and modern exploration. David Livingstone was the chief model for African missionary-explorers and inspirer of enthusiasm at home. Elsewhere, the voyages and journeys of colonial and missionary bishops had established a similar episcopal tradition, a tradition summed up exuberantly by an observer at the Pan-Anglican Congress in 'Romance in Gaiters' (1908):

> Strange things were all about us. Strange beings from strange places swarmed round every corner. Their titles stretched our spelling powers to breaking point... They carried about, in their names and in their talk, the fragrance of historic memories that had been to us fabulous, but which they had taken possession of... They had been rocked in bullock-carts:

[99] 'Our Friends and their Demands: A paper on Deputation Work', *MF* XX–VIII:444 (Dec 1892), 443.

> wrecked at sea: half-drowned in floods and fords: all but eaten alive by men and beasts. And here they were: and they were ours... Here was adventure, here was romance.[100]

With romance went hero-worship. Missionary work was "necessarily heroic work"[101] and high endeavour, suffering or death for the faith frequently moved others to offer themselves for service. It was, as one commentator noted in the 1880's, often "easier to fill up vacancies caused by fever in Africa than in our quiet country villages at home".[102] The death in the Sudan in 1885 of General Gordon, an ardent Evangelical with a missionary's zeal, was hailed in the most extravagant of terms and inspired a chain of Evangelical missions and a memorial cathedral in the land where he died.

Gordon was a soldier, not a missionary but to their contemporaries at home missionaries could appear in as noble guise. They seemed to move among the "dark perishing millions" in the "regions beyond" as "heroic men, brethren of a new order of knight errantry, the pioneers of the modern Church".[103] The heroic lives (and occasional martyrdoms) of pioneer bishops were a great stimulus to missionary enthusiasm.

The problem, however, from the point of view of the church, was that workers and support were needed for areas which lacked 'romance' as well as those which possessed it. Interest in certain areas and in types of work also waxed and waned among the missionary-minded public and so work abroad was subject to the "fickleness" of "fashion".[104]

Interest in South Africa, for example, ran high during and immediately after the Second South African War but by 1905 the "African boom" was over and the interest, even of missionary leaders, was shifting to Asia.[105] The World Missionary Conference at Edinburgh in 1910 therefore "paid curiously little attention to Africa"[106] and in the

---

[100] Henry Scott Holland, *A Bundle of Memories* (London: Wells Gardener, Darton & Co., Ltd, 1915), 233–4.

[101] Taylor, 'The Great Missionary Failure', 500.

[102] Bishop of Carlisle [Harvey Goodwin], 'The Church of the British Empire', *Murray's Magazine* 2:8 (August 1887), 160.

[103] E.C. Dawson, *James Hannington: First Bishop of Eastern Equatorial Africa: A History of his Life and Work (1847–1885)* (London: Seeley and Co., 1887), 160–1.

[104] S.T. Nevill, Bishop of Dunedin, *CCR* (1888), 239.

[105] LPL, Davidson, 106, H.H. Montgomery to Archbishop, October 10th, 1905, f. 250v.

[106] Hewitt, *The Problems of Success, I*, 413.

resolutions of the Lambeth Conference of 1908, work in Africa was not even mentioned.

Even interest in the East could be patchy, however: the diocese of Labuan (Borneo), founded in 1855, was finding it difficult at this very time to find new workers and raise funds, "for Borneo was no longer the land of romance, of pirates and head hunting".[107] Other Eastern countries also lacked appeal: it took the SPG two years (1904–6) to find six men prepared to go to Japan as missionaries.

Some areas of the mission field were never perceived as 'romantic': in 1891, William Carter, the new Bishop of Zululand had to grapple with the fact that his diocese did not have "that halo of romance" which made a mission such as the Universities Mission to Africa (UMCA) so attractive.[108] And as in Asia, so in Africa, the appeal of older work could diminish: even the UMCA, founded in the 1860's, was finding it difficult to sustain support in England by the end of the century.[109]

A further irony lay in the fact that as missionary work developed and the picturesque savages of popular imagination gave way to the sober scholars of the mission station, romance faded. The second phase of missionary work, of church buildings, schools and hospitals, was more costly than the first stage, yet was less appealing and missionary work where it was often most sorely needed, in the cities and great labour centres abroad such as the Rand, was devoid of romance. It was particularly difficult to arouse interest in work among de-tribalized city dwellers: they did not appeal.[110]

Missions of "discovery" (missions to the heathen), however, were said to be inherently more 'interesting' than missions of "recovery" (i.e. than colonial work)[111] for interest in the colonies, which had been high in mid-century had diminished as they had become better known, developed roads and telegraphs and self-government. By the late 1860s, they had lost what appeal they had once had to the imagination and

---

[107] Henry Paget Thompson, *Into All the Lands: The History of the Society for the Propagation of the Gospel in Foreign Parts 1701–1950* (London, S.P.C.K., 1951), 402.

[108] O.J. Hogarth and R.L. White, *Life of William Marlborough Carter* ([Dartmouth]: [O.J. Hogarth], 1952), 4.

[109] 'Church News in Brief', *CCM&PR* VI:2 (Feb 1898), 517.

[110] Thompson, *Into All the Lands*, 402; *Official Report of the Missionary Conference of the Anglican Communion* (London: Society for Promoting Christian Knowledge, 1894), 256.

[111] Archbishop of York [W.D. Maclagan], 'The Society's 196th Anniversary', *MF* XLII:500 (Aug 1897), 285–6.

their place was taken by 'missions to the heathen', in new and unexplored lands. When Mashonaland/SR was founded, colonial work was perceived as the least romantic of all work abroad and so had the most difficulty in attracting funds.

Earlier, it had been different, as one colonial bishop recalled, somewhat bitterly, in 1888. Forty or fifty years before, colonial work had had an "heroic element" about it. There were few colonial bishops and those who "first broke through the line of heredity and imagined dignity... and swam the rivers and climbed the mountains were looked upon as heroes for having defied the traditions of the past". People knew little of countries abroad and a man who came back from them, such as Selwyn, first Bishop of New Zealand (1841–65) was "looked upon as something like a demi-god descended from Olympus".[112] He, on his visit to England in 1854, "excited as much interest as some great potentate" and "threw a halo of heroism, and something like a light of poetry round the concept of a colonial bishop".[113]

Selwyn, however, bishop of both colonist and Maori, had fused the notions of colonial and missionary bishop in his own person in a way no subsequent bishop was able to do and after the middle years of the nineteenth century, colonial work lost its 'heroic' and 'romantic' associations. These qualities (and the designation 'missionary') now attached almost exclusively to missions to 'the heathen'.

Colonial work was no longer regarded as important, the subject "relegated to the fag-end of an evening meeting".[114] Colonial clergy complained that they were denied the title of missionary and that the English clergy would refuse to have them address a missionary meeting. People in England, said John Salt, a clergyman on furlough from Mashonaland in 1909, took "little interest" in "work among whites".[115] The depth of this indifference can be gauged by the fact that one society which was founded only to provide ministrations for colonists was forced to divert into 'missions to the heathen' for a period of some 40 years (c. 1860–1900) because they were more "picturesque" and so brought in support.[116]

---

[112] S.T. Nevill, Bishop of Dunedin, *CCR* (1888), 239.
[113] Bishop of Carlisle, 'The Church of the British Empire', 153–4.
[114] J.F. Stretch, Co-Adjutor Bishop of Brisbane, *CCR* (1898), 422.
[115] 'Annual General Meeting, Mashonaland Mission Association, July 9th, 1909', *MQP* LXIX (Aug 1909), 20.
[116] J.D. Mullins, *Our Beginnings: being a short sketch of the Colonial and Continental Church Society* (London: (n.p.), 1923), 25.

A similar prejudice operated in 1910 at the World Missionary Conference: the South African Church Railway Mission did not take part in the conference because the mission did not work among 'the heathen' but among white people and those of mixed ancestry.[117] The sum total of the English Church's work abroad was similarly ignored by the conference: only 'missions to the heathen' were reckoned as missionary and the English Church's extensive work among settlers was discounted. The result was to make the church's work abroad seem painfully small in comparison with that of other bodies.[118]

Even the SPG, founded originally to provide spiritual ministrations for settlers, increasingly downplayed the colonial side of its work. "'A missionary meeting': that will mean the heathen... and the heathen are black. They at least ought to be black. That is one of the few things we ask of them... in vain will the SPG speaker tell out his story. He is bound somehow after all to produce the usual 'properties'. He must have his dates and his palm trees and his mud huts and his beads and his bones and his blacks and all those things".[119]

VI *Colonial work; assumptions of establishment*

This bias in the home church against colonial work was felt abroad and resented. Bitter reproaches came from settlers themselves. From Australia in 1897: "If we were negroes in South Africa or South Sea Islanders... then we might hope for some attention: but because we are white men, forced out into the wild bush, no-one cares for us. We may lead the lives of animals and die the death of dogs".[120] From the "God-forsaken" vastness of Damaraland, South-West Africa (Namibia), in 1927: "Why is it that the Church at home leaves us in this country without the means of grace?"[121]

Colonial officials complained that the church was ignoring their needs: Shippard, for instance, Administrator of British Bechuanaland,

---

117 'Home Notes', *SARWMQP* 28 (July 1910), 20.

118 W.J. Conybeare, JCMA *46* (Nov 1910), 3.

119 RHO/USPG, X1001, Henry Scott Holland, 'The Church and the Mission Field', London Junior Clergy Missionary Association (in Association with the SPG), Great Evening Meeting, St. Andrew's Eve, 1894, 5.

120 [Letter to] Bishop of Riverina, in 'The Society's Grants for 1898', *MF* XLII:499 (July 1897), 253–4.

121 'The White Man in Lonely Outposts: Albert Hall Anniversary Meeting', *MF* LXXII:858 (June 1927), 158, 160.

complained about the neglect shown him and others by Knight-Bruce, when he was Bishop of Bloemfontein.[122] We have also seen earlier the resentment expressed by settlers in Mashonaland at Knight-Bruce and Powell's preference for 'native' work.

Scattered settlers, however, had been the haunting anxiety of colonial bishops since the days of Selwyn of New Zealand and such bishops continued to tell harrowing tales far into the twentieth century. They agonised over their inability to fulfil the responsibility undertaken at ordination, "to seek for Christ's sheep that are dispersed abroad"; and to "save the souls of baptised men from perishing".[123] It was pointed out, in 1898, that the worst spiritual destitution abroad was to be found, not on the missions, but in the colonies.[124]

In this, there was not only pathos but a certain irony, for the rapid increase in national activity abroad which took place in the late nineteenth century had presented the church and her extensions with a unique responsibility. In England, the Church of England, as the established church was charged with providing ministrations religious and pastoral to the entire population, regardless of religious affiliation. There was in the pastoral tradition of the English parish, "a real and recognised responsibility for the spiritual welfare of the whole body of the parishioners".[125] In any consideration of its duties the church was "bound to consider, not only the needs of [its] own members, but the whole nation and its spiritual requirements".[126]

By the end of the nineteenth century, as we have seen above, the English Church was rarely established abroad. This fact had very little influence on attitudes within the church: the assumptions of establishment were not so easily discarded. The Church in England continued to be the church of the nation and the corollary was that where the state and its people spread, as both did widely in the late nineteenth century, the church considered itself bound to follow.

---

[122] W/CPSA, AB/1162/A, 16, Bishop of Capetown to Sir Sidney Shippard, May 26th, 1887, f. 109.

[123] 'The Form and Manner of Ordering of Priests', Book of Common Prayer; Bishop of Pretoria [H.B. Bousfield], 'Notes of the Month', *MF* XXXV:416 (Aug 1890), 317.

[124] H.H. Kelly, *The History of a Religious Idea* (London: The Society of the Sacred Mission, 1898), 2.

[125] Herbert Hensley Henson, D.D., Lord Bishop of Durham, *Church and Parson in England* (London: Hodder and Stoughton Ltd., 1927), 72.

[126] *The Supply and Training for Holy Orders, Report to the Archbishop of Canterbury* (Poole: W.H. Hunt, 1908), 9.

At its simplest, this obligation was expressed in purely pastoral terms: "[W]herever our people go, their Church should follow them with the means of grace".[127] Or, as one churchman and colonial administrator put it, "The Empire follows its sons with protection of life and property. It is just imperative to follow them with protection of the soul."[128]

English assumptions of position and duty were also exported with the national diaspora. The massive immigration into Canada of the early 1900s, much of it from continental Europe, for instance, was greeted by the question: "[W]hose is the responsibility for the moral and religious future of this mixed multitude if it is not the national Church of the English speaking race?".[129] In 1889, similarly, a new Bishop of Tasmania arrived in his diocese "full of the sense of prestige and of the historical associations of the Church at home—her irresistible force and unquestioned position" and set to work, actuated by "a conviction that for the Anglo-Saxon race none but the English Church was adequate or gave a stable foundation for future years".[130]

In 1904, English clergymen on a 'mission of help' to the CPSA after the Second South African War appealed for home support in order to make it possible for the church there to assume her rightful place, to be "directly the first power in the land"[131] and an appeal for Mashonaland/SR, made in 1895, assumed that the English Church rather than any other religious body should "occupy" and "tend and cultivate" the ground there "by prescriptive right, and, it would seem, by the Divine Will".[132]

Even Knight-Bruce, licensing clergymen to accompany the BSA Company's expedition in 1890, did so on these grounds: "I have official information that the Company is recognised by the English Government. It is, therefore, my duty to send clergymen with their

[127] CE/CBM, *Third Annual Review of the Foreign Missions of the Church* (London: 1910), 57.

[128] Sir Horace Byatt, K.C.M.G., former Governor of Tanganyika, in 1930: D.M. Paton, *Reform of the Ministry: A Study in the work of Roland Allen* (London: Lutterworth Press, 1968), 100.

[129] Ven. G.E. Lloyd, Archdeacon of Saskatchewan, 'The Church's Mission among White Settlers in Canada', *Official Report of the Pan-Anglican Congress, VI* (London: S.P.C.K., 1908), S.E.1(g), 3.

[130] H.H. Montgomery, JCMA [*I*] (May 1899), 6–7.

[131] LPL, H56001, Mission of Help, Minutes of proceedings of a conference, Jerusalem Chamber, Westminster Abbey, 10 December 1903, 52.

[132] B.C. Durrad, South African Church Festival, *Combined Report* (London: [The Committee], 1895), 41.

men".[133] He was not alone, moreover, in this opinion of his duty, for distress was expressed in England at the time at the possibility of the pioneer column, or any other British expedition into the interior of Africa, not being accompanied by clergymen of the English Church,[134] and the directors of the BSA Company themselves asked, somewhat later, that a parson be sent to Fort Jameson in North-East Rhodesia, since they felt "the singularity" of a headquarters without a clergyman of the English Church.[135]

It can be seen, therefore, that the attempts made by successive Bishops of Mashonaland/SR to provide spiritual care for the settlers of the diocese, let alone for the 'heathen', had its roots in the pastoral assumptions and obligations of the church at home: all the settlers, without differentiation, were seen as their spiritual responsibility. The load of an itinerant clergyman in Mashonaland/SR was not lightened if he discovered that the majority of the employees on a mine were "dissenters or nothing".[136] They were, to him, as much his concern as they would be if members of his parish 'at home'.

For some ecclesiastical statesmen, the church's role was further extended by national imperial responsibility. God had called the English people to govern as he had called no other nation. The church, therefore, had to "cover the field marked out for it by the extent of our imperial responsibilities" and "become the most effective instrument for the conversion of the world".[137] For this to happen, however, for "the British Empire to further the Kingdom of God", the "primary condition" was that Britons abroad themselves "should be, and remain Christian".[138]

This was a large vision. Its realisation was another matter, however, as the struggles of the church in Mashonaland/SR to provide spiritual care for the settlers there show only too clearly. Those struggles had endless parallels elsewhere, in Canada, in Australia and New Zealand,

[133] 'The Bishop's Charge, Delivered in the Cathedral, Bloemfontein, at the Opening of the Diocesan Synod, 1890', *BQP* 89 (July 1890), 286.

[134] Commander V.L. Cameron R.N., *CCR* (1890), 237, 238; B.F. Westcott, Bishop of Durham, *CCR* (1890), 255.

[135] RHO/USPG, D Series, 148(b), 1903, D. Travers, Secretary UMCA, to Bishop Montgomery, May 28th, 1903.

[136] 'Letter from the Rev. J.W. Leary. St. Augustine's Mission, Gwanda, December 31st, 1898', *MQP* XXVIII (May 1899), 21.

[137] Wilson, 'The Church and the Empire', 383, 391–2.

[138] Dean of Ripon [W.H. Fremantle], 'Home Notes', *MF* XLV:530 (Feb 1900), 66.

in South America. "The mission of the English Church to the English speaking race" said a colonial bishop at the Church Congress of 1897, was "a sounding brass or a tinkling cymbal, a piece of grotesque irony, the more cruel because of the seriousness of the subject in its bearings on human life".[139]

He spoke, however, as attitudes towards the colonial church at home were beginning to change. From the 1890's onwards imperial feeling grew both in nation and church.

Some observers believed that this feeling was aroused by such events as the Royal Jubilee and the Imperial and Lambeth Conferences of 1897. In the great service for the Jubilee, held under the dome of St. Paul's in 1897, it was said, "*One felt the Empire*".[140]

Others thought that the Church of England was awoken to her wider responsibilities by the catastrophe of the Second South African War.[141] Still others noted that, at the time of the war, for the first time for forty years, colonial work began to appeal once more to the public imagination.[142]

Imperial feeling in the church, and more widely, was further aroused by evidence of colonial loyalty expressed at royal deaths and coronations and by colonial support for British forces in the Second South African War and in World War One. By 1914, the strength of imperial sentiment and imperial bonds was no longer in question, in church as well as nation. An appeal to restore St. Paul's, for example, launched in that year, described it as "the Cathedral of the Empire".[143]

At the turn of the century, therefore, imperialism was in vogue, "the Imperial idea...in the air", the expansion of empire "a subject of engrossing moment to the English Nation".[144] While much of this interest was roused by new areas of imperial rule and responsibility, by 'the White Man's Burden' (said to be "glowing topics" and to be fuelling a renewed interest in missions)[145] there was also a new interest in

[139] W.T. Thornhill Webber, Bishop of Brisbane, *CCR* (1897), 230.

[140] J.G. Lockhart, *Cosmo Gordon Lang* (London: Hodder and Stoughton Limited, 1949), 125.

[141] Bishop of Winchester [R.T. Davidson], 'Notes of the Month', *MF* XLV:529 (Jan 1900) 22–3; *CEYB* (1901), vii.

[142] Mullins, *Our Beginnings*, 25.

[143] Carpenter, *Winnington-Ingram*, 185.

[144] Dr. Welldon [Bishop of Calcutta], *MF* XLIV:517 (Jan 1899), 33; *CEYB* (1904), vii.

[145] JCMA [*11*] (Nov 1899), 9, *17* (Nov 1902), Chairman's address, (n.p.).

work among settlers. This work was now no longer entirely consigned to the prosaic category of "picket-duty"[146] or "sentry-go".[147]

New ventures in the colonies could even be described as 'romantic', if they were departures from the parochial norm. In Australia after 1898, work in the Bush Brotherhoods, groups of clergy formed to reach scattered settlers in the outback by itinerating from a common centre and living under a temporary rule was said to be 'romantic', as was work with the railway missions in South Africa and in Canada.[148] Wilfred Grenfell, a doctor who established a sea-borne medical mission to the isolated fishermen of the Labradorean coast, between 1892 and 1934, became one of the most romantic of missionary heroes. The very rapid emigration into Canada of some two million people between 1902 and 1912, also possessed its own appeal to the imagination.

This new interest in the colonies within the church and particularly within the SPG, was also the result of the existence of a colonial lobby. Its members had worked hard for a change in attitude since the 1890s and their efforts ran parallel to and sometime conflicted with the general attempt to publicise in England the needs of missionary work which has been examined above.

At the Lambeth Conference of 1897, for example, bishops in committee, the majority of them colonial bishops were very outspoken. Although the final word of the conference was to be that 'Foreign Missions' stood "in the first rank of all the tasks we have to fulfil",[149] in the opinion of these bishops, the claims of the colonies came "first in order".[150] There was "no more important subject" than "the duties of the Church to the Colonies" and, in the committee, "a strong feeling was manifested that the claims of our own colonists, our own kith and kin, have been at times somewhat unduly postponed...to the...duty...of ministering to the heathen". The opinion was expressed, furthermore, that "whereas originally [the SPG] was mainly intended to minister to our own people and give to them the means of grace...of later years...owing it may be to the greater popularity of the subject and

---

146 St. Clair Donaldson, Bishop-Elect of Brisbane, JCMA *21* (Nov 1904), 3.

147 [W.T. Gaul], 'Letter from the Bishop, Elm Bank, Leatherhead, July 15th, 1904', *MQP* XLIX (August 1904), 5.

148 H.St.J. Woollcombe, *Beneath the Southern Cross* (London: Longmans and Co., 1913), 71; Bishop of Stepney [H.L. Paget], 'The Annual Meeting. (Reprinted from the Church Times, March 4th, 1910)', *SACRMQP* (April 1910), 15.

149 Thomas, *The First Five Lambeth Conferences*, 195.

150 *Ibid.*, 277.

the degree to which it appeals more to the sympathies of missionary meetings, the duty of ministering to the heathen has been put more prominently forward and our duty to our own emigrants has been somewhat kept in the background".[151]

These bishops pointed out that England was pouring out people into the colonies with no idea of supporting the church there. "Thousands of our kith and kin" were "absolutely destitute of Church ministrations" and until this was realised the members of the church were living in "a fool's paradise". It was the duty of the conference to "get the SPG to remember the purpose for which they were originally intended".[152]

By then, moves were already afoot to restore the SPG to something closer to its original purpose, for in 1893 a group of London clergy had formed the Junior Clergy Missionary Association (JCMA) in connection with SPG, in order to stimulate a greater interest in the work of the society. Some of these men already had a connection with the colonial church and others were to become colonial bishops within a few years. While the missionary side of the SPG's work was not forgotten, the colonial side came into more prominence and in 1901 the effect of this group (and others) was felt in the appointment of a 'bush bishop', Montgomery of Tasmania, as the new secretary of the SPG.[153]

His appointment signified an attempt to change direction within the SPG. "No mission work in the world was more important" in his opinion, "than the Church following her flock" in the Empire.[154] Montgomery, however, in his plan to "imperialize" the mission of the church had failed to take sufficient account of such obstacles as the internal divisions of the Church of England and the desire for independence of her off-shoots.[155] He and his successors were only able to maintain but not to increase the proportion of money spent by the SPG on colonial work, which had begun to rise just before his arrival (from a quarter of the society's total annual income, in the early 1890s, to one third in 1897). During his seventeen-year secretaryship, however, he was able

---

151 LPL, Lambeth Conference (1897), Records, LC41, ff. 175–6.

152 *Ibid.*, ff. 187v–188v.

153 Thompson, *Into All the Lands*, 236.

154 *South African Church Railway Mission Year Book* (London: 1909), 18.

155 Steven Maughan, 'Imperial Christianity? Bishop Montgomery and the foreign missions of the Church of England, 1895–1915,' in Andrew Porter, ed., *The Imperial Horizons of British Protestant Missions, 1880–1914* (Grand Rapids, Michigan and Cambridge: W.B. Eerdmans, 2003), 36–54.

to make sure that the colonies "had the advantage in the matter of support" over missions to the heathen, in the supply of clergy.[156]

The continuing importance of the colonial church was further underlined in 1920, by the recall of St. Clair Donaldson, the Archbishop of Brisbane (one of the original members of the London JCMA) to be Bishop of Salisbury and head of the new Missionary Council of the Church Assembly. The SPG appointed as their new Secretary, in 1925, a cricketing Australian parson, Stacey Waddy and the hope was expressed that he would "help to keep the subject of Our People Overseas prominently before the mind and conscience of the Church".[157]

By the middle twenties, therefore, while the claims of the colonial churches and British abroad were still said to be largely unrecognised, there were strong cross-currents. The SPG was able to fill the Albert Hall for an annual meeting of supporters of "Our People Overseas" and a major report on missionary finance, published in 1927, stated that members of the Church of England, in general, appeared now to be far more ready to give money for the support of the colonial churches, than for missionary work.[158] The Empire and settlement within it were by then so extensive, however, that whatever money was raised did not meet the need. The English Church, said the SPG, was still not doing "a fraction" of what it ought to be doing.[159]

Missions to the heathen, moreover, remained the chief interest of the missionary-minded. When the general survey of the Church of England's responsibilities to the overseas church, the World Call, was first produced in 1925, for example, there was no report dealing with the needs of the colonial church. Only as a result of strong representations of protest and distress from their supporters was a report on 'Our People Overseas' published, two years after the other reports and when much of the excitement and interest had died down. Many people, it was said, felt "not without something approaching to indignation, that right in the foreground should have been a report about the Church's duty to go pioneering with the people, to give our settlers a reasonable chance to remain Christian".[160]

---

[156] This was not entirely a matter of principle, for colonial clergymen cost less to support than missionaries: H.H. Montgomery, JCMA *38* (April 1913), 21.

[157] SPG, [Annual Report] *The King's Business* (1926), ii.

[158] CE/CA/MC, *Missionary Finance*, 28.

[159] SPG, [Annual Report] *Onward* (1927), 18.

[160] SPG, [Annual Report] *The King's Business* (1926), ii.

The 'fashion principle' also still applied. Colonial work had to have a particular appeal to attract funds and not all settlers or groups of emigrants possessed the appeal of the sturdy homesteader of the lonely prairies or the hardy fishermen of the Labradorean coast, fighting for their existence against poverty and a harsh and dramatic climate. Colonial realities were often mundane or even antipathetic and seekers after land or gold tended to arouse hostility or contempt in home audiences, in spite of efforts by the colonial churches to emphasise the greater spiritual need of such "devotees of mammon".[161] They were dismissed as "adventurers"[162] or "mere money-grubbers",[163] especially if their interests were believed to conflict with the interests of local people and so of missionary work proper.

VII *Mashonaland/Southern Rhodesia*

The mysterious Central African interior of which Mashonaland/Southern Rhodesia was a part had held a romantic appeal for the missionary-minded since the 1850s, for it was associated with David Livingstone, the greatest of missionary-explorers: see Map 1, p. xxi, where the site of his death is marked. Knight-Bruce's journey of 1888 and an earlier attempt to explore Mashonaland for the church were both made within this particular tradition. William Greenstock, the clergyman from the Cape who made the first journey in 1874, had even arranged to travel in the company of Thomas Baines, the artist-companion of David Livingstone and had travelled on alone after tending Baines on his death-bed.

Knight-Bruce drew not only on the Livingstone tradition but on that of the heroic missionary or colonial bishop, in both his 1888 journey and his subsequent work: he modelled himself, openly, on Patteson, martyr-bishop of Melanesia (a bishop who lived among his missionaries)[164] and as we have seen earlier, on Selwyn of New Zealand. He and

---

[161] 'Letter from Rev. W.J. Roxburgh. Umtali, February 9th, 1901', *MQP* XXXVII (August 1901), 7–8.

[162] SPG, [Annual] *Report* (1889), 21.

[163] LPL, H5691.S7: Preliminary Expedition, Mission of Help to South Africa, *Report* (Private and Confidential) (1903), f. 28.

[164] 'Church News from South Africa', *MF* XXXV:419 (Nov 1890), 403.

his exploits were hailed in the familiar language of missionary romance, of 'heroism' and 'knight-errantry'.[165]

The 'romantic' aura of a missionary sort which Knight-Bruce established with such labour, however, did not survive the subsequent colonial and buccaneering element in the history of the diocese: Mashonaland/SR, after his time, was perceived as devoid of romance.

Even missionary work in the diocese became tainted by colonial associations, a colonial overlay. The work begun at Chief Makoni's town, for example, very soon became known as the twin missions of Epiphany and St. Faith's, in the colonial farming district of Rusapi. The name of the chief and the local identity of the people disappeared from view and with them went any exotic appeal. Some of the most successful work in the diocese, moreover, was among town dwellers and so was of small interest.

Mashonaland/SR did possess a second form of imaginative appeal, however, that of the heroic settler tradition: the BSA Company's advance into Central Africa in the 1890s, at a time of enthusiasm for Empire, held considerable romance for home audiences. The company also took care to see that favourable versions of its venture were published in the English newspapers. In these and other accounts, the settlers were portrayed as "sun-burnt... heroes, agents of 'a great civilising, Christianizing force', whose activity among 'savage races' could only bring light and life".[166] The settlers, therefore, had their brief hey-day, before critics of the type of imperialism they and Rhodes represented gained influence in England and the aura of romance which had surrounded them was thinned, if not entirely dispelled.

The church, however, was not able to capitalize to any great degree on this second tradition even when it was at its strongest, though there was some attempt to do so. In 1895, for instance, Gaul wrote of himself as, "carrying the old flag of the cross side by side with men like Jameson and Rhodes", who were "planting the Union Jack on the neck of tyranny and slavery".[167] This was, however, just before the débacle of the Jameson Raid, and the (temporary) eclipse of its perpetrators.

---

[165] Report, *The Standard* (January 4th, 1894), in 'Notes of the Month', *MF* XXXIX:458 (Feb 1894), 69; 'Presidential Address, May 10th, 1894', *MF* XXXIX:463 (July 1894), 243.

[166] J.A. Edwards, 'Two Kinds of Central African History', Central African Archives, *Occasional Papers*, No. 1 (Salisbury, Rhodesia, The Government Printer, 1965), 2–5.

[167] *Scottish Guardian* (September 13th, 1895), 444.

Gaul himself continued to propagate an idealistic version of imperialism, Beaven a benign one. Some 'romance' was also attached to work along the railway lines in Mashonaland/SR, as to all railway work abroad.

Knight-Bruce, however, was the chief publicist for the church at the time of the initial settler advance. His open disapproval of the settlers, which was continued by his associates and then by missionaries such as Arthur Shearly Cripps, prevented the 'heroic' version of the settler story from taking any real hold among supporters in England.

The settlers therefore, from the beginning, had a doubtful reputation among the missionary public and continued to be associated, primarily, with "rich companies",[168] with gold and with conquest—the exploitative rather than the serving or missionary aspect of empire. This prevented them, even when they most needed help (in the early, struggling years of the diocese) from attracting the support offered to such communities as the fishermen of Labrador. They were, on the contrary, dismissed out of hand, as "mere self-satisfied pirates".[169]

---

[168] SPG, [Annual] *Report* (1889), 21.

[169] RHO/USPG, D Series, 134(A) 1900, Will. Mashonaland, Manuscript of sermon, Salisbury, Shangani Day, December 4th, 1900.

CHAPTER FIVE

MASHONALAND/SOUTHERN RHODESIA: THE RECRUITMENT OF CLERGY

We have examined in Chapter Four the reasons why successive Bishops of Mashonaland/SR between 1890–1925 found it very difficult to obtain adequate financial help for the diocese from England and the 'mother church'. This chapter is concerned with a parallel difficulty experienced in finding and retaining clergymen. It is, therefore, primarily a study of recruits and recruiting.

I *Dependence, local vocations, sources of recruits*

In 1890 when work in Mashonaland began, all the branches of the overseas church, whether new or established, colonial or missionary, were dependent to some degree upon the Church of England for staff, just as they were for financial support. Only one area, Newfoundland, was producing all of its own clergy by 1925.[1]

The CPSA, to which Mashonaland/SR belonged, was one of the most heavily dependent of the overseas churches. In 1914, for instance, when there were 605 clergy serving in the CPSA, only 140 of them, fewer than a quarter, were locally-born (91 were black, 46 were white, 3 were 'coloured' or of mixed ancestry). In New Zealand in 1913, by comparison, more than two-thirds of the clergy, 249 out of 327, were local men (204 were white, 45 Maori). By 1925, New Zealand was almost as self-sufficient as Newfoundland but only about a third of the CPSA clergy were locally-born.[2]

The weakness of the CPSA lay chiefly in her colonial work: while the number of clergy produced by indigenous communities increased

[1] CE/CA/MC, *The Call from our Own People Overseas* (Westminster: 1927), 14.

[2] *Ibid.*, 14, 86; E.G.S. Gibson, 'The South African Church and the Church at Home', *ETW* XII (Oct 1914), 376; CE/CBM, *Missions Overseas, Eighth Annual Review* (London: 1915), 42.

significantly over the period,[3] very few came from her settler population. By 1925, only 60, barely a tenth, of the white clergy (615) were locally-born.[4] The CPSA therefore remained heavily dependent throughout the period of this study upon recruits from England, particularly for men to minister to her settler congregations.

She was also to some degree dependent on English emigrants to South Africa: the figures for colonial ordinations look less bleak if those for Englishmen who had emigrated to South Africa as laymen and subsequently been ordained are admitted. Such men numbered 30 in 1914, for example, when there were 46 locally-born white clergy and immigrants out-numbered colonials at the provincial theological college from its foundation in 1904 until the 1930s.[5]

A study of the origins of the one hundred clergy who served in Mashonaland/SR between 1890–1925[6] reveals the type of pattern that might be expected for a new diocese in the CPSA. There were (as we have seen earlier) only a handful of local vocations: six locally-born clergy were ordained between 1919 and 1925, five of them from indigenous communities and one from the settlers.

Mashonaland/SR, like the rest of Southern Africa, also produced a few vocations from English-born immigrants but these men returned to England to train and only one ever served in the diocese: W.J. Keates (the son of immigrants to the Eastern Cape) who was ordained in England in 1915 and returned, as a recruit, to work briefly in Southern Rhodesia in 1920 before being invalided out to a lower altitude in 1921.

There were also two groups of clergy serving in Mashonaland/SR in the period whose recruitment was not the responsibility of the diocese. These were nine members of the Community of the Resurrection (Mirfield), which took charge of Penhalonga in 1915 and nine men who worked for the South African Church Railway Mission. The remaining 76 men, however, three-quarters of the Mashonaland/SR clergy, had to be found outside the diocese.

---

[3] By 1933, 167 of the 696 serving clergy were indigenous: *With One Accord in South Africa, An Interim Statement circulated, with permission, before the Provincial Missionary Conference, 1933* (Johannesburg: Imprinted at the C.R. Press, Rosettenville, 1933), 23.

[4] CE/CA/MC, *The Call from our Own People Overseas*, 14, 86.

[5] Gibson, 'The South African Church', 376; *Ch.Ch.* (May 6th, 1904), 285; *The Paulatim*, 1 (Oct 1st, 1933), 3.

[6] See 'Clergy Recruits, Mashonaland/Southern Rhodesia, 1890–1935', pp. 190–193.

Several men, fifteen altogether, came from within the CPSA. Three of them served under Knight Bruce: Balfour, Trusted and Surridge. When Gaul first travelled up to the diocese in 1895 he took with him, and ordained, Douglas Pelly. He also recruited Beaven, who was then serving in the Capetown diocese and three South African-born clergymen: Hezekiah Mtobi (1896–1901); William Griffiths (1895–1896); and W.H. Robins (1897–1900). Six other men served in South Africa before going north: Nelson Fogarty (1897–1900); J.H. Selmes (1897–1902); Walter Leary (1898–1908); Arthur Shum (1906–11); R.J.J. Garrod (1920–7) and Herbert Heriot-Hill (1923–7).

The majority of the Mashonaland/SR clergy had to be sought in England, where there were two primary sources of recruitment. There were, first, various (party) missionary colleges which trained men for both colonial and strictly 'missionary' work, men who were expected to spend a lifetime's service abroad. The number of students at the colleges, however, in comparison with the need for both types of worker abroad, was very small: in 1899, when the church abroad was expanding rapidly, there were only 700 students in training.

A disturbing number of missionary college students, moreover, either never went abroad or, if they did go, did not stay but returned within a few years to work in England. This meant that the usefulness of these colleges to the church abroad was limited, as can be illustrated from the experience of Mashonaland/SR between 1890 and 1925: only 15 of the 76 recruits were trained at missionary colleges, W.J. Keates among them.

Clergy for 'foreign service' were also found through the missionary societies but the numbers here were also relatively small: in the mid-1890s, for example, there were only 600 or so English clergy serving abroad with the three largest societies, the SPG, CMS and the UMCA. (There were also 475 'native' clergy supported by the societies.) In 1921, there were 1,047 English clergy abroad with the societies (and 939 'natives'). Even these figures, however, do not give an accurate indication of men actually recruited for overseas church by the societies: in Mashonaland/SR, men found elsewhere were added to the SPG's lists once they were in the diocese and being paid from the society's grant. G.E.P. Broderick, for example, arrived in 1906. He was added to the SPG's lists in 1909 when he moved from colonial to missionary work.

Some fifteen of the 76 priests who were recruited externally for Mashonaland/SR in the period went out to Africa with the SPG. Three of them were also missionary college men. The colleges, with fifteen men and the SPG with twelve, therefore supplied Mashonaland with only 27 men between them, about a quarter of the diocese's clergy or under half the recruits found in England. This meant that the remainder had to be recruited elsewhere, from amongst the serving English clergy.

There were considerable hindrances to successful recruitment from this body of men. The first difficulty lay in the fact that, from about 1890, when the Mashonaland mission was first instigated and the overseas church generally began a particularly rapid expansion, the Church of England began to experience its own problems of 'clergy supply'.

We have seen in Chapter Three that the pastoral duties of the Church of England were not limited to its own members. This meant that clerical strength was assessed in relation to the entire population.[7] Between the 1840s and the 1880s, a reformed and revitalized church had kept pace with rapid demographic growth: large numbers of young men were ordained as deacons each year and as a result, whereas there had been 14,613 parsons in 1841, there were 25,363 in 1901. The ratio of parson to people stood at about 1:1,000 from 1841 until the last two decades of the century.

By this point, however, the numbers of men being ordained each year had begun to dwindle, with the result that the total number of parsons declined to under 25,000 in 1911. In 1921, after the lean recruitment years of the World War One (when there was a virtual moratorium on ordinations, except for men unable to fight in the war) the clergy numbered just over 23,000. Ordinations rose again in the 1920s but failed to keep pace with losses, let alone with demographic growth. There were 22,760 clergy in 1931 and the clergy/population ratio had dropped to 1:1,755.

The problem of 'clergy supply', moreover, was even more acute than these overall figures indicate. The church's work lay chiefly in her parishes and the numbers of the parish clergy declined even more steeply than the total numbers of clergy: since ordination is indelible, the decennial censuses included all clergy in their totals, whether they were in full-time work; did occasional 'duty'; or were retired. Clergy

[7] Unless otherwise stated, figures given for the English clergy are taken from the decennial censuses (occupational tables and population tables) although these include figures for Wales (the Welsh church was disestablished in 1919).

from these two latter groups formed about a quarter of all the clergy from 1911 onwards. In England, the numbers of clergy actually at work in the parishes dropped from a high point of over 20,000 in 1891, to under 17,000 in 1930.[8]

The church's ability to discharge its duty to the nation was severely threatened by this diminution in the numbers of clergy. Anxiety was widely expressed within the church from the 1880s onwards and official reports relating to 'clergy supply' were produced in 1898, 1900, 1908, 1910, 1923, and 1930. The overseas church, in Mashonaland as elsewhere, also watched the fall in numbers of the English clergy with dismay. On the whole however, what was seen as a "national calamity" in England[9] was viewed by the church overseas as something rather different.

In 1892, the ratio of parson to people abroad was estimated as 1:400,000 souls rather than the 1:1,288 of the English Church.[10] At the turn of the century, when there were more than 25,000 parsons 'at home', almost 21,000 of them in the parishes, there were only some 4,500 (working) clergy abroad. The numbers of the clergy abroad then grew to just over 5,000 in 1904 and some 5,500 in 1909 but when measured against the need abroad and the numbers of clergy in the home church, they were still pitifully small.

The sense of desperate helplessness over staffing experienced by successive bishops of Mashonaland/SR was shared by bishops from all parts of the world. It was particularly acute for those who could not count on the enthusiasm of the Evangelical party for the missionary cause. Some bishops, particularly High Church bishops, about to begin work could not attract any clergy at all. The bishop of the new diocese of Corea (1891), for example, spent a year in England after his consecration attempting to recruit clergy and then set sail for the east with a couple of laymen.[11] The foundation of the Diocese of Lebombo, in Portuguese East Africa, was delayed for two years (from 1891 to 1893) because the new bishop was unable to find any staff. He eventually

---

[8] R. Currie, A.D. Gilbert, and I. Horsley, *Churches and Churchgoers, Patterns of Church Growth in the British Isles since 1700* (Oxford: Oxford University Press, 1977), 197, 198.

[9] Preface, *CEYB* (1903), iv.

[10] 'A meditation on Missions', *MQP* I (June 1892), 9. This figure, and others given in this paragraph for the numbers of clergy overseas, are derived from the 'Statistical Returns of Church Work in the Indian, Colonial and Missionary Dioceses', published in the *Official Year Book of the Church of England*.

[11] M.N. Trollope, *The Church in Corea* (London: Mowbray and Co., 1915), 30.

began his work with one priest, a rescued slave from "Abyssinia", who had been trained at a missionary college in England.[12]

The position of the overseas church then became even more difficult during World War One, since very little recruitment was possible during the conflict and many overseas clergy were given to the war effort as military chaplains. The CPSA, for example, badly understaffed as it was, gave chaplains generously. Pretoria re-organised its entire ministerial structure in an attempt to continue its work while freeing men to serve as chaplains. Beaven supported the war effort so enthusiastically that Mashonaland needed at least 5 new priests in 1919 (20% of its clergy) just to bring numbers up to inadequate pre-war levels.

The situation was then further exacerbated in the 1920s, as missionary areas experienced mass conversions and post-war immigration swelled colonial populations. And yet there were no more clergy in the overseas church in 1923 than there had been in 1909 (some 5,500).

To the hard-pressed churches and missions abroad, therefore, even the post-war Church of England, with 2,000 fewer clergymen, was living in religious luxury. Throughout the period telling comparisons were made between undermanned work abroad and well-supplied English dioceses. The populations of the dioceses of Truro and Brisbane in 1897 were the same, although the area covered by Brisbane was 150 times that of Truro. Brisbane had only 52 clergy, however, while Truro had 330. In Lichfield, in 1914, there were at least 600 clergy but not even three could be induced to go to Mashonaland/SR. In 1923, a clergyman from South Africa resigned his English post to return home, "fed up with all this talk about lack of clergy and with the crowds of clergy" he had met.[13]

Churchmen abroad attributed the so-called 'dearth' in England simply to bad organisation and poor distribution and they accused the mother church of simply wasting her clergy. When 'clergy supply' began to fail in England, however, intense scrutiny was first given to possible causes of the failure and to ways in which it might be arrested. Only after World War One was much attention given to the best use of what clergymen there were and it was not until 1930 that an official report

[12] H.P. Thompson, *Into all the Lands: The History of the Society for the Propagation of the Gospel in Foreign Parts 1701–1950* (London: S.P.C.K., 1951), 321.

[13] F.A. Rogers, in 'Report of the Annual Meetings Held at the Church House, Westminster, SW1, on Wednesday, February 28th, at 3p.m. and 8p.m.', *SACRMQP* 76 (April 1923), 10.

conceded that before the war the Church of England had been overstaffed, as the overseas church had long maintained and that the real problem was, and had been, an "uneven distribution" of clergy.[14]

II *Clergy distribution, curates*

The cause of the uneven distribution of clergy in the Church of England lay in the massive urbanisation of the country over the course of the nineteenth century: by its end, the majority of the English people lived, not in the country, but in the towns.

The ancient parish system of the Church of England made it difficult for her to move with the people. Each parish was a separate legal entity, individually endowed and in individual patronage and was a civil as well as an ecclesiastical unit. Until mid-century, when new legislation was introduced, the division of a single parish required an individual Act of Parliament. The majority of the English clergy therefore remained in the countryside: in the diocese of Worcester, for instance, at the turn of the century, a rural population of 17,000 was served by 81 churches and 80 clergy while the industrial town of Birmingham had a population of 80,000 with about a dozen churches and mission rooms and only 20 clergy.[15]

The Victorian church nevertheless made strenuous, if uneven, efforts to provide more clergy and churches for the towns while avoiding a wholesale reform of the parochial system. Additional churches were built in undivided parishes: Longley, Bishop of Ripon between 1836 and 1857, consecrated one new church every two months during his twenty-year episcopate, for example.[16] After mid-century, many parishes were divided: in London, in St. Pancras, for instance, four ancient parishes were divided into thirty new ones.[17] There were some 10,000 parishes at the beginning of the nineteenth century and over 14,000 at its end.

---

[14] CE/CA, *Report of the Commission on Staffing of Parishes*, C.A. 334, (London and Westminster: Church Assembly and SPCK, 1930), 5.

[15] *Census Report for England and Wales for 1921* (1927), 115; E.A. Knox, *Reminiscences of an Octogenarian 1847–1934* (London: Hutchinson, 1935), 168.

[16] S. Meacham, *Lord Bishop: The Life of Samuel Wilberforce 1805–1873* (Cambridge, Massachussets: Harvard University Press, 1970), 129.

[17] Roger Lloyd, *The Church of England in the Twentieth Century, 1* (London: Longmans, 1946), 61, 63.

Many more clergy had also been deployed in the cities as curates: the post of assistant curate was a strategic creation of the Victorian church. Societies were formed to support curates in new, poorly-endowed, urban parishes and a new pastoral style was also created, in which a large urban parish was not divided but worked more cheaply and efficiently, under the direction of an incumbent, by a large group of helpers: district visitors, lay readers and, principally, curates. As a result of these strategies, the church of the 1890s was a church with many young clergy: in 1891 almost 6,000 men (5,771), a quarter of all the clergy, working and non-active, were under the age of 35.

This meant that the Church of England had become excessively reliant upon her younger clergy, a reliance which was then exposed by the drying up of 'clergy supply'. By 1907, 19% of curacies were vacant. In 1923, after World War One, the average age of the clergy was 52. The curate had become "as rare as the bittern or the bustard"[18] and town incumbents were struggling to look after parishes of several thousand souls single-handed.

The diminution in the numbers of curates in the Church of England also posed acute problems for the overseas churches. As has been seen above, a drop in the numbers of the English clergy overall was regarded overseas as less a question of numbers than one of distribution. The drop in the numbers of curates, however, over the period 1890–1930 and with it a marked change in the age-profile of the English clergy was a more serious obstacle to recruitment for work abroad, for the overseas church needed to recruit young men. Even overseas bishops were appointed when young: Knight-Bruce was in his early thirties when he became Bishop of Bloemfontein. William West Jones of Capetown (1874–1908) had refused two overseas bishoprics before he finally accepted Capetown at the age of thirty-five.

Missionaries 'to the heathen' needed to be young enough to learn languages and to be inculcated into a new way of life and work, since most missionary training was carried out in the field. Colonial clergy had to be able to adapt to the new society in which they were to work, particularly if they were going to the mining camp, the outback, the prairie. The churches overseas had discovered from (painful) experience that older clergy were seldom able to adjust satisfactorily to these new

[18] *Crockford Prefaces, 1922–44: The Editor Looks Back* (Oxford: Oxford University Press, 1947), 33.

societies. Two older men failed to adapt to life in early Bulawayo, for instance, one (E.A. Hammick) because he was appalled at the behaviour of the young men, most of whom were of his own social class and ought in his opinion to have behaved better (he was the son of a baronet, who was also a clergyman). The second (Anthony Bathe) was considered "too High Church" and he took with him to the colony the antagonism which existed between the church and Nonconformity in England but which had largely fallen away abroad.[19]

Too many men from the opposite end of the scale, very young or junior men, were not wanted either, however, as they could not be immediately useful. In the English system, a young clergyman was trained by working under the eye of a more experienced man and sole responsibility for a charge only came after many years as an assistant. Most posts abroad, however, were solitary and so junior men were of limited value. Nelson Fogarty, for instance, was recruited by Knight-Bruce while he was still a student at missionary college. He travelled out to South Africa in 1893 but it was considered inadvisable that he continue to Mashonaland, in spite of the desperate need for clergy there, as he was very young and there was no post which was not solitary. He served instead as a curate in the Diocese of Capetown for three years before going to Mashonaland to work with Gaul as his chaplain.

The men wanted overseas were reasonably mature, who had been some six to eight years in orders (the canonical age of ordination was 23). The ideal recruit was under thirty, in his second curacy, still young enough to be useful but sufficiently experienced to be able to cope alone. Such men, however, were in the shortest supply and the greatest demand at home over the period, which meant the churches abroad were attempting to recruit in direct competition not only with one another but with the mother church, for the men she most needed to keep for her urban curacies. Experienced men also found it easier to obtain benefices at home as the numbers of the English clergy shrank.

The overseas church as a result was forced to compromise in its recruiting. In Mashonaland, for instance, almost half of the 76 recruits were very young men, like Fogarty. Eighteen were ordinands or deacons and another twelve had been ordained for 3–4 years or less.

---

[19] RHO/USPG, D Series, 156(B), 1904, F.W. Mackenzie to SPG, June 12th, 1904.

Dioceses abroad also had often to accept men who, although mature enough to stand on their own, were not experienced clergyman: James Walker, for example, who travelled to Mashonaland in 1893 when he was 28. Walker had left Hatfield Hall, Durham, after theological training in 1892 and then worked as a private tutor. In Mashonaland he held sole charge, very successfully, first as a layman, then as deacon and priest at Makoni's, Fort Victoria, Umtali and Gwelo but he never had the opportunity of working under a senior priest. One reason for his return to England in 1903 was to learn "method" in church work.[20]

The churches abroad also usually wanted unmarried men and this requirement created a further barrier to recruitment, for after the turn of the century the younger clergy suffered from what was described as "an epidemic of marriage".[21] After World War One, there was no "strata (sic) of young, unmarried priests"[22] in the Church of England. The majority of the overseas dioceses, however, could not offer either stipends or conditions suitable for married men.

Mashonaland/SR was one such diocese. Men going there had to leave behind any thoughts of "sweethearts and perambulators",[23] unless they had private means. Of the 76 clergy who were recruited externally for Mashonaland/SR between 1890 and 1925, a mere 16 entered the diocese as married men, of whom two went to senior posts (Beaven, Archdeacon of Matabeleland, 1903; E.G. Harker, Dean of Salisbury, 1912). Only 17 clergy married while serving. Three single men were joined in Mashonaland/SR by their unmarried sisters and one by his mother.

Married clergy throughout the period were forced to leave the diocese for financial reasons. Nelson Fogarty, for example, married in 1899 a wife from his former parish in Claremont, Cape Town. When their first child was born in 1900 they left, as they could not afford to stay. Other clergy who left, wholly or partly, for the same reason were Hezekiah Mtobi (1896–1901); A.S. Robins (1901–10); J.W. Davies (1906–11); and H.C. Sandall (1913–1916).

---

[20] RHO/USPG, D Series, 148(B), 1903, W. Mashonaland to Bishop Montgomery, September 3rd, 1903.

[21] R.T. Gardner, JCMA, *19* (Nov 1903), 17.

[22] Bishop of Pretoria [Neville Talbot], *SACRMQP* 76 (April 1923), 12.

[23] RHO/USPG, D Series, 126(b), Will. Mashonaland to Mr Tucker, May 4th, 1898.

Married clergy could also be a heavy financial burden to parishes. In 1900, when recruitment was particularly difficult, Gaul accepted a married man with a family, J.S. Wimbush, for Bulawayo. The parish bought land and built a parsonage to accommodate them at a time of high prices caused by the South African war. The Wimbushes stayed only for three years but the rectory cost £2,500 and the parishioners were saddled with a debt which prevented them from building an adequate church until 1913.

Even where men had private means and could support their wives, churches overseas were reluctant to employ them, for English clergy wives seldom adapted well either to the conditions or societies they found abroad. This, however, does not seem to have been the case with Mashonaland/SR. There is no evidence that any wives who accompanied their husbands to the diocese from England failed to adapt to the circumstances in which they found themselves. Most, however, lived in the reasonably congenial environment of small colonial towns, as few of the missionary clergy were ever married: only nine out of 27 altogether.

The majority of women who married serving clergy were already living in the country and those of whom anything is known were women likely to be prepared to share the conditions of their husband's work. James Gillanders, for instance, missionary at St. Columba's, Bulawayo, married in 1899 Annie Garrett, the matron of the boarding house of St. John's, the church school. James Walker, in 1900 and J.W. Davies and A.S. Robins in 1908, married nurses. Edgar Lloyd in 1909 married Elaine Brewin, a missionary who was also a nurse and Thomas Beattie in 1916 married a Miss N.G. Pestance, who had formerly been a medical missionary in China. F.S. Salt married in 1906 Maude Reed, the South African-born daughter of a former miner and prospector in the Gwelo area; and Mia Mitchell, G.E.P. Broderick's wife, had grown up at Morven Mine, near St. Aidan's, Bembezi.

It should be noted, nevertheless, that even some of these women were defeated by the circumstances in which they found themselves: twice the loneliness of a wife, herself born in Africa, was a factor in the resignation of a man recruited in England: A. Dunley Owen left St. Faith's, Rusape in 1903 and G.E.P. Broderick left Bonda in 1916, in part for this reason. In both cases, the husbands shared the loneliness of their wives.

The health of wives and children appears to have been a more serious obstacle to the employment of married men in Mashonaland/SR than adaptation. More than one clergyman was compelled to leave for the sake of his wife's health or because of her death. Dunley Owen lost two wives while working for the diocese. He arrived in 1897 as a lay medical missionary, with his first wife Dorothy, to work at Zimunya's near Umtali. We have seen, in Chapter Two (p. 56), that they left the mission within months. Dorothy died on the journey. Owen returned to serve twice with his second wife, Kate. In 1901 they worked at Wreningham, near Enkeldoorn (Chivu) and then moved to St. Faith's, under Upcher, in 1902. They left St. Faith's in 1903, as detailed above. They returned for a second time in 1910 to the mission near Victoria. Owen then left Victoria when Kate died in 1912.

B.N.N. Woodard, priest at Hartley, Gatooma and Que Que, also left in 1926 with his four children, because his wife had died. J.L. Williams left St. Aidan's, Bembezi in 1915 and A.F.M. Maynard left Umtali in 1920 because their wives became ill. When the railway mission accepted the services of R.W.E. Robinson, a married man with children in 1925, because of a shortage of single recruits, he left within the year because his wife and children all suffered from fever.

III *Recruits: qualities needed*

The men wanted for service abroad were relatively young and preferably unmarried. They were also expected to be in good health, for they were wanted primarily for pioneering work on mission stations or the out-districts of colonies, work which was more physically demanding than work in England.

This expectation, however, was yet another bar to recruitment, for the health of the new urban populations of England was generally poor: in 1908, for instance, it was reported that a considerable percentage of applicants were being rejected by the missionary societies because they were medically unfit.[24] Serious suggestions were made as early as 1896 that missionary colleges should build swimming baths or gymnasia to enable students prepare for the physical demands of life abroad.[25] After World War One very few even of the newly ordained were in full physical health.

---

[24] Rev. E.J. Palmer, 'The Chairman's Address', JCMA *28* (May 1908), 6.

[25] Bishop of Zululand [W.M. Carter], 'Notes of the Month', *MF* XLI:487 (July 1896), 277.

The requirement that men should be physically robust, however, was not one which could be lightly dispensed with, as the experience of Mashonaland/SR showed. Not all the clergy were able, in Gaul's words, to "go anywhere and do anything, live on buffalo hide, sleep on thorns, love sand and delight in fever and come up smiling".[26] Many were invalided out: Frederick Lawrence (1893); William Griffiths (1896); Douglas Pelly (1899); J.A. Walker (1903); H.H. Foster, three times (1897, 1901 and 1912); J.A. Selmes (1902); William Roxburgh (1904); C.G.B. Turner (1906); James Gillanders (1910); A.C. Shum (1911); Percy Green (1920); W.J. Keates (1921); George Ashworth, twice (1919, 1921); R.J.J. Garrod (in 1927). Three clergymen died while serving: Wilson Trusted, in 1890, of dysentery; R.R.St.J. Hovell of a heart attack in 1919; and J.R. Powley, in 1925, of an unspecified illness.

Men going abroad also had to 'rough it', to be able to look after themselves without the comforts and conveniences of life in England. In Canada, even a bishop could find himself making bread and sweeping floors. Australian bush parsons had to feed, groom and harness their own horses, New Zealand clergy to grow their own potatoes. In Mashonaland/SR, clergy found themselves not only organising the building of their own churches and homes but themselves digging ditches and brick-making. On missions they had to look after cattle, plough and grow food crops and shoot for the pot. Occasionally they had to face (and even shoot) lions. Practical skills were, therefore, of paramount importance. By the early twentieth century, however, many applicants for foreign work were unsuitable because they were town-bred, unable to learn to look after themselves in new countries and unfamiliar conditions.

Men working abroad (outside the Evangelical fold) had also to contend with poverty. There was contemporary concern in England at increasing clerical poverty (it was believed to be the primary cause of the failure of 'clergy supply') but abroad conditions were worse. Missionaries lived, perforce, very simply or in actual poverty. The stipends of colonial clergy in Australia or Canada, £170 or so per annum, were little better than those of a farm labourer. In Mashonaland/SR, a clergyman on £200 a year earned less than a mechanic with his £40–50 a month. In New Zealand, many clergy lived on the edge of

[26] 'North-West Rhodesia', *Ch.Ch.* (July 12th, 1905), 427.

real destitution. The church abroad in fact, it was said, had "a sweated ministry".[27]

Recruits also had to cope with extreme isolation. In England, town clergy had colleagues or assistants and even country parsons had clerical neighbours. Abroad, however, the paucity of clergy and the size of districts meant that men worked on their own, with little or no support. In Southern Africa, most priests were stationed 50 to 100 miles away from any other priest. Clergy in Mashonaland/SR were as isolated as any, except for priests in the Australian outback. They rarely met as a group except at the tri-annual Diocesan Synods that were held after 1903. The first time as many as six met was ten years after the foundation of the diocese, in 1901, at an ordination.

Some clergy had a hermit's nature and relished their solitude, like Arthur Shearly Cripps. Other successful men possessed a buoyancy of temperament: Gaul, with his "unquenchable gaiety",[28] the breezy Upcher and Beaven, whose watch-word was "Serve God and be cheerful".[29] Knight-Bruce regarded the ability "never to be depressed" as the most important qualification for a missionary[30] and clergy for Mashonaland/SR were variously expected to have a sense of humour, to be "men of grit and go, men bright and cheery and full of the Holy Ghost".[31]

Foreign service clergy also had to be whole-heartedly dedicated to their work, to have "exceptional consecration and simplicity of aim".[32] Foundations for the future could only be laid if they were prepared to labour patiently for many years among a handful of people, settler or indigenous. It took a great deal of 'grit' to sustain "picket duty"[33] on the outskirts of the Empire or the "dust and drudgery divine",[34] which was all that places like Mashonaland could offer.

---

[27] Archbishop of Brisbane [St. Clair Donaldson], 'Editorial', *RCM* 16:10 (Oct 1919), 3.

[28] A. Pierce Jones, *A Procession of Witness* (Cape Town: [Printed by the Stewart Printing Company, Cape Town], 1947), 78.

[29] 'Enthronement of the Bishop', *RCM* 8:2 (Feb 1911), 3.

[30] G.W.H. Knight-Bruce, *Memories of Mashonaland* (1895) (Facsimile reproduction: Bulawayo, Books of Rhodesia, 1970), 214.

[31] 'Letter from the Dean [F.H. Beaven]. March 20th, 1910', *MQP* LXII (May 1910), 6.

[32] [W.T. Gaul], 'Mashonaland Diocese', *CCM&PR* V:2 (Feb 1897), 30.

[33] Bishop of Brisbane [St. Clair Donaldson], JCMA *21* (Nov 1904), 2.

[34] [W.T. Gaul], 'The Bishop's Letter. No. XXV. Church House, Bulawayo, September 24th, 1901', *MQP* XXXVIII (Nov 1901), 4.

A limited number of men, however, possessed the resilience to withstand such conditions. Many found it difficult to keep reading and mentally stimulated: as Knight-Bruce discovered in 1888, "intellectual standards" tended to drop "on the Zambezi".[35] Some parsons, in their solitariness, tended to lose any sense of the corporate strength of the church or the liturgical year or even their sense of belonging to a diocese. It was not easy to keep up "spiritual tone".[36] Many, Mashonaland clergy among them, after years of isolation began to feel alone and unsupported, became dispirited or depressed, broke down, or resigned.

James Toy, for instance, resigned in 1912, because he felt the need of "bracing up" in an English parish after six years of lonely and difficult work on the railway south of Francistown.[37] Harry Quinn (1901–14) worked almost entirely alone, at the Victoria mission and then in the Selukwe Reserve, for some thirteen years. His letters reek of loneliness. In 1914, he suddenly abandoned his post (for war service) and subsequently joined the Roman Catholic Church, which did not allow its missionaries to work alone. He served with them as a missionary priest in Southern Rhodesia for the rest of his life.

Clergy working abroad also had usually to adjust to social surroundings which were very different from those to which they were accustomed at home. There were "no traditions, no atmosphere, no high level of public opinion"[38] and very few outward reminders of religion, such as church buildings. Missionaries lived surrounded by "the dead weight of heathendom"[39] and the criticism or antagonism of settlers and officials. Colonial clergy had to live in societies where most people were indifferent to religion.

There was also usually a lack of class distinction in the colonies and no high social status was guaranteed to a clergyman, as in England. Settlers were "given to judge of the clergyman, not from his position or his cloth, but by his merits as a Christian and a man".[40] Even bishops,

---

[35] 'The Bishop's Journey to the Zambezi', *BQP* 87 (Jan 1890), 194.

[36] 'Letter from Rev. J. Hallward. St. Cyril's, Bulawayo, Sept. 20th, 1901', *MQP* XXXVIII (Nov 1901), 11.

[37] 'Letter from the Bishop [F.H. Beaven]. Salisbury, Rhodesia, July 15th, 1912', *MQP* LXXXI (Aug 1912), 4.

[38] D. Ellison, from Regina, Saskatchewan, JCMA *32* (April 1910), 15.

[39] 'Letter from the Archdeacon of Mashonaland [E.H. Etheridge]. St. Augustine's Mission, Penhalonga, September 21st, 1911', *MQP* LXXVII (Nov 1911), 6.

[40] Ven A.B. Sidwell, Bishop-Elect of George, 'The Work of the Church among the White Settlers of South Africa', *Official Report of the Pan-Anglican Congress*, VI (London: S.P.C.K., 1908), S.E.1(c), 3.

accustomed to deference at home, could find themselves treated with "an easy equality" in the colonies.[41] One clergyman wrote home from Southern Rhodesia, "What are you to do when a burly miner calls "Time!" in the middle of your sermon...? Such experiences either make the parson natural or make him clear out".[42]

Clergy, particularly missionary clergy, also needed to be capable of living among races generally considered inferior with respect, consideration and real kindness. Imperious or autocratic behaviour or racial pride were out of place. The ideal missionary was a man like Walter Leary in Matabeleland, who had a natural sympathy for the local people and spoke their language fluently (he had grown up in Pondoland, speaking Xhosa, which is akin to SiNdebele). He became known by them as Tanda Bantu, "lover of the people".[43]

A greater assimilation to local cultures, however, was not expected in Mashonaland/SR or elsewhere in this period: the 'civilising mission' of 'Church and Empire', with its assumption that 'native peoples' had everything to learn and little to give, precluded such adaptation. It is worth noting, nevertheless, that Mashonaland/SR was one of the few dioceses in the world where the clergy were expected to serve both indigenous and settler communities. "much sympathy for the varieties of Colonial and Native life" was essential.[44]

IV *The 'best men'*

It was widely agreed by those familiar with the overseas church that, given the conditions abroad, work there was both more difficult and "more important, more responsible" than work at home.[45] Demands grew, therefore, that recruits be of a higher calibre than had hitherto been the case. Missionaries needed to better trained for their work, for instance, or of a higher social class.

---

[41] J.B. Atlay, *The Life of the Rt. Rev. Ernest Roland Wilberforce* (London: Smith Elder, 1912), 317.

[42] 'Letter from the Rev. P.H. Green. Gatooma, Southern Rhodesia. Easter Monday, 1917', *SRQP* CX (Nov 1919), 8.

[43] NAZ, HMss, Misc/BE 4/1/1, T.O. Beattie, Reminiscences, f. 9.

[44] 'Letter from the Bishop [W.T. Gaul]. No. XIX. Bulawayo, September 23rd, 1899', *MQP* XXX (Nov 1899), 3.

[45] Rev. J.A. Sharrock, Principal of Caldwell College, Tutincorin, South India, *CCR* (1890), 25.

As for colonial work, the overseas churches protested against the assumption that any clergyman was adequate for such work or even that men who were of not much use in England could be sent to the colonies. Overseas bishops declared that they were no longer willing to take a low standard of clergy and that second-rate men could stay behind in England, where someone without exceptional qualities of intellect or leadership could do well enough. "Inferior souls", Gaul wrote, were simply a "burden" overseas.[46]

Abroad, only really capable men would do. "[G]ive us abroad your best" wrote the Bishop of Trinidad, in 1892,[47] He spoke for the other overseas bishops, for they all wanted 'the best men'. The overseas clerical ideal, however, did not correspond exactly to the English ideal.

In England at the time, although argument raged about many aspects of clerical life and work, certain general expectations of the clergy remained which related to their role in society. Parsons were expected to be social exemplars and leaders of thought. Whatever else he was, the 'best' clergyman was a gentleman and a well-educated one, a product of the universities of Oxford or Cambridge. Many overseas bishops adhered to this ideal, seeking to recruit "men of culture and breeding... **the cream of our Universities**", the "best and choicest" England could produce.[48]

It was also true however that, overseas, clergyman from widely differing backgrounds could be equally successful: Arthur Shearly Cripps and Edgar Lloyd, in Mashonaland/SR, for example, long-serving missionaries in the Charter district and at St. Faith's, respectively. Cripps was a Charterhouse and university man and a poet who won an Oxford prize for poetry on a sacred subject from his mission hut. Lloyd came from a humble background, had attended a SPCK college for lay assistants in London and was largely self-educated. The two men, however, were close friends and intellectual companions, notable missionaries and in their different ways both fighters for the rights of local people in Mashonaland/SR against settler exploitation.

Other examples from the diocese can be given: Nelson Wellesley Fogarty was of Irish extraction, the son of an army boot maker. He

[46] [W.T. Gaul], 'The Bishop's Letter. No. II. Buluwayo, Matabeleland, May 24th, 1895', *MQP* XIII (July 1895), 5.

[47] [J.T. Hayes], 'Notes of the Month', *MF* XXXVIII:440 (Aug 1892), 314.

[48] *Ibid.*, 314; and see RHO/USPG, X540, 'Resolutions', JCMA Federation Conference, Bristol, November 1897.

was born in Canterbury (a garrison town) and educated there, at King's School and St. Augustine's Missionary College, before going out to Africa in 1894. He became the first, and impressive, Bishop of Damaraland in 1924. Harold Etheridge, nephew and great-nephew of bishops, educated at Marlborough, Keble College, Oxford and Wells Theological College, was consecrated Bishop of St. John's, Kaffraria in 1923.

Breeding and education alone, therefore, did not suffice for places where the foundations of young nations and churches were being laid and individual clergy wielded an influence potentially far greater than that of clergy at home. Additional qualifications or attributes were needed.

First among these were "capacity and character".[49] For colonial work particularly, 'character' or personality was thought to count for very much more than it did in England. In societies which had lost the habit of church-going, people would only go to church, "give the parson a good show", if they liked him.[50] Nothing, it was said, unfitted a clergyman for colonial work more than lack of character.

This character, moreover, needed to be of a particular masculine kind, for in pioneering areas the clergy dealt very largely with men and men who led hard lives. Settlers were typified as "really strong and strenuous men"[51] or the "most virile members of their nationality".[52] Their parsons needed to be able to stand up to them and deal with the harsh world in which they lived.

Their gospel also had to be plain and straight-forward, one which spoke to vigorous men. Anything which savoured of "*weakness*, either in itself or in them", had to be avoided.[53] Beaven exhorted his clergy to preach a "strong Christ"[54] and care was taken, when a stained-glass representation of St. George was commissioned for the memorial chapel

---

[49] *The Supply and Training of Candidates for Holy Orders, Report to the Archbishop of Canterbury* (Poole: W.H. Hunt, 1908), 26.

[50] RHO/USPG, E Series, 57(A), 1902, J. Hallward, Report, Railway Mission, 30th June, 1902.

[51] D. Ellison, from Regina, Saskatchewan, JCMA *32* (April 1910), 15.

[52] H.H. Montgomery, 'The Church's Missions in Christendom', *Pan-Anglican Papers, Being Problems for consideration at the Pan-Anglican Congress, 1908* (London: S.P.C.K., 1907), No. 5 [5].

[53] W. Roxburgh, 'Salisbury', *MQP* L (Nov 1904), 9.

[54] 'The Synod', *RCM* 15:7 (July 1918), 4.

of Salisbury Cathedral, to make sure that the saint was pictured as a "manly warrior" and not "an anaemic-looking creature".[55]

Manliness was certainly expected of the clergy in Mashonaland/SR. The settlers liked the parson to be one of themselves and a priest had to be "a mixer, not a Puritan", if he was to draw them to church.[56] It helped if he were an athlete: advertisments for clergy for the diocese stipulated, *inter alia*, "A man among men" and "if an athlete, so much the better"[57] and a new recruit, A.S. Robins, wrote in 1901, "Out here one of the first things one has to be is a man, no pigeon-breasted, knock-kneed weakling, no mother's darling and cry-when-looked-at".

Robins himself, 6 foot tall and 13 stone, was almost immediately on arrival made captain of the Salisbury Football Club. He found that "men with rough exteriors, rough work, and rough surroundings, were willing to come together to worship God" under his leadership.[58] Other clergy in Mashonaland/SR joined settlers in shooting, cricket or golf: it all helped to "add credit to the parson as a man".[59] Play with your flock and they would pray with you.

The expectation that clergy for the church overseas should display a certain type of masculinity further narrowed the field of possible recruits, however, for there was considerable contemporary unease in England about many of the clergy, precisely because they did not meet the description of the young, vigorous and manly parson. When compared with 'virile' colonials the very "manhood of the Old Country" could seem almost "played out".[60]

In the early nineteenth century, English parsons had typically been men who were comfortable with other men and masculine pursuits, particularly those of the countryside. Clerical life and work had changed markedly, however, in the course of the century. The Evangelical movement demanded greater personal piety of the parson, the Oxford movement emphasized the separated and spiritual nature of the priestly calling. English clergy became less part of the fabric of ordinary society

[55] 'Diocesan Notes', *RCM* 16:5 (May 1919), 3.

[56] NAZ, HMss, Misc, BE 4/1/1, T.O. Beattie, Reminiscences, f. 5.

[57] RHO/USPG, X1007, CE/UBM, *CSA Quarterly Appeal*, 8th November, 1901.

[58] 'Letter from the Rev. A.S. Robins. Salisbury, June 22nd, 1901', *MQP* XXXVII (Aug 1901), 11, 13. Cf. (above, p. 17) the description of Frank Surridge.

[59] H.P. Hale, 'Diocese of Mashonaland', *SACRMQP* 12 (July 1906), 9.

[60] 'Letter from Rev. W. Roxburgh. Umtali, July 26th, 1900', *MQP* XXXIV (Nov 1900), 21. The reference is to Australian troops, in Southern Rhodesia *en route* to the Second South African War.

than the hunting parsons and JPs of earlier times, their work was more narrowly confined to their religious duties and they spent more time with women and children than did other men.

The majority of parsons, moreover, by the end of the century, were sons of clergy. Most had had a limited experience of life and of human nature. In the colonies, however, clergy could not escape seeing "human nature and especially male human nature, as it is".[61] The first visit an itinerant parson might make in a settlement was to a bar. If he did not, he would fail to meet and gather his congregation.

Contemporaries in England worried that the clergy were becoming "mere ecclesiastics not *men*", their work no longer seen as "a man's job".[62] Silly curates were music hall jokes and young men about to be ordained were anxious lest "he who would put off the Old man" might find himself putting on "the Old woman".[63] An inevitable reaction followed, in the direction of a more 'muscular Christianity': it was now greatly to a parson's credit if he had been an athlete at university or could, when necessary, knock a 'tough' down and the muscular young curate became as much of a stereotype in the music halls as his opposite.

Too many parsons, however, lost the man in the clergyman and developed alienating characteristics, mannerisms that were considered unmanly or a distinctive parsonical voice. Yet, for work abroad, clergy were wanted who were without such characteristics. Gaul wrote despairingly of one man who failed in the early days, "Oh why *will* men bring their dear sweet Rectorial ways out here?"[64] and dismissed another young man with, "We can do very well without Pratt and Co following the Crucified". (Pratt and Co were clerical outfitters). "What we want", wrote Gaul "is hardness as well as harness".[65]

Finally, recruits for work abroad were expected to possess moral and spiritual strength. They had to be deeply religious, the 'best' men in every sense if they were to minister successfully, for where there

---

[61] 'Service abroad by one who has tried it' (Anon.), *East and the West* X (July 1912), 323–4.

[62] Committee appointed by the Archbishops of Canterbury and York, *The Supply and Training of Candidates for Holy Orders* (Westminster, 1925), 12–3.

[63] G.W.E. Russell, *Afterthoughts* (London: Grant Richards Limited, 1912), 386.

[64] RHO/USPG, D Series, 163(b), 1905, W. Mashonaland to Bishop Montgomery, 8th February, 1905.

[65] RHO/USPG, D Series, 142(b), 1902, Will. Mashonaland to Bishop, 15th July, 1902.

were no other outward reminders of religion the parson was the only "visible emblem" of Christ.[66] Each had to "embody some adequate conception of the Church" in his own person.[67] Only men of first-hand conviction could do this, not those who had found themselves in the ministry simply because they had been born in a vicarage. These latter, moreover, tended to grow tired of the difficulties encountered abroad and the ministrations of clergy who took "a faint interest in religion" were at a discount there: life abroad was "too strenuous to permit of trifling".[68]

From the literature, therefore, a very clear picture emerges of the ideal parson wanted for overseas work in the period 1890–1925 and it is interesting to note that there was, towards the end of the period, a convergence between this overseas ideal and the English ideal, particularly in the requirement that the clergy should be men of personality and first-hand conviction, capable of embodying the faith and ministering under very difficult conditions. In England, this requirement became evident only in the trenches of the World War One: the war in fact, exposed the deficiencies of many of the English clergy.

It also revealed that men who had worked abroad successfully made excellent war chaplains. Such Mashonaland/SR clergy were swift to adjust to conditions on the Front, their time in Africa having provided them with a "splendid training".[69] Conversely, the diocese was able to recruit several war chaplains after the conflict was over, in spite of the shortage of clergy in England: some war chaplains, having experienced ministry in the trenches, were reluctant to return to the quieter life of an English parish.

V *Recruitment: commissaries, bishops and romance*

Overseas bishops had commissaries in England who acted as their recruiting agents. Some held influential positions in the church or at the universities of Oxford and Cambridge (which produced the majority of the English clergy) and so were relatively well-placed to find men. Most commissaries, however, were ordinary working clergymen

[66] J. Hallward, 'Annual Meeting', *SACRMQP* 51 (April 1916), 25.
[67] D. Ellison, from Regina, Saskatchewan, JCMA 32 (April 1910), 15–6.
[68] W. Gore-Browne, Rector of Pretoria, *SACRMQP* 2 (Jan 1904), 12.
[69] H.C. Sandall, in 'Editorial', *RCM* 14:3 (Mar 1917), 1.

with limited access to potential recruits and, frequently, no first-hand knowledge of dioceses abroad. Their recruiting depended "almost entirely upon advertisments in Church papers" and they had "little or no opportunity of appealing to heart and conscience".[70] Powell, for example, when a parish priest in England, was commissary for the Bishop of Kaffraria and as he later admitted, an unsuccessful one; "I was supposed to interview clergy who might be wishing to go out there, but nobody wished to go".[71]

Apart from Knight-Bruce's staff, several of whom were recruited for him by others (the records are incomplete), only five other men can be said, with certainty, to have been found for Mashonaland by commissaries: A.D. Owen (1897); James Gillanders (1897); E. Skagen (1897); Samuel Christelow (1909); and J.L. Williams (1910).

The overseas bishops themselves, therefore, were their own chief recruiting officers, forced to tour England in order to look for men and the competition between the bishops for staff was as fierce as that for finance. England was said to be "a crowded hunting ground for bishops from all parts of the globe".[72] The new Bishop of Brisbane described his experience in 1904: "I have found myself in company with others passionately appealing for the supply of needs at least as great. I have found myself in competition with commissaries of Bishops near and far...I do feel the misery of this competition, the shame and disgrace which it lays upon the Church of England".[73] One foreign bishop was succinct: "the whole business is reduced to grab".[74]

Naturally, and all too frequently, a bishop's personality or his connections rather than the actual needs of his diocese tended to be the determining factors in recruitment, as in the raising of funds. The Bishop of Labuan and Sarawak expressed his view of this situation, in 1912, in "a few plain words": "[W]e bishops are tumbling over each other in our efforts to find men and money and very often the least deserving is the most successful. This is certainly the case when the man

---

[70] J.H. Ellison, in *Official Report of the Missionary Conference of the Anglican Communion* (London: S.P.C.K., 1894), 563.

[71] 'The New Bishop of Mashonaland', *South Africa* 76 (Oct 19 1907), 157.

[72] Editorial, 'Scarcity of Clergy', *RCM* 9:12 (Dec 1912), 1.

[73] Bishop of Brisbane [St. Clair Donaldson], JCMA *21* (Nov 1904), 2.

[74] Michael Furse, Bishop of Pretoria, in C. Lewis, and G.E. Edwards, *Historical Records of the Church of the Province of South Africa* (London: S.P.C.K., 1934), 617.

is an expert mendicant".[75] A report printed for private circulation, in 1903, made much the same point: "If a colonial bishop comes home to seek for men... and happens to have a number of influential friends, and is possessed of an attractive personality, he will in all probability get a certain number of men to volunteer to go out to him".[76]

A South African bishop who was recruiting at that very time provides a case in point: William Carter, who was translated from Zululand to Pretoria, after the South African War, was able to recruit over 60 clergy for the re-construction of his new (and difficult) diocese between 1902 and 1908, at a time when competition for clergy in England was made particularly acute by the needs of the church in Western Canada, overwhelmed by immigrants to the prairies. Carter, however, had been at Eton and Oxford, he was a nephew of one of the great Tractarians, T.T. Carter of Clewer and he was a friend and associate of Charles Gore, the leading High Churchmen of the day. He had been a successful slum priest and was an outstanding leader who could attract good men.

Bishops who had been unable to keep up their English connections, perhaps because they had been many years abroad, were at a disadvantage when it came to recruitment. "If [a colonial bishop] has not many influential friends, if he has been long abroad and therefore lost touch with the Church at home, if he has not an attractive personality, even though the needs of his diocese may be far greater than that of his brother bishop, he will probably get no one to come, or certainly fewer than his brother with the friends and the personality".[77] At the very time Carter was successfully collecting men for Pretoria, the ageing Archbishop of Capetown, William West Jones, wrote sadly from his diocese, "We are in aweful (sic) straits for want of men, and I cannot keep the work going" and "This poor diocese seems to offer no attraction to anybody. Perhaps it is my own fault".[78] West Jones had originally had many of the 'right connections' among the High Church party, had been an Oxford fellow and held an Oxford benefice, was an able man, with a warm and loveable personality but he had, by this time, been 31 years in Africa.

---

[75] LPL, Davidson, 425, Memo from Bishop of Labuan and Sarawak [W.R. Mounsey] to Summer Meeting of CBM, June 1912, f. 98.

[76] LPL, H5691.S7, Preliminary Expedition, Mission of Help, f. 27.

[77] *Ibid.*

[78] W/CPSA, AB/1162/A, Diocese of Capetown, Letter books, Archbishop of Capetown to Bishop of Southwell, August 30th, 1905, f. 184; to Lady Loch, September 27th, 1905, f. 229.

Even new bishops with connections could struggle to find men, however: the unsuccessful new bishop of Lebombo in 1893, W.E. Smyth, for example, (above, pp. 160–61) was a product of Eton and King's College Cambridge, took First Class in the Theological Tripos and was the recipient of various University honours. Bishops without 'friends' were rarely able to find sufficient clergy, let alone men of the calibre they sought and commentators lamented the tragedy of these less successful bishops, "losing heart and hope" on a furlough spent, not resting, but fruitlessly travelling the country, looking for men.[79]

Gaul, for example, returned to Mashonaland in 1896, ill and tired after months of hard work in England and Ireland, having failed to find staff even for his most important district, Bulawayo. This failure was described by his metropolitan, West Jones of Capetown, publicly, at the 196th anniversary meeting of the SPG, as "appalling and heart-rending". He pointed out that the creation of missionary sees was of little use if their bishops were left unsupported by clergy.[80]

It was also acknowledged (and deplored) that a significant element in recruiting, as in the raising of money, was 'romance', or the relative attractiveness of the work itself. It is instructive, in this regard, to note that the new Bishop of Brisbane in 1904, St. Clair Donaldson, came from the same circles as Carter of Pretoria. They were friends and former colleagues: Donaldson had earlier succeeded Carter as Head of the Eton Mission in the East End of London. Donaldson's commissaries had previously been commissaries for Carter.

The two bishops were recruiting at the same time but one had considerably more success than the other in attracting men. Weight must therefore be given to the probability that Pretoria won over Brisbane (and over Western Canada) not only because of the episcopal personalities or qualities of leadership concerned but also because the work offered in Pretoria also had its own attractions. Public attention had been captured by the events of the South African War. Now men, young men of the right sort, were wanted in the newly-conquered Transvaal to rebuild the church, much as young men of the same sort were wanted for Milner's 'kindergarten' to reconstruct the administration. Pretoria

[79] Woollcombe, *Under the Southern Cross*, 106.
[80] 'The Society's 196th Anniversary', *MF* XLII:500 (Aug 1897), 291.

could also offer mission work. Brisbane had only routine colonial work to offer.

There was little prospect of 'heroism and romance' to draw men to such dioceses as Lebombo or Mashonaland/SR except, as we have seen in Chapter Four, where there was a railway mission. The desire for 'romance' among recruits, as among missionary supporters, however, seemed nothing but frivolous to men already at work in these dioceses.

Samuel Christelow, the missionary at Bonda, for example, on hearing that someone writing in "a leading Church paper" in Britain, in 1922, had dismissed the area as "lacking in romance", responded, "[He] knows nothing of Rhodesia. What greater romance can one have other than that of winning a child-race for the Kingdom of God?"[81] Leary, attempting to set up the mission at Bembezi in 1901, with the help of a single catechist, wrote, "we need priests, *devoted* priests, who will not look back upon the flesh-pots of Egypt when they come out here and find life on a mission station unromantic, commonplace and lonely".[82] Etheridge, at Penhalonga, wrote in 1904, "there is but little that is heroic, romantic or exciting, but just a simple round of commonplace and elementary duties. And these are the things that men find hard".[83] A new missionary to the diocese in 1910, J.L. Williams, could confess to having had the 'romance' knocked out of him very soon after arrival.[84]

Mashonaland had its own share of "charm", moreover, if it lacked a stereotypical 'romance':[85] Gaul, in 1896, encouraging clergy to come out, promised they "would find the fascination of the colonies lasting".[86] Many who did venture out discovered this to be true: they found a delightful new land and work with its own deep satisfactions. H.H. Foster, for instance, in 1897, wrote of the "indescribable fascination of

---

[81] 'Letter from the Rev. S.J. Christelow. St. David's, Bonda, July 13th, 1922', *SRQP* CXXI (Aug 1922), 14.

[82] 'Letter from the Rev. J.W. Leary. St. Aidan's, Bembezi, September 5th, 1901', *MQP* XXXVIII (Nov 1901), 8.

[83] 'Letter from the Rev. E.H. Etheridge. St. Augustine's Mission, Panhalonga, August 24th, 1904', *MQP* L (Nov 1904), 12.

[84] 'Letter from the Rev. J.L. Williams, St. Augustine's Mission, Penhalonga, June 1910, *MQP* LXXIII (Aug 1910), 14.

[85] A.S. Cripps, 'Annual Meeting [Mashonaland Mission Association]: Work in Southern Rhodesia', *SRQP* CXII (May 1920), 9.

[86] 'Notes of the Month', *MF* XLI:486 (June 1896), 232.

life in Rhodesia" and the "fierce pleasure of pioneer work".[87] Thomas Beattie, in 1910, after two weeks in the diocese, wrote that he felt "already the strange fascinations of this great country which has gripped so many".[88] Others were impressed by the beauty and strange silence of the bush, by wild and rugged landscapes and the open veld.

VI *A lack of volunteers, reactions, remedial action*

However appealing the work overseas or heartrending the calls, however, very few of the English clergy responded. Their failure to do so produced sheer exasperation in supporters of the overseas church and particularly, as we have seen, in men themselves serving overseas. This had been the case since Selwyn of New Zealand had poured scorn on clergy who, instead of going abroad, sat down, in the prime of life, to do nothing more exacting than "collect butterflies".[89]

Other overseas churchmen continued in the same vein. They professed themselves "appalled" that young men were prepared to "stagnate", to settle down in the "very tiniest sphere" at home rather than volunteer for work abroad.[90] The reluctance of the English clergy to venture abroad was attributed to a "craven, diffident and un-enterprising spirit"[91] and the day-to-day duties of an English parish were unfavourably compared with the demands and physical hardships of the colonial church. Even the best men in England, it was said, were facing small issues compared with those faced abroad.

The younger clergy seemed to have "no force" to "fulfil the Mission of the Church to the English speaking race",[92] were unwilling to offer for the mission field. It was pointed out, frequently, that they seemed to be the only group of Englishmen unwilling to go abroad: others went readily enough, particularly to the Empire, as settlers, soldiers, officials

---

[87] 'Letter from Rev. Herbert Foster. U.S.S. Giaka, N. Lat.43. October 14th, 1897', *MQP* XXII (Nov 1897), 12–3.

[88] 'Letter from the Rev. T.O. Beattie. St. John's Rectory, Bulawayo, June 10th, 1910', *MQP* LXXIV (Nov 1910), 18.

[89] The Revd. H.W. Tucker, M.A., *Memoir of the Life and Episcopate of George Augustus Selwyn D.D. Bishop of New Zealand, 1841–1869; Bishop of Lichfield, 1867–1878* (London: William Wells Gardner, 1879), *I*, 327.

[90] C.F. Andrews (Cambridge Mission to Delhi), JCMA *33* (Nov 1905), 6.

[91] Letter from A.L. Keith, The Parsonage, Talawakele, Ceylon, January 9th, 1907, *Guardian* (Feb 20th, 1907), 326.

[92] Bishop of Brisbane [W.T.T. Webber], JCMA [*12*] (April 1900), 17–8.

or businessmen. Where were the clergy of "adventurous faith", with "a sporting instinct on their spiritual side" who were needed to man the overseas church?[93]

Churchmen in Mashonaland/SR were as vocal as others. Gaul described England as a mere "suburb" of the Empire, with its vast colonial dioceses.[94] He failed to understand how young men could bear the "humdrum and almost pathetic respectability" of clerical life at home.[95] They ought to come out to Africa, become "large-minded", get "lost on the veldt"[96] and be prepared to be "crucified for Christ" as settlers were for the world.[97] Upcher declared that a "vigorous young country" like Rhodesia suited a "vigorous parson" better than "a prebend's stall" or a "soft billet" in England.[98] Beaven wrote that the clergy in cathedral towns in England were "not overworked", were "cramping and narrowing their lives" while there was acute need abroad.[99]

Struggling clergy abroad were tormented by the reluctance of clergy in England to come out and help them. Leary, in 1901, asked, "Are the clergy...going to be forever content with standing on missionary platforms and pointing the way with soul-stirring eloquence to the dark mass of ignorant heathenism in foreign lands and ever find a ready excuse why *they* should not go themselves? It is sickening. What has been the result in South Africa of all your missionary enthusiasm? A miserable handful of priests...."[100] Couldn't England spare some of its thousands of men for Mashonaland, where men were breaking down from overwork? asked Harry Buck, from Penhalonga, in 1913.[101]

---

[93] D.F. Ellison, *God's Highwaymen: the Story of the South African Church Railway Mission* (London: S.P.C.K., 1930), 64, 66.

[94] RHO/USPG, D Series, 130(a), 1899, Will. Mashonaland to Mr Tucker, January 16th, 1899.

[95] RHO/USPG, E Series, 54A, 1899, Will. Mashonaland, 'Dangers and Why Not?', To the Editor *MF* (n.d.) [April], 1899.

[96] RHO/USPG, D Series, 134(A), 1900, W. M'land to Mr Tucker, Bulawayo, July (n.d.), 1900.

[97] RHO/USPG, D Series, 163(b), 1905, W. Mashonaland to Bishop, February 13th, 1905.

[98] 'Letter from Archdeacon Upcher', *MQP* XXXVII (Aug 1901), 21.

[99] 'Letter from the Archdeacon of Matabeleland. St. John's Rectory, Bulawayo, (n.d.)', *MQP* LVI (May 1906), 6.

[100] 'Letter from Rev. J.W. Leary, St. Aidan's Bembezi, September 5th, 1901', *MQP* XXXVIII (Nov 1901), 8.

[101] RHO/USPG, E Series, 68(B), 1913, H.C. Buck, Report, Quarter ending December 31st, 1913.

These men believed that the Church of England was responsible for their plight and held the answer to their needs, a view widely held by those concerned with the overseas church throughout the period 1890–1925 and beyond. The matter was raised constantly, not only in correspondence, church papers and publications but also whenever representatives of the church gathered, at the 1897 Lambeth Conference for example and the Pan-Anglican Congress in 1908.

The supply (and better training) of workers for the overseas Church was the first on the list of all the topics proposed for the Pan-Anglican Congress, for instance and when a suggestion was made that the responsibility for these lay with the mother church, there was no dissent. As with money, so with men, what needed to be recognised was a principle of re-distribution or fairness. The church's work, at home and abroad, needed to be seen as a whole, men (and means) to be shared and England ought to be prepared to make sacrifices to help the church abroad.

Unified action was, however, as difficult to achieve in recruiting as in fund-raising, but not entirely for the same reasons. Central fundraising was hampered largely by the de-centralised nature of the Church of England and by the independence of the missionary societies. Central recruiting was hindered chiefly by the professional independence of the clergy of the Church of England. Unlike clergymen in dioceses abroad, where others decided a man's sphere of work, English clergymen could only be invited, not directed, to a course of action. They could not be 'sent' to the mission field, as so many desired.

The lack of definite policy and haphazardness in recruiting, which had been lamented since the mid-nineteenth century, therefore continued into the twentieth, with some modifications. After its formation in 1920, for example, the Missionary Council of the Church Assembly gathered and disseminated information about the needs of the overseas church. The various dioceses of the CPSA made attempts to co-ordinate recruiting from 1911, formed a South African Church League in 1914 and a South African Church Institute in London in 1925. These bodies could not relieve the bishops of the need to make their own recruiting tours but did render them and their commissaries considerable assistance. Responsibility for recruiting otherwise continued to be left, very largely, to individuals.

Various efforts were made in England, however, to increase the numbers of men available for work overseas. These attempts were directed, in the first instance, towards the supply of permanent workers, men who were committed to a lifetime abroad. This was done by providing the means for their training, for it had become clear by the turn of the century and continued to be true into the 1920s, that a significant hindrance to a supply of permanent workers for the overseas church was financial. Training for the ministry was very expensive. Missionary or theological colleges which provided free or heavily subsidised training were oversubscribed and there was no lack of suitable applicants.

The CMS began to pay for the training of its missionaries in 1887 and thenceforward was able to supply as many missionaries as the society was able to support. In 1904, the SPG broke with two hundred years of tradition and followed suit. A Five-Shilling Fund was launched, with the initial aim of assisting 40 candidates to acquire a first-class preparation for their work: three years at university and two at training college. The response exceeded expectation: £4,500 was raised in the first sixteen months. By 1906, 83 candidates were being supported, some wholly, some partly. By 1922, £55,500 had been raised and by 1926 no candidate had to be refused for lack of money. The scheme was highly successful, in its own terms. The numbers of English clergy serving with the SPG abroad increased from some 260 in 1894 to 603 in 1924. In comparison to the need abroad, however, such increases were still inadequate: in 1925, it was estimated that double that number of recruits (some 600 men), were wanted to meet only the immediate needs of the overseas church.

Another initiative grew out of the difficulties of recruiting encountered by the first Bishop of Corea in 1890 (above, p. 160). The one clergyman who had shown an interest in joining him, Herbert Kelly, was left behind in England to find and train staff for Corea. Kelly founded both a religious order, the Society of the Sacred Mission and a theological college, at Kelham. He and the clergy who joined him trained young men, mainly young men who would otherwise have become clerks, for both lay and ordained work abroad.

The Kelham initiative won wide-spread praise at home as well as abroad, although clergy from the lower classes were not normally acceptable at home. In fact, as Kelly himself realised early on, many candidates were applying to him for training not because they had a missionary vocation but because there was no other way that men from their social class could become clergymen.[102] The training given to

---

[102] H.H. Kelly, *England and the Church: Her calling and its fulfilment considered in relation to the increase and efficiency of her ministry* (London: Longmans and Co., 1902), 59.

candidates at Kelham, however, was long and hard. Social deficiencies were removed, Kelham products, if not 'gentlemen' in the true sense, nevertheless able to conduct themselves with ease in society.

In the end, however, the very success of the scheme told against the church overseas: when Kelham men became acceptable at home as well as abroad, the initiative suffered from capture by the home church. In 1903, Kelham ceased to be a purely missionary college: by 1914, while the college had produced 82 students, 70 were serving in the home church and only 12 overseas; by 1930 Kelham was producing more ordinands for the home church than any other theological college.

Efforts were also made to assist the churches overseas with short service schemes. A man might not wish to commit himself to work abroad for life but still be prepared to spend a few years in a colonial diocese while young. Accredited schemes were necessary, because it had become clear that one reason why the English clergy were reluctant to go abroad was because it was difficult for a man who had done so, on his own initiative, to find a position if he attempted to return home: "returned empties" were regarded with some suspicion.[103]

The first recognised scheme, the five-year scheme, was begun for the Brisbane diocese in 1887 and met with considerable success. After 1894, therefore, when the Junior Clergy Missionary Association (JCMA) was formed in connection with SPG, pressure grew for a wider scheme for short service in the church abroad. Such a scheme was endorsed in 1897 by the bishops of the Lambeth Conference and in 1899 a Council for Service Abroad was created, with high hopes of a flood of recruits.

It was expected that young men would be fired by the idea of serving as "curates of the Empire" and that a movement would develop between England and the colonies which would rival the earlier 'slum movement' at home.[104] A senior overseas clergyman, F.S. Baines, recently Archdeacon of Durban, was seconded to run the Council and was immediately besieged by the overseas bishops with requests for men. The expected flood, however, was no more than a trickle and by the time Baines was recalled to Africa to become Bishop of Natal in 1901, the Council was virtually moribund.

The JCMA itself had been formed with hopes that through its activities many of the younger clergy would develop an interest in mission

[103] LPL, RD, 128, R.T. Gardner, Hon. Sec. Council for Service Abroad (United Board of Missions), to Archbishop, April 16th, 1906, f. 319.

[104] RHO/USPG, X1002, London JCMA, Minutes (Nov 1899), f. 8.

and consider service abroad. Very few of its members did volunteer, however: in 1904, for example, the association had 5,176 members but only 273 of them were serving abroad.

Other attempts to attract large offers of service were made at the time of the Pan-Anglican Conference in 1908; in 1919, when a Recruiting Campaign for Service in the Kingdom of God was launched (also led by an experienced overseas clergyman); and at the publication of the World Call in 1925. None of these was conspicuously successful. The only large-scale scheme to attract a reasonable number of suitable volunteers was that for Western Canada in 1910, which was backed by an unprecedented appeal by the Archbishops of Canterbury and York. The scheme, when implemented, however, was a very limited success (one critic described it as "a melancholy lesson" for the home church)[105] as it had in many respects been ill thought-out and many volunteers went to unsuitable posts.

Nevertheless, although individual schemes were less than successful, their existence and their endorsement did create a greater overall acceptance of short service abroad by the church at home. A few more of the English bishops than before were prepared to encourage their clergy to go abroad, particularly after men with overseas experience began to be appointed to English sees: when George Wyndham Kennion returned to Bath and Wells from Adelaide in 1894, for example, or St. Clair Donaldson to Salisbury from Brisbane, in 1920.

Short service became almost the norm in certain sections of the church abroad, particularly in Australia and Southern Africa. The majority of the men serving in the CPSA in 1911, for instance, were single or short service men. A very high proportion of the Mashonaland/SR clergy served short terms (for a variety of reasons, including illness): thirty-nine of the seventy-six men recruited for Mashonaland served for under six years. Thirteen served for a year or less.

Short service clergy, therefore, became essential to the survival of the church abroad but the system had its limitations. Men returning to England could still be at a disadvantage when it came to finding a position and the system was costly for the overseas churches, since it usually took at least two years before an English clergyman had adapted sufficiently to become useful in the colonies. Endless chopping and

[105] J.H.F. Peile, 'The Case for Voluntary Clergy,' [review of book by the same name, by Roland Allen], *Church Quarterly Review* 110 (July 1930), 337–8.

changing, moreover, meant that the work of the church abroad lacked stability and continuity.

A tiny handful of clergy (recruited in the period 1890–1925) served 20 years or more in Mashonaland/SR. Five were missionaries, James Hay Upcher (1892–1931), Edgar Lloyd (1902–36), Arthur Shearly Cripps (1901–1926, 1930–52), Ernest Simpson (1907–32) and Samuel Christelow (1909–45). Two were colonial clergymen: Beaven, and Ernest Parker (1902–32), at Salisbury for almost 30 years. Only four men, all of them missionaries, Upcher, Lloyd, Cripps, and G.E.P. Broderick, spent the rest of their lives in the diocese and 'left their bones' there.[106]

Continuity in church affairs in Mashonaland/SR, therefore, was provided more by dedicated members of the laity than by the clergy. This was certainly so among the settlers: many of the same names appear on church committees and councils, diocesan boards and Synod lists from the 1890's to well beyond the period of this study. R.A. Letts, for example, a member of St. John's Bulawayo, left the diocese in 1938, after 40 years as an active layman. Godfrey King, the Diocesan Registrar, served from 1906 until his death in 1946.

These lay people also gave a much-needed unity to the scattered work of the church: the names of officials and Company police, in particular, recur in the church's records as they are posted around the country. Captain L.C. Masterson of the BSA police, for instance, was a leading layman in Selukwe, Melsetter, Victoria and Hartley, between 1910 and 1921. J.P.L. de Schmidt, Civil Commissioner and Magistrate, was an active layman at Gwanda, Enkeldoorn, Gwelo and Salisbury between 1902 and 1925.

VII *The Mashonaland/SR clerical recruits*

When what is known of the clergy who were recruited for Mashonaland/SR is analysed, they show no great divergence in background from the generality of English clergy (if the 15 missionary college men, men intended only for work abroad, are excluded). Forty-eight percent of the rest of the recruits (29 out of 61) were Oxford and Cambridge graduates, for instance, a reasonable proportion, given

[106] In local understanding, the final act of identification with Africa and its people: see, D.V. Steere, *God's Irregular: Arthur Shearly Cripps: A Rhodesian Epic* (London: S.P.C.K., 1973), 151.

that the percentage of such men among ordinands in England itself dropped from over 60%, in the 1890s to 42%, in the post-war period (1920–30). A fair number were from clerical families, as were the majority of English parsons.

It can be surmised that some clergy who served in the diocese (missionary college men included) may have been attracted by its 'patriotism', or high level of English feeling (see, below, p. 196). It can also be stated that all were willing to serve in a diocese with a moderate degree of High Church or Anglo-Catholic practice.

Two other factors distinguish the recruits as a group, however, and it is likely that these two factors were particularly important in influencing them to serve. The first is that many of them had links with others and so the Mashonaland clergy of this period can be said to have been, to a degree, self-recruiting. The second factor is that many had some kind of colonial connection or experience abroad.

If the links between the clergy are traced, they show both chains and clusters of connections. Beaven, for example, himself recruited by Gaul, was largely responsible for the arrival in the diocese of J.F. Salt in 1903. Salt then recruited A.S. Shum in 1905. Shum came to Mashonaland from Bloemfontein but had earlier been, like Salt, a curate in the Lichfield Diocese. He, in his turn, was followed out in 1907 by George Ashworth, the man who had succeeded him as curate in his Lichfield parish in 1902. George Ashworth then recruited his brother, Frederick Ashworth, in 1910.

Other groups of recruits were drawn to Mashonaland by the influence of the same man. Several came through William Roxburgh, priest at Umtali from 1898 to 1904. Roxburgh was himself recruited by Douglas Pelly (originally for Penhalonga). Roxburgh's presence in Mashonaland was influential in the recruitment, in 1901, of Arthur Shearly Cripps, with whom he had been at Trinity College, Oxford and who expected to work with him.[107] Roxburgh also, once in the diocese, made contact with another Trinity friend, Harry Buck and Buck arrived to work at Penhalonga in 1903. Roxburgh was further responsible for recruiting, through his sister, who ran a branch of the Mashonaland Mission Association, two men who had been schoolmasters at St. David's College, Lampeter: John Wright Davies (1906–1911) and G.E.P. Broderick (1906–1919).

---

[107] A.S. Cripps, 'Stray Glimpses of a Prophet', *RCM* 16:10 (Oct 1919), 5.

A significant number of recruits had colonial connections or experience abroad. Thirteen, including some ordained in England, had been born in the colonies. Eight of these were South African-born: Hezekiah Mtobi (1896–1901), William Griffiths (1895–6), W.H. Robins (1897–1900), Walter Leary (1898–1908), G.E.P. Broderick (1906–1919); Thomas Beattie (1910–300); Pieter Abraham de Wit (1911–2) and R.J.J. Garrod (1920–27). Three men were Canadians: F.W. Ritchie (1893), Edward Skagen (1897) and Harry Quinn (1901–14). One was a New Zealander, R.R.St.J. Hovell (1910–13, 1914–19).

Twenty-six of the 76 recruits, though English-born, had lived abroad before going to Mashonaland/SR. Ten had served as clergy in the CPSA. Of the others, B.N. Woodard (1920–23) had previously been a miner in the diocese; Douglas Pelly (1892–3, 1895–9) and Ronald Alexander (1898–1908) had farmed as young laymen in Canada; and Anthony Bathe (1898–9) had been a chaplain in Egypt. Several men had been parsons in Australia or Canada and others had missionary experience: O.C. MacMahon (1909–10), for example, was the son of a missionary in Madagascar; A.S. Robins (1901–10) had served with the SPG as a layman. Three men had worked with the UMCA: James Gillanders (1897–1910), as a layman; J.S. Wimbush (1900–03); W.G. Webster (1912–25).

Some of the clergy had relatives in South Africa or in Mashonaland/SR itself: John Hallward (1900–15) and J.H. Selmes (1897–1902) both joined brothers in Matabeleland. Hovell, the New Zealander, had a sister who was married to a Rhodesian miner. J.C. Forrester, who served as a locum at Bulawayo in 1919, had a brother living in the town and J.R. Powley (1924–5) was the brother of a Native Commissioner at Mount Darwin. H. Heriot-Hill (1923–7), a middle-aged man who came to the diocese in 1923, joined a son who was living in Salisbury.

Clergy Recruits: Mashonaland/Southern Rhodesia, 1890–1925

No	Name	Service in Mashonaland	Education: Oxford or Cambridge/ Theological College (non-graduate)/ Missionary College/Other	Clerical status: ordinand/ deacon/ lay/years since ordained deacon	Marital status: married recruit or married while serving	Connection: bishop/ cleric/ commisary/SPG	Colonial connection/ foreign experience
1	Trusted, W.	1890	TC:Queen's College, Birmingham (+ B.A. Durham)	7		Bp	X
2	Balfour, F.R.T.	1890–2	C:Trinity	18		Bp	X
3	Surridge, F.H.	1890	TC:Sarum	5			X
4	Sewell, J.R.	1891–2	O:Merton	6			
5	Lawrence, F.	1892–3	MC:Burgh	Ord			
6	Upcher, J.H.	1892–1931	C:Trinity	15		Bp/SPG	
7	Sylvester, A.D.	1892–4	King's College, London; King's College, Windsor, Nova Scotia	Deacon (Nova Scotia) 6			X
8	Ritchie, F.W.	1893	Bishop's College, Lennox	Deacon (Guiana) 8			X
9	Walker, J.A.	1893–1903	Durham	Lay/ord	M(s)		
10	Pelly, D.R.	1892–3, 1895–9	C:Emmanuel	Lay/ord	M(s)	Bp/cl	X
11	Hammick, E.A.	1895–7	O:Exeter	21			
12	Foster, H.H.	1895–1901 1908–13	O:Pembroke	8	[sister]		X
13	Griffiths, W.	1895–6	St.Cyprian's College, Bloemfontein	14		Bp	X
14	Mtobi, H.	1896–1901	[Diocese of Grahamstown]	9	M(r)	[Bp]	X
15	Jones, H.W.	1896	SDC, Lampeter: B.A.	6		Bp/SPG	
16	Fogarty, N.W.	1897–1900	MC:Canterbury	3	M(s)	Bp	[X]

No	Name	Service	Education	Clerical status	Marital status	Connection: Bishop/ cleric/ SPG/commisary	Connection: colonial/ foreign
17	Robins, W.H.	1897–1900	St.Cyprian's, Bloemfontein	18		Bp	X
18	Skagen, E.	1897	St. John's College, Manitoba	Deacon (Rupertsland 3		Comm	X
19	Selmes, J.H.	1897–1902	O:Merton	8		Cl	X
20	Gillanders, J.	1897–1910	[Scotland/ UMCA]	Lay/ord	M(s)	Comm	X
21	Caulfeild, L.	1897–99	SDC, Lampeter: B.A.	Lay/ord		Cl/SPG	
22	Bathe, A.	1898–9	O:Brasenose	27		Bp	X
23	Leary, J.W.	1898–1908	O:Keble	3		Cl	X
24	Roxburgh, W.J.	1898–1904	O:Trinity	8		Cl	
25	Alexander, R.	1898–1908	MC:Canterbury	Lay/ord		Cl/SPG	X
26	Etheridge, E.H.	1900–1923	O:Keble	5		Cl	X
27	Hallward, J.	1900–1915	O:Brasenose	5	[sister]	Cl	X
28	Wimbush, J.S.	1900–1903	O:Oriel	9	M(r)		X
29	Cripps, A.S.	1901–26 (1932–52)	O:Trinity	10		Cl/SPG	
30	Robins, A.S.	1901–10	MC:Canterbury	Ord	M(s)	SPG	X
31	Quinn, H.R.	1901–14	MC:Canterbury	3 (Niagara)			X
32	Owen, A.D. [lay 1897]	1901–3 1910–12	London: MRCS LRCP	Lay	M(r)	Comm/cl	
33	Lloyd, E.W.	1902–36	[SPCK College]	Lay	M(s)		
34	Parker, E.J.	1902–32	O:Brasenose	7	M(s)		
35	Urch, F.	1902–4	O:Christ church	5	M(r)		
36	Salt, F.J.	1903–9	O:Christ church	6	M(s)	Cl/SPG	
37	Beaven, F.H.	1903–10 (Bishop 1910–24)	TC: St.Bees, (+Durham)	25	M(r)	Bp	X

No	Name	Service	Education	Clerical status	Marital status	Connection: Bishop/ cleric/ SPG/commisary	Connection: colonial/ foreign
38	Buck, H.A.	1905–15 (1920–49 with C.R)	O:Trinity	Ord		Cl/SPG	
39	Turner, C.G.B.	1905–6	[Literate]	3		SPG	
40	Shum, A.C.	1905–11	TC:Lichfield	5		Cl	X
41	Broderick, G.E.P.	1906–19	London (B.Sc)	1	M(s)	Cl/SPG	X
42	Wright Davies, J.	1906–11	SDC, Lampeter: B.A.	5	M(s)	Cl/SPG	
43	Toy, J.	1906–11	TC: Manchester "Scholae Episcopi"	3			
44	Simpson, E.J.	1907–32	MC:Canterbury	Lay	M(s)		
45	Ashworth, G.L.	1907–21	Durham: B.A.	8		Cl	
46	Christelow, S.J.	1909–45	MC:Warminster	Ord	M(s)	SPG	
47	McMahon, O.C.	1909–10	MC:Canterbury	Ord			X
48	Beattie, T.O.	1910–30	MC:Burgh	3	M(s)	Cl/comm	X
49	Williams, J.L.	1910–15	SDC, Lampeter: B.A.	7	M(s)	Comm	
50	Davies, R.B.	1910–11	C:St.John's	26	[sister]		X
51	Hovell, R. St.J.H.	1910–13 1914–19	University of New Zealand: B.A.	4	[mother]		X
52	Harker, E.G.	1911–28	O:Exeter	18	M(r)	Cl	
53	Ashworth, F.L.	1911–20	C:Selwyn	4	–	Cl	
54	Goldring, C.	1911–12	O:Exeter	7			
55	de Wit, P.A.	1911–12	University of the Cape	12	M(r)		X
56	Lack, W.F.	1912–15	TC:Can.Schol. Linc.	3	–		
57	Green, P.H.	1912–19 1922–25	TC:Lichfield	3	M(r)	Bp	
58	Knyaston, P.E.	1912–23	C:King's	21	M(r)	Cl	
59	Webster, W.G.	1912–25	MC:Canterbury (+ Durham B.A.)	12	M(s)	Cl	X
60	Wilson, J.W.	1912–25	MC:Burgh (+ L.Th. Durham)	Ord	–	Cl	

No	Name	Service	Education	Clerical status	Marital status	Connection: Bishop/ cleric/ SPG/com-misary	Connection: colonial/ foreign
61	Sandall, H.C.	1913–16	C:St.John's	10	M(r)		
62	Maynard, A.C.M.	1914–16 1919–29	C:Queen's	7	M(s)		
63	Scogings, F.	1914–28	MC:Burgh (+ L.Th. Durham)	Deacon	M(s)	Cl	
64	Clissold, W.J.	1916–22	C:St.John's	9	–		
65	Forrester, J.C.	1919 (locum)	Trinity, Dublin: B.A.	20	?		X
66	Keates, W.J.	1920–21	MC:Burgh (+ L.Th. Durham)	5	–		X
67	Woodward, B.N.N.	1920–23	TC:Bishop's Hostel, Farnham	6	M(r)	Cl	X
68	Garrod, R.J.J.	1920–27	TC:St. Paul's, Grahamstown	10	–		X
69	Clarke, G.S.	1920–25	TC:Can.Schol. Linc.	9	–	Bp	
70	Crane, E.W.J.	1920–44	O:University	8	–	Bp	
71	Knights, A.C.	1921–31 1934–39	MC:Burgh (+ L.Th. Durham)	Deacon	–		
72	Young, A.D.	1922–27	London: B.A.	8	M(r)		
73	Heriot-Hill, H.	1924–28	TC:Can. Schol.Linc.	32	M(r)		X
74	Powley, J.R.	1924–5	O:Queen's	19	–		X
75	Le Suer, A.B.	1924–34 1939–x	MC:Burgh (+ L.Th. Durham)	Deacon	–	SPG	
76	Chambers, B.F.	1925–31	C:Trinity	5	–		

Principal sources: *Crockford's Clerical Directory*, 1890–1944; *Mashonaland Quarterly Paper*, 1892–1915; *Southern Rhodesia Quarterly Paper*, 1915–1926; *Rhodesia Church Magazine*, 1901–1925; *Church Chronicle*, 1904–1927; USPG archives, Bodleian Library of Commonwealth and African Studies at Rhodes House, Oxford; Diocesan records, National Archives of Zimbabwe; CPSA archives, Department of Historical Manuscripts, University of the Witwatersrand Library.

CHAPTER SIX

RELIGIOUS PRACTICE IN MASHONALAND/SOUTHERN RHODESIA: ENGLISH MODELS AND SOUTH AFRICAN INFLUENCES; LOCAL ADAPTATIONS; AND 'RELIGION ON THE VELD'

I *English models, South African influences*

The primary models for the institutions and religious practice of the Diocese of Mashonaland/SR, in the period 1890–1925, were those of the 'mother church', the Church of England. This was most clearly the case where ministry to settlers was concerned: Knight-Bruce and Powell, for example, both assumed it was their duty to provide the settlers with both pastoral care (churches and clergy) and education (church schools), on English lines.

Gaul proposed to recreate English home life (where the social, religious and the cultural were intertwined) for the settler community. Upcher wrote that parsons like himself were "pioneers and supporters of civilisation, trying to make men's lives in colonies such as ours less of an exile, more of an England over the sea";[1] and colonial clergy set themselves to establish the best English parochial forms and traditions (with some adaptations) in raw frontier towns.

These aspirations were not entirely out of keeping with the circumstances of the diocese. The largest settler group within it was that of the white community of (Southern) Rhodesia, a colony which was founded (the British government legitimized the ambitions of Cecil Rhodes) in order to increase Imperial influence in the region. This white community was built up between 1890 and 1925 by selective immigration, mainly from Britain and South Africa. By 1921, 95.8% of the settlers were, technically at least, of British nationality.[2]

They formed a community with its own marked characteristics. Flux (movement in and out of the country, as well as within it) was

---

[1] 'Letter from Archdeacon Upcher. Wreningham, Wymondham, January 8th, 1896', *MQP* XV (Feb 1896), 12.

[2] Barry M. Schutz, 'European Population Patterns, Cultural Persistence, and Political Change in Rhodesia', *Canadian Journal of African Studies* VII:1 (1923), 9.

one of them, for real 'settlement' only began to take place towards the end of the period. This was also a predominantly male society even into the 1920s and so its composition was considerably affected by the shifts in occupation of the men which have been considered in earlier chapters.

There was also, fairly early in its history, a rough division of the community into two classes: the respectable (mainly, though not exclusively, town-dwellers) and the rowdy (represented by small-workers, traders, early farmers and transport-riders) and there was a marked contrast, even among the respectable, between the society of the first decade or so, which was made up largely of young Englishmen, most of them 'gentlemen' and that which succeeded it. The settler population of 1911 was less wealthy and well-educated than that of 1904,[3] for instance and although immigration requirements were subsequently tightened, there were few English public school accents to be heard among the men of the 1920s.[4] Less is known about the origins or social mix of the settler women but anecdotal evidence indicates that women from English-speaking communities in South Africa as well as the 'home-born' were to be found at all points on the colonial social spectrum.

There were also distinctive minorities among the settlers: a Jewish community, which produced two early mayors; a small Roman Catholic community, with Irish, French and German religious, who were held in unusually high regard for a British colony; a tiny Greek community, with its own Archimandrite, with whom the Anglicans were on the most cordial of terms;[5] and several considerable communities of 'Dutch' farmers.[6] This was therefore a society which differed in many respects from the community of ultimate origin, from Britain. A majority of the settlers throughout the period, however, were always, nominally at least, members of the English Church.[7]

---

[3] *Report of the Director of Census, regarding the Census taken on 7th May, 1911* (Salisbury: Government Printer, 1912), 9.

[4] Tawse Jollie, *The Real Rhodesia* (1924) (Facsimile reproduction: Bulawayo: Books of Rhodesia, 1971), 5–6. And see below, p. 219.

[5] There were 39,174 white settlers in 1926, 1,546 (3.9%) of whom were Jewish; 7.7%, Roman Catholic; and 1%, Greek: *Report of the Director of Census for 1926* (Salisbury: The Government Printer, 1927), *Part II*, 18–19.

[6] The proportion of (South African) 'Dutch' was at its highest in 1921, at 20% of the white settler population and then began to decline: R.S. Roberts, 'The Settlers', *Rhodesiana* 39 (September 1978), 57.

[7] English Church members were estimated at 60–80% of the settler population in the early 1890s but reliable figures are only available from 1904: membership grew from 42% in 1904, to 45% (or 55.6% of the non-Dutch settler population) in 1926.

They were also, whether members of the English Church or not, culturally conservative, heavily dependent upon the culture of 'home' like other small white communities in Africa, those of East Africa, for instance or the scattered English-speaking settlers of the south. While, therefore the white settlers established a local identity (they became proudly "Rhodesian" as early as 1900)[8] they were also deeply "patriotic", could be described by the early 1920s as "British" and "intensely" so.[9]

At the heart of the Diocese of Mashonaland/SR and dominant within it, was a colony in which a "young, national life, loyal to the traditions of the home land" was being built up.[10] The religion which had done so much to shape the traditions of 'home' was expected to present a familiar face, the Anglican church in South Central Africa to be recognisable as the church of the English people.

In missionary work, on the other hand, the English model was less dominant. The Church of England itself stood for the "right of national independence within Catholic unity" (as expressed in its own break from Rome)[11] and in Mashonaland/SR, as throughout the missionary extensions of the church abroad, indigenous people were expected to develop an appropriate religious identity. Nevertheless, most of the missionaries came to the diocese directly from 'home' and their presuppositions were English (or British). The daily round of a mission station could be modelled on that of an English parish, as at St. Faith's, in 1914.[12]

In matters cultural too, converts could not escape a certain degree of Anglicising for the task of the missionaries was to 'civilise' as well as Christianise. In the Selukwe area in 1915, a clergyman could notice with satisfaction, as a sign of advancement, the substitution of clothes made from imported cotton for traditional garments made from skins. Other aspects of English life such as traditional forms of play were introduced. On St. Stephen's day in 1898, at St. Augustine's Penha-

---

[8] O.N. Ransford and H.W. Kinsey, 'The Seige of Elands River', *Rhodesiana* 40 (1979), 9.

[9] Tawse Jollie, *The Real Rhodesia* (1924) (Facsimile reproduction: Bulawayo: Books of Rhodesia, 1971), xv, 7.

[10] 'Letter from the Archdeacon of Matabeleland [H.H. Foster], February 24th, 1912', *MQP* LXXX (May 1912), 19.

[11] Cf. Rev. M.N. Trollope (Corea), *MF* XL:474 (June 1895), 232.

[12] RHO/USPG, E Series, 69(B), 1914, Elaine Lloyd to Miss Sanders, December 31st, 1914.

longa, local women competed in an 'egg-and-spoon' race, using *majanji* fruit instead of eggs. At St. Faith's, in 1906, Upcher organised games of 'oranges and lemons'.

In the conduct of worship, however, it was accepted without question that the 'mother-church' was the primary model for both settler and convert wings of the church. Worship in the Church of England by the late-nineteenth century (and across all party divides) was characterized by formality or dignity. Services were rich, even ornate. What was sought was true reverence, a reverence achieved not only by the disposition of clergymen and worshippers but by a variety of other means: solemn processions, ceremony, robed or vested clergyman and altars, decorated churches, surpliced choirs, anthems and organ music.

Services in Mashonaland/SR showed a faithful continuation of English practice: formal and dignified worship was expected, whatever the circumstances. The bishops and clergy robed to conduct services in the veld or burials on the battlefield: Knight-Bruce, for instance, robed to bury the dead in the Anglo-Ndebele war. Itinerant clergy travelling down the railway lines or on bicycles through the bush and wading through rivers to conduct services might be informally clad but they carried their robes with them. The catechists too and the later settler lay-readers wore robes (cassock and surplice) and not only in church buildings but to lend solemnity to other religious occasions. There is an account of Upcher travelling with a catechist in 1924 and coming across a threshing party at an out-station. The harvest is blessed and both Upcher and the catechist don their robes for the occasion.[13]

The early clergy and particularly those ministering to settlers set themselves to conduct reverent worship in the most incongruous of settings: station waiting rooms or railway platforms, hotel dining-rooms, miner's huts. In these varied situations they had to contend with clouds of insects, wandering chickens, noise from adjoining rooms (a game of billiards, for instance) and invariably the company of dogs, often several of them.

When communities moved out of the frontier stage and churches were built which made decent worship possible, not only was clergy relief palpable but attempts were then made to reproduce the circumstances

[13] Extracts of Letters from Archdeacon Upcher. S. Francis' Mission [Selukwe], June 27th, SRQP LXXIX (August 1924), 6.

of worship 'at home': appeals were made locally or to supporters in England for help with vestments, altar frontals, candlesticks and stained glass windows. Even the early hut churches were supplied with appropriate church furniture, a prayer-desk constructed from whisky boxes, a cross made out of cigar boxes. At Fort Victoria and Umtali the early churches were given rood or Gothic screens.

The organs and church bells characteristic of English churches also made their appearance very early in the history of the diocese: a church bell (for Victoria) travelled with Knight-Bruce in his waggon on his return journey to the diocese in 1893, for example. Umtali, Bulawayo and Salisbury had harmoniums or American organs within a year or so of settlement. Small organs or harmoniums were even presented to mission stations (to St. Faith's in 1902 and St. Aidan's, Bembezi in 1905) although a variety of instruments accompanied settler worship in the out-districts: banjoes, violins, pianos, an autoharp played by the cyanide manager of a mine. Surpliced settler choirs were established in 1893 in Salisbury, by 1897 in Bulawayo and in 1918 in Que Que. St. Matthew's, the 'native' church in Gwelo, formed a surpliced choir in 1914.

Quasi-religious English customs, such as the variety of rituals which went to make up a late-Victorian or Edwardian wedding, also persisted among the settlers of the diocese. Wedding cakes were often sent out from England, as for the wedding of the Reverend John Salt at Gwelo in 1906 (although the presents reflect a local setting: they included gold nuggets, a leopard skin and a lion's claw set in gold).[14] Cakes could be carried in their boxes for many miles through the bush, on the heads of bearers, to farm weddings and a presiding clergyman could find himself taking out, to a distant wedding, not only food for the feast but traditional orange-blossom for the bride.

Such semi-religious English customs were also often adopted by local people and could be sanctioned even by missionaries most protective of them and their ways. A photograph of the first (double) wedding of converts solemnised by the radical missionary, Arthur Shearly Cripps, for instance, in 1905 shows the brides dressed in white wedding gowns and veils, the grooms in (white) suits and ties, in front of an African hut-church.[15]

---

[14] Salt Scrapbooks, (in the possession of Mrs. Nicky Salt), Literary Scraps 1905–1912, [April 20, 1906], ff. 2–3.

[15] 'First Christian marriages at Wreningham', *Letters to the Children* [supplement to MQP] (Nov 1905), 1.

The character of the diocese was also affected by the fact that it was part of the Church of the Province of South Africa: it was governed by diocesan and provincial Synods and its bishops were elected and not appointed by the Crown as in England.

Its religious practice was also influenced to some degree by that of the 'High', or Anglo-Catholic, tradition of the CPSA. This was itself English in origin and the CPSA maintained strong links with the 'Advanced' church party in England. In Mashonaland/SR, however, the CPSA tradition was only partially superimposed upon the broader and more diverse traditions of England. The style of religion which resulted was somewhat mixed and there were local variations. In Gwelo, for instance, (unlicensed) settler laymen taking a service in the absence of the parson, in 1907, robed in cassock and surplice. At Fort Victoria, in the same period, laymen would similarly take a service but not robe: that was "only for the Fathers".[16]

The CPSA tradition also tended to be more influential on the missions than in settler congregations. This was largely because the missionary clergy in this period faced no informed challenges to their authority in religious matters from their convert flocks and were free to introduce practices which were more 'extreme' than those likely to be acceptable in settler congregations: individual confession was expected of converts, for instance, but not of settler Christians. Missionary clergy could wear birettas, Roman-style, mission churches be decorated with Marian devices such as the Crown of Mary (St. Faith's).

The settler laity, however, had more say in church matters than the people of the missions and most were considerably 'lower' in churchmanship than the majority of the clergy.[17] There were a few High Churchmen, like Captain Masterman, a stalwart of the Salisbury congregation who was a convert of the famous Father Dolling of Portsea, one of the most 'Ritualistic' clergy in the Church of England. There were also a few people from the opposite end of the spectrum, Colonel Flint, for example, an eccentric Evangelical churchman in Fort Victoria who was accustomed to take services on alternate Sundays evenings for "some who are not of our way of thinking", while the priest who

---

[16] 'Victoria', *RCM* 4:12 (Dec 1907), 9.

[17] LPL, Temple, 41, Evelyn Cecil M.P. to Archbishop Frederick Temple, July 13th, 1900, f. 379; Sir Charles Warren, *CCR* (1904), 412.

served the town was on his mission thirty miles away.[18] In 1907, Flint led a public outcry against the way in which the church hall (which was also a school) was (newly) decorated and the style of services held.

Not many of the laity took things as far as Colonel Flint, however, (there are no other public defections on record) although 'extreme' tendencies on the part of clergy did generate a certain amount of criticism throughout the period. Beaven, for instance, himself a moderate in these matters, discussed with his Chapter in 1910 criticisms of "invocations" and other unauthorised interpolations in services.[19] Some lay people voiced their opinions to the SPG: we have seen, above, in Chapter Five (p. 164), the disapproval shown of Anthony Bathe, in Bulawayo in 1898.

Local newspapers could also be openly critical: the newcomer John Salt was pilloried in a local newspaper, the *Bulawayo Chronicle*, in 1903 for a lack of broadmindedness (towards other churches). There was not a great deal of controversy over these matters in the period, however, possibly because (it can be surmised with certainty) those who were disaffected either voted with their feet and stayed away from church or joined one of the other churches. More important, perhaps, was the fact that significant numbers of church members over the period were immigrants from South Africa, whether South African or 'home-born' and were therefore accustomed to High Church worship. The 'High' party also began moving into the ascendant in the Church of England in the 1890s, which meant that for many more English parishioners—and emigrants to Central Africa—a moderate degree of High Church practice was deemed acceptable or even fashionable by the early twentieth century.

The bitter battles over ritual which were still taking place in the Church of England also tended to make 'Advanced' clergy there, and in Africa, intransigent and unwilling to compromise very far. Such evidence as exists indicates that it was the settler laity who, in liturgical matters at least, moved nearer to the position of the clergy over time: by 1924, the laity could be said to "rather like High Church ways".[20]

As far as 'broadmindedness' or relations with other churches went, however, movement tended to be in the other direction: John Salt, for

[18] 'Letter from the Rev. H.R. Quinn. Mission of the Transfiguration, December 28th, 1906', *MQP* LIX (Feb 1907), 15.

[19] NAZ, HMss, ANG 1/4/6/1, Cathedral Chapter, Minutes, February 17th, 1910.

[20] 'Letter from Mr. Beresford', *SACRMQP* 79 (April 1924), 5.

instance, who arrived in 1903 as an uncompromising High Churchman was, by the time he left in 1909, a most cordial friend of the local Nonconformist minister in his district of Gwelo.

II *The need for modification*

We have seen, in the last section, the significant role played by cultural conservatism in the shaping of religion, particularly settler religion, in Mashonaland/SR. After the turn of the century, however, attempts such as these, to reproduce the "dear old Church of England wherever we go",[21] began to be questioned by some. The nostalgia which so often drew settlers to church in Southern Africa because it reminded them of 'home', for instance, could be criticised as a very inadequate motive for church-going and one cause of the church's weakness in the area.

In general, the CPSA was seen by such commentators as having failed to take deep root in Southern Africa, especially among settlers, precisely because it had not adapted to its setting. It had, on the contrary, remained "almost exotic" and this 'exotic' quality was blamed, among other things, for the lack of vocations to the ministry from colonial congregations: by 1907, it was pointed out, there had been no clergy produced by any of the leading settler families of Natal, one of the most 'English' of the South African colonies.[22] In 1921, it was suggested in debate in the Southern Rhodesia Synod that the CPSA could not be called "indigenous" until it was providing its own clergy[23] and similar criticisms were made of the church elsewhere in the Empire. Many importations from England were seen as inappropriate, such as deans in gaiters for remote Australian dioceses or the cultivation of a lofty English episcopal dignity.[24]

In Mashonaland/SR, it could be asserted by 1913 that daughter churches of the Church of England did not have to be "exact copies" of their mother but could "combine with her essential nature such

[21] LPL, Ms 1713, E.J. Palmer to JCMA Conference, Hereford, November 1907, f. 23.

[22] *Ibid.*, f. 17.

[23] Canon Parker, 'New System for Clergy Stipends', *RCM* 18:10 (Oct 1921), 8.

[24] H.St.J. Woollcombe, *Beneath the Southern Cross* (London: Longmans and Co., 1913), 116–7.

other qualities as their environment draws out and makes necessary".[25] After all, the people of the diocese were engaged in a process of "re-founding their Mother-Church in a new environment, and...planting it also in the untried soil of native peoples".[26]

Beaven put it this way: "all that is insular and merely Anglican in time drops off from us but that which is Catholic remains and takes new forms"[27] and when the records of the diocese are examined, they show that English religious tradition did undergo significant change in both settler and indigenous communities and not merely in the direction of High Church practice. Indigenous converts, for example, were usually baptised by total immersion in local rivers (following early Christian practice) rather than in the waters of a font within a church building, as was the case in England (and among the settlers). This custom was even perpetuated in urban missions: at St. Columba, in the Bulawayo location, where there was no river, a six-foot bath was used for baptism by total immersion.

Entirely new forms of religious behaviour also developed, created as much by the people and their circumstances as by the missionaries. Powell visiting outstations north of St. Augustine's, Penhalonga was greeted at one village by a crowd of people singing and dancing, much, as he remarked, as King David must have danced before the ark.[28] At St. Faith's, at great festivals, hundreds of members of the out-stations would converge on the central church in processions, behind their catechist-teachers and their banners. Worshippers would often camp out at a mission overnight, worshipping, feasting.

Local exigencies could even affect the keeping of the liturgical calendar: Christmas and Easter in Central Africa, for instance, were times for guarding crops in the field from the depredations of animals. The greatest gatherings at the central mission stations therefore took place, not at these most important Christian festivals but at lesser festivals, such as patronal festivals, which fell at times of agricultural quiet.

The settler wing of church also produced its own variations even after small town life on the English model had developed and the frontier

---

[25] 'Letter from the Rev. E.N. Parker, Rowledge Vicarage, Farnham, April 28th, 1913', *MQP* LXXXIV (May 1913), 8.

[26] 'Religion and Empire', *RCM* 9:9 (Sept 1912), 2.

[27] 'Installation of the Dean at Salisbury', *MQP* LXXVII (Aug 1911), 6.

[28] RHL/USPG, E Series, 63(B), 1908, Report from Bishop Powell (n.d.), 1908.

characteristics of the early days of the diocese were said to be found only in the outlying districts.

Metropolitan ideals of decorum, for instance, were hard to achieve. Even where churches had been built, the difficulties under which the early and itinerant clergy laboured in their efforts to lead reverent worship, followed them into the buildings. Fowls wandered into the early churches, dogs chewed the matting on the floor or chased one another under the altar. As late as 1922, when the first part of the cathedral in Salisbury had been built, worshippers had to be asked not to bring their dogs into church, for dogs accompanied settlers everywhere. They were accepted as necessary colonial appurtenances, much as guns were in other frontier societies: they were needed for protection. They were, however less easily left at the door, especially in a country with a hot climate where the doors of buildings were left open for ventilation.

Many hallowed English customs also disappeared under Southern hemisphere conditions. At Christmas, while some settlers ate plum pudding and communities decorated 'Christmas trees' for the children, for many the festival became a time for open-air sport and picnicking in the veld rather than an attempt to reproduce a traditional, English Christmas. Rogation Days had to be moved from May to November, the season of Advent; Harvest Festivals were celebrated uncertainly, now at harvest, then at the time of the settler agricultural shows. Women sang in the surpliced choirs, which were all-male in England.

A distinct modification of English patterns of religion can also be discerned in settler attendance at worship. In the towns, the times of services customary in England were adhered to: an early Holy Communion at 8; the main service of Matins at 11; and an evening service, usually at 8. Attendance, however, was very unlike that of England.

At Umtali in 1912, only three or four people, rarely as many as a dozen, went to Matins, which indicated to the parson that the service was little more than "a relic...of imported English custom which had not taken deep root".[29] Nevertheless, there and elsewhere, the few for whom Matins was the norm in England continued to attend at the accustomed hour of 11, in spite of the blazing morning heat and the small stuffy churches.

[29] 'Letter from Canon Hallward. Umtali, Christmas-time', *MQP* LXXVII (Feb 1912), 11.

A few others, too few in the opinion of the clergy, attended the early communion services, anything between six and twenty in Umtali in 1912 and an average of seven in Gatooma in 1913 when, in the parson's opinion, there ought to have been 30. The vast majority of worshippers, however, went to the evening service: at Umtali in 1912 the evening service averaged 70 to 80. 'At home', however, the evening service was never the main service of the day and very seldom was it a Eucharist.

The clergy were much perturbed by this behaviour: it is a frequent topic of discussion in the literature. Many of them would happily have dispensed with Matins and substituted a mid-morning Eucharist, in approved 'Advanced' fashion and some did so occasionally: a Sung Eucharist replaced Matins as the main service once a month in Salisbury in 1907 and in Selukwe twice a year by 1918 (at the major festivals of Christmas and Easter). Few parsons, however, were ever really reconciled to the settlers' habit of going to church in the evening rather than the morning and rarely, if ever, making their communion.

Yet an evening rather than a mid-morning service often better suited the religious needs of the settlers, as Gaul pointed out in 1907. Most of them were young men who worked "shut up in offices and shops and mines" during the week. "Why should we expect men, and especially young men to spend the hottest part of the day in Church, when their whole instincts rebel against it?" asked Gaul.[30]

An evening service was also never a Eucharist in Mashonaland/SR and so carried no obligation for worshippers to be confirmed members of the English Church. This was a pastoral advantage in small settlements, where there might be no other churches or services. On the mines, for instance, as one travelling parson wrote in 1913, it did not matter which denomination a man belonged to: if he was off-duty he came along. The evening service at Francistown was attended by Presbyterians and Wesleyans. The miners of Penhalonga Valley, near St. Augustine's, to whom the missionaries ministered, were mostly Scotsmen and Presbyterians. At the Jumbo mine, Mazoe, in 1916 the congregation included the Jewish hotelier and his wife.

An evening service also did not require, as a Eucharist did, that those who attended should be in a state of grace or at least not in a state

[30] RHO/USPG, D Series, 178(b), 1907, W. Mashonaland to the Right Rev. the Secretary, SPG, Report, January 13th, 1907.

of open sin. This was an important consideration in a society where sexual immorality was common and where the travelling parson could be met with the greeting, "You'll find us drunk... give it to us strong!"[31] Evening services were services to which 'all sorts and conditions of men' could, and did, come.

The normal pattern of settler worship that developed in Mashonaland/SR and particularly in the out-districts was a communion service for the known faithful in the early morning and perhaps a Matins, but certainly a service open to all, even the 'hard cases', at night. At the tiny settlement of Tuli, where there were 20 white men in 1903, only two attended the early morning Holy Communion but almost all turned out for the evening service. At the Arcturus mine, 22 miles from Salisbury, only the doctor's wife and one young man made their communion when the parson visited in June 1911 but 25 or 26 men put in an appearance at the service held in the evening.

The clergy were well aware that many men attended such services simply because they had a novelty value where life was monotonous and unvaried. It was not unknown, for instance, for an itinerant parson to face the prospect of losing his congregation to the rival attractions of a travelling conjuror. Many parsons, however, found "the crust of apathy and unbelief" among settlers in Mashonaland (as elsewhere in Southern Africa) thinner than had been thought[32] and properly handled, as Gaul pointed out, these evening services became important pastoral and evangelistic occasions: "if he [the parson] knows how to use his opportunity their hearts are in his hands".[33]

It was through these evening services, moreover, and others like them, such as the (morning) farm services which followed the development of colonial agriculture, that a need for further modification of English models became evident—and in the opposite direction from modifications made by indigenous worshippers.

On the missions, services became longer, slower, attuned to the pace of a people who lived "by the sun".[34] For settlers, it became clear that the language of the Prayer Book and the length of services needed to be modified on the lines of what were known in England as 'mission

[31] NAZ, HMss, HA 4/1/1, H.A. Hale, Letter Book, ff. 37,132.
[32] Editorial, 'The Mission of Help: Deo Gratias', *Ch.Ch.* (Nov 4th, 1904), 697.
[33] RHO/USPG, E Series, 54(A), 1899, Will. Mashonaland, 'Dangers and Why Not?', To the Editor *MF* (n.d.) [April], 1899.
[34] Osmund Victor, C.R., *The Salient of South Africa* (London: S.P.G., 1931), 86.

services' or elsewhere in the world as 'bush services'—briefer, simplified services. The formality of English worship also too easily became something stiff and dull, too far removed from the casual camaraderie of colonial life: worship for settlers needed to be "less formal, more intelligent and better adapted" as William Carter, Archbishop of Capetown put it, in 1917.[35]

Music was also modified: convert Christians made English hymn tunes their own by adding an African *timbre*, harmonies and counter-rhythms and, for settler worship, traditional Anglican chant was replaced by a simplified musical version of the psalms, composed by Ernest Parker, one of the Salisbury clergy.

Church life was also affected by the fact that freemasonry was extraordinarily strong at all levels of settler society, from railway men to Rhodes himself.[36] Many of the clergy, including Gaul, Beaven and Upcher were masons, several were chaplains to lodges. There was therefore a more open and comfortable association between the church and freemasonry than was the case in England. Masonic services were held in churches and foundation stones (in Bulawayo and Gwelo) laid with masonic ritual.

The years 1890–1925 also saw another novelty: sport, or organised games, was brought within the sphere of religion. Initially, sport was simply perceived as one form of healthy recreation, recreation which was much needed to counter the demoralising conditions in which so many settlers lived, in drab and comfortless huts, "without amusements, comfort or society", their only resort the canteen, or bar.[37] The church, therefore, provided or encouraged various forms of innocent social activity, most of them familiar from England: libraries and reading rooms, church socials in the larger settlements, bicycling clubs, concerts, Sunday School picnics.

The clergy acted as chaplains to such organizations as the boy scouts, cadets and the Sons of England and they welcomed the formation in 1902 of the Volunteer Movement, a militia for colonial males, as "a good step forward", anticipating the disciplined activity it would bring:

---

[35] William M. Capetown, January 17th, 1917, 'To the Bishops, Clergy and Members of the English Church in South Africa', 14:3 (March 1917), 6.

[36] Robert Rotberg, *The Founder: Cecil Rhodes and the Pursuit of Power* (Oxford: Oxford University Press, 1988), 244; Jon Lunn, *Capital and Labour on the Rhodesian Railway System, 1888–1947* (Oxford: Oxford University Press, 1997), 87.

[37] 'Letter from the Rev. A. Bathe. Church House, Buluwayo, March 10th, 1899', *MQP* XXVIII (May 1899), 16.

"the tramp of armed men and the manoeuvering of horses on the parade ground".[38] Leading laymen were officers in the force. Upcher became both a chaplain and a trooper from his mission at Rusape; other clergy became chaplains to local bands. Regular church parades were held for the Volunteers (as for the BSA Company police). The bishops, Gaul and Beaven in particular, enthusiastically supported the movement.

The playing of sport, however, was particularly encouraged in both wings of the church. Gatherings at mission stations on great festivals or state occasions, as to celebrate the coronation of Edward VII in 1902, had a sporting component, as we have seen earlier—races or a game of football. Among settlers, however, healthy exercise was promoted not merely as part of an occasional celebration but as a regular ministry to the bodies as well as the souls of men, as in England. There, among the lower classes, sport was believed to have an elevating effect, to assist the development and protection of good morals. Among the middle and upper classes, sport was believed to develop personal character.

It was also seen as a fitting antidote to idleness or "loafing". "Better is the open air for us than the air of the canteen" and "far better that we should play cricket or tennis, take a long walk over the veld with gun and dogs, than loll about the house in pyjamas, reading poor novels, smoking to excess, and the ever-present "Perfection" [whisky] at our elbow".[39] A youthful community which showed little enthusiasm for sport could be reprimanded by the parson and working hours, shifts on a mine for example, which prevented men from playing team games were regarded with disfavour. Employers such as the later (and larger) mining companies who provided opportunities for recreation were commended, as was the BSA Company for its provision of public amenities such as parks in the colonial townships.

Sport gradually came to be so highly regarded in both church and community that the church in Mashonaland even worked its way away from English notions of Sabbath observance. Gaul, for instance, declared the traditional antithesis between Sunday sport and religion to be a false one. Sport on Sunday became acceptable and even encouraged, provided only that the players began and ended their day with worship and Holy Days were not desecrated (as they often were).

---

[38] [J.H. Upcher], 'Rusapi', *RCM* 2:11 (Nov 1902), 4.
[39] H.R. Quinn, 'A Few words on Sunday Sport,' *RCM* 9:3 (March 1912), 4.

By 1912 religion and 'recreation' were openly associated and prowess at sport had taken on the quality of a virtue, as tributes and memorials to leading settlers bear witness. In 1908 the retiring Resident Commissioner, Colonel Chester Master, was described as "a constant and strenuous supporter of the Church, as of all healthy sports and social and philanthropic activity".[40] In St. John's Bulawayo, one brass plaque reads, "Alfred Perry/ A man greatly beloved/ Tender and true in friendship/ In bodily exercise superb/ And as chivalrous as strong/ 1908–1936". Two others read, "Sportsman, benefactor and beloved friend" (G.W.A. Chubb, 1911–1987); and "Sportsman, soldier and benefactor" (Colonel John de Lisle Thompson, O.B.E., 1908–1997).

III *Church architecture and decoration*

The setting of the diocese in Central Africa also brought about modifications in ecclesiastical architecture. The first churches, like Balfour's at Salisbury, were 'pole-and-dagha' huts and such churches continued to be built in the mission out-districts well beyond the period of this study. Even Balfour's church, however, with its extraordinarily high-pitched thatch, was an attempt to reproduce an English style of architecture (see photograph, above, p. xxii). In the main centres, therefore, hut-churches were soon succeeded by churches in 'builder's' or 'carpenter's' 'Gothic'. The first St. John's in Bulawayo was an attempt at "Early English style".[41]

This pattern of building then tended to give way to a third style, more in keeping with local need and the limited finances of the diocese. Plain churches, often made of wood and corrugated iron like many other colonial buildings, were erected. They took the form of aisleless naves and were essentially halls rather than churches with nave and chancel. Some were simply called church halls. They could be used for school classes and other meetings during the week with the top section of the hall, the chancel area, curtained off. Many became, as was the intention, the social centre of a colonial settlement. Those which served indigenous congregations were also used invariably as schools.

---

[40] 'Archdeaconry of Mashonaland', *RCM* 5:3 (March 1908), 2.

[41] 'Extracts from Letters from Archdeacon Upcher. Bulawayo, (n.d.)', *MQP* XIII (July 1895), 12.

The problem with these buildings, however, was not only that they were hot and uncomfortable in a country where life was lived in the open air but they lacked beauty and the ability to inspire awe or remind people of the existence and majesty of God. Arrivals from England, accustomed to exquisite historic churches and the achievements of Victorian church architects found them sadly deficient. Even Gaul, who encouraged the building of church halls rather than churches in the early days of the diocese, was aware of their lack of religious feeling: "three things are absolutely necessary in a country like this to give a real *religious* tone to any church building—curves, shadows and high lights. Our churches are too like square toy houses, with staring light on the walls, hitting you in the face: sharp angles with no sense of rest: and great low windows, with big panes of glass that blind, dazzle and hurt you."[42]

He went on to recommend as a design for the new cathedral to be built at Salisbury, a church of seven huts erected on the mission run by Arthur Shearly Cripps at Wreningham: "In the crude group of common, native-made hut buildings... there is *thought*, *vision* and *repose*—a sense of mystery and reserve and quiet that we all need in this loud steaming tide of human noise, competition and restlessness".[43] Gaul also suggested that the school chapel proposed for Plumtree should be modelled on a similar three-hut church at the mission at Francistown.

Gaul's suggestions were too radical, however, for a settler church which was both conservative and dismissive of indigenous cultures and the two hut-churches mentioned above were themselves unusual even among mission churches which were normally designed, like the settler churches, on English lines. In the fourth stage of church building in the diocese, therefore (except on the missions of Cripps) there was a reversion to familiar models: the church built at Beira in 1922, for instance, was "quite a gem in the Gothic style".[44] The new St. John's, Bulawayo (1912) was described as a fine example of "Gothic with a touch of Romanesque".[45]

Many of these buildings, however, were subtly modified to suit the area and the climate: they ceased to face East, into the morning sun,

---

[42] 'The Bishop's Notes', *RCM* 4:5 (May 1907), 2.
[43] *Ibid.*
[44] 'Letter from the Bishop. Beira, St. Michael and All Angels (n.d.)', *SRQP* CXII (Nov 1922), 3.
[45] 'Bulawayo', *RCM* 10:5 (May 1913), 10.

for instance. Permanent churches that were cool, dark and welcoming, whatever their architectural style, gradually replaced the hot, bright church halls. When a cathedral was eventually begun in Salisbury, English models were deliberately avoided. The architect was Herbert Baker, who had much experience of South African conditions and his design drew on Mediterranean models, that is, on cathedrals built in lands which had similar problems with light but were still 'European'. The windows of Salisbury cathedral were small and high and an apse and ambulatory replaced the traditional English East wall. The great East window of the English cathedrals disappeared.

The cathedral also contained slight but significant references to the land in which it was built. It was made of granite, the "native stone of the country", of which the Zimbabwe and other "prehistoric" remains were built. In the original design, the tower was an "unusual circular form", a "gesture of recognition of Rhodesia's one old building, the conical tower of Zimbabwe"[46] (thus linking the cathedral to a putative earlier 'Northern' civilisation in Africa).[47] Baker also intended there to be a further reference to Zimbabwe on the tower: eight carved stone birds, like those found in the fort or acropolis of Zimbabwe, were to be placed above the square base (see architectural drawing, above, p. xxiii). When the tower was finally built many years later, however, a more conventional, straight-sided tower was substituted for the circular tower and there were no birds.

The period 1890–1925 also saw some departure from English tradition in the building of chapels or 'oratories'. It was early suggested that the religious needs of settlers, widely dispersed as they were, would be better met by a series of tiny churches such as existed in the Tyrol than a few large district churches, based on the parish churches of England. Among settlers, however, the English ideal proved hard to dislodge and only a few small churches were built: one by the farming community of Essexvale (Esigodini) in 1923; and three in the suburbs of Salisbury, at Avondale (1909), Park Town (1914) and Rhodesville (1918). Indigenous people, however, from the beginning were taught that the local presence of believers was signified by the existence of a

---

[46] *Diocese of Southern Rhodesia Church Magazine* IV:6 (Oct 5th, 1938), 8.

[47] Herbert Baker, *Cecil Rhodes: by his Architect* [1934], in Herbert Baker and W.T. Stead, *Cecil Rhodes, The Man and His Dream* (Bulawayo: Books of Rhodesia, 1977), frontispiece, 103–5.

structure dedicated to worship and so the mission districts were scattered with little hut-churches.

The decoration and fittings of the churches also showed the gradual development in the diocese of a distinct, local character. Initially all decoration, like the architecture, was tied to English conventions. Even on the missions, the fittings of the earlier churches tended to reflect English styles: the first church at St. Augustine's, Penhalonga had an altar of carved oak, which had been sent out from England.

However, as here and there new directions began to be taken in the shape of buildings, so also new departures began to be made in decoration. The new 'native' church in Salisbury, St Michael's (1907), was painted with appropriate murals, albeit by an English female missionary. Local Christians also began to use their initiative and creativity in the service of their religion: at Bonda in 1915, Beaven visiting for a confirmation was presented with a new pastoral staff, decorated with African beadwork. Most striking was the new church at St. Faith's, Rusape (1913) where the missionaries were beginning to encourage local arts and crafts: it was fitted and decorated, throughout, in indigenous style.

The settler churches continued to hark back to England in decoration: what were wanted were stained glass windows, carved wooden pulpits, brass lecterns. English convention, however, was put to local use, particularly in the cathedral. In the English cathedrals, the country's famous dead are honoured. The Black Prince lies buried at Canterbury with his armour above his tomb. The illustrious from all walks of life are buried or commemorated in Westminster Abbey and St. Paul's Cathedral.

In Mashonaland/SR, as early as 1897, the very building of a cathedral at Salisbury was proposed as a memorial to those who had died in the early days of settlement (by Gaul). Beaven subsequently suggested, as we have seen earlier, that a chapel be dedicated to the memory of Rhodes alone as founder of the country and St. George's chapel was eventually built as a memorial both to him and those others who had "laid down their lives in the pioneer work of occupation".[48]

The cathedral, in fact, became the chief repository and shrine for the country's significant settler past, for it contained what were for many

[48] RHO/USPG, D Series, 201(B), 1910, Leaflet, appeal for cathedral, enc., Frederic H. Beaven to Mr Pascoe, July 22nd, 1910.

years almost the only records of local settler history: memorials to those who died in the 1896–7 risings and the Second South African War. A 5 cwt bell and a brass, for instance, which arrived from England in 1909 were given in memory of a mining commissioner, Arthur Jamieson, the son of an Irish clergyman who had been murdered at Lomagundi in 1896. The torn colours from a memorable engagement of the Second South African War, the battle of Elands' River on 4th August 1900, in which a tiny contingent of BSA Police (and some Australian 'Bushmen') held their position against the attack of some five or six hundred Boers, were hung in the cathedral, as were the flags of the First and Second Rhodesia Regiments and the First Rhodesia Native Regiment of World War One. The majority of the stained glass windows of St. George's chapel were memorials to the dead of World War One.

Fittings of other churches were also commemorative of the country's history. In the church at Umtali, the pulpit was a memorial to railwaymen who had died in the construction of the Beira line and a stained glass window commemorated fever victims of the Second South African War. The flag of the Second Rhodesia Native Regiment was lodged in St. Columba's in the Bulawayo location.

In these commemorations a particular emphasis was given to the most significant incident in local settler history, the death of Allan Wilson and his men on the Shangani in 1893 (see Chapter One, p. 36). The English Church took a leading part both in the obsequies of the patrol and then in the enshrining of a central settler myth or foundation story.

The 'last stand' on the Shangani was an event of enormous significance to the settler community, as can be seen in the abundance of memorials it inspired. A hospital was built at Bulawayo at the end of the Anglo-Ndebele War as a memorial to all those who had died in the conflict but particularly to the patrol. A lodge of masons in Bulawayo was named the Allan Wilson Lodge. Offerings were made to the churches as memorials for individual members of the patrol: a font and brass lectern to the cathedral; a carved oak pulpit, also to the cathedral, in memory of Henry Borrow, by two of his friends; a chalice, the 'Shangani chalice', in memory of H. Arthur Carey, to St. John's, Bulawayo.

Both at the time and subsequently, the members of the Allan Wilson patrol were celebrated primarily for the sheer courage with which they were reported to have fought and died. Their first short epitaph, carved on a tree by the Shangani River where they fell, was repeated on their final monument: "To Brave Men". They were said to have received a similar accolade from Ndebele who witnessed their last stand, "They were men of men and their fathers were men before them".[49]

The conflict of 1893, however, in which the members of the patrol were the chief settler casualties, was succeeded by the uprisings of 1896–7, in which almost a tenth of the settlers were massacred. In the aftermath of these uprisings, the deaths of the Allan Wilson patrol came to be regarded as symbols of all those other deaths and so of the entire colonial enterprise in that part of Africa, the "indomitable courage and fearless enterprise of the English race...in the contest between progress and stagnation".[50]

In 1896 the incident was brought within the sphere of official and public religion: the Administrator appointed December 4th, Shangani Day, the day on which the patrol died, as a day for commemoration by church services of all those who had died in the occupation and holding of the country in the previous six years.

The single grave in which the remains of the patrol had been buried near Fort Victoria, however, had become a place of pilgrimage for travellers as early as 1894. In 1895, one wreath for each member of the patrol sent from Cape Town (undoubtedly by Rhodes) was laid on their grave by John Burgin, the English Church lay minister at Fort Victoria, on Good Friday at a service attended by the local judge and twenty other men. Gaul made a point of visiting the grave and holding a service with the Resident Magistrate on his arrival in his diocese soon afterwards. In 1896 he sanctioned a special form of service to be used on Shangani Day and preached at many such services himself to crowded churches, as did Upcher, Beaven and other clergymen of the diocese.

To Beaven, the men of the patrol were heroes, splendid examples of duty honoured and death willingly undertaken for their country. To Upcher and particularly to Gaul, Allan Wilson and his men were something more. Upcher, for example, in a Shangani Day service in 1907 read the lament of David over Saul and Jonathan ("How are the mighty fallen!") and spoke of the patrol as a gallant band triumphing over barbarism, as the Hebrew "warriors" had triumphed over the

[49] Katherine Sayce, *A Town Called Victoria: or the Rise and Fall of the Thatched House Hotel* (Bulawayo: Books of Rhodesia, 1978), 57.

[50] *The Times* (November (n.d.), 1896), in *MQP XIX* (Feb 1897), 23.

Philistines, "upholding the cause of truth and righteousness against the hords (sic) symbolical of barbarism and evil of that day".[51] Carter of Capetown, taking a service in 1913 at the dedication of the new Bulawayo church building, was more specific: "Bulawayo... The very name spoke of bloodshed, spoke of cruelty, spoke of heathendom. What a contrast between twenty-five years ago and now!"[52]

Gaul, however, produced the most thorough-going theology of all. He was one of those churchmen for whom the whole imperial enterprise was part of "the redeeming of the earth from captivity to freedom, from barbarian to Christian civilisation". A "true colonist" was prepared, like Allan Wilson and his men, to follow a "religion of self-sacrifice" in the service of this ideal[53] and Gaul linked with the commemoration of the patrol not only those other settlers whose graves "bore silent witness to the splendid self-sacrifice which won and kept the country" but also the workers who had died in the service of the church.[54]

There is, furthermore, in the archives of the SPG, a map annotated by Gaul in 1903, which reveals the significance he attributed to the deaths on the Shangani. Four sites are marked: the burial place of David Livingstone; the grave of Bishop Mackenzie, first bishop of the UMCA, across the Zambezi (the mission launched in response to Livingstone's appeal for the liberation of Africa); the place where Bishop Chauncey Maples, also of the UMCA, was drowned in 1895; and the place where Allan Wilson and his men fell.[55] The map is sacred geography: these are the graves of the local heroes of Gaul's religion. All but the patrol were missionaries.

Allan Wilson and his men were also commemorated in stained glass in the new St. John's, Bulawayo and so were brought into association with a whole cluster of Christian and patriotic ideas and ideals. The East Window of St. John's is a memorial to "the early pioneers who fell in the [Matabele] war, including the Shangani heroes". The figure of Christ is in the centre of five lights: on his left are Joshua and David,

---

[51] 'Shangani Day', *RCM* 4:12 (Dec 1907), 2.

[52] 'Sermon preached by the Archbishop of Capetown, On the occasion of the Dedication of the Church of S. John the Baptist at Bulawayo, 24th June, 1913', *RCM* 10:7 (July 1913), 2.

[53] RHO/USPG, D Series, 134(A), 1900, Will. Mashonaland, Manuscript of sermon, Shangani Day, Salisbury, December 4th, 1900.

[54] 'The Bishop's Charge to Synod (continued): Rhodesia and our Responsibilities', *MQP* XLVI (Nov 1903), 5.

[55] RHO/USPG, D Series, 148(b), 1903, [40], map, annotated, Gaul's hand.

"a leader of men and a warrior"; on his right, St. Alban, the first English martyr and St. George, "patron saint of the men who died in the war". Other smaller lights depicted the Matabeleland pioneers; Service; St. John the Baptist, to whom the church was dedicated; Sacrifice; and the victory of Good over Evil. Above in the tracery were other lights including the New Jerusalem and the River of Life, "all in keeping with the spirit and design of the main part of the work".[56] The windows were unveiled by Sir Leander Starr Jameson in December 1913, in the presence of an overflowing congregation which included large numbers of Volunteers and a contingent of the BSA Police.

Well before 1913, however, the custom of commemorating the patrol and others by annual services had fallen into disuse. Shangani Day had become more of a holiday than a holy day and even the Volunteers could not be persuaded to turn out for religious services on a weekday. After 1914, the greater slaughter and sacrifice of World War One eclipsed those of the patrol in the commemorations of the church.

There had also been a shift in thinking, by some, away from the simple view of men like Gaul who saw the imperial venture, imperfect though it was, as guided by Providence. Archbishop Carter, for instance, had in 1895 shared Gaul's views but in 1913 he distinguished carefully between sacrifices, however courageous, which were made "For the Empire's sake" and those made for very much higher ideals, those of "the Kingdom of God and His *righteousness*".[57] The men of the Allan Wilson patrol were still lauded by him as heroes but the cause for which they died was no longer identified with that of the Kingdom of God.

IV *The land*

The commemoration of settler heroes such as the Allan Wilson patrol by religious means was significant in itself for the settler wing of the church in Mashonaland/SR. As a religious phenomenon, however, it was nothing new. There was ample precedent in English tradition and there were contemporary parallels elsewhere in the Empire: St. George's chapel in Salisbury cathedral, built and furnished in memory of Rhodes and the early pioneers, had its counterpart in a chapel in

[56] *Morning Post*, in 'Bulawayo', *RCM* 11:3 (March 1914), 18.
[57] 'Sermon preached by the Archbishop of Capetown', *RCM* 10:7 (July 1913), 2.

Khartoum cathedral (consecrated in 1912) which was a memorial to the imperial and Christian hero General Gordon and others who had died in the Sudan. The altar frontal was fringed with gold braid from Gordon's uniform and his prayer-mat lay nearby.[58]

To find a distinctive development in the settler religion of Mashonaland/SR, therefore, one has to look outside church buildings to the landscape: what did emerge in the religious sensibility of the settlers was a new attitude to the land and specifically, among Rhodesians, to the country in which they were settled.

This new attitude had roots in metropolitan English and European tradition—there were some continuities—and these continuities can be seen, for instance, in the reactions of early visitors to a particularly magnificent spectacle in the north-west of the country, the Victoria Falls. The railway reached the Falls in 1904 and thereafter many settlers and travellers from England took the opportunity to visit them.

Members of the church (and others) were predisposed to find the experience a religious one, for nineteenth century Europe had learned from the Romantic movement and the earlier, eighteenth century love of 'the sublime', to marvel at wild and untamed landscapes and to recognise God in nature as well as in grace. The first white man to see the Falls, moreover, had been the missionary and explorer David Livingstone and his well-publicised reaction had been one of religious awe: "Scenes so lovely must have been gazed upon by angels in their flight".[59]

Subsequent visitors echoed Livingstone. Baden-Powell wrote, "here was God manifest in Nature".[60] Gaul, deeply moved, called the Falls "an illuminated chapter of [the Book of] Revelation" making visible "the transcendant (sic) Beauty of God in Creation".[61] One "gallant colonel" summarised his reaction as "God created the Heaven and the Earth and the Victoria Falls".[62] Frank Rhodes and a few friends

---

[58] H.C. Jackson, *Pastor on the Nile Being some account of The Life and Letters of Llewellyn H. Gwynne, C.M.G., C.B.E., D.D., LL.D., Formerly Bishop in the Sudan and Deputy Chaplain-General in France in the First World War* (London: S.P.C.K., 1960), 128–9, 130–2, 135.

[59] Tim Jeal, *Livingstone* (London: Pimlico, 1993 c.1985), 149.

[60] Lord Baden-Powell of Gilwell, *African Adventures* (London: C. Arthur Pearson Ltd (n.d.)), 150.

[61] [W.T. Gaul], 'Diocese of Mashonaland: North-West Rhodesia', *Ch.Ch.* (July 12th, 1905), 427.

[62] D.B. Ellison, 'Letter from the Head of the Mission. Grahamstown, December 6th, 1909', *SACRMQP* 26 (Jan 1910), 3.

agreed to use the word "stupendous" only to describe the Falls.[63] Lord Selborne, the High Commissioner, gave them the supreme accolade of 'sublime' and believed that word should be reserved for them alone. His cousin E.J. Palmer, soon to be Bishop of Bombay, wrote in his diary in 1907, "I wish Dante had seen this place".[64] Percy Clark, a settler who arrived at the Falls in 1903 before there was a railway and lived beside them until his death in 1937, wrote of his first encounter, "It was like entering some wonderful cathedral...I felt as if I stood in the presence of some majestic Power quite ineffable".[65]

These reactions, however, though genuine, were educated responses to a particular spectacle which corresponded to Europe's ideas of the beautiful and the grand. The only two other landscapes singled out for approbation, the mountainous border between Rhodesia and Portuguese East Africa and the Matopos/Matobo Hills ('The Matopos'), a wild and dramatic outcrop of rocks which lies 20 miles south-east of Bulawayo, also corresponded to European notions of what was appealing. The wonderful views and vistas of the Eastern Highlands reminded visitors from Europe and newcomers of picturesque parts of Scotland and Wales and they struggled to find words adequate to describe the fantastic jumble of rocks that form the Matopos.

They tended to be less enthusiastic about the rest of the vast, rolling plateau which formed the interior of Southern and Central Africa. The more knowledgeable made a distinction between the greener landscapes of Rhodesia with its higher rainfall and more abundant vegetation and the dry and often treeless plains of the territories to the south and east of the country. Even Rhodesia could disappoint, however: the overall impression was of an unending, empty, landscape. The phrase which is used in the literature, repeatedly, to describe the landscape of the interior is 'the illimitable veldt'. The primary impression, even of Rhodesia, was simply of "vastness" and "hundreds of miles of veldt".[66]

This endless expanse was usually experienced as monotonous, dreary, lonely, even threatening. The impression was the more acute as most visitors travelled into the interior in winter, when the veld was dry.

---

[63] LPL, H5046.1.22: Mission of Help, *End of the Mission* (1904), 35.

[64] LPL, Ms 3013, E.J. Palmer, Journal of a visit to South Africa, Sunday, September 1st, 1907.

[65] Percy M. Clark, *The Autobiography of an Old Drifter* (1936) (Facsimile reproduction: Bulawayo: Books of Rhodesia, 1972), Publisher's Introduction, 120–1.

[66] 'Letter from the Rev. Percy H. Green. Gatooma, Southern Rhodesia, November 14th, 1912', *MQP* LXXXIII (Feb 1913), 10.

"Only those who have seen the high veld of Rhodesia can realise its unutterable dreariness", wrote one newcomer, of his arrival in Rhodesia in 1898.[67]

In religious terms, the veld was seen as 'a wilderness', a Biblical term for a lonely and forsaken place: it was both the cause and symbol of spiritual desolation. Mashonaland/SR was described in 1892 as "a wilderness-diocese".[68] Missioners of the South African Church Railway Mission, which was founded specifically to minister to isolated settlers, saw their work as reminding settlers of "the existence of things spiritual", could describe it as "rain in the wilderness"[69] or as spreading "God's table in the wilderness".[70]

The attitudes of those who lived on the veld, however, tended to diverge from those of visitors from Europe. While the land retained its lonely and daunting aspects, it nevertheless exercised over them a "nameless fascination".[71] Many became deeply attached to a landscape they initially experienced as alien. Others had come to Africa in search of wide horizons. "I am happy when on the broad veld and feel a sense of freedom which no money can purchase" runs a typical comment from an early settler.[72]

Incidental evidence in settler writings, moreover, points to the veld as the primary shaping agent of settler consciousness, religious or otherwise. This was most obviously the case for the true 'backvelders', those who lived outside the towns. Kingsley Fairbridge, for example, who wrote one of the few settler autobiographies of the time, was the son of a surveyor and wandered the veld of the east of the country with only his servant-companion and his dog from the age of twelve. The formative effect of both those landcapes and those of his earlier

---

[67] Stanley Portal Hyatt, *The Old Transport Road* (1914) (Facsimile reproduction: Bulawayo: Books of Rhodesia, 1969), 55–6. Only BSA Company apologists described Rhodesia as lush: see Percy F. Hone, *Southern Rhodesia* (London: George Bell and Sons, 1909), 5–12.

[68] 'Mashonaland: Bishop's Visit to England', *MF* XXXVII:434 (Feb 1892), 60.

[69] H.P. Hale, 'Diocese of Mashonaland', *SACRMQP* 4 (July 1904), 8.

[70] E. Winnington-Ingram, in 'Annual Meeting', *SACRMQP* 62 (April 1919), 9.

[71] Tawse Jollie, *The Real Rhodesia*, 2. Terence Ranger, in *Voices from the Rocks: Nature, Culture and History in the Matopos Hills of Zimbabwe* (Harare, Bloomington and Indianapolis: Oxford, Baobab, Indiana University Press and James Currie, 1999), 11, claims an "unrivalled" capacity to affect settler sensibility for the landscape of the Matopos Hills. This, however, was true only for those from the vicinity.

[72] Hylda M. Richards, *False Dawn: The Story of Dan Judson, Pioneer: Based on the diaries of Dan and Maynie Judson* (Bulawayo: Books of Rhodesia, 1974), 19, 219.

childhood in South Africa can be seen quite clearly in his account of his life and in his verse.[73]

Other settlers, particularly town-dwellers, showed an early tendency to domesticate or suburbanize their surroundings, to introduce the spirit of South Kensington or Surbiton. But, as was pointed out, this provided little more than a "veneer", for the open veld, stretching away in every direction, was the background to all settler life in the period.[74] Even in 1921, houses near the centre of Salisbury were surrounded by long grass. The Bulawayo houses were widely scattered on the veld.

For settler children, in particular, who were deprived of the "comfortable civilisation" and "pageantry" of their British "heritage", "inspiration" had to come "from Nature, from the veld and from the sky"[75] and by 1921, even among adult settlers, those with such a childhood were in the majority: 60% had been born in Africa, 25% in Rhodesia itself (in 1911, approximately 49% had been born in Europe, 46% in Africa).[76] Many had grown up running completely wild on the veld—and 'wild' was the term normally reserved to describe indigenous people who had had no contact with so-called 'civilisation'.

By the end of the period of this study, a change in attitude and perception had also occurred among observers in Europe. It had come to be recognised by the wider church that wild and 'uncivilised' landscapes such as the veld were not necessarily hostile to the religious impulse. On the contrary, wherever in the world people originally from Europe lived scattered in wide-open spaces, they were now acknowledged to be facing, daily, "the mysteries and perplexities of the universe".[77] Their surroundings therefore came to be seen as potentially productive of spiritual things rather than as inimical to them.

The primary characteristic of the Central African landscape, for instance, its "true beauty", lay in its "sense of space", "vast unconfined"

---

[73] Kingsley Fairbridge, *His Life and Verse* (Reprint of the 1927 edition of *The Autobiography of Kingsley Fairbridge* with additional text and new illustrations; and selections from the 1909 and 1928 editions of his *Veld Verse*) (Bulawayo: Books of Rhodesia, 1974), *passim*.

[74] Tawse Jollie, *The Real Rhodesia*, 3–4, 126.

[75] *Ibid.*, 3, 4, 123, 124, 192, 240.

[76] *Report of the Director of Census for 1921*, (Salisbury: 1922), 21.

[77] CE/CA/MC, *The Call from Our Own People Overseas* (Westminster: Published for the Missionary Council by the Press and Publications Board of the Church Assembly, 1927), 34.

space[78] and it came to be recognised in the church there that "there was a power and appeal" in wide-open spaces.[79] Distant dwellers in loneliness and silence under the great sky of Africa could become more aware of the divine rather than grow half-crazy or deteriorate morally and spiritually. These "hermit[s]" of the veld could become deeper thinkers because of their solitude, grow more open to receive the travelling parson or missionary, more ready to talk about their faith, more charitable towards their only neighbours, the indigenous people of the land.[80] The clergy, too, often found in the services they conducted for these isolated people a reality which was often greater than could be experienced 'at home'.

The wild, or the land, of the Southern and Central African plateau, moreover, came to be recognised as providing more than merely surroundings in which settlers could grasp the truths of revealed religion more clearly. It was itself acknowledged as a source of spiritual experience, of the sacred: in the "vastness and silence of the veldt", "the Presence of God in nature" was evident, as Fr. Bull C.R., a chaplain to Imperial troops in the Second South African War, wrote in 1901.[81] In the great spaces and the loneliness, one could see "Visions of God" as a railway missioner testified in 1921.[82]

An early farmer at Darwendale, whose cattle grazed among elephant by day and who 'trekked' with his herd deep into the veld in the winter months in search of pasture for them, wrote: "Living in such close contact with nature in all its aspects, and sleeping on a grass bed under the heavens, covered with stars, deepens one's sense of religion and makes one realise the vastness and mystery which surrounds us."[83] A new settler tradition, in which the wild was a *locus* of religious apprehension, therefore grew up beside tradition inherited from England, where such encounter normally took place in a sacred building.

---

[78] Henri Rolin, *Rolin's Rhodesia* (New translation of 1913 edition: Bulawayo: Books of Rhodesia, 1978), 4–5.

[79] 'Letter from the Rev. E.W. Lloyd. Rusape (n.d.)', *SRQP* 117 (Aug 1921), 10.

[80] E. Lloyd, 'Mission of the Epiphany and St. Faith's (n.d.)', *MQP* LXIII (Feb 1908), 14.

[81] Paul B. Bull, Community of the Resurrection, Mirfield, 'God and our Soldiers', *Goodwill* VIII:7 (July 1901), 152.

[82] 'Letter from the Rev. Stenson-Stenson. As from 9th Avenue, Bulawayo. 31st August, 1921', *SACRMQP* 71 (Oct 1921), 10.

[83] O.C. Rawson, in Colin Black, *The Legend of Lomagundi* (Salisbury: North-Western Development Association, 1976), 39.

Traces of this development in individuals can be seen in the writings of some of the clergy who served in Mashonaland/SR, the railway missioner cited above, for instance, or Philip Knyaston, the scholarly Etonian who served at Umtali between 1912 and 1919. "There is in the back of my heart an ache for the wilderness", he wrote in 1914.[84] Percy Green, who served at Gatooma, wrote in a similar vein in 1917: "the wilds call me".[85] That such experiences were widespread can be gauged by the publication of a warning, in 1915, in both the South African *Church Chronicle* and the *Rhodesian Church Magazine*, against neglecting the duty of corporate worship in favour of solitary religion and "solemn" feelings "under the stars".[86]

What is interesting, however, is the way in which the English Church adapted, albeit unevenly, to this dimension of its new environment in Central Africa: a partial accommodation was made to settler religious sensibility. In a country where life was lived outside buildings, in what was widely regarded as the finest climate in the world, it became acceptable, for instance, to hold corporate worship in the open air rather than in a building.

Such worship was often begun out of necessity, because there was no church. Surridge, accompanying the BSA police into the country in 1890, celebrated Holy Communion in the open air with a biscuit box for an altar. Some of his successors, itinerant parsons and missionaries, celebrated on rock altars in the open air. In 1913 in Gwelo, before the new 'native' church was built, the parson gathered the congregation for Communion in the open air.

Sometimes services were held outside buildings because the churches were too small or simply to accommodate a local community: at Bonda mission in 1915, a large confirmation was held under a tree and at Christmas in 1911, the Gatooma parson found himself perched on a whisky box on the sports ground of a large mine, conducting an open-air service for three hundred people. Civic services on public occasions, led jointly by the leaders of the several churches, were often held in public squares.

In farming areas, services were occasionally held in the garden but more usually on the large and airy verandahs of the farmhouses, rather

---

[84] P.E. Knyaston, 'Umtali. (n.d.). A Visit to Melsetter', *MQP* XC (Nov 1914), 17.

[85] 'Letter from the Rev. P.H. Green, Gatooma, Southern Rhodesia, Easter Monday, 1917', *SRQP* CI (Aug 1917), 9.

[86] 'Religion on the Veld', *RCM* 12:9 (Sept 1915), 8.

than inside the house itself. At Fort Usher in Matabeleland, on at least two occasions, itinerant parsons held evening services, not inside the building they had been lent (the court house) but outside, on the steps and 'under the stars'.

These open-air services held both old and new religious traditions together and the combination could be a powerful one. There was considerable appeal, as one new parson wrote after a verandah service, "in old, familiar hymns sung in the open air and in brilliant sunshine".[87] A service held by Beaven on a stoep (verandah) in the Melsetter district in 1913, against the spectacular back-drop of the mountains of the Eastern Districts, part of "God's unwritten book of Nature", was judged, by the BSA police captain present, to be "one of the most impressive he had ever attended".[88]

V *Burial customs*

A distinctive settler attitude to the land was also revealed in the development of burial customs which diverged from those of England.[89] In English or metropolitan tradition, the graveyard lay next to the church and public cemeteries formed part of towns. The famous, as we have seen above, were buried within or near important churches and cathedrals. These metropolitan customs were followed in Mashonaland/SR: the early settlers buried their friends whenever possible in graveyards, official or unofficial, with or without parsons and funeral services. Each colonial settlement set aside land for a cemetery.

When, as so often happened, settlers died at a distance from a settlement, attempts were made to give them decent burial. The graves were marked and protected by piles of stones. Some were given small fences or walls. Rough crosses were placed on them or carved in the bark of a nearby tree. Itinerant clergy were often asked to bless the grave of someone who had been so buried.

Many of these isolated graves were marked with the intention that arrangements would subsequently be made for the re-burial of the dead, in places of permanent reservation. The remains of many

87 H.C. Sandall, 'Itinerary: Bindura and Shamva,' *RCM* 11:9 (Sept 1914), 11.

88 'Bishop's Notes', *RCM* 10:11 (Nov 1913), 1.

89 The stimulus for this section was provided by T.O. Ranger, in 'Taking Hold of the Land'. Ranger, however, is concerned with an "imaginative appropriation of the land" by missionaries (p. 161), rather than with the religious experience of settlers.

settlers who died in the out-districts in the 1896–7 uprisings were later retrieved and buried in the Salisbury cemetery. Other graves were left as they were, to become places of pilgrimage. Gaul visited the grave of a respected pioneer in the Rusape district in 1905, for instance, while the train he was travelling in waited for him. Lord Buxton, the High Commissioner, in 1919, visited the graves of those who had fallen in the punitive expedition against Chief Makoni in 1896.

Very early in the history of the diocese, however, a different and distinctive burial custom arose in which settlers were buried, not by accident but by design in the veld or open country, rather than in cemeteries or near churches. The first official and clearly documented burial of this nature was that of the Allan Wilson patrol: in February 1894, the men who had been sent out to find the remains of the patrol gave them a bush burial where they had fallen the previous December on the Shangani River. Not many months afterwards the remains were retrieved and taken to the little English Church in Fort Victoria where they lay in state. They then were taken out of the town and re-buried within the stone-walled fortress of Zimbabwe, eighteen miles away.

Fort Victoria already had two cemeteries, one at the existing and one at the earlier site of the settlement. The remains of the patrol were re-buried, however, according to the instructions of Cecil Rhodes and his intention, as he wrote to the widow of A.B. Kirton, a member of the patrol, was to place their remains "in a spot where their record would have the most lasting remembrance". He believed that "Zimbabye" would, "for many future centuries" be "the chief object of interest"[90] in the new country and his intention was to turn "the ruins... those inscrutable masses of hard bare stone" into "a Walhalla for South Africa", for those who had "deserved well of their country". Rhodes expressed his hope to his associates that "in time to come it would be as difficult to obtain sepulture in Zimbabye as it now is in Westminster Abbey".[91] In 1894, he intended to be buried there himself.

Rhodes' plan was hailed in the British press as "very striking and picturesque", "as original as it is imaginative". A comparison was also made between the fascination exerted by the stone ruins of Zimbabwe on "men of English race" and that of the "great prehistoric remains"

[90] Facsimile, autograph letter, May 6th, 1894, C.J. Rhodes to Mrs Kirton, *Rhodesiana* 31 (September 1974), 8, 8–9.

[91] *Spectator*, (July 14th, 1894), 35.

at Stonehenge. What saved the plan from censure as pagan, however, was that the burial was to be outside the supposed temple enclosure of 'Zimbabye', the ground of burial was to be consecrated and a chapel erected, at Rhodes's expense.[92] Established religious tradition and the new were thereby to be held together.

The remains of the Shangani patrol were buried on a small eminence between the temple area of Great Zimbabwe and what was known as 'the fort'. The ground of the grave was consecrated but no chapel was built nor any other memorial. Rhodes himself, moreover, was buried eight years later (in 1902) in a different place altogether, high in the Matopos (Matobo) Hills near Bulawayo. He had become familiar with the hills and fascinated by them, while negotiating an end to the conflict of 1896, with Ndebele who had taken refuge there.

That Rhodes' new choice of burial site was influenced by political considerations is undoubted. The former king of the Ndebele, Mzilikazi, Lobengula's father, had been buried in a cave in the hills a few miles from the site Rhodes chose for himself. Contemporary accounts, as for instance those of Rhodes' negotiations with the Ndebele 'indunas' (leaders) in 1896 or the role played by Ndebele warriors at Rhodes' funeral (when they gave him the royal salute, 'Bayete'), also show Rhodes assuming or being accorded the position of great man, chief or Father of the Ndebele nation.

Rhodes also chose to be buried facing North, the direction in which he had wished to extend the British Empire and in 1904, by a provision of his will, the remains of the first of his colonial heroes, men who had "deserved well of their country", the Allan Wilson patrol, joined him in the Matopos Hills. A magnificent (if inappropriate) granite monument, with bas-reliefs by Tweed, was finally provided for them, near his grave and they were re-interred there.[93]

In Rhodes' choice of burial sites, first in the mysterious remains of what he believed to be an earlier, ancient civilization of 'the North' and then in hills sacred to a defeated enemy, the burial site of an Ndebele king, the instinct of the conqueror and coloniser can be seen. There is

[92] *Ibid.*, Rhodes' letter to Mrs Kirton mentions rumours that the burial was to be in the temple enclosure.

[93] The memorial appears to be the adapted base of an obelisk, originally designed for the Zimbabwe site: see Robert Cary, letter to the Editor, *Rhodesiana* 33 (Sept 1975), 92.

grandiosity in these gestures and a desire to dominate even in death: Kipling's funeral ode to Rhodes was as revealing as it was adulatory,

> The immense and brooding spirit
> Still shall quicken and control.
> Living he was the land, and dead
> His soul shall be her soul.

The grave immediately became a place of regular pilgrimage for both settlers and visitors, as was no doubt intended by Rhodes. 'The founder's grave', in fact, displaced that of the Shangani patrol as the burial site of primary significance for the settler community.[94] Services were now held at his graveside, as they had earlier been held at the grave of the patrol in 'Zimbabye'. The British Association for the Advancement of Science, for example, some 380 strong, visiting in 1905, was only one of many groups who climbed to the site to hold a service there.

Rhodes' associate and the second BSA Company Administrator, Leander Starr Jameson, who died in 1917, was re-buried at the Matopos site, not far from Rhodes, in 1920; and the last time the site was used was when Sir Charles Coghlan, the country's first prime minister (1924–7), who had died in office, was re-buried there in 1930. Metropolitan burial tradition had re-asserted itself, however, well before this point and imposing permanent churches and cathedrals worthy to house settler memorials had been built in the colonial towns. Rhodes' dream of a colonial Walhalla did not survive for very long and his open-air 'Westminster Abbey' for the settler community was never crowded, as he had hoped it would be.

It is the contention of this study, however, that Rhodes' choice of final burial site had a significance other than the political and that when he chose the 'view of the world' in the Matopos Hills, over the ruins of Great Zimbabwe, a deeper instinct than that of the Empire builder was at work. His recorded reaction to the view from the site was a religious one, entirely in line with the responses of contemporaries to similar spectacles, such as the Victoria Falls (which Rhodes himself never saw). He was very deeply moved. The "peacefulness"

[94] The Zimbabwe grave-site retained its significance for the people of Victoria, who were outraged by the (secret) exhumation and removal of the remains of the patrol. They placed a memorial stone and plaque on the site: Sayce, *A Town Called Victoria*, 96.

and "chaotic grandeur" of the hills awed him: "it brings home to us how very small we are", he said.[95]

The difference between Rhodes and his contemporaries, however, was that he chose to be buried in the midst of a wild magnificence. An isolated, hill-top burial in Christian England was inconceivable. Elsewhere in the literature, the lonely graves of pioneers in Africa are lamented. *The Times*, for instance, in November 1896 mourned the "three hundred lonely graves" caused by the 'native' risings of that year.[96] Another, earlier, colonial incident which had resulted in death was commemorated in verse in a pioneer newspaper, *The Nugget*, with similar feeling: "There's a lone grave on the veldt now, far from hamlets, town or city".[97] There was, as Eduard Mohr, an early traveller wrote, "a peculiar poetry about a lonely grave in the wilderness", productive of "the very spirit of melancholy".[98]

Rhodes' will, however, revealed that he had chosen the Matopos site as much for its "loneliness" as for its "grandeur".[99] He had been accustomed to spend hours in solitude ("alone with the Alone", as he put it) on the veld, which he loved, or on Table Mountain, at the Cape. He said openly that, to him, the mountain was his chapel or church.[100]

It is significant, therefore, that the chapel which had been proposed for the original burial site at Zimbabwe is never mentioned in connection with the Matopos site: it simply disappears. Rhodes' burial therefore completes a radical break with English or metropolitan tradition which was first given public expression when the Allan Wilson patrol were buried at Great Zimbabwe.

Since Rhodes' religious observance was not conventional, his choice of burial sites and style could be dismissed as a mere idiosyncracy. What indicates that it was not is that these departures from tradition were accepted without demur by the church. Rhodes' funeral and subsequent burial service were conducted by William West Jones, the then Archbishop, in Cape Town and William Gaul in the Matopos Hills. Gaul also conducted Jameson's funeral. James Walker, the English Church deacon stationed at Fort Victoria, presided over the first interment of

[95] MacDonald, *Rhodes: A Heritage*, 49.
[96] *The Times* (November (n.d.), 1896), in *MQP* XIX (Feb 1897), 22.
[97] Sayce, *A Town Called Victoria*, 11, 14.
[98] Eduard Mohr, *To the Victoria Falls of the Zambezi* (1876) (Facsimile reproduction: Bulawayo: Books of Rhodesia, 1973), 386.
[99] Baker and Stead, *Cecil Rhodes*, Part Two, 3–4, 86.
[100] J.G. Lockhart and C.M. Woodhouse, *Rhodes* (London: Hodder and Stoughton, 1963), 30–31; and see McDonald, *Rhodes—A Life*, 332, 349.

the Shangani patrol and William West Jones, with Beaven, Archdeacon of Matabeleland, assisting, conducted the second. Coghlan was re-buried with Roman Catholic rite. This would suggest that Rhodes was not alone in his instinct and that the experience of the land as sacred place, which has been discussed above, was widespread among settlers at least as early as 1894.

VI *'Religion on the Veld'*

The new settler religious tradition was not strong enough to displace earlier, metropolitan tradition as is evident from the discontinuation of burials at the Matopos site; the persistence of the cemetery or graveyard tradition among the settlers; and also in the extension of the graveyard tradition to the local people by missionaries. It was in 1906 that Upcher at St. Faith's reported the burial of one Barnabas, a headman and the first Christian to die on the mission, in a grave rather than in a cave on a nearby hill, as was the local custom for men of his rank. Barnabas' grave was the first in a new Christian cemetery at Rusapi and similar cemeteries were to be provided at the other mission stations.

It is suggested here, however, that in settler sensibility the old and the new religious traditions came to co-exist, much as old and new religious traditions came to co-exist in the religion of convert Christians. That traditional beliefs continued to be held alongside Christian beliefs in the religion of converts has been well-established by modern research. A similar co-existence can be traced in settler sensibility, that of the 'civilised' or the metropolis and of 'the veld' or 'wild'.

Veld or bush burials, for instance, survived the re-assertion of metropolitan tradition: some settlers, particularly those who had spent most of their lives in the veld, continued to be buried outside towns, churchyards and cemeteries. Danie Viljoen, for example, a hunter killed by a buffalo in 1910 was buried, at the request of his family, on the southern bank of the Zambezi River, his accustomed hunting ground.[101] "Donkey" Reid, a prospector, died alone in the veld at much the same time and was buried at his last camp "as he would have wished".[102] The hunter

---

[101] *The Victoria Falls Advertiser* (Monday, October 3rd, 1910), (n.p.), reproduction in Keith Meadows, *Sometimes When It Rains, White Africans in Black Africa* (Bulawayo: Thorntree Press, 2000), plates, 118–9.

[102] The Right Hon. Sir Robert C. Tredgold, *The Rhodesia That Was My Life* (London: George Allen and Unwin, 1968), 26.

Frederick Courtney Selous, who led the BSA Company's pioneer column into Mashonaland in 1890, was buried where he fell in 1917 during the East Africa campaign of World War One, with a simple wooden cross on the grave. The bodies of those who died with him were later exhumed for re-burial but—in spite of the fact that his wife was the daughter of an English parson—Selous was left where he lay in the wild, his grave now surmounted with a slab and inscription.[103]

The majority of these distinctive bush burials, however, followed the development of settler agriculture. Many early farmers, like other early travellers, hunters, miners and men laying the railways, were buried where they had died (in their case, on the farm) for purely practical reasons such as the need for a swift interment in the heat and difficulties and cost of transport. One parson serving in early Salisbury, for instance, gives a vivid account of struggling 42 miles out to a farm to take a funeral and being overtaken as he did so by a bearer carrying the coffin on his head.

Subsequently, however, just as weddings and even baptisms and occasional confirmations were held on farms rather than in a building in a settlement near or far, so also the dead were buried, with Christian rite, on farms, even when there were cemeteries within reach. Hendrina Magdalena Southey, for instance, mother of an English Church family, was buried in 1900 "in a lonely grave beneath a tree she loved, near her home at Borrowdale", a farm only eleven miles from Salisbury.[104] On other farms, also within reach of settlements, family graveyards were established. At Ceres Farm near Shamva, for example, after 1913, A.R. Morkel set aside and tended "God's Acre", "in the shade of trees and within the sound of running water". He was buried there himself (in 1937).[105] There was a cemetery at Shamva and, well before 1937, a church he himself had helped to furnish.

It is possible that this custom of farm burials owed something to Boer or 'Dutch' tradition: the Southey and Morkel families, cited above, had previously farmed in South Africa, like the majority of settler farmers and so would have been familiar with Boer tradition.[106] Many of their

---

[103] Stephen Taylor, *The Mighty Nimrod: A Life of Frederick Courtney Selous: African Hunter and Adventurer 1851–1917* (London: Collins, 1989), 208–9, 290–1.

[104] Marjory Dick Davies (compiler), *Twin Trails: The Story of the Fynn and Southey families* (Salisbury: K.B. Davies (Pvt.) Ltd., 1974), 239–40.

[105] *Ibid.*, 273–4.

[106] It was estimated in 1913 that 95% of farmers had come from South Africa and of these 70% were of British origin: Rolin, *Rolin's Rhodesia*, 226.

new neighbours, moreover, as we have seen above, were 'Dutch' (see, above, p. 196). Boer farmers had practised veld burial for generations. The custom was so strong that bodies were returned to the ancestral farm for burial whenever possible, whatever difficulties such a journey imposed.

There is no evidence, however, to indicate that the custom of burying their dead (and performing other rites of passage) on farms was taken by 'English' settlers from their Dutch neighbours. English-speaking settlers in Southern Africa and particularly in Rhodesia tended to hold aloof from the Dutch[107] and no such transfer of custom is discussed in the literature, even though comparisons are made from time to time, especially by the clergy, between the religion of the Dutch and that of English settlers. It was often observed that various aspects of Boer religious practice could be adopted by other settlers with advantage: their deep piety, for instance, and family prayers.

It is more likely therefore that English settler and Boer farm burial had similar origins, in the practicalities forced on farmers by isolation. The English farmers then developed their own custom of veld burial, some of them within a generation. The novelist and farmer's wife, Gertrude Page, for example, who was born in England in 1872, emigrated to Rhodesia in 1904 and died in Salisbury in 1922. Her funeral was held at the cathedral but she was buried on a *kopje* (a small, rocky hill) on her Umvukwes (Mvurwe) farm, some 70 miles away.

These burials suggest that for such farmers, as for Rhodes and others who preferred the veld to life in the towns, the *locus* of the sacred had come to be found as much, or more, in the land which surrounded them than in the consecrated building and burial ground of inherited tradition.

The development of a growing awareness among settlers of the land as sacred place which is revealed by the custom of veld burial can also be traced in the language which came to be used to describe it. It can be seen in Gaul's burial sermon for Rhodes. There was no physical chapel or church at the site but in its stead the rocks of the Matopos Hills themselves and the surrounding landscape are described in terms of that familiar sacred building, an ancient cathedral: "we leave our

[107] Roberts, 57, 59; Donal Lowry, "'White Woman's Country': Ethel Tawse Jollie and the making of White Rhodesia', *Journal of Southern African Studies* 23:2 (June 1997), 268–9.

friend and chief at rest in his rocky tomb in God's great Cathedral, with the sapphire vault of heaven above him and the old grey granite walls around him".[108] A similar sensibility can be seen in the writings of the missionary Arthur Shearly Cripps. The African landscape he walked though was to him as the interior of a church: when he celebrated the Eucharist every morning of his journeys, in the open-air, with a slab of rock for an altar, the sky was his altarpiece. He also wished to be buried on a hill (on his mission station), with the rites of "the Church of England".[109]

Another parson, William Roxburgh, attempting to describe the effect on him of the landscape around Rusape could only describe it in the language of his religion: it did not have "the pleading beauty of the British" nor the "emotional grandeur" of the Swiss but it did have an "impressive dignity". It was a "landscape of the Resurrection—grave, solemn, dignified, majestic".[110]

For other men, the land became what it is in some of the psalms, the temple of the Lord: an itinerant parson coming across a plain teeming with game near Tuli, in 1902, for instance, used psalm 39, which exults at the presence and power of God in nature, "In His temple everything saith 'Glory!'".[111] Less well-educated settlers could describe Rhodesia as "God's really own country".[112] It was Beaven, however, the settler's bishop, who produced the most striking tribute to the religious power that "this vast, this wonderful land"[113] had over the settler imagination. In a memorial address given by him in 1921, heaven itself takes on the characteristics of a Central African landscape: "that land of life, of far and spacious distances to which they [the departed] have gone".[114]

---

[108] Philip Jourdan, *Cecil Rhodes, His Private Life by his Private Secretary* (London: John Lane, The Bodley Head, 1910), 281.

[109] A.S. Cripps, Wreningham, Enkeldoorn, 'The Open Way', *RCM* 5:11 (Nov 1908), 5; D.V. Steere, *God's Irregular: Arthur Shearly Cripps: A Rhodesian Epic* (London, S.P.C.K., 1973), 151; and see Ranger, 'Taking Hold of the Land', 181. Cripps' wish was not known at the time of his death and he was buried in the chancel of his church: Steere, 152.

[110] 'Letter from the Rev. W.J. Roxburgh, Epiphany, September 17th, 1904', *MQP* LI (Feb 1905), 11.

[111] [J.S. Wimbush], 'Bulawayo', *RCM* 2:1 (Nov 1902), 1.

[112] Vivian Meik, *Zambezi Interlude* (London: Philip Allan, 1932), 2.

[113] 'Letter from the Archdeacon of Matabeleland [F.H. Beaven], (n.d.)', *MQP* LXVI (May 1908), 7.

[114] 'Dedication of Memorial Windows: Address given by the Bishop at the dedication of the memorial windows at the Cathedral on Sunday, 9th October', *RCM* 8:11 (Nov 1921), 4.

CONCLUSION

The existence of the Diocese of Mashonaland/Southern Rhodesia was precarious for most of the period 1890–1925, although a degree of stability (symbolized by the building of substantial churches) had been achieved by 1925. Development, however, was uneven and often less the result of policy than the pressure of circumstances and the initiatives of individuals: bishops, converts, clergy and settlers.

Difficult conditions, among them division within society and church on racial lines, saw the premature retirement of the first three bishops: Gaul, on doctor's orders; Knight-Bruce and Powell, because of failure and discouragement, masked by illness. There was little to show for Powell's brief tenure but Knight-Bruce's episcopate left the diocese with a distinct missionary character and Gaul was able to establish rudimentary institutions.

Beaven, the fourth bishop, worked under somewhat easier conditions than those faced by his predecessors. His episcopate therefore saw a greater development of the institutional life of the church. It also, paradoxically, saw both an advance in the status of indigenous Christians and also the endorsement of an effective, if incomplete, separation into settler and 'mission' wings.

Development was always hampered, however, by an insufficiency of funds and each bishop in turn looked to the Church of England for assistance, only to encounter competition in fund-raising, both from philanthropic societies 'at home' and from other branches of the church abroad. Only in Knight-Bruce's time did Mashonaland/SR have the specific, 'romantic' appeal which was necessary to attract funds in such a competitive environment.

The diocese was also heavily dependent upon England for clergy throughout the period, for few could be found elsewhere in Southern Africa and local communities, both settler and indigenous, only began to produce clergy, and then in very small numbers, in 1919. Recruits, however, had to be found in the face of a competition which was as fierce as that for funds. When what is known of the clergy who were recruited for Mashonaland/SR is examined, in order to establish what might have influenced them to serve there, it shows that many were either recruited by a colleague, had a personal connection with the diocese, or had previously lived or worked abroad. There never were sufficient clergy to meet the needs of the diocese, however and only a few gave long service.

Members of the 'English Church' expected to re-create in Africa the ecclesiastical life of England, where the Church of England was pre-eminent, both ecclesiastically and in the field of education. Since a very 'British' colony, that of (Southern) Rhodesia, lay at the heart of the diocese these expectations were not entirely inappropriate. By 1925, however, the work of the church among indigenous peoples had been outstripped by that of other bodies; and lay ministry, by catechist-teachers, supplemented by occasional visits from ordained missionaries, had become the norm.

The paucity of clergy also resulted in settlers outside the major towns becoming accustomed either to infrequent worship or to a (limited) lay ministry. A high turnover of clergy also meant that stability and continuity were very largely provided by the settler laity. It also proved impossible, in this period, to sustain church schools on the English scale. Religious education, however, was provided for by a right of entry for the clergy to all schools for settler children.

Many of the religious practices of the Church of England persisted in Mashonaland/SR but others were modified and new forms of religious expression also emerged. By the end of the period, therefore, a distinct, local, religious identity had emerged, which could be seen, for example, in the architecture and decoration of both settler and mission churches. Among settlers, a new religious sensibility, in which the land became the *locus* of the sacred, had also developed alongside tradition inherited from England, in which religious encounter normally took place in a sacred building. This new sensibility was revealed in the language which settlers came to use about the land but it was most clearly expressed in their custom of bush or 'veld' burial.

This study has only been able to sketch in the outlines of work amongst the indigenous peoples of the diocese and other minority settler groups: a comprehensive history of this work is needed. Studies of individual mission districts are also needed, if the extraordinary variety of Anglican missionary work in the period is to be explored. The examination made here of the wider background of the search for finance and staff, has also revealed a need for greater study of the part played by the High Church or Anglo-Catholic party of the Church of England in the development of the overseas church, which has been overshadowed by academic investigation into Evangelical and Protestant activity. Too is little known, furthermore, about the relationship, in this period, between the Church of England and the colonial churches (and ministries to Britons abroad, outside the Empire), as most recent scholarly attention has been devoted to the history of missions and the supporters of missions in England.

The social history of the white settler community of the diocese has also been insufficiently studied: more investigation is needed of its origins, make-up and character at any one point in this period. Future studies might also compare what has been discovered here, about settler religion, with contemporary developments in other colonies and British communities abroad.

SELECT BIBLIOGRAPHY

This bibliography is arranged as follows:

PRIMARY SOURCES

A: *Archival*

- I: The National Archives of Zimbabwe.
- II: Department of Historical Manuscripts, University of the Witwatersrand Library, Johannesburg, South Africa.
- III: The Bodleian Library of Commonwealth and African Studies at Rhodes House, Oxford.
- IV: Lambeth Palace Library.
- V: General Synod of the Church of England, Record Centre.
- VI: The Scottish Record Office.
- VII: Derbyshire County Archives.
- VIII: Papers in private possession.

B: *Reports*

- I: Reports of Proceedings.
- II: Reports.
  - a) On the supply and training of the clergy.
  - b) On the work of the Church overseas.
  - c) Church of the Province of South Africa: Reports, Episcopal Charges, Acts and Resolutions.
  - d) Reports, miscellaneous.

C: *Journals and periodicals*

D: *Books, pamphlets and articles*

SECONDARY SOURCES

A: *Archival*

I: *National Archives of Zimbabwe*
Historical Manuscripts Collection

a) Records of the Anglican Church, Diocese of Mashonaland/Southern Rhodesia

ANG 1/2/2: Albums: Diocese of Mashonaland, 1890–1943.

ANG 1/4/4: First Diocesan Conference, St. Augustine's College, Panhalonga, August 21, 1902.

ANG 1/4/6/1: Bishop's Senate, (subsequently Cathedral Chapter), Minutes, 1910–28.

ANG 5/2/1: Anglican Church, Parish of St. John the Baptist, Umtali. Out Letter Book, 1904–14.

ANG 5/3/1–3: Anglican Church, Parish of St. John the Baptist, Umtali. Albums, 1893–1946.

ANG 5/4/1: Anglican Church, Parish of St. John the Baptist, Umtali. Balance Sheets, 1900–22.

ANG 5/5/1–3: Anglican Church, Parish of St. John the Baptist, Umtali. Minutes, Church Council and Easter Vestry, 1896–1940; Church Building Committee, 1894–95.
ANG 5/7/1: Anglican Church, Parish of St. John the Baptist, Umtali. Reminiscences.
ANG 5/8/1: Anglican Church, Parish of St. John the Baptist, Umtali. Report by the Treasurer, 1913.
ANG 5/8/1: Anglican Church, Parish of St. John the Baptist, Umtali. Returns, 1916–30.
ANG 9/1/1: Anglican Church, Parish of St. Edmund, Hartley. Nominal Rolls and other papers, 1909.
ANG 9/2/1/1: Anglican Church, Parish of St. Edmund, Hartley. Minutes, Church Council and Easter Vestry, 1908–1924.
ANG 9/1/2: Anglican Church, Parish of St. Edmund, Hartley. Books of Account, (April) 1916–(December) 1948.
ANG 9/4/5/2: Anglican Church, Parish of St. Edmund, Hartley. Register of Services, Sept 17 1919–Dec 25, 1943.
ANG 3/1/1: Anglican Church, Parish of All Saints, Gatooma. Minutes, Church Council and Easter Vestry, 1910–34.
ANG 29/2/1: Pelly, Rev. D.R. A Short History of the Knight-Bruce Memorial College for Natives at St. Augustine's Mission in Rhodesia.
MS 1036/3: Diocese of Mashonaland/Southern Rhodesia, Board of Finance, Minute Books, 1903–25, 1925–1939.
MS 1036/5/1: Diocese of Mashonaland/Southern Rhodesia, Synod, Minute Book, April 1903–Jan 1927.

b) Memoirs, correspondence, reminiscences
AL 3/1/1: Alexander, Ronald Perry Goodwin. Memoranda, August 1936.
ANG 1/10/1: Bishop E.H. Etheridge, Memoirs. 1954.
AS 1/1/1–6: Ashworth, George Leopold. Correspondence.
BL 7/2/1: Nurse Hewitt's Memoirs.
BO 11/1/1: Borrow, John Henry. Correspondence, 1881–95.
BR 3/1/1: Broderick, George Edward Peach. Correspondence and other papers, 1906–1945.
BR 8/1/1: Knight-Bruce, Bishop G.W.H., Correspondence, 1886–94.
CR 4/1/1: Cripps, Arthur Shearly. Correspondence, general, 1922–1954.
HA 4/1/1: Hale, Herbert Percy. Letter Book, 1903–05. [Continued in AS 1/1/6].
JO 3/1/1: Johnson, Sir Frank William Frederick. Correspondence and other papers, 1886–1943.
LE 4/1/1: Leary, Walter James. Reminiscences: 'Southern Rhodesia after 40 years'.
Misc/BE 4/1/1: Beattie, Thomas Oliver. Reminiscences, 1910–22.
MS 354: Bruce, Bishop G.W.H. Knight. Correspondence and other papers: general: 1885–1889.
PE 3/1/1: Pelly, Douglas Raymond. Correspondence, 1892–1934.
PE 3/1/2: Pelly, Douglas Raymond. Correspondence, 1896–1934.
PE 3/1/2: Pelly, Douglas Raymond. Reminiscences, 1891–1900.
SO/5/2: Southey, Charles William Ritchie. Reminiscences, Jan 1943.
VI/2/2/4: Osmund Victor, C.R., Historical Notes: The Stanley Society: 12th February, 1939.

c) Miscellaneous
Information file 92.283(8): Some material for a life of Bishop Knight-Bruce [prepared by R.R. Langham-Carter, c. 1967].
Public Records: E2/11/18/(3) Department of Education, Schools, European, Fort Victoria Public School.

II: *Department of Historical Manuscripts, University of the Witwatersrand Library, Johannesburg, South Africa*

Records of the Church of the Province of South Africa

AB/184: Source material, for C. Lewis and G.E. Edwards, *Historical Records of the Church of the Province of South Africa* (1934).

AB/307: Mission of Help to South Africa, Records, 1904, 2 vols. Minute book, Scrap book.

AB/186: Carter, W.M., (Bishop of Zululand, 1891–1902, Bishop of Pretoria, 1902–1909, Archbishop of Capetown 1909–1931), Papers, 1891–1930.

AB/355f: Bishop Knight-Bruce. Papers. [Letters, extracts made by Mrs. Knight-Bruce, 1930].

AB/636: William Thomas Gaul, Scrapbook, 1874–1931.

AB/707,Cb3: South African Church Institute, London. Records, 1914–70.

AB/867/aa, 4:2: Zambezi Bishopric, 1902–1919. Correspondence relating to.

AB/1107: Church of the Province of South Africa, Association of Women Workers (previously Society of Women Missionaries), Records, 1918–1977.

AB/1162: Diocese of Capetown, Letter books, Bishops, letters from, 1886–1896; [Archbishops], letters from, 1897–1908.

AB/1225: Church of the Province of South Africa, Diocese of Southern Rhodesia, Records, 1905–1955.

III: *Bodleian Library of Commonwealth and African Studies at Rhodes House, Oxford*

Records of the United Society for the Propagation of the Gospel

E Series: Reports from Africa, 1890–1925.

D Series: Letters from Africa, 1890–1925.

[All correspondence in D and E Series filed under 'M', for Mashonaland, or 'S' for Southern Rhodesia.]

X215: Colonial Bishoprics Fund, Centenary Memorial Volume, 1941.

X362: Mashonaland Mission Committee, Minutes, 1893–1903 [Minutes of first meeting of Committee (January 23rd, 1893), thereafter minutes of Council].

X363: Mashonaland Mission Executive Committee, Minute book, Feb 1893–July 1902.

X573: Mashonaland Mission Executive Committee, Minute book, Oct 1902–April 1912.

X405: London Junior Clergy Missionary Association, Minute Book (no. 1), 1899–1903.

X540: [Federation of] Junior Clergy Missionary Associations, Conferences, Minute Book, 1896–1910.

X1000: London Junior Clergy Missionary Association, *Fourth Report and List of Members* (pamphlet), 1896.

X1001: London Junior Clergy Missionary Association, Report of Evening Meeting, November 29th, 1894 (pamphlet) (1894).

X1002: Federation of Junior Clergy Missionary Associations, Conferences, resumés of proceedings, 1899–1904; Annual reports, 1898–1904. [Includes: Junior Clergy Missionary Association. *Missionary Preparation (Church of England)* (April 1902)].

X1003: Federation of Junior Clergy Missionary Associations, Annual Reports, 1896–1898, 1902–1919.

X1004: Federation of Junior Clergy Missionary Associations: Conferences, Printed resumés of proceedings, 1904–1924.

X1005: Junior Clergy Missionary Association, Miscellaneous printed papers, re. conferences etc., 1900–1920.

X1007: Junior Clergy Missionary Association, Council for Service Abroad, 1901–1915.

X1008: "Recruiting Campaign for Service in the Kingdom of God" (correspondence and papers), c. 1917–1920.

X1010: Junior Clergy Missionary Association, Miscellaneous correspondence, 1910–1921.

IV: *Lambeth Palace Library*
Papers of the Archbishops of Canterbury:
Edward White Benson (1883–1896).
Frederick Temple (1896–1902).
Randall Davidson (1903–1928).
BM 3: Bishop's Meetings, 1896.
BM 4: Bishop's Meetings, 1897.
Lambeth Conference, 1888, Records: LC 17, 18, 19, 25, 26, 28.
Lambeth Conference, 1897, Records: LC 40, 41, 46, 55.
MS 1713: E.J. Palmer [subsequently Bishop of Bombay], Address on the Church in South Africa, to Junior Clergy Missionary Association, Hereford, 1907.
MS 2927: Church Education in South Africa, 1901–3.
MS 2928–9: Archbishop's South African Education Fund, Committee, Minute Books, 1905–11.
MS 3013: E.J. Palmer, Journal of a visit to South Africa, April–October, 1907.
H5133.1067, No. 8: Junior Clergy Missionary Association (in connection with the SPG), printed *resumés* of proceedings: [11th] Conference, (Nov 1899); [12th] Conference, (April 1900).
H56001.7: Mission of Help, Minutes of proceedings of a conference, Jerusalem Chamber, Westminster Abbey, December 10th, 1903.
H5046.1.22: Mission of Help, *End of the Mission* (1904).
H5691.S7: Preliminary Expedition, Mission of Help to South Africa, *Report* (Private and Confidential) (1903) [printed, galleys].
YC912.63.3: Archbishop of Canterbury's Oxford and Cambridge Missionary Exhibition Fund, 1905.

V: *General Synod of the Church of England, Record Centre*
CACTM/COU/D/1/5: Central Advisory Council of Training for the Ministry, *Diocesan Ordination Candidates' Funds, Confidential*, (1913).
CACTM/COU/D/1/24: Central Advisory Council of Training for the Ministry, *Report of Committee appointed at the preliminary meeting of the Central Advisory Council of Training for the Ministry on February 19th, 1913, Confidential*, (n.d.) [March 1913].
CACTM/COU/D/1/19: Central Advisory Council of Training for the Ministry, No. 24, *Kelham Theological College, Confidential*, (1914).
CACTM/COU/D/1/22: Central Advisory Council of Training for the Ministry, *Agenda, Feb 13th & 14th, 1914*. [Feb. 3rd, 1914].
CACTM/COU/D/1/32: Central Advisory Council of Training for the Ministry, *Minutes*, Feb 13th & 14th, 1914, *Confidential*.
CACTM/COU/D/1/38: Central Advisory Council of Training for the Ministry, *Minutes, 7th Ordinary Meeting*, Feb 4th, 1915, *Confidential*.
CACTM/COU/D/1/38: Central Advisory Council of Training for the Ministry, No. 38, *Special Meeting July 13th, 1915*, [*Report on the Present Condition and Prospects of the Theological Colleges.*], *Confidential*, (1915).
CACTM/COU/D/1/41: Central Advisory Council of Training for the Ministry, No. 41, *Conference on Preparation for Ordination* [*Report of committee appointed at the fourth ordinary meeting, February 13 and 14, 1914, to organise a conference on the testing and training for ordination of those who have had little early education.*] (1915).
CACTM/COU/D/1/46: Central Advisory Council of Training for the Ministry, No. 46, *Conference on Preparation for Ordination* [*Report (Revised) of committee appointed at the fourth ordinary meeting, February 13th and 14th, 1914, to organise a conference on the testing and training for ordination of those who have had little early education.*] (1916).

CACTM/COU/D/1/91: Central Advisory Council of Training for the Ministry, No. 91, *Correspondence on Service Overseas*, [*Memorandum, &, on a proposal to require a period of service overseas from all candidates after their ordination.*] *Confidential*, (1918).
CACTM/COU/D/1/93: Central Advisory Council of Training for the Ministry, *Minutes, Ordinary Meeting*, May 17th, 1918.
CACTM/COU/D/1/94: Central Advisory Council of Training for the Ministry, No. 94, *Resolutions on Missionary Colleges*, (1918).
CACTM/COU/D/1/97: Central Advisory Council of Training for the Ministry, No. 97, *Memorandum on Oxford and Cambridge Schemes*, (1918).
CACTM/COU/D/1/98: Central Advisory Council of Training for the Ministry, No. 98, *Minutes, Ordinary Meeting*, October 24th, 1918.
CACTM/COU/D/2/126: Central Advisory Council of Training for the Ministry, No. 126, *Selection of Civilian Candidates*, (1920).
CACTM/COU/D/2/161: Central Advisory Council of Training for the Ministry, No. 161, *Summary of Proceedings for 1923*, (1924).
CACTM/COU/D/2/188: Central Advisory Council of Training for the Ministry, No. 188, *Archbishops' Committee on the Supply of Candidates for Holy Orders*, (1926).
CACTM/COU/D/3: 'Archbishops' Commission on Training for the Ministry, Memorandum', by The Rev. Canon B.R. Brasnett, D.D., Principal of Edinburgh Theological College, 9th March, 1937, [Typescript].
UBM/BD/1, Minutes of the Board of Canterbury Province from 4th July, 1887–16th May, 1895 with the minutes of Boards of Missions of Canterbury and York from January 20th, 1893.

VI: *Scottish Record Office*
Loch, Henry Brougham, Baron. Papers, 1827–1900.
Walpole, G.H.S., Bishop of Edinburgh 1910–1926. Papers.

VII: *Derbyshire County Archives*
Gell Collection.

VIII: *Papers in private possession*
a) Mrs. Elizabeth Hinde, papers of the late Canon Richard Holderness:
– 'Con and Jim in Rhodesia' (typescript).
– sundry photographs.
b) Mrs. Nicky Salt; Salt Scrapbooks (compiled by her father-in-law, Rev. John Frederick Salt):
– Scrapbook, (1899–1902).
– Literary Scraps, (1905–1912).
– Literary Scraps, (1914–c. 1924).
– Literary Scraps, (1925–c. 1939).
– News cuttings, (1938–c. 1944).
c) Miss Olga Ward (niece of James Hay Upcher):
– *In Memoriam, James Hay Upcher: Archdeacon of Mashonaland, Diocese of Southern Rhodesia 1892–1931* [1931]. [Pamphlet, annotated].

B: *Reports*

I: *Reports of proceedings*
Church Congress, 1880–1927.
Convocation, Province of Canterbury, 1860–70, 1885–1930, (*Chronicle of the Convocation of Canterbury*).
Convocation, Province of York, 1890–1907, (*Journal of Convocation of York*).
Representative Church Council, Church of England, 1904–18.

Church Assembly [National Assembly] of the Church of England, 1919–1930.
Royal Colonial Institute, 1891.
Southern Rhodesia Missionary Conference, 1926–30.

II: *Reports*

a) On the supply and training of the clergy (in order of date of publication)

Convocation of Canterbury, Lower House, Report 318, *Assistant Curates* (Westminster, 1898).

Convocation of York, *The Training of Candidates for Holy Orders* (York, 1899).

Convocation of Canterbury, Lower House, Report 343, *Supply and Training of Candidates for Holy Orders*, Westminster, 1900).

Report of a Committee of Bishops appointed on the Training of Non-graduate Ordination Candidates (Confidential) (*1905).

Supply and Training of Candidates for Holy Orders, Report to the Archbishop of Canterbury (Poole: W.H. Hunt, 1908).

Convocation of Canterbury, Lower House, Report 436, *Supply and Training of Candidates for Holy Orders*, (1910).

Committee appointed by the Archbishops of Canterbury and York, *The Supply and Training of Candidates for Holy Orders* (Westminster: 1925).

Lambeth Conference, 1930, Report V, 'The Ministry of the Church', in *Report of the 1920 and 1930 Lambeth Conferences: With select resolutions from The Conferences of 1867, 1878, 1888, 1897, and 1908* (London: S.P.C.K., 1948).

Church of England, Church Assembly, *Report of the Commission on Staffing of Parishes*, CA 334 (1930).

Convocation of Canterbury, Lower House, Report 571, *Status of Unbeneficed Clergy* (1930).

b) On the work of the Church overseas

Church of England, Central Board of Missions. *Annual Review of Missions Overseas*, 1910–1911.

Church of England, Central Board of Missions. *Missions Overseas, Annual Review*, 1912–1922.

Church of England, Central Board of Missions. *Supplement to Missions Overseas, 11th Annual Review* (1919).

Church of England, United Board of Missions. *A Study of Some Missionary Problems* (1903).

Church of England, United Boards of Missions. *Annual Review of the Foreign Missions of the Church*, 1907–1909.

Church of England, Church Assembly, Missionary Council. *The World Call to the Church: The Call from Africa* (Westminster: 1926).

Church of England, Church Assembly, Missionary Council. *The World Call to the Church: The Call from Our Own People Overseas* (Westminster: 1927).

Church of England, Church Assembly, Missionary Council, *The World Call to the Church: The Call to East and West* (Westminster: 1928).

Church of England, Church Assembly, Overseas Council, *Missionary Finance: Being the report of the Missionary Finance Commission set up by the Missionary Council of the Church Assembly* (London: 1932).

Church of England, Church Assembly, Missionary Council, *WITH ONE ACCORD: A unified and authoritative statement of the needs of the Church overseas, consisting of surveys and statistical tables based upon information supplied by the overseas bishops and the recognised missionary societies and agencies of the Church of England, together with a statement of what the Church is asked to do in 1933* (Westminster: 1933).

Church of England, Church Assembly, Missionary Council, *The World Wide Church 1934–5: Second unified statement*...(Westminster: 1934).

Church of England, Church Assembly, Missionary Council, *World Wide Witness 1935–6: Third unified statement*...(Westminster: 1935).

Church of England, Church Assembly, Missionary Council, *The World Quest 1936–7: Fourth unified Statement*...(Westminster: 1936).

(London) Missionary Conference, *Official Report of the Missionary Conference of the Anglican Communion* on May 28th, 29th, 30th, 31th and June 1st, 1894. Edited by George A. Spottiswoode (London: S.P.C.K., 1894).

Official Report of the Pan-Anglican Congress, VII Volumes (London: S.P.C.K., 1908).

Report addressed to the Lord Bishop of Lincoln, as Visitor of St. Paul's Missionary College, Burgh; of an enquiry as to the advisability of undertaking the training of men for lay-work in the mission field abroad (Liverpool: 1893).

Report of the 1920 and 1930 Lambeth Conferences: with select resolutions from the Conferences of 1867, 1878, 1888, 1897, and 1908 (1948).

Society for the Propagation of the Gospel [SPG]. [Annual] *Reports*, 1890–1936 (Westminster).

World Missionary Conference, *Report of the Commissions*, 9 Volumes, (Edinburgh: 1910).

c) Church of the Province of South Africa: Reports, Episcopal Charges, Acts and Resolutions

Acts and Resolutions together with certain documents of the Diocese of Mashonaland, authorised by the First Diocesan Synod and confirmed by the Provincial Synod of 1904 and promulgated by the Lord Bishop of the Diocese, in the Cathedral of Salisbury On Wednesday, April 22nd, 1903 (Fakenham, Norfolk: [n.d.])

Charge delivered to the Pretoria Diocesan Synod, by William, Bishop of Pretoria, in the Cathedral Church of St.Alban, Pretoria, in June 21, 1905, together with the Acts and Resolutions of the Diocesan Synod (Pretoria, 1905).

Official Report of the Tenth Provincial Missionary Conference of the Church of the Province of South Africa, Holden at Port Elizabeth October 25th–28th 1933 (Johannesburg, Imprinted at the C.R. Press, Rosettenville, 1933).

Resolutions passed by the Episcopal Synod, Between the Years 1993 and 1935 and now Published by Order of the Synod for the information of the Church (Cape Town: 1936).

South African Church Festival [varies, as South African Church United Festival]. *Combined Report*, 1894–1911 (London: [The Committee]).

With One Accord in South Africa, An Interim Statement circulated, with permission, before the Provincial Missionary Conference, 1933 [Osmund Victor, C.R., Provincial Commissary] (Johannesburg: Imprinted at the C.R. Press, Rosettenville, 1933).

United Festival of the Home Organisations in Aid of the Funds of the Ten Dioceses of the Province of South Africa, *Combined Report, to be presented to the General Meeting* (London: [The Committee], 1892, 1893).

d) Reports, miscellaneous

British Association for the Advancement of Science [Annual] *Report* (1903–5).

Census for England and Wales, *General Report with Indices*, 1891, 1901, 1911, 1921, 1931.

Report of the Director of Census, regarding the Census taken on 7th May, 1911 (Salisbury, [Southern Rhodesia]: Government Printer, 1912).

Report of the Director of Census, regarding the European Census taken on 3rd May, 1921 (Salisbury [Southern Rhodesia]: Government Printer, 1922).

Report of the Director of Census for 1926, (Salisbury [Southern Rhodesia]: The Government Printer, 1927).

Report of the Archbishops' Committee on Church and State: With Appendices (Poole: 1916).
The Teaching Office of the Church: Being the Report of the Archbishops' First Committee of Inquiry: with Appendices (London: Published for the National Mission by the Society for Promoting Christian Knowledge, 1919).

C: *Journals and periodicals*

NB. It was not possible to consult contemporary newspapers (specifically, the *Bulawayo Chronicle* and the *Rhodesia Herald*). Most items of interest in these publications, however, are preserved or discussed in the church records which have been examined.

African World.
Anglican, The [Diocese of Pretoria], 1903–5.
Bloemfontein Quarterly Paper.
Cape Church Monthly and Parish Record.
Cape to the Zambezi: Quarterly Paper for the Church of the Province of South Africa.
Children of the Church Magazine [SPG].
Chronicle of the Central Board of Missions (Church of England).
Church Chronicle for the Province of South Africa.
Church Quarterly Review.
Church Magazine for South Africa.
Church Times.
Colonial Church Chronicle, Missionary Intelligencer and Foreign Ecclesiastical Reporter.
Contemporary Review.
C.R.: A Chronicle of the Community of the Resurrection [Mirfield].
East and the West: Quarterly Review for the Study for Missions.
Fortnightly Review.
Goodwill.
Guardian.
Homeworker's Gazette.
International Review of Missions.
Kingdom, The [Magazine of the Diocese of Pretoria, from 1905].
Light for the Line [South African Church Railway Mission Magazine, Grahamstown].
Link [Diocese of Southern Rhodesia].
Mashonaland Quarterly Paper.
MESSAGE from the parishes of The Cathedral, Avondale and Highlands [Diocese of Southern Rhodesia].
Mission Field: Monthly Record of the Proceedings of the Society for the Propagation of the Gospel at Home and Abroad.
Murray's Magazine: a home and colonial periodical for the general reader.
National Church [journal of the Church Institution].
National Review.
Net, Cast in Many Waters, The [Association in Aid of the Mission to Zululand].
New Quarterly.
Nineteenth Century.
Nineteenth Century and After.
Paulatim [Annual Magazine of St. Paul's Theological College, Grahamstown] [from 1933].
Quarterly Review: Community of the Resurrection, Grahamstown.
Quarterly Review.
Rhodesian Church Magazine.
Rhodesia Review: Independent Quarterly for Settlers and Shareholders, 1905–6.
St. John's Monthly Magazine [Bulawayo].
St. Paul's College Magazine, Grahamstown [Annual Magazine of St. Paul's Theological College, Grahamstown] [from 1925].

St. Peter's Home: Quarterly Letters 1903–1925, Community of the Resurrection, Grahamstown.
Scottish Chronicle.
Scottish Guardian.
South Africa.
South African Church Mission Quarterly Paper.
Southern Rhodesia Church Magazine.
Southern Rhodesia Quarterly Paper.
Souvenir [Magazine of St. Paul's Theological College, Grahamstown] [for 1932].
Transvaal and Southern Rhodesia Missions Quarterly Magazine.

D: *Books, pamphlets and articles*

A Dominican Sister. *In God's White-Robed Army: The Chronicle of the Dominican Sisters in Rhodesia 1890–1934* (Cape Town: Maskew Miller Limited, 1947).
Alban, Edgar [Edgar Jacob, Bishop of St. Alban's]. 'The Lambeth Conference and the Pan-Anglican Congress' *The Church Quarterly Review* CXXX (Jan 1908): 256–77.
Alderson, E.A.H. Lieut-Col. *With the Mounted Infantry and the Mashonaland Field Force 1896* (Facsimile reproduction of the 1898 edition with additions) (Bulawayo: Books of Rhodesia, 1971).
Alexander, Eleanor, ed. *Primate Alexander, Archbishop of Armagh: a Memoir: With Portraits* (London: Edward Arnold, 1914).
Allen, Roland. *Missionary Methods: St. Paul's or ours: a study of the Church in the four provinces* (London: Robert Scolt, 1912).
——. *The Case for Voluntary Clergy* (London: Eyre and Spottiswood, 1930).
Anderson, Daphne. *The Toe-Rags: the story of a strange up-bringing in Southern Rhodesia* (London: Deutsch, 1989).
Andrew, Father, S.D.C. *My Year in Rhodesia* (London: S.P.G., 1933).
Andrews, C.F. 'The Junior Clergy Missionary Associations', *East and the West* V (April 1907): 166–173.
——. *John White of Mashonaland* (London: Hodder and Stoughton, 1935).
Atlay, J.B. *The Life of the Rt. Rev. Ernest Roland Wilberforce* (London: Smith Elder, 1912).
Baden-Powell, Lord, of Gilwell. *African Adventures* (London: C. Arthur Pearson Ltd, [n.d.]).
Baillie, Albert Victor, K.C.V.O., D.D., Formerly Dean of Windsor. *My First Eighty Years* (London: John Murray, 1951).
Baker, Herbert, and Stead, W.T. *Cecil Rhodes: The Man and His Dream* (A newly arranged and newly titled, two-part work comprising facsimile reproduction of the 1934 edition of *Cecil Rhodes: by his Architect*; and the 1902 edition of *The Last Will And Testament of Cecil John Rhodes*, with additional chapters by W.T. Stead, ed., and incorporating a new Foreward and additional Illustrations (Bulawayo: Books of Rhodesia, 1977).
Balfour, Alice Blanche. *Twelve Hundred Miles in a Waggon* (A facsimile reprint of the 1895 edition) (Salisbury, Rhodesia: The Pioneer Head, 1970).
Barry, A. 'The function of the colonial churches in our missionary expansion', *East and the West*, I (April 1903): 182–194.
Baxter, E.C., Comptroller of Customs, Bulawayo. 'The Church's Mission among White Settlers in South Africa', *Official Report of the Pan-Anglican Congress*, VI (London: S.P.C.K., 1908), S.E.1(c).
——, comp. *A Short History of the Diocese of Mashonaland (Southern Rhodesia)* (Bulawayo: [published for the Diocese of Southern Rhodesia by O. Ellis Allen], 1922).
Bent, J. Theodore, F.S.A., F.R.G.S. *The Ruined Cities of Mashonaland* (Facsimile reproduction of the third Edition [1896]) (Bulawayo: Books of Rhodesia, 1969).
Bernard Robert Wilson of Portsea and Brisbane, A Memoir [n.a.] (Portsmouth: W.H. Barrell, 1910).
Bishop of St. Albans, see Jacob, Edgar.

Bishops of London, St. Albans, Southwark, St. Andrews and Stepney. *The Foreign Mission Work of the Church, Addresses to Business Men* (London: Society for the Propagation of the Gospel, 1906).

Black, Colin. *The Legend of Lomagundi* (Salisbury, North-Western Development Association, 1976).

Blackwood Lewis, see *Mrs Mary Blackwood Lewis.*

Blennerhasset, Rose and Sleeman, Lucy. *Adventures In Mashonaland* (Facsimile reproduction of the 1893 edition with additions and illustrations) (Bulawayo: Books of Rhodesia, 1969).

Blomfield, A. *A Memoir of C.J. Blomfield, Bishop of London: With Selections from his Correspondence, edited by his son, A. Blomfield, with a portrait*, 2 vols. (London: John Murray, 1863).

Boggis, R.J.E. *A History of St Augustine's College, Canterbury* (Canterbury: Cross and Jackman, 1907).

——. *I Remember: Reminiscences of an Octogenarian* (Exeter: W.V. Cole and Sons, 1947).

Boutflower, C.H. (Bishop of Dorking). 'What is wrong? Where are the people to go abroad?', *East and the West*, IV (April 1906): 169–178.

Boyd, Mary R. *The Veld, Bardic Poem, South African Eisteddfod, 1921* (Cape Town: T. Maskew Miller, 1921).

Brabant, F.H. *Neville Stuart Talbot 1879–1943: A Memoir* (London: SCM Press, 1949).

Brettell, Noel. *Side-gate and Stile. An Essay in Autobiography* (Bulawayo: Books of Rhodesia, 1981).

Brough, J.S.B. 'The Training of the Missionary', *East and the West* XVI (January 1918): 68–81.

Bullock-Webster, Canon. 'Church Finance', in *Official Report of the Pan-Anglican Congress*, VI (London: S.P.C.K., 1908), S.C.Gp3, Sc.1.c.

Burnham, F.R. *Scouting on Two Continents* (Facsimile Reproduction of the 1927 edition with new Foreward and Index) (Bulawayo: Books of Rhodesia, 1975).

Burnley, Alfred [Alfred Pearson, Bishop of Burnley] 'Autonomy in Anglican Churches', *The Nineteenth Century and After* LXIV:378 (Nov 1908): 258–265.

Can England's Church Win England's Manhood? A study in camp, field and hospital of the spiritual condition of English soldiers. By an Army Chaplain (London: Macmillan & Co., 1917).

Carey, W.J., Bishop of Bloemfontein, *My Priesthood* (London: Longmans and Co., 1915).

Carey, W. *Goodbye To My Generation* (London: A.R. Mowbray, 1951).

Carlisle, Bishop of, [Harvey Goodwin]. 'The Church of the British Empire', *Murray's Magazine* 2:8 (August 1887): 145–164.

Chester-Master, Lieut-Col. R., Resident Commissioner and Commandant General of Rhodesia. 'Missions in South Africa as affected by Racial Problems' in *Official Report of the Pan-Anglican Congress*, VI, (London: S.P.C.K., 1908), S.E.3 a(d).

'Church and Empire', A Reprint of The Special Number of The Times June 25th, 1930 (July MCMXXX).

Church and Life of Today, by the Bishop of Bristol, the Dean of Manchester, and others (London: Hodder and Stoughton, 1910).

'Church in Newfoundland, The', (n.a.), *Church Quarterly Review* 60, 1905 (July 1905): 355–371.

'Church in South Africa, The', (n.a.), *Church Quarterly Review* 114, 1904 (Jan 1904): 241–257.

Church of England, The: A Practical Survey, (by a Parish Worker) (London: Simpkin, Marshall, Hamilton Kent and Co., 1910).

Churchill, Lord Randolph S., M.P. *Men, Mines and Minerals in South Africa* (Facsimile reproduction of the third edition, [1893]) (Bulawayo: Books of Rhodesia, 1969).

Churton, E.T., Bishop of Nassau, *Foreign Missions* (London: Longmans, Green, 1901).

Clark, Percy M. *The Autobiography of an Old Drifter* (Facsimile reproduction of the 1936 edition, with new Publisher's Introduction) (Bulawayo: Books of Rhodesia, 1972).

Clayton, P.B. *Plain Tales from Flanders* (London: Longmans, Green and Co., 1930).

Cleveland. M.E. 'Reminiscences, from 1899–1920, with introductory notes by Ann Andersen', *Heritage of Zimbabwe* 19 (2000): 81–107.

Colonial and Continental Church Society. *Church Work Abroad (Extracted from 'The Rock', Oct 14th, 1887)* (1887).

'Colonial Bishoprics' Fund, The', *Mission Life* V:II (New Series) (London 1874), 445–50.

'Colonial Bishoprics' Fund, The', *Church Magazine for South Africa* VI:67 (July 1891), liii–liv.

Colquhoun, Archibald. *Dan to Beersheba: Work and Travel in Four Continents* (London: William Heinemann, 1908).

Cooper-Chadwick, J. *Three Years with Lobengula and Experiences in South Africa* (Facsimile reproduction of the 1894 edition with new Foreward and illustrations) (Bulawayo: Books of Rhodesia, 1975).

Cope-Christie, J.A. 'Looking Back Over Fifty Years: Portions of an address given . . . on 15th June 1944', *Heritage of Zimbabwe 6* (1986): 1–14.

Creighton, Louisa. 'Ministry of Women: Its relation at the present time to work done by men', *Pan-Anglican Papers Papers: Being Problems for Consideration at the Pan-Anglican Congress, 1908* (London: Society for Promoting Christian Knowledge, 1907), S.C.iii(a)

Cripps, Arthur Shearly. *Faery Lands Forlorn: African Tales* (Oxford: B.H. Blackwell, 1910).

——. *The Brooding Earth: A Story of Mashonaland* (Oxford: B.H. Blackwell, 1912).

Crockford's Clerical Directory.

Crockford's Prefaces 1922–4: The Editor Looks Back (Oxford: Oxford University Press, 1947).

Cross, F.L. *Darwell Stone: Churchman and Counsellor* (Westminster: Dacre Press, 1949)

Curteis, G.H. *Bishop Selwyn of New Zealand and Lichfield: A sketch of his life and work with further gleanings from his letters, sermons, and speeches* (London: Kegan, Paul, Trench, 1889).

Cust, R.N. *Observations and Reflections on Matters Connected with Missionary Societies and Missionaries of All Countries etc.* (London: [n.p.], 1885).

——. *Notes on Missionary Subjects*, Part I (1888), Part II (London: Elliot Stock, 1889).

——. *Essay on Prevailing Methods of the Evangelisation of the Non-Christian World* (London: Luzac and Co., 1894).

Darter, Adrian. *The Pioneers of Mashonaland* (Facsimile reproduction of the 1914 edition with new illustrations, Foreword, nominal rolls and route map; and list of corrections to the original edition (Bulawayo: Books of Rhodesia, 1977).

David, A.E. *Australia: With illustrations and maps* [Handbooks of English Church Expansion. No. 4] (London and Oxford: A.R. Mowbray and Co., 1908).

Davidson, R.T., comp. *The Lambeth Conferences of 1867, 1878, and 1888: The official reports and resolutions together with the sermons preached at the Conference* (London: Christian Knowledge Society, 1896).

Davidson, Randall, Archbishop of Canterbury. 'Missionary Problems', *East and the West* II (Jan 1904): 1–3.

Davies, Marjory Dick, comp. *Twin Trails: the Story of the Fynn and Southey families* (Salisbury: K.B. Davies (Pvt.) Ltd., 1974).

Dawson, E.C. *James Hannington: First Bishop of Eastern Equatorial Africa: A History of his Life and Work 1847–1885* (London: Seeley and Co., 1887).

Dawson, Christopher. *The Spirit of the Oxford Movement* (London: Sheed and Ward, 1933).

Dawson W. (Missions to Seamen) 'Ecclesiastical Hydrophobia or Where are the Men?', *East and the West* IV (April 1906): 179–188.

Deane, Anthony C. 'The Falling-Off in the Quantity and Quality of the Clergy', *The Nineteenth Century* XLV:268 (April 1899): 1023–30.

'Dearth of Clergy, The', (n.a.), *Church Quarterly Review* 67, 1909 (Jan 1909): 405–27.

Decle, Lionel. *Three Years in Savage Africa* (Facsimile reproduction of the 1900 edition with new Publisher's Introduction and Foreward) (Bulawayo: Books of Rhodesia, 1974).

De Waal, D.C., M.L.A. *With Rhodes in Mashonaland* (Translated from the original Dutch by Jan H. Hofmeyer de Waal). (Facsimile reproduction of the 1896 edition, with new Foreward, Publisher's Introduction and illustrations) (Bulawayo: Books of Rhodesia, 1974).

Dimont, C.T. and Batty, F. de Witt, *St. Clair Donaldson: Archbishop of Brisbane 1904–1921, Bishop of Salisbury 1921–1935* (London: Faber and Faber, 1939).

Doane, G.W. (D.D.). *The Missionary Bishop: The Sermon at the Consecration of the Right Reverend Jackson Kemper, D.D., Missionary Bishop for Missouri and Indiana; in St. Peter's Church Philadelphia, September 25th, 1835* (Burlington, New Jersey: [n.p.], 1835).

Donaldson, St. Clair, Archbishop of Brisbane, 'The idea of a Bush Brotherhood', *East and the West* XII (April 1914): 193–8.

Donaldson, St. Clair George Alfred, *The Missionary Policy of the Church in the Existing World Situation, An Address to the Enrolled Electors of the Parish of Wimbledon, Monday May 1, 1922* (London: S.P.C.K., 1922).

Donaldson, S.A. 'Education in South Africa: our opportunity and our duty', *East and the West* I (October 1903): 390–401.

Donovan, C.H.W. *With Wilson in Matabeleland: or Sport And War in Zambezia* (Facsimile reproduction of the 1894 edition with a new Frontispiece, Foreword, Appendix and Index) (Bulawayo: Books of Rhodesia, 1979).

Duckworth, Sir Dyce Bt., M.D., Ll.D. 'Lapses from Christian Conduct in the lives of young men in the tropics and how to deal with them', *East and the West* X (Oct 1912): 377–381.

Du Toit, S.J. *Rhodesia Past and Present* (Facsimile reproduction of the 1897 edition with a new Foreward and Index) (Bulawayo: Books of Rhodesia, 1977).

'Edward Coleridge and the Rise of Missionary Colleges' [n.a.], *Church Quarterly Review* 20 (1885): 109–25.

Ellison, D. *The Pioneer Work of the Church: A Plea for the Gripping of the Railways: a paper read at the Pan-Anglican Congress* (London: Christian Knowledge Society, 1909).

Ellison, D.F. *God's Highwaymen: the Story of the South African Church Railway Mission* (London, S.P.C.K, 1930).

Ellison, J.H.J., and Walpole, G.H.S., eds. *Church and Empire: A Series of Essays on the Responsibilities of Empire* (London: Longmans and Co., 1907).

English, Pat. *Lushington: A Fragment of Time, Being a Tale of happy endeavour along the Marandellas Watershed and the Lushington Loop in earlier days* (n.p. [Harare]: (Private publication), 1995).

Every, E.F. *The Anglican Church in South America* (London: S.P.C.K., 1915).

Fairbridge, Kingsley. *His Life and Verse* (Reprint of the 1927 edition of *The Autobiography of Kingsley Fairbridge* with additional text and new ilustrations; and selections from the 1909 and 1928 editions of his *Veld Verse*) (Bulawayo: Books of Rhodesia, 1974).

Ffrench, G.E. 'The Supply of Clergy', *The Nineteenth Century and After* LXIV:381 (Nov 1908): 852–863.

Finaughty, William. *The Recollections of William Finaughty Elephant Hunter 1864–1875* (Reprint of the 1916 edition with additional sketch map, illustrations, and new Foreward and Notes by Edward C. Tabler) (Bulawayo: Books of Rhodesia, 1973).

Finlason, C.E. *A Nobody in Mashonaland* (Facsimile reproduction of the 1893 edition) (Bulawayo: Books of Rhodesia, 1973).

The Foreign Mission Work of the Church (1906): see Bishops of London, St. Albans, Southwark, St. Andrews and Stepney.

Fort, G. Seymour. *Alfred Beit: A Study of the Man and his Work* (London: Ivor Nicholson and Watson, 1932).

Fripp, C.E. and Hiller V.W., eds. *Gold and the Gospel in Mashonaland 1888: being the journals of 1. The Mashonaland Mission of Bishop Knight-Bruce 2. The Concession journey of Charles Dunell Rudd.* Central African Archives, Oppenheimer Series, Number Four (London: Chatto and Windus, 1949).

Frodsham, George H. *A Bishop's Pleasaunce* (London: Smith, Elder, 1915).

From the Cape to Buluwayo or How to Travel to Rhodesia Through British Territory By One who has done it (Facsimile reproduction of the 1896 edition with a new Publisher's Introduction and Illustrations) (Bulawayo: Books of Rhodesia, 1979).

Fuller, Latimer. 'Separation of Black and White in Church', *East and the West* X (October 1912): 382–394.

Furse, Michael, Formerly Bishop of Pretoria and later Bishop of St. Alban's. *Stand Therefore! A Bishop's Testimony of Faith in the Church of England* (London: S.P.C.K., 1953).

Gale, W.D. *One Man's Vision: The Story of Rhodesia* (Facsimile reproduction of the 1935 edition to a reduced format and incorporating new Author's Preface and Illustrations) (Bulawayo: Books of Rhodesia, 1976).

Garlick, Phyllis. *Six Great Missionaries* (London: Hamish Hamilton, 1955).

Gaul, William, Bishop of Mashonaland. 'The Possibilities of an African Kraal', *East and the West III* (April 1905): 121–9.

——. 'Vocation and Preparation for Missionary Work', *East and the West* III (October 1905): 407–410.

——. 'South Africa: The Anglican Church and Imperial Ideals', in J.H.J. Ellison and G.H.S. Walpole, eds. *Church And Empire: A Series of Essays on the Responsibilities of Empire* (London: Longmans and Co., 1907): 216–240.

——. 'Vocation, recruiting and training of candidates for Holy Orders with special reference to South Africa', *Official Report of the Pan-Anglican Congress*, IV (London: S.P.C.K., 1908), S.C.i(a).

Gell, P.L. *The Maintenance of the Parochial System Being a survey of the requirements, resources and possible unification of diocesan finance prepared for the Southwell Diocesan Agencies*, (2nd edition, London: Henry Frowde, 1909).

Gibson, A.G.S. 'Some thoughts on the Native Question in South Africa', *East and the West* II (October 1904): 452–458.

——, ed. *Sketches of Church Life and Work in the Diocese of Capetown* (Capetown: The S.A. "Electric" Printing and Publishing Co., 1900).

——. 'The Training of South African Missionaries', *East and the West* X (July 1912): 262–274.

——. 'The South African Church and the Church at Home', *East and the West* XII (October 1914): 374–382.

Goodwin Green, Elsa. *Raiders and Rebels in South Africa* (Facsimile reproduction of the 1898 edition with new Foreward and Index) (Bulawayo: Books of Rhodesia, 1976).

Gollock, G.A., comp. *In the Year of the World Call* (London: Overseas Council (Church of England), 1927).

Gordon-Cumming, C.F. *"The Last Commandment": A word to every Christian* (London: [Church Missionary Society], 1887).

Gore, Charles, D.D. *The Incarnation of the Son of God* (Bampton Lectures, 1891) (2nd Edition, London: John Murray, 1892).

Gott, J. *The Parish Priest of the Town* (2nd edition, London: Christian Knowledge Society, 1889).

Gouldsbury, Cullen. *Rhodesian Rhymes* (Reprint of the 1932 edition with additions) (Bulawayo, Books of Rhodesia, 1969).

Grant, Anthony. *The Past and Prospective Extension of the Gospel by Missions to the Heathen* [Bampton Lectures, 1843] (London: 1844).

——. *The Ramsden Sermon on the Extension of The Church in the Colonies and Dependencies of the British Empire: A Sermon on Matthew XXVIII:19* (London: 1852).

Greenup. A.W., Litt. D. [Principal of St. John's Hall, Highbury]. *The Supply and Training of Candidates for Holy Orders. Papers read at the Town-Hall, Folkestone, on June 25th, 1909, by A.W. Greenup and J.E. Watts-Ditchfield. Extracted from the report of The Clerical and Lay Church Alliance for the Dioceses of Canterbury, Chichester and Rochester* (1910).

Grenfell, Wilfred. *A Labrador Doctor: The Autobiography of Wilfred Thomason Grenfell* (5th Edition, London: Hodder and Stoughton, 1922).

Gumprich, Mrs. O. and Yates, Mrs E., comps. *Women in Central Africa* ([Salisbury], The Committee of Press, Publicity and Broadcasting of the National Council of Women of Southern Rhodesia) [1951]).

Rev. G.D. Halford, former Archdeacon of Rockhampton, Queensland. 'The Church's Ministry among White Settlers', *Official Report of the Pan-Anglican Congress*, VI (London: S.P.C.K., 1908), SE.1(f).

Hamilton, C. Frederick. 'The Englishman in Canada', *National Review* 50:295 (Sept 1907): 116–127.

Hamilton, J.A.I. Agar. *A Transvaal Jubilee: being a History of the Church of the Province of South Africa in the Transvaal* (London: S.P.C.K., 1928).

Hastings, L. *Dragons Are Extra* (Harmondsworth: Penguin, 1947).

Hawtrey, Sir Charles Henry. *The Private Secretary: a farcical comedy in three acts* [An English version of *'Der Bibliothekar'* by Gustav von Moser] (London: [n.p.], 1884].

Heald, Madeline, comp. *Down Memory Lane with SOME EARLY RHODESIAN WOMEN 1897–1923* (Bulawayo: Books of Rhodesia, 1979).

Heanley, R.M. *A Memoir of Edward Steere, D.D., LL.D, Third Missionary Bishop in Central Africa 1873–1888* (London: George Bell and Sons, 1888).

Heinrich, H.R. and Thompson, H.P. *On Distant Trails: The Story of the Church in Canada and Australia* (Westminster: Junior Work Department, S.P.G., 1926).

Hemans, H.N. *The Log of a Native Commissioner* (Facsimile reproduction of the 1935 edition) (Bulawayo: Books of Rhodesia, 1971).

Hendriks, Katie. *The Bend in the River* (Cape Town: Howard Timmins, [n.d.] [1930?]).

Henson, Herbert Hensley, ed. *Church Problems, A View of Modern Anglicanism. By various authors* (London: J. Murray, 1900).

——. *The Ethics of Empire* (London: Oxford University Press, 1927).

——, D.D. Lord Bishop of Durham. *Church and Parson in England* (London: Hodder and Stoughton Ltd., 1927).

——. Successively Bishop of Hereford and Durham, *Bishoprick Papers* (London: Oxford University Press, 1946).

——. *Retrospect of an Unimportant Life, Volume One 1863–1920* (1942), *Volume Two 1920–1939* (1943), *Volume Three 1939–46, The Years of Retirement* (1950) (London: Oxford University Press).

Henson, Herbert Hensley, Letters of: Chosen and Edited with an Introduction by Evelyn Foley Braley (London: S.P.C.K., 1950).

Henson, Herbert Hensley, More Letters of: Chosen and Edited with an Introduction by Evelyn Foley Braley (London: S.P.C.K., 1954).

Hickman, Colonel A.S. *Men Who Made Rhodesia, A Register of Those who Served in the British South Africa Company's Police* (Salisbury: The British South Africa Company, 1960).

Hirtzel, Sir Arthur, K.C.B. 'Imperial Christianity', *East and the West* XI (October 1913): 361–382.

Hirtzel, Sir Frederick Arthur. *The Church, the Empire and The World: Addresses on the Work of the Church Abroad* (London: S.P.C.K., 1919).

Hobhouse, Walter. *The Church and the World in Idea and in History* [Bampton Lectures for 1909] (London: Macmillan and Co., 1910).

Hocking, W.J., ed. (With a preface and introduction by), *The Church And New Century Problems* (London: Wells Gardener, Darton and Co., 1901).

Hole, Hugh Marshall, C.M.G. *The Jameson Raid* (Facsimile reproduction of the 1930 edition, with new Publisher's Introduction and additional illustrations (Bulawayo: Books of Rhodesia, 1973).

——. *Old Rhodesian Days* (Facsimile reproduction of the 1928 edition with a new Foreward and Frontispiece) (Bulawayo: Books of Rhodesia, 1976).
——, C.M.G. *The Passing of the Black Kings* (Facsimile reproduction of the 1932 edition with a new Foreward) (Bulawayo: Books of Rhodesia, 1978).
Holland, Henry Scott. *George Howard Wilkinson: Bishop of St. Andrews, Primus of the Episcopal Church* ([n.p.], [n.p.], 1909).
Holland, Henry Scott. *A Bundle of Memories* (London: Wells Gardener, Darton & Co., Ltd, 1915).
——. *The Call of Empire and other papers* ([Westminster]: [n.p.], 1917).
Hone, Percy F. *Southern Rhodesia* (London: George Bell and Sons, 1909).
Hulley, C.M. *Where lions once roamed* (Salisbury, Rhodesia: The Pioneer Head, 1969).
Hyatt, Stanley Portal. *The Old Transport Road* (Facsimile reproduction of the first edition, 1914) (Bulawayo: Books of Rhodesia, 1969).
Jackson, H.C. *Pastor on the Nile: Being some account of The Life and Letters of Llewellyn H. Gwynne, C.M.G., C.B.E., D.D., LL.D., Formerly Bishop in the Sudan and Deputy Chaplain-General in France in the First World War* (London: S.P.C.K., 1960).
Jacob, Edgar. *The Divine Society or the Church's Care of Large Populations*: Second edition with additions (London: Christian Knowledge Society, 1903).
——, D.D., Bishop of St. Alban's. *Charge delivered to the clergy and churchwardens of the Diocese of St. Alban's at his second visitation* ([n.p.]: [n.p.], May 1911).
'John Kapuya-An Expedition to the land of the Crocodile-Eaters', (As told to Jean Farrant by John Kapuya), *Rhodesiana* 20 (July 1969), 81.
Johnson, Edward E., Metropolitan of India. 'The United Boards of Missions of the Dioceses of Canterbury and York', *East and the West* IV (Jan 1906): 36–49.
Johnson, Frank, Lieut-Col. D.S.O. *Great Days: The Autobiography of an Empire Pioneer* (Facsimile reproduction of the 1940 edition with New Publisher's Introduction) (Bulawayo: Books of Rhodesia, 1978).
Johnston, Sir Harry. 'Are Our Foreign Missions a Success?', *Fortnightly Review* 45: CCCXVIII (April 1889): 481–489.
Jones, Harry. *Priest and Parish* (Essays reprinted, with One exception, from *Fraser's Magazine*) (London: [n.p.], 1866).
——. *Fifty Years: or Dead Leaves and Living Seeds* (London: Smith Elder, 1895).
Jones, Neville. *Rhodesian Genesis: The Story of the Early Days*, compiled from the Reminiscences of some of the *Pioneers for the Rhodesian Pioneer's and Early Settler's Society* (Bulawayo: Books of Rhodesia, 1953).
Jourdan, Philip. *Cecil Rhodes, His Private Life by his Private Secretary* (London: The Bodley Head, 1910).
Kelly, Herbert Hamilton. *England and the Church: Her calling and its fulfilment considered in relation to the increase and efficiency of her ministry* (London: Longmans and Co., 1902).
Kelly, H.H. *The History of a Religious Idea* (London: Society of the Sacred Mission, 1898).
——. 'Methods of mission work in South Africa: a criticism', *East and the West* I (April 1903): 156–180.
Knight, E.F. *Rhodesia of Today: A description of the Present condition and the Prospects of Mashonaland and Matabeleland* (Facsimile reproduction of the 1895 edition with new Foreward and Illustrations) (Bulawayo: Books of Rhodesia, 1975).
Knight-Bruce, G.W.H. *Journals of the Mashonaland Mission 1888–1892* (London: Society for the Propagation of the Gospel in Foreign Parts, 1892).
——. *Memories of Mashonaland* (Facsimile reproduction of the 1895 edition) (Bulawayo: Books of Rhodesia, 1970).
Knox, E.A. *Reminscences of an Octogenarian 1847–1934* (London: Hutchinson, 1935).
Lancelot, J.B. *Francis James Chavasse: Bishop of Liverpool* (Oxford: Basil Blackwell, 1929).
Lax His Book, The Autobiography of Lax of Poplar (London: The Epworth Press, 1937).

Leonard, Major A.G. *How We Made Rhodesia* (Facsimile reproduction of the 1896 edition with new Publisher's introduction, Foreward and Illustrations) (Bulawayo: Books of Rhodesia, 1973).

Letcher, Owen. *When Life Was Rusted Through, A Tale of Northern Rhodesia and of the Beira and Mashonaland Railways* (First published in book form 1934) (Bulawayo: Books of Rhodesia, 1973).

'Letter printed by request of the Bishop if too late for the May magazine', April 18th, 1900, (loose in *Mashonaland Quarterly Paper* XXXII (May 1900): 1–4.

Lloyd, Ven. G.E., Archdeacon of Saskatchewan. 'The Church's Mission among White Settlers in Canada', *Official Report of the Pan-Anglican Congress*, VI (London: S.P.C.K., 1908), S.E.1(g).

Lucas, H.J. 'Early Days on a Small Working', *Rhodesiana* 20 (July 1969): 14–22.

McDonald, J.G. *Rhodes: A Heritage* (London: Chatto and Windus, 1943).

——. *Rhodes, A Life* (Facsimile reproduction of the 1927 edition) (Bulawayo: Books of Rhodesia, 1971).

MacDonald, Shelia. *Martie and Others in Rhodesia* (London: Cassell and Company, Ltd., 1927).

——. *Sally in Rhodesia* (Reprint of the 1927 edition with additional illustrations) (Bulawayo: Books of Rhodesia, 1970).

Macleane, Douglas 'The Church as a Profession', *National Review* XXXIII:198 (August 1899): 945–55.

McClemens, Ven T. 'The Work of the Church among the Miners of West Australia', *Official Report of the Pan-Anglican Congress*, VI (London: S.P.C.K., 1908), SE1(b).

Mandell Creighton, Life and Letters, by his wife, Two Volumes (London: Longmans, Green and Co., 1905).

Mason A.J. *The Church of England and Episcopacy* (Cambridge: at the University Press, 1914).

——. *George Howard Wilkinson, A Memoir.* Two volumes (New York: Longmans, Green and Co., 1909).

——, D.D. *Life of William Edward Collins: Bishop of Gibraltar* (London: Longmans, Green and Co., 1912).

'"Matabele Jim"—the Trials and Tribulations of an 1894 Settler, with annnotations by J.R.A. Burton', *Heritage of Zimbabwe* 15 (1996): 70–115.

Mathers, E.P. *Zambezia: England's Eldorado in Africa* (Facsimile reproduction of the 1891 edition with a new Foreward) (Bulawayo: Books of Rhodesia, 1977).

Maud, J.P. 'The Supply and Training of Clergy', *East and the West* IV (July 1906): 341–349.

Meadows, Keith. *Sometimes When It Rains: White Africans In Black Africa* (Bulawayo: Thorntree Press, 2000).

Meik, Vivian. *Zambezi Interlude* (London: Philip Allan, 1932).

Melbourne, H.L. [H.L. Clarke, Bishop of Melbourne]. 'Church of England in Australia', *Church Quarterly Review* 85, 1917 (Oct 1917): 55–72.

Melina Rorke: Told by Herself (Facsimile Reproduction of the 1939 edition) (Bulawayo: Books of Rhodesia, 1971).

Men, Money and the Ministry: (A Plea for Economic Reform in the Church of England) [n.a.] (London: Longmans, Green and Co., 1937).

Michell, Sir Lewis. *The Life of the Right Honourable Cecil John Rhodes*, Two Volumes (London: Edward Arnold, 1910).

Mohr, Eduard. *To the Victoria Falls of the Zambezi* (Facsimile reproduction of the English edition of 1876, with new Publishers's Introduction) (Bulawayo: Books of Rhodesia, 1973).

Montgomery, Henry Hutchinson. 'The Church's Missions in Christendom', No. 5 of *Pan-Anglican Papers: Being Problems for Consideration at the Pan-Anglican Congress, 1908* (London: Society for Promoting Christian Knowledge, 1907).

——. *Foreign Missions*, New edition (London: Longmans, Green, 1904).
——. 'The Pan-Anglican Congress of 1908', *East and the West* IV (Jan 1906): 27–35.
——, ed. *Mankind and the Church: Being an Attempt to estimate the Contribution of Great Races to the Fullness of the Church of God By Seven Bishops* (London: Longmans and Co., 1907).
——. *Service Abroad: lectures delivered in the Divinity School of the University of Cambridge* (London: Longmans and Co., 1910).
——. *Visions for Missionaries and Others* (London: Society for the Propagation of the Gospel in Foreign Parts, 1916).
——. *Francis Balfour: of Basutoland: Evangelist and Bishop* (London: S.P.G., 1925).
——. *The Spirit of the S.P.G.* (London: S.P.C.K., 1929).
Montgomery, Maud. *Bishop Montgomery: A Memoir* (Westminster: Society for the Propagation of the Gospel in Foreign Parts, 1933).
Mott, John R. *The Home Ministry and Modern Missions* (London: Hodder and Stoughton, 1908).
'Mrs. Mary Blackwood Lewis's letters about Mashonaland, 1897–1901'. *Rhodesiana* 1:5 (1960): 14–53.
Mullins, J.D. *Our Beginnings: being a short sketch of the Colonial and Continental Church Society* (London: [n.p.], 1923).
Neligan M.R., Bishop of Auckland, 'New Zealand: an ill-constructed quadilateral' in J.H.J. Ellison and G.H.S. Walpole, eds. *Church and Empire: A Series of Essays on the Responsibilities of Empire* (1907): 169–171.
Official Yearbook of the Church of England.
Oldham, J.H. *Christianity and the Race Problem* (London: Student Christian Movement, 1925).
'*Open Letter to the Clergy at Home*' (n.a.) (London: Society for Promoting Christian Knowledge, 1917).
Page, Gertrude. *Jill On A Ranch* (London: Cassell and Co., 1921).
——. *The Silent Rancher* (London: Hurst and Blackett, 1909).
Palmer E.J. 'Vocation to Missionary Service', *East and the West* III (October 1905): 411–432.
Pan-Anglican Congress. *Official Handbook* (London: Society for Promoting Christian Knowledge, 1908).
——. *Who's Who at the Pan-Anglican Congress, With numerous portraits and other illustrations* (London and Oxford: A.R. Mowbray and Co., 1908).
Pan-Anglican Papers: Being Problems for consideration at the Pan-Anglican Congress, 1908 (London: Society for Promoting Christian Knowledge, 1907).
Pascoe, C.F. *Two Hundred Years of the S.P.G.: An historical account of the Society 1701–1900: Based on a digest of the Society's Records* (London: Published at the Society's Office, 1901).
Pauling, George. *The Chronicles of a Contractor, Being The Autobiography of the late George Pauling* (Facsimile Reproduction of the first edition) (Bulawayo: Books of Rhodesia, 1969).
Peile, J.H.F. 'The Case for Voluntary Clergy,' *Church Quarterly Review* 110, 1930 (July 1930): 333–340.
Plomer, William. *Double Lives: An Autobiography* (London: Jonathan Cape, 1943).
Posselt, F.W.T. *Fact and Fiction* (Facsimile reproduction of the 1935 edition with a new Foreward) (Bulawayo: Books of Rhodesia, 1978).
Prestige, G.L. *The Life of Charles Gore: a Great Englishman* (London: William Heinemann Limited, 1935).
Priest and Parish in India (European Congregations) [n.a.] (London: S.P.C.K., 1928).
Rangoon, Bishop of, (Arthur Mesac Knight). 'The Church's Ministry, Distribution of Spheres', (2), in *Official Report of the Pan-Anglican Congress*, IV (London: S.P.C.K., 1908), SCi.B.6.

Redhead, Aida E. 'Our "Home from Home"', *Heritage of Zimbabwe* 19 (2000): 46–52.
Reynolds, Bernard. *Church Work* (London: Longmans, 1905).
Rhodes, Cecil John. Facsimile, autograph letter, May 6th, 1894, to Mrs Kirton, *Rhodesiana* 31 (September 1974): 88–9.
Richards, Hylda M. *False Dawn: The Story of Dan Judson, Pioneer: Based on the diaries of Dan and Maynie Judson* (Bulawayo: Books of Rhodesia, 1974).
Riley, J.A.L. *Qualifications of Missionary Agents: the best means of obtaining them, together with some reflections on the estates of virginity and matrimony in connexion with foreign missionary work: A paper read before the Church Congress held at Rhyl, 1891* (Derby and London: Bemrose and Sons,1891).
Roberts, Revd. Canon Page. 'Is the Broad Church Party Extinct?', *National Review* XXXV:210 (August 1900): 1017–1024.
Robertson, Rev. W.A. Scott. *British Contributions to Foreign Missions* (London: Church Printing Co., 1890).
Robinson, Arthur W. 'The Policy of the Church with Regard to Education in South Africa', *The East and The West*, 2 (January 1904): 21–31.
——. *The Mission of Help to South Africa, What it has done, and what it has taught us* (London: Longmans & Co., 1906).
Rolin, Henri. *Rolin's Rhodesia* (translated by Deborah Kirkwood) (Newly-set English translation of Les Lois et l'Administration de la Rhodésie, published in Brussels in 1913. With new introductory material and Illustrations) (Bulawayo: Books of Rhodesia, 1978).
Roxburgh, Mrs., of Rhodesia, South Africa. 'Women's Industrial Work in Native Missions Abroad', *Official Report of the Pan-Anglican Congress, V* (London: S.P.C.K., 1908), S.D.2(v).
Russell, G.W.E. *Afterthoughts* (London: Grant Richards Limited, 1912).
Ruzawi: The Founding of a School (Ruzawi Old Boy's Association, Salisbury, Rhodesia), (n.a.)[Robert Grinham and Maurice Carver] (n.p.) [Salisbury] (n.d.) [1968].
Sandford E.G., ed. *Memoirs of Archbishop Temple: By Seven Friends*, Two volumes (London: Macmillan, 1906).
Sauer, Hans. *Ex Africa* (Facsimile reproduction of the 1937 edition, with new Publisher's Introduction) (Bulawayo, Books of Rhodesia, 1973).
Saunders, C.R. 'Geoffrey Musgrave of "The Chrome"—Selukwe's Master Miner', *Heritage of Zimbabwe* 17 (1998): 121–5.
Sayce, Katherine. *A Town Called Victoria: or the Rise and Fall of the Thatched House Hotel* (Bulawayo: Books of Rhodesia, 1978).
Schreiner, Olive. *Trooper Peter Halket of Mashonaland* (1897) (1959 edition: London: Ernest Benn Limited).
Scott Moncrieff, C.I.E. *Eastern Missions from a Soldier's Standpoint* (London: The Religious Tract Society, 1907).
Selous, F.C. *Sunshine and Storm in Rhodesia* (Facsimile reproduction of the second edition [1896]) (Bulawayo: Books of Rhodesia, 1968).
——. *Travel and Adventure in South-East Africa* (Facsimile reproduction of the 1893 edition, with new Publisher's Introduction and Foreward) (Bulawayo: Books of Rhodesia, 1972).
Selwyn, George Augustus. *The Work of Christ in the World: Four Sermons preached before the University of Cambridge on the four Sundays preceding Advent in the year of Our Lord 1854* (Cambridge: [n.p.], 1855).
'Service abroad by one who has tried it', (Anon.) *East and the West* X (July 1912): 322–328.
Sheppard, H.R.L. *The Impatience of a Parson, A Plea for The Recovery of Vital Christianity* (London: Hodder and Stoughton, n.d. [1927?]).
Sidwell, Ven A.B., Archdeacon of Pretoria, Bishop-Elect of George. 'The Work of the Church among the White Settlers of South Africa', *Official Report of the Pan-Anglican Congress*, VI, (London: S.P.C.K., 1908), S.E.1(c).

Smith, E.W. *The Way of the White Fields in Rhodesia: A survey of Christian enterprise in Northern and Southern Rhodesia* (London: [n.p.], 1928).

Smith, H. Maynard. *Frank, Bishop of Zanzibar: Life of Frank Weston, D.D. 1871–1924* (London: Society for Promoting Christian Knowledge, 1926).

'Some Notes on the Church in Australia' [n.a.], *Church Quarterly Review* 157 (Oct 1903): 146–66.

St. Aidan's Church, Yeoville, Johannesburg. *Rev. W.J. Roxburgh: In Memoriam* (1919).

Stent, Vere. *A Personal Record of Some Incidents in the Life of Cecil Rhodes* (Reprint of the 1925 edition with additional illustrations) (Bulawayo: Books of Rhodesia, 1970).

Stephens, W.R.W. *The Life and Letters of Walter Farquhar Hook D.D., F.R.S. by his son-in-law* (Sixth Edition, London: Richard Bentley and Son, 1881).

Studholme, J. 'The Church's Mission among the Settlers in New Zealand', *Official Report of the Pan-Anglican Congress*, VI (London: S.P.C.K., 1908), S.E.1(h).

Sykes, Frank W. *With Plumer in Matabeleland* (Facsimile reproduction of the 1897 edition with new Publisher's introduction) (Bulawayo: Books of Rhodesia, 1976).

Tabler, E.C., ed. *To the Victoria Falls via Matabeleland: The Diary of Major Henry Stabb 1875* (Cape Town: Struik, 1967).

Talbot, The Right Reverend Ethelbert, D.D., S.T.D. Bishop of Central Pennsylvania, *My People of the Plains* (New York and London: Harper Brothers, 1906).

Tanser, G.H. *A Scantling of Time: The Story of Salisbury, Rhodesia 1890–1900* (Salisbury, Rhodesia: Pioneer Head, 1965).

——. *A Sequence of Time: The Story of Salisbury, Rhodesia 1900 to 1914* (Salisbury: Rhodesia, Pioneer Head, 1974).

Tatlow, Tissington. *The Story of the Student Christian Movement of Great Britain and Ireland* (London: Student Christian Movement Press, 1933).

Tawse Jollie, Ethel, M.L.A. *The Real Rhodesia* (Facsimile reproduction of the 1924 edition) (Bulawayo: Books of Rhodesia, 1971).

Taylor, Isaac. 'The Great Missionary Failure', *Fortnightly Review* 44:CCLXII (Oct 1888): 488–500.

——. 'Missionary Finance', *Fortnightly Review* 44:CCLXII (Nov 1888): 581–589.

Taylor, R.D. 'Passenger Trains on the Harare Branch Lines', *Heritage of Zimbabwe* 17 (1998): 77–87.

The '96 Rebellions: Originally published as The British South Africa Company Reports on the Native Disturbances in Rhodesia, 1896–97 (Facsimile reproduction of the 1898 Reports, with new Foreward and illustrations) (Bulawayo: Books of Rhodesia, 1975).

Thomas, H., comp. *The Five Lambeth Conferences, etc.* (London: S.P.C.K., 1929).

Thompson, Doris. *Priest and Pioneer, A Memoir of Father Osmund Victor, C.R., of South Africa* (Westminster: Faith Press, 1958).

Thompson, Matabele. An Autobiography: Edited by his daughter Nancy Rouillard (Facsimile reproduction of the 1936 edition with a new Foreward) (Bulawayo: Books of Rhodesia, 1977).

Townsend, Hazel. *The History of the Umvukwes: Written on behalf of THE UMVUKWE WOMEN'S INSTITUTE* ([n.p., n.p. n.d.]).

Tredgold, The Right Hon. Sir Robert C. *The Rhodesia That Was My Life* (London: George Allen and Unwin, 1968).

Trollope, M.N. Bishop in Corea, *The Church in Corea* (London: Mowbray and Co., 1915).

Tucker, H.W. *Under His Banner: papers on the missionary work of modern times* (London: Christian Knowledge Society, 1872).

——, M.A., The Revd. *Memoir of the Life and Episcopate of George Augustus Selwyn D.D. Bishop of New Zealand, 1841–1869; Bishop of Lichfield, 1867–1878, In Two Volumes* (London: William Wells Gardner, (1879).

——. *The English Church in Other Lands, or the Spiritual Expansion of England.* Vol. 13 of Professor Mandell Creighton, ed. *Epochs of Church History*) (London: Longmans, Green and Co., 1886).

Upcher, James Hay. *Notes on the Story of the English Church Mission in the Diocese of Mashonaland* [Salisbury: Diocese of Southern Rhodesia, 1903].
Varian, H.F. *Some African Milestones* (Wheately, Oxford: George Ronald, 1953).
Victor, Osmund C.R. *The Salient of South Africa* (London: S.P.G, 1931).
Waddy, Etheldred. *Stacy Waddy: Cricket, Travel and the Church* (London: The Sheldon Press, 1938).
Wallis, J.P. *One Man's Hand* (Facsimile reproduction of the 1950 edition with new Publisher's Introduction and portrait of the author) (Bulawayo: Books of Rhodesia, 1972).
Watney, Charles. 'Why the Englishman is Despised in Canada', *National Review* 50:297 (Nov 1907): 422–443.
Welldon, J.E.C. [Bishop of Calcutta, 1898–1901]. 'An Imperial Conference of the Church and It's Significance', *The Nineteenth Century and After* LXII:376 (June 1908): 888–902.
Westcott, B.F., Bishop of Durham. 'The Empire', in W.J. Hocking, ed. *The Church and New Century Problems* (London: Wells Gardener, Darton and Co., 1901): 19–31.
——. *Lessons from Work* (London: Macmillan and Co., 1901).
——. *The Responsibility of Churchmen with Respect to Foreign Missions* (1888) in Edgar Jacob, *The Divine Society: or the Church's Care of Large Populations* ([1890], 2nd Edition, 1903).
White, Arnold.'Britannia and the Colonist', *National Review* 35:208 (June 1900): 635–645.
White, John. 'The Rationale of the Missionary Conference of Southern Rhodesia', *Native Affairs Department Annual* 2 (1924): 67–9.
White, Gilbert [Bishop of Carpentaria]. *Some Problems of Northern Australia: Being a paper read before the Victorian Branch of the Royal Geographical Society of Australia, Sept 13, 1907* (Melbourne: Uruquhart and Nicholson, 1907).
Whitham, Arthur Richard. *Holy Orders* (London: Longmans, Green and Co., 1903).
Whitington, F.T., *William Grant Broughton: Bishop of Australia: With Some Account of the Earliest Australian Clergy* (Sydney: Angus and Robertson, 1936).
Wilkinson, D.H.D., Secretary, Church Missionary Society. 'The Church's Ministry, Vocation and Recruiting', *Official Report of the Pan-Anglican Congress*, IV (London: S.P.C.K., 1908), Sc.1A.
Willis, W.A. and Collingridge, L.T. *The Downfall of Lobengula* (Facsimile reproduction of the 1894 edition) (Bulawayo: Books of Rhodesia, 1971).
Wilson, Bernard Robert, see also *Bernard Robert Wilson.*
Wilson, Bernard. 'The Church and the Empire', in Herbert Hensley Henson, *Church Problems: A View of Modern Anglicanism* (1900): 348–393.
Wilson, G.H. *The History of the Universities Mission to Central Africa* (Westminster: Universities Mission to Central Africa, 1936).
Wilson, Muriel Talbot. *The History of the English Church in Rome from 1816 to 1916* (Rome: Printing House "La Sperenza", 1916).
Winnington-Ingram, Arthur Foley. *Fifty Years of Work in London 1889–1839* (London: Longmans Green and Co., 1940).
——. *Work in Great Cities: Six lectures on pastoral theology* (London: Wells Gardener and Co., 1896).
Wood, Michael Henry Mansel. *A Father in God: The Episcopate of William West Jones . . . Metropolitan of South Africa, 1874–1908* (London: Macmillan and Co., 1913).
Wood, Col. J.G., M.L.A. *Through Matabeleland: Ten Months In a Waggon* (Facsimile Reproduction of the 1893 Edition with additional portraits, and a new Foreward by Edward Tabler) (Bulawayo: Books of Rhodesia, 1974).
Woollcombe, H.S. *Beneath the Southern Cross: being the impressions gained on a tour through Australasia and South Africa on behalf of the Church of England Men's Society* (London: Longmans and Co., 1913).

Wymer, Norman. *Father of Nobody's Children: A Portrait of Dr. Barnardo* (London: Hutchinson, 1954).

Wynne, George Robert. *The Church in Greater Britain* (Donnellan lectures, University of Dublin 1900–1901) (London: Kegan Paul and Co., 1901).

Secondary sources

Addison, William. *The English Country Parson* (London: Dent, 1947).

Alexander, Jocelyn and McGregor, JoAnn. 'Modernity and Ethnicity in a Frontier Society: Understanding Difference in Northwestern Zimbabwe', *Journal of Southern African Studies* 23:2 (June 1997): 187–201.

Atkinson, Muriel. 'History of the Globe and Phoenix Mine', *Heritage of Zimbabwe* 16 (1997): 67–72.

Atkinson, N.D. *Teaching Rhodesians: A History of Educational Policy in Rhodesia* (London: Longman, 1972).

Arnold, W.E. *Here to Stay: The Story of the Anglican Church in Zimbabwe* (Lewes, Sussex: The Book Guild Limited, 1985).

Baker, Jill. *Beloved African* (Weltevreden Park, South Africa: Covos-Day Books, 2000).

Bamber, Shielagh. 'Gertrude Page: Authoress and Farmer's Wife, being the transcript of a talk given at Mvurwe on Sunday 3 August 1986', *Heritage of Zimbabwe* 6 (1986).

Banana, Canaan Sodindo. *A Century of Methodism: I, Zimbabwe 1891–1991* (Harare: Methodist Church in Zimbabwe, 1991).

Barnes, J.C. 'The Battle of Massi-Kessi', *Rhodesiana* 32 (March 1975): 1–26.

——. 'The Beira-Mashonaland Railway', *Rhodesiana* 37 (Sept 1977): 1–15.

Beach, D.N. '"Chimurenga": the Shona Rising of 1896–97', *Journal of African History*, 20:3 (1979): 395–420.

——. 'The historiography of the people of Zimbabwe in the 1960s', *Rhodesian History* 4 (1973): 21–30.

——. *Mapondera 1840–1904* (Gweru: Mambo Press, 1989).

——. 'The Early History of Harare to 1890', *Heritage of Zimbabwe* 9 (1990): 5–27.

——. *The Shona and their Neighbours* (Oxford: Blackwell, 1994).

Bell, G.K.A. *Randall Davidson: Archbishop of Canterbury* (London: Oxford University Press, 1938).

Bentley, James. *Ritualism and Politics in Victorian Britain* (Oxford: Oxford University Press, 1978).

Best, G.F.A. *Temporal Pillars: Queen Anne's Bounty, The Ecclesiastical Commissioners and the Church of England* (Cambridge: Cambridge University Press, 1964).

Blake, Robert. *A History of Rhodesia* (London: Eyre Methuen, 1977).

Blow, Norman J. 'The Theology of Missions', in E.R. Morgan and Roger Lloyd, eds., *The Mission of the Anglican Communion* (London: S.P.C.K. & S.P.G., 1948): 1–17.

Blunden, M.A. 'The Anglican clergy and the politics of Southern Africa 1888–1909' (D.Phil., Oxford University, 1980).

Bourdillon, M.F.C., ed. *Christianity South of the Zambezi, 2* (Gwelo: Mambo Press, 1977).

——. *Religion and Society: A Text for Africa* (Gweru: Mambo Press, 1900).

Bowen, Desmond. *The Idea of the Victorian Church: A Study Of the Church of England 1833–1889* (Montreal: McGill University Press, 1968).

Bowman, Larry W. *Politics in Rhodesia: White Power in an African State* (Cambridge, Massachusetts: Harvard University Press, 1973).

Bousfield, J.W. 'The Pieter Van Der Byl Trek', *Heritage of Zimbabwe* 10 (1991): 102–4.

Breward, Ian. *A History of the Churches in Australasia* (New York, Oxford: Oxford University Press, 2001).

Broderick, G.E.P. 'A History of the Diocese of Southern Rhodesia (formerly the Diocese of Mashonaland) 1874–1952' (Compiled for the USPG, 1953). Copies deposited in the Bodleian Library of Commonwealth and African Studies at Rhodes House, Oxford and the National Archives of Zimbabwe (Historical Manuscripts, BR 3/3/1).

Brooke, Audrey. *Robert Gray: First Bishop of Cape Town* (Oxford and Cape Town: Oxford University Press, 1947).

Bullock, F.W.B. *A History of Training for the Ministry of the Church of England in England and Wales from 1875 to 1974* (London: Home Words Printing and Publishing Co. Ltd., 1976).

Burrett, Robert. 'Eldorado Mine: a faded "Premier Producer"', *Heritage of Zimbabwe* 16 (1997): 37–46.

——. 'Lomagundi Genesis', *Heritage of Zimbabwe* 12 (1993): 39–60.

——. 'The Eyre Brothers: Arthur and Herbert', *Heritage of Zimbabwe* 9 (1990): 37–46.

——. 'The Optimistic Years: The Ayrshire Mine, 1892–1909 and Beyond', *Heritage of Zimbabwe* 10 (1991): 17–30.

Butler, Guy. *The Prophetic Nun: Sister Margaret CR, Sister Pauline CR, Sister Dorothy Raphael CSMV* (Johannesburg: Random House, 2000).

Carpenter, S.C. *Church and People, 1798–1889: A History of the Church of England from William Wilberforce to "Lux Mundi"* (London: Society for Promoting Christian Knowledge, 1933).

——. *Winnington-Ingram: The Biography of Arthur Foley Winnington-Ingram, Bishop of London 1901–1939* (London: Hodder and Stoughton, 1949).

Carrington, Philip. *The Anglican Church in Canada: A History* (Toronto: Collins, 1963).

Chadwick, Owen. *Mackenzie's Grave* (London: Hodder and Stoughton, 1959).

——, ed. *The Mind of the Oxford Movement* (Stanford, California: Stanford University Press, 1960).

——. *The Victorian Church: Part One* (3rd edition) (1971), *Part Two* (2nd edition) (1972) (London: Adam and Charles Black).

——. *Hensley Henson: A study in the friction between Church and State* (Norwich: The Canterbury Press, 1994).

Chennells, A.J. 'Anglicans and Roman Catholics before and after Independence', Essay Review, *Zambezia* XV:I (1988): 75–85.

Cherer-Smith, R. 'Notes on Some of Zimbabwe's Mines', *Heritage* 4 (1984): 13–24.

——. 'Rezende Mine', *Rhodesiana* 34 (March 1976): 21–7.

Clark, Kitson G.S.R. *Churchmen and the Condition of England 1832–1885* (London: Methuen, 1973).

Clarke, Alison. *Holiday Seasons: Christmas, New Year and Easter in Nineteenth-Century New Zealand* (Auckland: Auckland University Press: 2007).

Clarke, J.B. 'The Early Years of Plumtree School', *Heritage of Zimbabwe* 4 (1984): 1–12.

Cleary, Frederick and Field, Ann. *Kamoto: The Life of Winston John Field, C.M.G., M.B.E. (Mil), 1904–1969* (St. Arnaud, Victoria, Australia: [Private publication], 1998).

Cnattingius, Hans. *Bishops and Societies: A Study of Anglican Colonial and Missionary Expansion 1698–1850* (London: Published for the Church Historical Society by S.P.C.K., 1952).

Cobbing, Julian. 'The Absent Priesthood: Another Look at the Rhodesian Risings of 1896–7', *Journal of African History* 18:1 (1977): 61–84.

Cockshutt, A.O.J. *Anglican Attitudes: A Study of Victorian Religious Controversies* (London: Collins, 1959).

Colloms, Brenda. *Victorian Country Parsons* (London: Constable, 1977).

Cox, Jeffrey. *The English Churches in a Secular Society: Lambeth 1870–1930* (New York and Oxford: Oxford University Press, 1982).

Crowther, M.A. *Church Embattled: Religious Controversy in Mid-Victorian England* (USA: Archon, 1970).
Currie, R., Gilbert, A.D. and Horsley, L. *Churches and Churchgoers, Patterns of Church Growth in the British Isles since 1700* (Oxford: Oxford University Press, 1977).
Dachs, A.J., ed. *Christianity South of the Zambezi, 1* (Gwelo: Mambo Press, 1973).
——. and Rea, W.F. *The Catholic Church and Zimbabwe, 1879–1979* (Gwelo: Mambo Press, 1979).
Davis, Pat. 'The History of Gwelo. Part 1', *Rhodesiana* 34 (March 1976): 9–20.
——. 'The History of Gwelo. Part 2', *Rhodesiana* 35 (September 1976): 4–15.
——. 'The History of Gwelo. Part 3', *Rhodesiana* 36 (March 1977): 26–36.
Daw, E.D. *Church and State in the Empire: The Evolution of Imperial Policy 1846–1856*. Occasional Monograph No. 1, Department of Government, Faculty of Military Studies, University of New South Wales (Canberra: 1977).
De Bruijn, H.S., and Louisa. 'Aspects of the Early History of Chimanimani', *Heritage of Zimbabwe* 10 (1991): 149–58.
Douglas, R.G.S. 'The Development of the Department of Immigration to 1953', (undated and unpublished typescript, National Archives of Zimbabwe).
Edwards, D.L. *Christian England (Volume 3) From the Eighteenth Century to the First World War* (London: Collins, 1984).
Edwards, J.A. 'Two Kinds of Central African History', Central African Archives, *Occasional Papers*, 1 (Salisbury, Rhodesia: The Government Printer, 1965).
Edwards, Pat. 'Early Settlers in Chipinge', *Heritage of Zimbabwe* 10 (1991): 159–62.
Ellert, H. *Rivers of Gold* (*Zambeziana*: XXII, A Series on Culture and Society in Zimbabwe) (Gweru: Mambo Press, 1993).
Etherington, Norman. 'Recent Trends in the Historiography of Christianity in Southern Africa', *Journal of Southern African Studies* 22:2 (June 1996): 201–9.
Evans, H.St.J.T. *The Church in Southern Rhodesia* (Westminster and London: S.P.G. and S.P.C.K., 1945).
Ewbank, R.A.B. *The Forerunners: An Account of the Founding of the Anglican Church in Bulawayo* ([Bulawayo]: (n.p.), (n.d.) [1985]).
——. *Love Bade Me Welcome: A History of St. John's Cathedral, Bulawayo* ([Bulawayo]: (n.p.), (n.d.), 1995?]).
Farrant, J. *Mashonaland Martyr: Bernard Mizeki and the Pioneer Church* (Cape Town, London, Salisbury: Oxford University Press, 1966).
Fleming, Mary. 'How The Railway Came To Gwanda', *Heritage* 4 (1984): 25–6.
France, W.R. *The Overseas Episcopate: Centenary History of the Colonial Bishoprics' Fund 1841–1941* [1941].
Franks, R.D. 'Jumbo Mine: A Brief History', *Rhodesiana* 32 (March 1975): 36–42.
Gann, L.H. *A History of Southern Rhodesia: Early Days to 1934* (London: Chatto and Windus, 1965).
——. 'The White Settler: A Changing Image', *Race* 2:2 (1961): 28–40.
——. and Duignan P. *White Settlers in Tropical Africa* (Harmondsworth: Penguin, 1962).
——. and Gelfand, M. *Huggins of Rhodesia: The man and his country* (London: George Allan and Unwin Ltd, 1964).
Garlake, P.S. 'Cran Cooke and the Monuments Commission' *Heritage of Zimbabwe* 11 (1992): 101–5.
Gibbon, Geoffrey. *Paget of Rhodesia: A Memoir of Edward, 5th Bishop of Mashonaland* (Johannesburg: Africana Book Society (Pty.) Ltd., 1973).
Gifford, P. *The Religious Right in Southern Africa* (Harare: Baobab Books and University of Zimbabwe Publications, 1988).
Girouard, Mark. *The Return to Camelot: Chivalry and the English Gentleman* (New Haven and London: Yale, 1981).

Glass, Stafford. *The Matabele War* (London: Longmans, 1968).

Grain, A.E. *Mission Unaccomplished: Stories of the Travelling Church in Southern Africa 1890–1980: An Account of the Work of Railway Missions in Southern Africa 1890–1980* (Published by the Revd. A.E. Grain, College of St. Barnabas, Lingfield, Surrey) (n.d.) [1989?].

Grant, David. 'The Shangani Story', *Heritage of Zimbabwe* Publication No. 13 (1994): 81–96.

——. 'Focus on Aspects of the Last Stand of the Wilson Patrol and its Aftermath', *Heritage of Zimbabwe* Publication No. 13 (1994): 97–100.

Gray, Richard. *Black Christians and White Missionaries* (New Haven and London: Yale University Press, 1990).

——. 'Christianity', in Andrew Roberts, ed. *Cambridge History of Africa, VII, From 1905 to 1940* (Cambridge, Cambridge University Press, 1986): 140–90.

Gutsche, Thelma. *The Bishop's Lady* (Cape Town: Howard Timmins, 1970).

Guy, J. *The Heretic: A Study of the Life of John William Colenso 1814–1883* (Johannesburg and Pietermaritzburg: Ravan Press and University of Natal Press, 1983).

Haig, A. *The Victorian Clergy* (London & Sydney: Croom Helm, 1984).

Hallencreutz, C.F., and Moyo, A.M., eds. *Church and State in Zimbabwe: Christianity South of the Zambesi*, 3 (Gweru: Mambo Press, 1988).

Hart, A. Tindal, *The Curate's Lot: The story of the unbeneficed English clergy* (London: J. Baker, 1970).

Harvey, R.K. 'Felixburg—a Dream That Faded—but Legends Live On', *Heritage of Zimbabwe* 14 (1995): 83–6.

Hastings, Adrian. *The Church in Africa 1450–1950* (Oxford: Oxford University Press, 1994).

——. *A History of English Christianity 1920–1990* (London and Philadelphia: Collins, 1991).

——. 'African Christian Studies, 1967–1999: Reflections of an Editor', *Journal of Religion in Africa* XXX:1 (2000): 30–44.

Heeney, Brian. *A Different Kind of Gentleman: Parish Clergy as Professional Men in early and mid-Victorian England* (Hampden, Connecticut: Archon Books, 1976).

Hewitt, Gordon. *The Problems of Success: A History of the Church Missionary Society 1910–1942: Volume I, In Tropical Africa, The Middle East, At Home* (1971): *Volume II, Asia, Overseas Partners* (1972), (London: SCM Press Ltd.).

Hinchliff, Peter. 'The Selection and Training of Missionaries in the Early Nineteenth Century', in G.J. Cuming, ed., *Studies in Church History* 6 (1970): 131–35.

——. *The Anglican Church in South Africa: An account of the history and development of the Church of the Province of South Africa* (London: Darton, Longman and Todd, 1963).

Hodder-Williams, Richard. *White Farmers in Rhodesia 1890–1965: A History of the Marandellas District* (London: Macmillan, 1983).

Hogarth, O.J. and White, R.L. *Life of William Marlborough Carter, Third Archbishop of Capetown* ([Dartmouth]: [O.J. Hogarth], 1952).

Holderness, Hardwicke. *Lost Chance: Southern Rhodesia 1945–58* (Harare: Zimbabwe Publishing House (Pvt.) Ltd., 1985).

Howman, Roger. 'Patriotism and Pioneering Problems', *Heritage of Zimbabwe* 9 (1990): 75–102.

Iliffe, John. *Famine in Zimbabwe 1890–1960* (Gweru: Mambo Press, 1990).

Iremonger F.A. *William Temple: Archbishop of Canterbury: His Life and Letters* (London: Geoffrey Cumberledge, Oxford University Press, 1948).

Isaacman, Allen. 'Social Banditry in Zimbabwe (Rhodesia) and Mozambique, 1894–1907: An Expression of Early Peasant Protest', *Journal of Southern African Studies* 4:1 (Oct. 1977): 1–30.

Isichei, Elizabeth. *A History of Christianity in Africa: from antiquity to the present* (London: SPCK, 1995).

Jacob, W.M. *The Making of the Anglican Church Worldwide* (London: SPCK, 1997).
Jeal, Tim. *Livingstone* (London: Pimlico, 1993).
Jones, A. Pierce. *A Procession of Witness* (Cape Town: [Printed by the Stewart Printing Company, Cape Town], 1947).
Kelsey, B.L. 'The Education of the Anglican Clergy 1830–1914' (Ph.D. thesis, University of Leicester, 1982).
Kemple, Monica. 'The Chakari District in the 1920s and 1930s', *Heritage of Zimbabwe* 14 (1995): 113–7.
Kennedy, Dane. 'Climatic Theories and Culture in Colonial Kenya and Rhodesia', *Journal of Imperial and Commonwealth History* X:1 (Oct 1981): 50–66.
——. *Islands of White: Settler Society and Social Control in Southern Rhodesia 1890–1939* (Durham, North Carolina: Duke University Press, 1987).
——. 'Imperial History and Post-Colonial Theory', *Journal of Imperial and Commonwealth History* XXIV:3 (1996): 345–363.
Keppel-Jones, Arthur. *Rhodes and Rhodesia: The White Conquest of Zimbabwe 1884–1902* (Pietermaritzburg: University of Natal Press, 1983).
Killingray, David. "To Suffer Grief in All Kinds of Trials': Persecution and Martyrdom in the African Church in the Twentieth Century', in Diana Woods, ed., *Studies in Church History* 30 (1993): 465–82.
Kimberley, Michael. 'Sir Joseph Vintcent—Rhodesia's First Judge', *Rhodesiana* 38 (March 1978): 1–13.
——. 'Swynnerton of Gungunyana: a Pioneer Zimbabwean Natural Historian', *Heritage of Zimbabwe* 9 (1990): 47–61.
Kirk, Kenneth E. *The Apostolic Ministry: essays on the history and doctrine of episcopacy* (London: Hodder and Stoughton, 1946).
Kosmin, B.A. 'Ethnic Groups and the qualified franchise', *Rhodesian History* 8 (1977): 35–70.
——. *Majuta: A History of the Jewish Community of Zimbabwe* (Gweru: Mambo Press, 1981).
——. 'The Pioneer Community of Salisbury in November 1897', *Rhodesian History* 2 (1971): 25–37.
Langham-Carter, R.R. 'The Manica Frontier Dispute: Major Sapte's Mission', *Rhodesiana* 30 (June 1974): 38–43.
——. 'M.P. Bowden: Pioneer, and H.W.M. Paulet: Early Settler', *Rhodesiana* 32 (March 1975): 48–53.
——. *Knight Bruce: First Bishop and Founder of the Anglican Church in Rhodesia* (Salisbury, Rhodesia: Christchurch, Borrowdale, (n.d.) [1975]).
Lee, M.E. 'Politics and Pressure Groups in Southern Rhodesia 1898–1923 (Ph.D. thesis, University of London, 1974).
Lewis, C., and Edwards, G.E. *Historical Records of the Church of the Province of South Africa* (London: S.P.C.K., 1934).
Leys, Colin. *European Politics in Southern Rhodesia* (Oxford: Clarendon Press, 1959).
Linden, Ian. 'Missions Ancient and Modern', [review article], *Zimbabwean History* VIII (1980): 87–90.
Liptz, Paul. 'The Jewish Community in Zimbabwe', *Zimbabwean History* 12 (1981): 67–70.
Lloyd, Cormac. 'Fort Charter', *Heritage of Zimbabwe* 11 (1992): 123–30.
——, and Graves, Benedicta. 'Ayrshire District, 1909–1946', *Heritage of Zimbabwe* 12 (1993): 87–93.
Lloyd, Roger. *The Church of England in the Twentieth Century*, Two Volumes. First Edition (London: Longmans Green, 1946).
Lockhart, J.G. *Cosmo Gordon Lang* (London: Hodder and Stoughton Limited, 1949).
——, and Woodhouse, The Hon. C.M. *Rhodes, A new biography based, for the first time, on unrestricted use of the Rhodes papers* (London: Hodder and Stoughton, 1963).

Logan, E.A. 'The Shamva Story', *Heritage of Zimbabwe* 5 (1985): 17–30.

Lowry, Donal. '"White Woman's Country": Ethel Tawse Jollie and the making of White Rhodesia', *Journal of Southern African Studies* 23:2 (June 1997): 258–281.

Lunn, Jon. *Capital and Labour on the Rhodesian Railway System, 1888–1947* (Oxford: Oxford University Press, 1997).

Maclean, L.S. 'Earlier Days in Salisbury', *Rhodesiana* 36 (March 1977): 62–4.

Mckelvie, Graham D. 'The development of official Anglican interest in world mission, 1783–1809, with special reference to Bishop Beilby Porteous' (Ph.D. thesis, University of Aberdeen, 1984).

McLaughlin, Peter. *Ragtime Soldiers, The Rhodesian Experience in the First World War* (Bulawayo: Books of Zimbabwe, 1980).

Malmgreen, G. *Religion in the lives of English Women 1760–1930* (London and Sydney: Croom Helm, 1986).

Martin, Keith. 'The Pioneer Cemetery', *Heritage of Zimbabwe* 16 (1997): 115–127.

Mashonaland Branch of the Rhodesiana Society, *Occasional Paper I, A Record of the Proceedings at a Series of 5 Lectures on Rhodesia 1896 to 1923, Held at the National Gallery of Rhodesia, Salisbury During September and October 1975* [containing]: *The Beginning*—G.H. Tanser; *The Stewards*—J.G. Storry; *The Carriers*—A.F.H. Baxter; *The Guardians*—H.R.G. Howman M.B.E.; *The People*—W.D. Gale.

Mason, Alastair. *History of the Society of the Sacred Mission* (Norwich: The Canterbury Press, 1993).

Mason, Philip. *The Birth of a Dilemma: The Conquest and Settlement of Rhodesia* (Oxford: Institute of Race Relations and Oxford University Press, 1958).

Maughan, Steven. '"Mighty England Do Good": The Major English Denominations and Organisations for the Support of Foreign Missions in the Nineteenth Century', in Robert A. Bickers and Rosemary Seaton, eds. *Missionary Encounters: Sources and Issues* (Richmond, United Kingdom: Curzon Press, 1996).

——. 'Imperial Christianity? Bishop Montgomery and the foreign missions of the Church of England, 1895–1915', in Andrew Porter, ed., *The Imperial Horizons of British Protestant Missions, 1880–1914* (Grand Rapids, Michigan and Cambridge: W.B. Eerdmans, 2003), 32–57.

Maxwell, David. 'New Perspectives in the History of African Christianity', *Journal of Southern African Studies* 23:1 (March 1997): 141–148.

——. 'The Spirit and the Scapular: Pentecostal and Catholic Interactions in Northern Nyanga District, Zimbabwe in the 1950s and Early 1960s', *Journal of Southern African Studies* 23:2 (June 1997): 283–300.

Meacham, S. *Lord Bishop: The Life of Samuel Wilberforce* (Cambridge, Massachussets: Harvard University Press, 1970).

Megahey, Alan. *Humphrey Gibbs: Beleaguered Governor: Southern Rhodesia, 1929–69* (Basingstoke and London, New York: Macmillan and St. Martins Press, Inc., 1998).

Mews, Stuart P. 'Kikuyu and Edinburgh: the Interaction of Attitudes to Two Conferences', in J.G. Cuming and D. Baker, eds., *Studies in Church History* 7 (1971): 345–59.

——. 'Religion and English Society in the First World War' (Ph.D., University of Cambridge, 1973).

Mlambo, Alois S. 'Building a White Man's Country: Aspects of White Immigration to Rhodesia 1890–1910', Paper presented to the Conference on the Zimbabwean Economy 1930–1990, University of Zimbabwe, 4th–7th August 1997.

Morgan, E.R. and Lloyd, Roger, eds. *The Mission of the Anglican Communion* (London: S.P.C.K. & S.P.G., 1948).

Mossop, R.T. 'Malaria and Blackwater Fever', *Heritage of Zimbabwe* 14 (1995): 11–16.

Murray, D.J. *The Governmental System in Southern Rhodesia* (Oxford: Clarendon Press, 1970).

Mutambirwa, J.A. Chamunorwa. *The Rise of Settler Power in Southern Rhodesia (Zimbabwe) 1898–1923* (Cranbury, New Jersey, London and Toronto: Associated University Presses, 1980).
Neill, Stephen. *A History of Christian Missions* (Harmsworth: Penguin, 1964).
——. 'The History of Missions: An Academic Discipline', in G.J. Cuming, ed., *Studies in Church History* 6 (1970): 149–170.
——. *Anglicanism* (Fourth Edition, London: Mowbray, 1977).
Nicolls, P.L. 'The social expectations of Anglican Clergy in England and Australia in the period 1850–1910 (D. Phil., University of Oxford, 1988).
Noll, Mark A. *A History of Christianity in the United States and Canada* (Michigan and London: SPCK, 1992).
Norman, E.R. *Church and Society in England 1770–1970: A Historical Study* (Oxford: Clarendon Press, 1976).
——. *Christianity in the Southern Hemisphere: the churches in Latin America and Southern Africa* (Oxford: Oxford University Press, 1981).
O'Connor, Daniel, ed., and others. *Three Centuries of Mission: The United Society for the Propagation of the Gospel 1701–2000* (New York, London: Continuum, 2000).
O'Day, Rosemary. 'The Clerical Renaissance in Victorian England and Wales', in Gerald Parsons, ed. *Religion in Victorian Britain, Vol. 1, Traditions* (Manchester: Manchester University Press in association with the Open University, 1988): 184–212.
Oliver, S.P. *Many Treks Made Rhodesia* (Facsimile reproduction of the 1957 edition with the addition of a new Foreward and an Index, and a revised List of Illustrations) (Bulawayo: Books of Rhodesia, 1975).
Orr, K.W. 'Changes in the methods of financing of the Church of England c. 1870–1914, with special reference to the parochial clergy (D. Phil.,University of Oxford, 1983).
Palmer, Robin. *Land and Racial Domination in Rhodesia* (London: Heinemann Educational, 1977).
Parkinson, D.K. 'The Pioneer Road: Tuli to Fort Victoria in the Chibi District: 1890–1966, *Rhodesiana* 37 (Sept 1977): 44–53.
Peaden, W.R. 'Christian Missions in Mashonaland 1890–1927' (Ph.D. thesis, University of Bristol, 1974).
Petheram, R.W. 'Inyanga: with special reference to the Rhodes Inyanga Estate', *Rhodesiana* 31 (September 1974): 36–50.
Phimister, Ian. 'Meat and Monopolies: Beef Cattle in Southern Rhodesia 1890–1938', *Journal of African History* 19:3 (1978): 391–414.
——. 'Towards a history of Zimbabwe's Railways', *Zimbabwean History* 12 (1981): 71–99.
——. 'Zimbabwean Economic and Social Historiography since 1970', *African Affairs*, 78, (1979): 253–268.
——, and van Onselen, C. *Studies in the History of African Mine Labour in Colonial Zimbabwe* (Gwelo: Mambo Press, 1978).
——. 'Accommodating Imperialism: the compromise of the settler state in Southern Rhodesia, 1923–1929', *Journal of African History*, 25, (1984): 279–294.
——. *An Economic and Social History of Zimbabwe 1890–1948: Capital Accumulation and Class Struggle* (London: Longman, 1988).
Pichanik, J., Chennells, A.J., and Rix, L.B. *Rhodesian Literature in English: A Bibliography (1890–1974/5)* (Gwelo: Mambo Press, 1977).
Potter, S.C. 'The Social Origins and recruitment of English Protestant Missionaries in the Nineteenth Century' (Ph.D., University of London, 1975).
Piggin, Stuart. 'Assessing Nineteenth-Century Missionary Motivation: Some Considerations of Theory and Method', in D. Baker, ed., *Studies in Church History* 15 (1978): 327–337.

Porter, A.N. 'Late Nineteenth-Century Anglican missionary expansion: a consideration of some non-Anglican sources of inspration', in D. Baker, ed., *Studies in Church History* 15 (1978): 349–365.
——. '"Commerce and Christianity": the rise and fall of a nineteenth-century missionary slogan', *The Historical Journal* 28:3 (1985): 597–621.
——. 'Religion and empire: British expansion in the Long Nineteenth Century', *Journal of Imperial and Commonwealth History* XX:3 (1992): 370–386.
——. '"Cultural Imperialism" and Protestant Missionary Enterprise, 1780–1914', *Journal of Imperial and Commonwealth History* XXV:3 (1997): 367–391.
——. 'Religion, Missionary Enthusiasm and Empire', in A.N. Porter, ed. *The Oxford History of the British Empire, Vol 3: The Nineteenth Century* (Oxford University Press, 1999): 222–246.
Presler, Titus. 'Missionary Anglicanism Meets An African Religion: A retrospect of the centenary of Bishop Knight-Bruce's entry into Zimbabwe', *Missionalia* 17:3 (November 1989): 162–175.
Ranger, T.O. 'Church and State in Southern Rhodesia 1919–1939', Central African Historical Association, Local Series, 4, (Salisbury, 1961).
——. *Revolt in Southern Rhodesia, 1896–7* (London: Heinemann, 1967).
——. *The African Voice in Southern Rhodesia 1898 to 1930* (London: Heinemann, 1970).
——. 'The Historiography of Southern Rhodesia', *Transafrican Journal of History*, I, (1971): 63–76.
——. 'White Presence and Power in Africa', *Journal of African History*, 20 (1979): 463–469.
——. 'Literature and the Political Economy: Arthur Shearly Cripps and the Makoni Labour Crisis of 1911', *Southern African Studies* 9:1 (Oct 1982): 33–53.
——. 'Taking Hold of the Land: Holy Places and Pilgrimages in Twentieth-Century Zimbabwe', *Past and Present* 117 (November, 1987): 158–194.
——. *Voices from the Rocks: Nature, Culture And History in the Matopos Hills of Zimbabwe* (Harare, Bloomington and Indianapolis, Oxford: Baobab, Indiana University Press and James Currie, 1999).
——. and Weller J., eds. *Themes in the Christian History of Central Africa* (London: Heinemann Educational, 1975).
Ransford, O.N. and Kinsey, H.W. 'The Seige of Elands River', *Rhodesiana* 40 (1979): 1–10.
Rea, W.F., S.J. *Seventy-Five Years in Two Cities: The Story of St. George's 1896–1971* ([Salisbury]: [St. George's College], [1971?]).
Rennie, J.K. 'White Farmers, Black Tenants and Landlord Legislation: Southern Rhodesia 1890–1930', *Journal of Southern African Studies* 5:1 (Oct 1978): 86–98.
Roberts, A.D. 'The earlier historiography of Colonial Africa', *History in Africa* V (1978): 153–67.
Roberts, R.S. 'A Neglected Source of Pioneer History', *Rhodesiana* 40 (1979): 11–3.
——. 'The Settlers', *Rhodesiana* 39 (September 1978): 55–61.
Ross, Andrew C. *David Livingstone: Mission and Empire* (London: Hambledon and London, 2002).
Rotberg, Robert. *The Founder: Cecil Rhodes and the Pursuit of Power* (Oxford: Oxford University Press, 1988).
Russell, Anthony. *The Clerical Profession* (London: SPCK, 1980).
Sachs, William L. *The Transformation of Anglicanism: From State Church to Global Communion* (Cambridge: Cambridge University Press, 1993).
Samkange, Stanlake J.T. *Origins of Rhodesia* (London: Heinemann Educational, 1969).
Sayce, Katherine. *A Town Called Victoria: or the Rise and Fall of the Thatched House Hotel* (Bulawayo: Books of Rhodesia, 1978).
Schutz, Barry M. 'European Population Patterns, Cultural Persistence, and Political Change in Rhodesia', *Canadian Journal of African Studies* VII:1 (1923): 3–25.

Shinn, Allison. 'The Early European Settlement of the South Western Districts of Rhodesia. Part 1', *Rhodesiana* 30 (June 1974): 13–33.

——. 'The Early European Settlement of the South Western Districts of Rhodesia. Part 2', *Rhodesiana* 30 (June 1974): 13–33.

Sinclair, David. *The White Tide* [The story of Alfred Musson] ([Bulawayo]: (private publication), 2002).

Sohmer, Sara. 'Anglican tradition and mission: sources for mission methodology in the nineteenth-century Pacific', in Daniel O'Connor and others, *Three Centuries of Mission, The United Society for the Propagation of the Gospel 1701–2000* (New York, London: Continuum, 2000): 301–3.

Stebbing, Dorothy. 'The Past that Slipped Away', *Rhodesiana* 33 (September 1975): 62–7.

Steele, Murray. 'Arthur Shearly Cripps', in Daniel O'Connor and others, *Three Centuries of Mission, The United Society for the Propagation of the Gospel 1701–2000* (New York, London: Continuum, 2000): 371–381.

——. '"With hope unconquered and unconquerable..." Arthur Shearly Cripps, 1869–1952', in T.O. Ranger and J. Weller, eds. *Themes in the Christian History of Central Africa* (London: Heinemann Educational, 1975): 152–174.

Steere, D.V. *God's Irregular: Arthur Shearly Cripps: A Rhodesian Epic* (London: SPCK, 1973).

Stephenson, Alan M.G. *Anglicanism and the Lambeth Conferences* (London: S.P.C.K., 1978).

Stigger P. 'The Land Commission of 1894 and Cattle', *Zimbabwean History* 11 (1980): 20–43.

——. 'The Land Commission of 1894 and its Membership', *Rhodesian History* 8 (1977): 99–110.

Sundkler, Bengt and Steed, Christopher. *A History of the Church in Africa* (Cambridge: Cambridge University Press, 2000).

Taylor, R.D. 'The Planet Arcturus Railway', *Heritage of Zimbabwe* 17 (1998): 74–9.

——. 'Gweru, a Railway Centre', *Heritage of Zimbabwe* 20 (2001): 61–81.

Taylor, Stephen. *The Mighty Nimrod, A Life of Frederick Courtney Selous, African Hunter and Adventurer 1851–1917* (London: Collins, 1989).

Thompson, Henry Paget. *Into All the Lands: The History of The Society for the Propagation of the Gospel in Foreign Parts 1701–1950* (London: S.P.C.K., 1951).

——. *Thomas Bray* (London: S.P.C.K., 1954).

Thorpe, C. *Limpopo to Zambezi, 60 years of Methodism in Southern Rhodesia* (London: Cargate Press, 1951).

Vambe, Lawrence. *An Ill-fated People: Zimbabwe Before and After Rhodes* (London: Heinemann Educational, 1972).

Van Onselen, Charles. *Chibaro: African Mine Labour in Southern Rhodesia 1900–1933* (London: Pluto Press 1976).

Varney, Beverley Jayne. 'The Role of the African Catechist—Teachers and Priests in Anglican Mission Strategy in Rhodesia-Zimbabwe 1890–1950' (B.A., Hons., University of Manchester, 1980).

Vassilatos, Enetia. 'Race and class: The development and influence of white images of blacks in Southern Rhodesia 1890–1923' (M.A., University of Zimbabwe, 1977).

Walls, A.F. 'African Church History: Some Recent Studies', *Journal of Ecclesiastical History* XXIII:2 (April 1972): 161–169.

——. '"The Best Thinking of the Best Heathen": Humane Learning and the Missionary Movement', K. Robins, ed., *Studies in Church History* 17 (1981): 341–353.

——. 'Black Europeans, White Africans: Some Missionary Motives in West Africa', D. Baker, ed., *Studies in Church History* 15 (1978): 339–348.

Wauchope, George. 'Healing in a Religious Context: A Comparative Analysis', (M.Phil., University of Zimbabwe, 1987).

Webb, Lorna. *Chintali: The Life and Times of Sir Thomas Page, CBE, KB* (Swindon: Newton Publishers, 1995).

Weller, J.C. *Anglican Centenary in Zimbabwe 1891–1991* (Mutare: (n.p), 1991).

Weller, John. 'The Influence on National Affairs of Alston May, Bishop of Northern Rhodesia, 1914–40', in T.O. Ranger and J. Weller, eds., *Themes in the Christian History of Central Africa* (London: Heinemann Educational, 1975): 195–211.

——, & Linden, Jane. *Mainstream Christianity to 1980: in Malawi, Zambia and Zimbabwe* (Gweru: Mambo Press, 1984).

Wetherell, H.I. 'Political History in colonial Zimbabwe: the problem of perspective', *Zimbabwean History* II 1980): 95–9.

White, Gavin. *How the Churches Got to Be the Way they Are* (London and Philadelphia: SCM Press and Trinity Press International, 1990).

——. 'Religious Patterns in the Diaspora of the British', *The Diaspora of the British: Papers of the SSRC Conference on the Diaspora of the British, held at Rutherford College, University of Kent, on July 6th–8th, 1981* (London: Institute of Commonwealth Studies, University of London, 1982): 200–209.

Wilkinson, Alan. *The Church of England and the First World War* (London: S.P.C.K., 1978).

——. *The Community of the Resurrection: A Centenary History* (London: SCM Press Ltd., 1992).

Williams, C.P. "Not Quite Gentlemen': an Examination of 'Middling Class' Protestant Missionaries from Britain, c. 1850–1900', *Journal of Ecclesiastical History* 31:3 (July 1980): 301–15.

Wood, R.H. 'A Visit to Mazoe', *Heritage* 5 (1985): 83–90.

Yates, T.E. *Henry Venn and Victorian Bishops Abroad: the missionary policies of Henry Venn and their repercussions upon the Anglican Episcopate of the colonial period 1841–1872* (Uppsala and London: Swedish Institute of Missionary Research and SPCK, 1978).

Zvogbo, C.J.M. *A History of Christian Missions in Zimbabwe 1890–1939* (Gweru: Mambo Press, 1996).

——. *The Wesleyan Methodist Missions in Zimbabwe 1891–1945* (Supplement to *Zambezia*, The Journal of the University of Zimbabwe) (Harare: University of Zimbabwe Publications, 1991).

INDEX